INTERNATIONAL JOURNAL
OF URBAN AND REGIONAL RESEARCH

ISSN 0309-1317

Anthropology
Architecture
Cultural Studies
Economics
Environment
Geography
History
Planning
Political Economy
Political Science
Science and Technology Studies
Sociology
Urban Studies

WILEY

International Journal of Urban and Regional Research

IJURR is the leading social science journal for urban studies. It publishes articles from a variety of disciplines and from many countries, including many articles on comparative topics. It is not restricted to any theoretical perspective but has consistently published articles which take a critical stance towards existing theories and policies, and which apply theories and analyse empirical data in a rigorous way. IJURR's Debates section presents shorter, sometimes contentious essays on recent developments in the field–policy, practice and theory–and occasional coverage of truly groundbreaking convocations, mobilizations and reports. The Book Reviews section is a valuable resource for researchers, providing an informed, critical overview of important new publications. With a commitment to global and local issues, a cutting-edge approach to linking theoretical development and empirical research, and a consistent demand for quality, IJURR is a groundbreaking force for intellectual debate. It is written and read by scholars and practitioners with a concern for the complex, changing roles of cities and regions.

Intending contributors are asked to consult the author guidelines which are published on the journal website at www.ijurr.org.

All articles and Debates essays must be submitted online at http://mc.manuscriptcentral.com/ijurr.

Symposium proposal guidelines are also available on the journal website.

All books for review and book reviews should be sent to Matthias Bernt, Leibniz Institute for Research on Society and Space, Flakenstraße 29-31, 15537 Erkner, Germany, Matthias.Bernt@leibniz-irs.de

Published by
John Wiley & Sons Ltd

Printed by
Hobbs the Printers Ltd, UK

Designed by
Atelier Dreibholz, Typography and Graphic Design, London/Vienna

VOLUME 41   NUMBER 6   NOVEMBER 2017

Contents

— SUNKEN CITIES: Climate Change, Urban Futures and the Imagination of Submergence

PAUL DOBRASZCZYK

Abstract

Climate change presents multiple challenges to cities—not only in terms of the resilience and sustainability of the urban fabric, but also in relation to how urban inhabitants imagine they might adapt to a future transformed environment. This article explores imaginative modes of thinking in relation to future cities and climate change, focusing on representations of urban drowning or submergence. It considers, in turn, climate-change fictions—from J.G. Ballard's 1962 novel The Drowned World *to Paulo Bacigalupi's* The Drowned Cities, *published in 2012; visual representations from Gustave Doré's* The New Zealander *in 1872 to Alexis Rockman's 2004* Manifest Destiny; *and architectural conjecture, from Wolf Hilbertz's Autopia Ampere project from 1970 onwards to CRAB Studio's Soak City in 2009. The article draws out how these imaginaries intersect with theoretical understandings of science fiction and ecology, contending that an emphasis on* multiple *imaginaries of climate change is critical to expanding the narrow range of possibilities that currently characterize the literature on cities and climate change. Imaginative texts, images and designs mutually inform each other to encourage holistic ways of approaching how we think about the prospect of urban submergence and to incubate radical responses to it.*

Introduction

Despite the fact that climate change is already affecting cities across the world—principally based on the increased incidence and severity of urban flooding—it nevertheless remains a discourse dominated by future predictions. Even by the cautious estimates of the most recent report of the IPCC (Intergovernmental Panel on Climate Change) in 2013, cities are in for a rough ride in this and the next century. By 2100, the rise in global temperatures is likely to exceed 2 degrees Celsius above pre-industrial levels—temperatures reached that level for a short time in early 2016 (Holthaus, 2016). Sea levels will rise by anything up to a metre, and even more, if current predictions prove to be over-optimistic. The sea will warm and become more acidic, and turbulence in the atmosphere will intensify, leading to ever more extreme weather events and a greater risk of flooding (IPCC, 2013). As much as these climate reports are grounded in empirical evidence, they are nevertheless essentially predictive in their discourse, laying out a whole host of possible futures that rely as much on our ability to imagine those futures, even with the help of a welter of facts and figures (Yusoff and Gabrys, 2011). The overwhelmingly future-orientated discourse of climate change is perhaps the principal reason why it has been and continues to be so difficult to find common agreement on how to act in the face of such fundamentally uncertain futures (Hulme, 2009; Machin, 2013).

It is no wonder, then, that the focus of much of the current literature on climate change and cities is on mitigation rather than adaptation, with Bulkeley (2013: 143) admitting that, even as the effects of climate change are already being felt, international

The work presented here forms part of a larger independent research project on urban futures and the imagination, supported in its early stages by an Independent Scholar Research Fellowship from the Independent Social Research Foundation. I am grateful to the three anonymous IJURR reviewers who provided such constructive feedback on an earlier draft of the article, and to Richard Breen, Paul Cureton, Marrikka Trotter and Jason Nguyen for comments and advice on the work of Wolf Hilbertz. Thanks also to Paul Cureton, Alexis Rockman and Squint/Opera for kindly giving me permission to reproduce their work. A small section of this article was published in revised form in my book *The Dead City: Urban Ruins and the Spectacle of Decay* (IB Tauris, London, 2017).

and national policy-making communities remain more concerned with mitigating these effects than with adapting to them (this formed the focus of the landmark international climate change agreement in Paris at the end of 2015). Even the emerging body of literature on climate change and urban resilience, perhaps most notably the ongoing Resilient Cities congress and its associated publications (Otto-Zimmermann, 2011), which seeks to shift the focus from mitigation to adaptation, remains firmly grounded in instrumental thinking—whether that centres on the adaptation of the built fabric through long-term strategic planning (Watson and Adams, 2010) or the reshaping of urban governance and socio-political life towards sustainable ends (Pelling, 2011). While these objectives are laudable, what is underplayed in much of this work is the role of the creative imagination in thinking through the relationship between urban futures and climate change. Engaging the imagination—'the human power to connote absence into presence, actuality into possibility' (Kearney, 1991)—with the discourse of climate change and cities is critical because the imagination is a powerful tool for articulating radical new possibilities for urban life in the face of equally radically uncertain futures. Thus, despite the denigration of future-orientated modes of urban planning in architectural modernism (and their perceived authoritarian utopianism), there is obviously a pressing need to re-engage the imagination of future cities in ways that draw on 'blue-sky thinking', as Vidal and Cornils (2014) term it. Indeed, the impulse for radical urban change has been recently reassessed by critics such as Harvey (2000), Jameson (2008) and Levitas (2013). They regard an invigorated form of utopian futurism as a necessary response to the apparent hegemony of global capitalism, which has arguably contributed most to the engines that are driving climate change. Far from escaping into fantasies of alternate yet implausible worlds, the utopian mode (and its close cousin dystopia) might be the only way of arguing that radical difference is possible and that alternatives to global capitalism are achievable (Jameson, 2008: 231–32).

In this article, I explore imaginative modes of thinking—both utopian and dystopian—in relation to future cities and climate change, focusing on representations of drowning or submergence. The investigation centres on representations produced by fiction writers, visual artists and architects as ways of thinking through the range of possibilities for urban life in a world radically transformed by rising sea levels. The first section focuses on climate-change novels and the pervasive motif of urban flooding in these fictions; the second section investigates visual corollaries to these fictions, from flood maps issued by governmental organizations to post-apocalyptic images produced by artists. The final section considers radical architectural approaches to submergence—from underwater building to self-generating structures that grow out of the sea—that have emerged in experimental practices and that are fundamentally concerned with adaptation rather than mitigation. The urban centres that ground these imaginative engagements—in this article the focus is on London, Washington DC, Melbourne, Bangkok and New York—are undoubtedly dominated by global 'landmark' cities, even as more peripheral and impoverished cities will likely be the first to be affected by rising sea levels and more severe and frequent flooding. This reflects the fact that the imaginative discourse of climate change—whether expressed in novels, films, art or architectural speculation—has largely emerged from those landmark cities themselves, probably because there is a sense that the threats that climate change pose to the affluent West are still held at bay—a future possibility rather than a clear and present risk. It remains to be seen how the imagination of climate change will evolve as the threat to these cities continues to grow.

The multiple urban imaginaries that form the focus of this article contribute to a contemporary re-evaluation of science fiction as an important tool in the discourse of urban planning. For example, Stephen Graham's recent work on vertical urbanism has argued that science fiction cities are 'pivotal in constituting the materialities of contemporary cities' because 'built projects, material cities, sci-fi texts, imaginary futures, architectural schemes and urban theories mingle and resonate together in complex and unpredictable ways' (Graham, 2016: 388). This intermingling is crucial to the power of science fiction in that it produces what Darko Suvin has termed 'cognitive estrangement', namely the process of temporarily taking readers and viewers out of the real world they inhabit into an imagined one that seems strange and disjointed, but nevertheless convincing in its familiarity (Suvin, 1972). When we read a text, watch a film or look at an image of a future city, we are not escaping from the real, but rather redefining its parameters by creating links between imagined and real cityscapes that make any clear separation between the two categories untenable. In Graham's estimation, 'real and imagined sci-fi cities ... offer powerful opportunities for progressively challenging contemporary urban transformation' because they hold, at their core, the value of multiplicity rather than the homogeneity of urbanism under global capitalism, and they emphasize the forging of linkages rather than the cutting of ties in an increasingly fragmented world (Graham, 2016: 395).

Taken together, the themes and works explored here aim to establish resonances between a wide range of urban imaginaries that engage, whether explicitly or obliquely, with the transformed urban environments that will likely be brought about by climate change. I contend that the emphasis on *multiple* imaginaries of climate change—here represented through literature, art and architecture—is critical in expanding the narrow range of possibilities that currently characterize the literature on cities and climate change. To expand these possibilities is not merely to add another layer of interpretation onto the scientific or instrumentalist—an aesthetic embellishment of the pragmatic; rather, it contributes to the redrawing of the boundaries of the entire field of thinking about climate change, particularly with respect to how it affects our psyches—our thinking and feeling about the subject. This emphasis on the mind is important because it chimes with philosopher Félix Guattari's reading of ecology—or what he terms 'ecosophy'—as the coming together of individual subjectivity, social relations and the environment (Guatarri, 2000). For Guattari, an ecology of the mind means one that resists the tendency of contemporary capitalism or, by implication, any dominating worldview, to limit the human imagination by subjugating it to ideological dictates. In correlation with Jacques Rancière's understanding of aesthetics as inseparable from politics (Rancière, 2004), Guattari argues that the imagination is already politicized because, as a faculty that only flourishes when set free, it is inherently antithetical to such subjugation. Furthermore, as an emancipatory tactic, the imagination gives credence to multiple subjectivities—whether Guattari's heterogeneous mental ecologies or Rancière's modes of being and 'forms of visibility'—making it harder for any single narrative to dominate our understanding of a given historical event, place or group of people. Of course, cohering these subjectivities into a collective form is intensely problematic and always risks diminishing the multiple into something lesser. Yet, in order to fully embrace what happens when we encounter the future-orientated discourse of climate change, we must begin in the only place we can, that is, facing outwards from our own subjective imaginative worlds, ready to engage with whatever we encounter. From that place, we can aim to find resonances with others' subjectivities and build a collective basis for re-inhabiting our cities in new and inventive ways.

Climate-change fictions

Even as the recent knowledge of climate change has generated many future imaginings of drowned cities, particularly coastal or low-lying conurbations, these are also part of a long history of collective fears of apocalyptic inundations that date back to pre-history, namely in countless stories of devastating deluges that characterize so many of the world's religious and spiritual traditions (Withington, 2013: 9–32). These ur-floods may have grown from myths and legends but their almost universal presence in diverse geographical locations and cultural traditions reflect the fact that floods are the most common disasters known to humankind (*ibid.*, 19–20). Thus, even as the most famous submerged city of Atlantis was probably a mythic assemblage of classical architectures buried under the city's namesake ocean, it was probably also inspired by real urban drownings in the ancient world, whether cities that were submerged by flood waters or buried by Vesuvius's ash and mud (Donnelly, 2006). Throughout history, vulnerable cities have been literally obliterated by the seas—the archaeologist and scuba diver's paradise off the coast of Alexandria is testament to rising sea levels that drowned ancient cities;[1] the city of Saeftinghe in the Netherlands and Dunwich in England are more recent ones, the former being devastated in the All Saints Flood of 1750 (never to be recovered), the latter slowly erased by relentless coastal erosion (Anderson, 2015: 198–205). More recently, some cities have been given up to others in the demand for fresh water—for example, Shi Cheng, the Lion City, which lies in ruins at the bottom of a hydroelectric dam in China, or the city of Igarata in Brazil, submerged since 1969 after the creation of a reservoir, and which recently started re-emerging as a result of one of the worst droughts in recent history (Osborne, 2015).

The prospect of future drownings owing to the effects of climate change, principally rising sea levels caused by melting ice in the polar regions and Greenland, has been a dominant motif in climate-change fictions, probably because it chimes with this long history of real and imagined drowned cities, while at the same time providing a way of rendering climate change in a local context and as a powerful, if often exaggerated, effect (Trexler, 2015: 83–84; Abbott, 2016: 160–70). Within this body of work, two types of narrative dominate: on the one hand, post-diluvian cityscapes imagined in the future after a catastrophic flood, and on the other, the progress of a flood that gradually transforms an urban environment. In the first category, the most influential precedent is J.G. Ballard's early novel *The Drowned World*, published in 1962. Although written long before global warming was even coined as a term (in 1975), the novel has become regarded as a major influence on more recent climate-change fictions and also prescient of real climate-related disasters, such as the devastation of New Orleans after Hurricane Katrina in 2005 (Gandy, 2006: 86; Ballard, 2009). Ballard also self-consciously positioned the novel within an existing English literary tradition of imagining London's death by water, from Richard Jefferies's 1885 fantasia *After London* to John Wyndham's *The Kraken Wakes* from 1953. Yet, in explicit contrast to Wyndham's novel, which emphasizes survival and rebuilding, and to the more recent reconstruction in post-Katrina New Orleans, where flood defences have been strengthened, *The Drowned World* posits a transformed urban world that must be adapted to in order for an authentic human experience to emerge (Sellars and O'Hara, 2014: 83, 90).

Ballard's novel presents a hallucinatory vision of a future London that has been sunk beneath vast flood waters created by the melting of the polar ice sheets, the latter caused by rapid global warming that resulted from a sudden increase in solar radiation. *The Drowned World* imagines London as a city that has been literally swamped by exotic flora and fauna that has reverted back to resemble that of the Paleozoic era: an 'impenetrable Matto Grosso sometimes three hundred feet high' (Ballard, 2011: 19) that consumed the city's half-submerged steel-supported tower blocks; giant iguanas that made their homes in the boardrooms of former offices; outsized bats that created their eyries in the ruined buildings; and, in between the last vestiges of the city, a network of lagoons filled with rotting vegetation and the carcasses of dead animals. The novel's isolated protagonist, Kerans, lives in the former Ritz Hotel and is a member of a group

---

1   The sunken cities off the coast of Alexandria were the subject of the exhibition *Sunken Cities: Egypt's Lost Worlds* held at the British Museum, London, 19 May to 27 September 2016.

of scientists who are gathering information about the world's drowned cities before heading to the last remaining place fit for human habitation—the Arctic—where the remnants of humanity have gathered. With temperatures and humidity rising each day, Kerans experiences his own psychic equivalent of regression, eventually embracing the new jungle before him, the novel concluding with this 'second Adam' heading south towards his certain death. Key to Ballard's vision and the power of his prose lies in the way the transformed urban environment functions as a mirror image of the processes going on in Kerans's psyche, whether in his constant confrontation with the submerged city itself (an obvious metaphor for the unconscious mind), the abandoned clock towers he sees, their faces without hands (*ibid*.: 63), or a chalk-white colonnade he visits that reminds him of an Egyptian necropolis (*ibid*.: 68).

The Drowned World uses 'the external transformation of the urban landscape to reflect and marry with the internal transformation' of Kerans, who is the only character in the novel to fully embrace both of these transformed worlds (Sellars and O'Hara, 2014: 90). Indeed, as Ballard has also argued, perhaps the extreme urban transformation he depicted in *The Drowned World*—by any other estimation a catastrophe—might provide the *only* environment in which genuine human transformation might occur (*ibid*.: 202–203). Yet there is no denying the extreme subjectivity of Ballard's future drowned city, a post-urban environment in which conventional social relations are completely severed. It is clear that Ballard believed that individual psyches have the potential for transformation, but this transformation occurs in almost total isolation. There is also a sense in which Ballard's vision elides human responsibility for the transformed environment—it is the sun that causes London to be drowned, not human activity. As Trexler (2015: 28) has argued, this has proved a problematic precedent for fictions that address anthropogenic climate change because it 'acts as a terrific form of compression, homogenizing a whole world of ecological and climatic variation into a single, distorted disaster'. Yet vivid images of submerged cities that draw their inspiration from Ballard's novel have characterized a number of recent climate-change fictions. Paolo Bacigalupi's *The Drowned Cities* (2012) is similar to *The Drowned World* in both its self-explanatory title and also the fact that the identity of the city it depicts—Washington, DC—is, like Ballard's future London, only revealed towards the end of the novel. The American capital, mirroring Ballard's post-diluvian London, has been overtaken by tropical vegetation but, unlike Ballard's uninhabited city, this one has become home to rival warlords and scavengers. With its Chinese counterpart, Shanghai Island, remaining a bastion of civilization, Bacigalupi inverts conventional contemporary Western assumptions about America's enlightened democracy versus China's repressive political regime. No less savage in its politics, but more satirical, is Will Self's *The Book of Dave* (2008), where London, 400 years into the future, has been submerged by 100 metres of sea water, turning the city into an archipelago. With its social and political life based on the eponymous book, the rantings of a London cabbie that are revealed in the segments of the book set in our present-day era, the imagined future world extends Dave's bigoted views, cockney dialect and text messages to form an entire social and linguistic world. Yet the novel's fantastic premise is also grounded in Self's own encyclopaedic knowledge of London, one that closely links this future city to London in the here and now, with all its current dystopian tendencies—increasing social division, the rise in right-wing nationalism, and the globalization of finance and culture—imagined to be played out as a reactionary future *in extremis*. Although the submerged cities in these novels host social lives we can barely imagine, they nevertheless draw those lives firmly within the orbit of the familiar, whether through landmarks such as the Washington Monument and White House in *The Drowned Cities*, or the myriad familiar-yet-different street and place names of a future London in *The Book of Dave*. As already stated in the introduction to this article, the play of strangeness and familiarity in such future-orientated fictional narratives is important because it disrupts the ways we relate to the familiar real urban world, thus shifting the parameters of what that real might actually be. In Rancière's estimation, this kind of estrangement opens up new realms of possibility because it 'rearranges the rules of the game by making two things interdependent: the blurring of the borders between the logic of facts and the logic of fiction' (Rancière, 2004: 36).

In contrast to these post-diluvian future cities, some recent climate-change fictions have used the image of flooded cities to articulate a different kind of narrative, namely that of flood-as-duration. These have sought to imagine social relations in future cities that are being slowly transformed by rising sea levels, and notable examples include Melbourne in George Turner's *The Sea and Summer* (published in 1987 when awareness of climate change was only just emerging), Bangkok in Bacigalupi's *The Windup Girl* (2010), and London in Maggie Gee's *The Flood* (2004) and Stephen Baxter's *Flood* (2008). In all of these city-based climate-change fictions, the relationships between characters in a transforming urban environment take precedence over dramatic descriptions of submerged cities. Yet they do so for varied reasons. In *The Sea and Summer* the emphasis is on relations between sharply divided classes—as sea levels inexorably rise, Melbourne's tiny urban elite retreat to high ground in secure compounds, while the 90% poor and unemployed eke out a third-world existence in flood-prone tower blocks. *The Windup Girl* focuses on the relationships between human beings and their artificially created cousins (the windup girl of the book's title) in a future Bangkok, an island-city ringed by enormous defensive sea walls protecting it temporarily from a flooded outside world in violent turmoil (Trexler, 2015: 211–19; Abbott, 2016: 165–68). Gee and Baxter's London-based novels centre on near-contemporaneous urbanites dealing with an ongoing crisis—unending rain and rising flood waters—and an impending catastrophe, namely an apocalyptic tsunami in *The Flood* that engulfs the entire city in the final moments of the novel, and an even greater apocalypse in *Flood* as sea levels continue to rise until they submerge the entire planet. In contrast to *The Drowned World*, the cityscapes in these novels function more as backdrops to social interactions and character development and therefore lack the hallucinatory power of Ballard's post-diluvian London; yet, this is precisely the result of their emphasis on the relationships between people in a transformed urban environment rather than the intense subjectivity of a solitary inhabitant. As Trexler (2015: 117) has argued in relation to Gee's *The Flood*, this focus on social relations suggests that 'human connections are wholly dependent on material place, that climate change has decimated the characters with whom the reader has identified, and that it also threatens to kill real people we love in *this* world'. In this way, the near-future London depicted in *The Flood* draws us back to the present-day city that we know and experience, rather than forward to a transformation that is only seen as destructive and diminishing.

Taken together, climate-change fictions that imagine future drowned cities invite multiple ways of working through possible apocalyptic scenarios. Although most of these fictions exaggerate the scale and shorten the timescale of future flooding for dramatic effect, they do so in order to galvanize the apocalyptic imagination towards redemptive rather than reactive ends, whether the transformation of the individual psyche when confronted with radical change or social relations during the progression towards catastrophe. These multiple ways of apprehending urban futures are important because they flag up the fact that discourses on climate change are inevitably both real and fabricated, relying as they do on the work of the imagination as much as scientific enquiry; many non-fictional accounts of climate change also draw on exaggerated apocalyptic imagery for rhetorical effect (Lynas, 2008; Oreskes, 2014). Climate-change fictions also point to the need for the human imagination to think through *adapting* to the future effects of climate change on cities. Indeed, these novels demonstrate a wealth of adaptive strategies taken up by human subjects in the face of catastrophe, from the total acceptance of the solitary contemplative in *The Drowned World* to the communal struggles of *The Flood* and *The Sea and Summer* and other contemporary novels.[2] Finally, even as these fictions project the city forward in time—whether the far future of Ballard's novel or the near-contemporary London of *The Flood*—they nevertheless, through their narratives and characters, draw readers back into the world they inhabit in the present, a world that is already set on a future course that they will—individually, collectively, and all together with the changing climate—play a part in bringing into being. In this sense, they can contribute much to what Guattari (2000) has identified as an ecology of mind. For Guattari, cultivating a mental ecology is as important as an ecology that focuses on environmental or social concerns, and he sees this as primarily achieved by abandoning 'scientific (or pseudo-scientific) paradigms and returning to aesthetic ones' (*ibid.*: 37). This may seem like an extreme reaction against scientific enquiry which, after all, has led us to the point of knowing about climate change, but for Guattari, it is science that has denigrated and almost extinguished the value of human subjectivity and the aesthetic dimension of human experience (*ibid.*: 28). For the ecological revolution to occur that is urgently required to address climate change, the 'sensibility, intelligence and desire' of the human mind must be reshaped, just as much as the political, economic and social aspects of the human world. It is precisely in the realm of the imagination that human subjectivity might begin to build its own resilient ecology of mind. Such mental resilience on the part of the urban populace is equally important as that of the built fabric of the city—whether buildings or infrastructure—in the face of the threats and transformations that will be brought about by climate change.

Postcards from the future

One of the most enduring images of London in ruins is an engraving by Gustave Doré from 1872 (see Figure 1)—the final illustration in Blanchard Jerrold's book *London: A Pilgrimage*. Depicting what was then the world's largest city and the centre of a global empire, Doré's image was a late expression of the nineteenth-century obsession with the figure of the New Zealander, an imagined New World successor to the British who would, in the far distant future, come to gaze upon the ruins of London just as Victorian travellers gazed upon those of ancient Rome (Nead, 2000: 212–15; Skilton, 2004). It is also a powerful image of submergence—the city slowly succumbing to ruin from above (its buildings sinking into the ground) and below, from the waters of the river Thames, long released from their human-made embankments. This image, which tapped into late-nineteenth-century anxieties about both imperial decline and London's seemingly intractable social divisions, was an early precursor to cinema's enduring obsession with picturing urban destruction. Thus, apocalyptic flood disaster films, from Felix E. Feist's *Deluge* (1933) to Roland Emmerich's *The Day After Tomorrow* (2004), use New York's landmarks, such as the Statue of Liberty, in the same way as Doré's image uses the sunken pillars of Blackfriars Bridge and the ruined dome of St Paul's Cathedral beyond to provide memorable visual reference points for an otherwise wholly unfamiliar apocalyptic narrative (Page, 2008: 74–76, 89–91, 196, 220–26; Withington, 2014: 107–16). At the same time, the sense of flood waters as restoring untamed nature back to the city resonates with cinematic images of post-apocalyptic cities, such as New York City in *I am Legend* (2008), directed by Francis Lawrence, and London in *The Girl with all the Gifts* (2016), directed by Colm McCarthy. Indeed, these two aspects of deluge imagery—the apocalyptic and post-apocalyptic—mirror the two strands already identified above in relation to climate-change fictions, namely the imagination of cities after a catastrophic

---

2   Other notable examples of city-based climate fictions that use the flood-as-duration motif are Donna McMahon's *Dance of Knives* in 2001, set in a flooded Vancouver; Kim Stanley's Robinson's *Forty Signs of Rain* in 2004, the first in his *Science in the Capital* trilogy and set in Washington DC; Saci Lloyd's London-based *The Carbon Diaries 2015* in 2009 and its 2010 sequel; and David Brin's *Existence* from 2012, which takes place in the Huangpu estuary on the edge of a flooded Shanghai. Robinson's novel, *New York 2140*, published in 2017, set in a flooded future New York City, was published too recently for inclusion in this article.

FIGURE 1 *The New Zealander* by Gustave Doré, wood-engraved print in Blanchard Jerrold and Gustave Doré's *London: A Pilgrimage* (London, 1872)

flood and those that focus on the apocalyptic flooding event or events themselves. As with fiction, these images tend to emphasize, on the one hand, the experiences of a solitary survivor (the New Zealander in Doré's image) and, on the other, the attempts by urban inhabitants to come to terms with flooding, even if, in the cinematic tradition, this usually focuses on rebuilding cities rather than adapting to their submergence.

In relation to more recent predictions about the impact of sea level rises on low-lying cities, visual imagery is characterized by two dominant viewpoints, namely the view from above and the view from below. The first category includes scientifically produced images, such as predictive flood maps issued by the UK Environment Agency (*Daily Mail*, 2011)—conventional map views of cities such as London overlaid with swathes of blue indicating areas at risk from future flooding—and more creative adaptations of maps seen in Jeffery Linn's series of sea rise maps, in which the artist has shown how world cities such as London, Los Angeles, Vancouver and Hong Kong would virtually disappear if sea levels rose by 66 metres, the highest level currently predicted by the IPCC (Linn, 2016). Views from above also include bird's-eye views of cities showing how sea level rises might alter the skyline, shore and riverscapes of iconic landmarks, for example, the Houses of Parliament in one image from the artists Didier Madoc-Jones and Robert Graves's series *Postcards From the Future* (2010),[3] and John Upton's digital photomontage of Manhattan skyscrapers used in Al Gore's polemical film *An Inconvenient Truth*, released in 2007. There is no doubting the rhetorical effect such imagery has, providing, as it does, a dramatic at-a-glance picture of what cities might look like if flooded by a significant rise in sea levels; yet, these images distance viewers from the catastrophic effects of such flooding by showing only the end results in the far future and also, in the case of many of the images from the *Postcards from the Future* series, by casting the future inhabitants of inundated cities as racially 'other' (Baldwin, 2015). Indeed, what we see in these images are effectively urban stage sets—cities emptied of inhabitants bar orientalized migrants and submergence cast as an inevitable and unstoppable apocalyptic event, even as the processes leading to flooding on such a scale would take centuries to work themselves out.

Views from below actually situate viewers beneath the flood waters—a discomforting position because such an environment would be much more hostile to human habitation than the dry land that would remain above the flood water level. They include digital images of submerged urban landscapes, such as Francois Ronsiaux's Times Square in New York enveloped in submarine blue (Azzarello, 2015) and Nickolay Lamm's similarly rendered image of Miami under a 25-foot rise in sea levels (Bennett-Smith, 2013). These images present desolate urban vistas, devoid of any life bar the observer, even as the flood waters are rendered crystal clear. In contrast, in one of a series of five images produced by the UK media production studio Squint/Opera, London's future flood waters support a rich marine ecosystem (see Figure 2). This image shows a view from the bottom of a new shallow sea towards the half-submerged Church of St Mary's on London's Strand, providing an unfamiliar counter to the otherwise predominantly pessimistic representations of urban futures underwater (Fairs, 2008; Gandy, 2014). Exhibited as part of a series at the London Architecture Festival in 2008, this view from below offers a sense of optimism—in Squint/Opera's London of the future, 'far from being a tragedy, the floods have brought about an improved way in life in the capital' (Fairs, 2008). Yet, just how such an improved way of life will come about is far from clear in the image, bar the inclusion of a manned boat that suggests a tranquil human presence. The image's depiction of a thriving marine ecosystem in pure waters is entirely at odds with most literary fictions that represent the progress of future urban floods. Thus, in Gee's *The Flood* (2004: 189), the rising waters smell 'of rot, of toilets'; in Turner's *The Sea and Summer*, they are filthy, 'full of floating, nameless debris, stinking rubbish' and 'soft slops of slime that touched and clung'; while in Baxter's *Flood* (2008: 172, 244), they are choked with bodies and wastes, 'murky grey-brown', 'slick with oil' and 'littered with garbage, plastic scraps and bursting bin liners'. These fictions undermine the image of any future flood waters as restorative or regenerative, mirroring

3   This series of digital images was presented as large-scale back-lit transparencies in the exhibition *Postcards from the Future* at the Museum of London, October 2010 to March 2011.

FIGURE 2   *St Mary Woolnath–Rich Pickings*, digital image from the series *Flooded London*, 2008 (reproduced by permission of Squint/Opera)

the experience of many dealing with the aftermath of real urban floods, when raw sewage often rises up from underground sewers.

At first glance, the flood waters in Alexis Rockman's painting *Manifest Destiny* from 2004 (see Figure 3), seem to be supporting an equal abundance of life as in Squint/Opera's image of a bucolic flooded London (Figure 2).[4] Indeed, they do, but this is not

---

4   *Manifest Destiny* was first exhibited in 2004 at the Brooklyn Museum of Art, which had commissioned the work. It was subsequently acquired by the Smithsonian American Art Museum in Washington DC.

FIGURE 3 *Manifest Destiny* by Alexis Rockman, 2003–2004, oil on board (Smithsonian American Art Museum; reproduced by permission of Alexis Rockman)

life as we know it; rather, the painting shows an extraordinary array of organisms made up of a mixture of recognizable flora and fauna (algae, coral, seals, lampreys, carp, an enormous jellyfish, sunfish and lionfish underwater; and gulls, cormorants, egrets and pelicans above) and strange new bioengineered species, including fish sprouting pustules, outsized deadly viruses (identified by the artist as HIV, West Nile and SARS) and other bacteria-like creatures and mutant crustaceans (Rockman, 2005: 6; Page, 2008: 226–28). Indeed, most of the non-human life included in *Manifest Destiny* seems alien, for this is a split-level panorama of the New York district of Brooklyn in the year 5000, after global warming has not only submerged the city but also transformed its climate from temperate to tropical. Despite the fact that the landscape is empty of human beings, the legacy of the latter is evident everywhere. Here, the remains of the human-constructed environment—the Brooklyn Bridge on the right, vestigial skyscrapers in the distance and, perhaps most strikingly, the city's subterranean infrastructure of tunnels, storage vaults, sewers, and gas and water pipes—not only linger in the far distant future, but have played a key role in the evolution of the organisms that now inhabit them. Scattered throughout the image are also the products of present-day accelerated capitalism that mock the hubris that characterizes our technological age—a floating oil barrel, sunken oil tanker, stealth bomber and submarine. Finally, Rockman also includes in his painting the remains of projects yet-to-be built (in 2004), most notably dykes and sea walls meant to protect the city against sea level rises, but which, in the far distant future, have long been overwhelmed by the inexorable flood waters.

In its extraordinary attention to detail and concern with accuracy—during the process of creating the work Rockman consulted with palaeontologists, biologists, archaeologists and architects—*Manifest Destiny* not only presents a dire warning to a pervasive contemporary reluctance to change the destructive course of industrial capitalism, but also a compelling image of how the human-built world will continue to influence the evolution of the environment long after humans themselves have disappeared. With its mixture of tropical and bioengineered flora and fauna, the intensity of its sunlight and the absence of the human, Rockman's vision mirrors Ballard's hallucinogenic image of a future London in *The Drowned World*. Yet, unlike the novel, it points us back to ourselves in the here-and-now, challenging us to think more seriously and more imaginatively about the long-terms effects our collective actions now will have on the world to come. As such, *Manifest Destiny* chimes strongly with the emergence of the idea of the Anthropocene in the 2000s as defining a new epoch in geological time in which human activity, and particularly an accelerating urbanism, is as 'geologic' a force as natural ones (Chakrabarty, 2009: 206–207). Even though the painting transports the viewer a barely conceivable 3,000 years into the future, it nevertheless spells out clearly the connections between our own time and this long span into the future. It also breaks down the entrenched humanist distinction between natural and human history; in *Manifest Destiny*, both the future of the city and of nature are thoroughly intertwined. As such, the painting clearly flags up the need to think through those connections today and to recognize that they are already putting us on the road to the future envisaged in the painting. However, as the painting's ironic title suggests, such a future is not inevitable; rather, *Manifest Destiny* invites us to think through how our own small actions are interwoven with the world and how they might be changed to co-create a more sustainable future. The painting also calls into question the current tendency to combat urban inundations with more effective flood defences, as seen in both post-Katrina New Orleans (Burnett, 2015) and in many towns in the UK affected by recent flooding.[5] With New York's own future-built flood defences swallowed by the

---

5   On responses to the recent UK floods, see the 2016 report published by the Department for Environment, Food and Rural Affairs, and the Environment Agency at https://www.gov.uk/government/news/700m-boost-for-flood-defences-brings-150m-more-for-yorkshire-and-cumbria (accessed 18 July 2016).

sea, the painting clearly shows the folly of such an approach in its unwillingness to make deeper changes to both mitigate and adapt to global warming, a point that is perhaps at last being recognized in a shift towards ideas of resilience in the UK government's 2016 National Flood Resilience Review (HM Government, 2016). Such warnings are also characteristic of the climate-change fictions discussed previously: the vast sea walls that surround Melbourne in the mid-twenty-first century in *The Sea and Summer* are eventually overwhelmed; the relocation of New York to higher ground in *Flood* proves fruitless; and the seemingly impregnable walls and pumps encircling Bangkok in *The Windup Girl* are finally destroyed as a result of the inhabitants' inability to peacefully resolve their conflicts.

How we negotiate the prospect of a future urban life radically transformed by flooding is critical to the formation of the imagination today. In both literary and visual depictions of submerged urban futures, the intention is clearly to engage our imaginations in thinking through such possibilities. But does such apocalyptic deluge imagery have the effect of paralyzing us in the face of overwhelming, and perhaps inevitable, catastrophe, as Swyngedouw (2010, 2013) has argued? Even though the urban transformations depicted in many fictions and images of the effects of future climate change might be extreme or exaggerated, they nonetheless provide intimations of what might be required for genuine human and social transformation to occur. This idea closely reflects the original meaning of the word 'apocalypse'—namely the Greek *apokalupsis*, meaning revelation or disclosure. In this sense, apocalyptic urban drownings in texts and images are not orientated towards a terminal point in the future but rather produce an ongoing revelation that transforms. As Skrimshire (2010: 228) has highlighted, the notion of apocalypse as revelation is embedded in how climate change is portrayed today, namely 'as a discourse of the future that is at once the revelation of ends, or limits, as well as the symbol of necessary transformation itself'. What images in particular contribute to this discourse are representations that open up an ambiguous aesthetics where a transformed future urban environment can be temporarily *lived in* by readers/viewers in order to establish resonances between their inner and outer worlds. Based on Rancière's understanding of aesthetics as the visual forms of the world that present themselves to our sensory experience, these images can be understood as interventions that disrupt the existing aesthetic field, rendering it more heterogeneous and therefore richer in its potentiality. These images not only affect how we sense the urban world now but also how we negotiate our relationship to a future urban reality they open a window onto: a coming 'real' that 'must be fictionalized in order to be thought' (Rancière, 2004: 38). As images like *Manifest Destiny* suggest, such a future urban environment will be co-produced by both human and non-human forces, each with their own histories and future trajectories, whether the short spans of individual and collective human history or the 'deep' geological and ecological time of the earth. As Chakrabarty (2009: 213) has forcefully argued, the realization that anthropocentric climate change will transform the future environment necessarily 'requires us to bring together ... the planetary and the global; deep and recorded histories; species thinking and critiques of capital'.

Submarine cities

Although the climate-change fictions and imagery examined so far describe urban environments radically transformed by rising sea levels, their architectures tend to remain cast in relatively conventional terms: familiar concrete slum-like tower blocks and skyscrapers in *The Sea and Summer*, *The Flood* and *Flood* sink beneath the flood waters rather than being adapted in terms of their design; cities are abandoned for giant cruise ships that eventually prove just as vulnerable in *Flood*; while even the futuristic architectures included in *Manifest Destiny*, such as Santiago Calatrava's proposed remodelling of the Washington Bridge in New York, are shown to be wholly inadequate responses to the threat of climate change.[6] By contrast, in architectural practice, some have imagined and even partially realized urban communities that adapt to rising sea levels by floating on water (Miéville, 2007; Olthus and Keuning, 2010), while others envisage cities creating 'soft' edges to peacefully coexist with what are projected to become permanently flooded zones (Beatley, 2014; Barker and Coutts, 2016). These approaches attempt to mitigate rising sea levels in urban areas by accommodating water in innovative ways; yet, they tell us very little about how architects might respond to buildings becoming partially or completely submerged. How might future urban communities embrace the sea as an environment to be lived *in* rather than *on*? Just as the images discussed above often fail to produce convincing representations of the submarine urban environments that will likely be newly created by rising sea levels, so architecture has often struggled to envisage let alone realize underwater habitats. As Sandra Kaji-O'Grady and Peter Raisbeck (2005: 448) have argued, the submarine environment is one that is as hostile to human habitation as alien planets or outer space; under water, the human body is extraordinarily vulnerable, not only losing its ability to respire naturally but also its orientation to the vertical, to the horizon.

Yet, despite these challenges, the exploration and habitation of the submarine environment has long held a fascination for many writers and designers, from Jules Verne in *Twenty Thousand Leagues Under the Sea*, originally published in 1870, to the development of scientific and military underwater habitats in the second half of the twentieth century, whether research laboratories such as the US-Navy-designed Sealab series in the 1960s, or through Jacques Cousteau's experimental Conshelf communities. Stimulated by these technological developments, architects in the 1960s began to imagine the building of entire cities under water. These included a submarine hotel complex displayed as part of General Motors' 1964 Futurama exhibit at the World's Fair in New York (Samuel, 2007: 106–109), Warren Chalke's interconnecting spheres in his Underwater City project for Archigram in the same year (Sadler, 2005: 38–41), and Jacques and Edith Rougerie's projects in the early 1970s for a submarine village, museum, and a deep-sea research laboratory (Rougerie and Rougerie, 1974).

In recent years, a renewed interest in underwater living has been stimulated by both the threat of rising sea levels and the extreme overcrowding of existing terrestrial cities. In the popular media, National Geographic produced *City Under the Sea* (2011), a pseudo-documentary charting the construction of an imagined future submarine city built in response to global warming and comprised of communal domes on the sea bed linked to rows of living pods for the 'aquanaut' families. In architectural discourse, designers have published their own proposals for underwater cities of the future, including Phil Pauley's Sub Biosphere 2 project, a semi-submerged settlement of eight biodomes connected to a central spherical support structure (Garvey, 2010); Shimizu Corporation's Ocean Spiral scheme from 2015, a 500-metre-wide underwater sphere that would support a tower filled with homes, shops, offices, a hotel and research facilities (Shimzu Corporation, 2014); and Ocean City by Alanna Howe and Alexander Hespe (Hespe and How, 2010), exhibited as part of the Australian *Now + When* entry at the 2010 Venice Biennale, made up of clusters of floating platforms with submerged living quarters that resemble jellyfish in their design. In thrall to a technological optimism in the face of ecological crisis, as well as a libertarian politics that seeks to create new autonomous territories for social elites, these projects demonstrate the enduring appeal of the idea of the sea as a hostile environment to be conquered—a frontier for the melding of individual freedom and unfettered technological innovation (Miéville, 2007). Although these projected cities claim to create truly sustainable

---

6   During the production of *Manifest Destiny*, Calatrava's scheme was commissioned by New York's Port Authority, only to be controversially rejected by the Authority's commissioners in 2011 (Hutchinson, 2011).

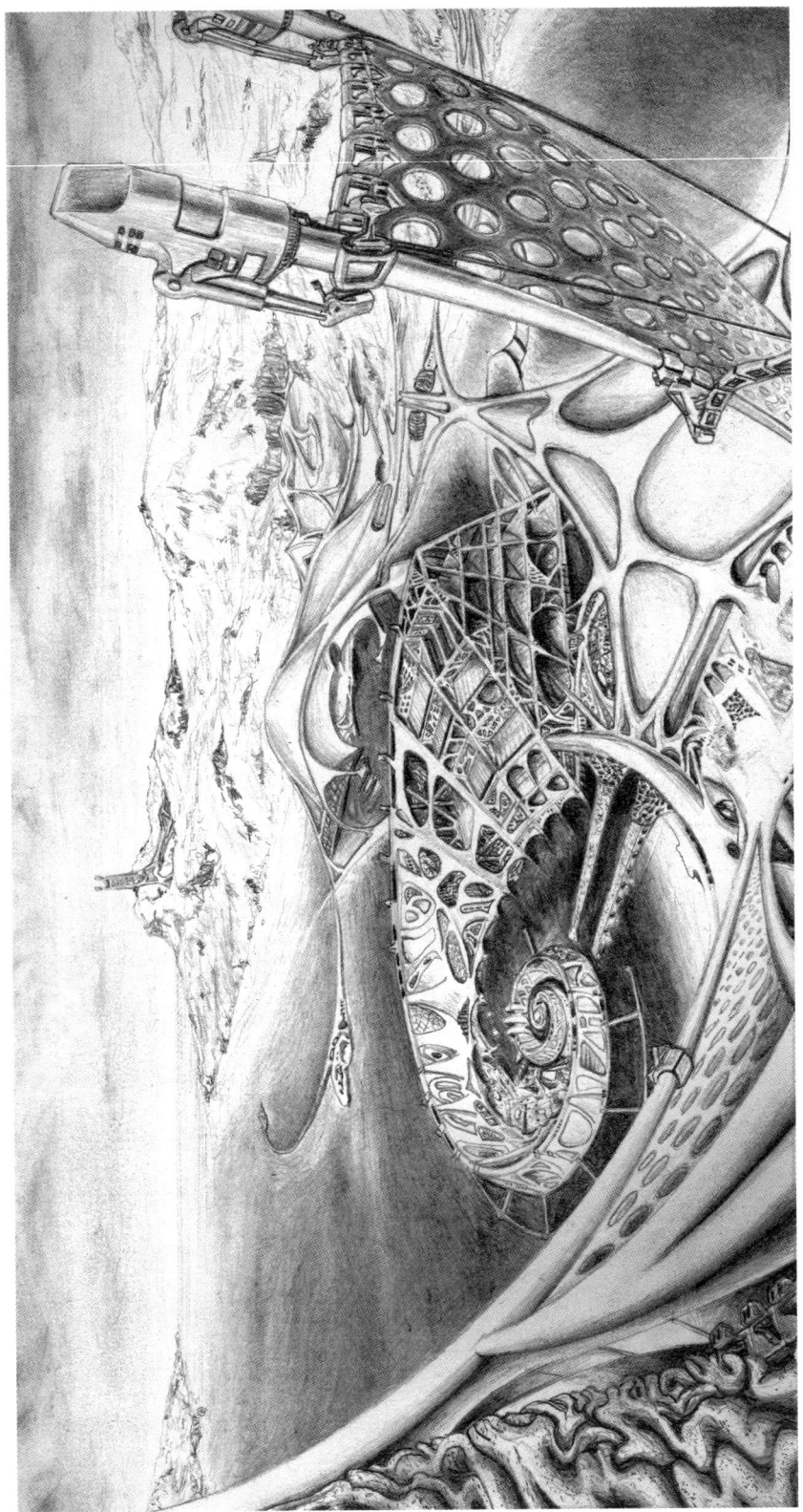

FIGURE 4 *Perspective view of Autopia Ampere (after Newton Fallis)* by Paul Cureton, 2013, pencil and ink on paper (reproduced by permission of Paul Cureton)

habitats—self-sufficient communities that recycle all wastes, generate their energy entirely from renewable sources, and grow their own food—they nevertheless fail to articulate any kind of progressive social programme, instead falling back on the elitist libertarian ideals that have characterized utopias of this kind from the early twentieth century onwards. They also fail to engage with the sea as a dynamic environment, one that we know is rapidly changing as it absorbs the carbon dioxide we continue to release into the atmosphere. As the recent wave of mass coral bleaching events in Australia's Great Barrier Reef testify, the sea is becoming both warmer and more acidic, factors that will irrevocably alter the entire marine ecosystem. To assume that humans can colonize a pristine new environment (as most of these projects do) is a dangerous illusion, one that has been parodied in 2K Boston's video game *Bioshock* (2007), in which the high-tech submarine city Rapture turns from a libertarian dream into a savage dystopia (Anderson, 2015: 205).

Yet, there are currents within the architectural imagination of submerged urban environments that suggest a richer engagement with the sea as it might become in a warming climate. Back in 1970—as many first became consumed with fear about the likelihood of grim urban futures of environmental pollution and overpopulation—the architect Wolf Hilbertz and artist Newton Fallis first sketched out a proposal for their Autopia Ampere project (see Figure 4), a marine city that would literally grow out of the sea at Seamount Ampere, a site of shallow waters situated about halfway between the Madeira Islands and the tip of Portugal (Hilbertz, 1970; Cureton, 2013). The city would begin as a series of underwater wire-mesh armatures anchored on top of a sea mountain. Once in place, the wire mesh would be connected to a supply of low-voltage direct current produced by solar panels. Over time, electrochemical reactions would draw minerals from the sea to the armatures, creating walls of calcium carbonate—a natural spiral-shaped dam that would emerge from the sea to both protect and contain a sizeable population from the otherwise hostile marine environment. Although Autopia Ampere was never realized, Hilbertz's visionary 'growing' architecture eventually led to his development, in collaboration with the coral scientist Thomas Goreau, of Biorock in 1979 (also known as Seacrete or Seament), a substance formed by the electro-accumulation of materials dissolved in sea water (Hilbertz, 1979). This material has found a viable use in the restoration of damaged coral reefs, with the Biorock grown to attract corals and other marine life in order to rebuild submarine ecosystems and make them more resilient to changes in the constitution and temperature of sea water (Spenhoff, 2010). In a world where coral has already become one of the first casualties of climate change, Biorock is likely to become an important material that is able to create new submarine environments out of the ruins of the old. In this sense, Hilbertz's submarine-grown building material is very different from any proposed in more conventional designs for underwater habitats; because it is able to adapt to changes in the constitution of the sea, it is a material that is ideally suited to the age of the Anthropocene. It provides a pertinent model for an urban design practice that seeks to adapt to the waters that will eventually inundate many cities. As many of the future fictions discussed above make clear, such water will not be pristine and undefiled, but rather filled with a host of human-made substances, whether dissolved carbon dioxide, indestructible plastic or urban wastes. It may become evident that the only building material that will be able to adapt to submerged cities will be one like Biorock, that can be grown in the transformed environment.

Hilbertz's Biorock is an important precursor to the current trend in architectural design that seeks to engineer biomorphic materials that mimic nature, thereby questioning conventional interpretations of what sustainable and resilient architecture might be (Agkathidis, 2016; Pawlyn, 2016). Such an approach has led to some radical urban design proposals that directly address the prospect of rising sea levels. The synthetic biologist Rachel Armstrong (2009) has proposed using protocells (chemical agents that behave in lifelike ways) to grow an immense artificial limestone reef structure under Venice to save the city from sinking into the sea. In a different vein, CRAB Studio (led by architects Peter Cook and Gavin Robotham) addressed the prospect of a future flooded London with their Soak City project (2009), a series of towers sited in East London that would be hand-built from the remains of former buildings and other salvaged materials (Cook, 2013: 86–87).[7] The towers themselves were developed from Cook and Robotham's earlier projects for vegetated dwellings, which conceived of buildings taking plants into themselves as part of their ongoing evolution and growth, eventually resulting in hybrid architectures that meld nature and artifice (Cook, 2016: 142–45). Enveloped in the dense vegetation that has grown out of the flood waters themselves, the Soak City towers suggest a future semi-submerged urban environment that allows continued habitation by means of a radical form of adaptation. Soak's City's vegetated towers mirror the verdant ruins of the Brooklyn Bridge in *Manifest Destiny* and the vine-choked apartment blocks and offices in Ballard's *The Drowned World* but, in contrast to both, also envisage a thriving human presence that responds to the flooded city with complete acceptance, resulting in a dynamic coexistence with the transformed urban environment.

The kind of architectural conjecture seen in Hilbertz's Autopia Ampere and Crab Studio's Soak City radically departs from conventional notions of building as deriving from the fabrication of construction materials; rather, making in these projects is fundamentally a process of growth. As such, it chimes strongly with the arguments put forward by anthropologist Tim Ingold (2013: 21), who has sought a renewal of the notion of design as a process of making that intervenes in 'worldly processes that are already going on, and which give rise to the forms of the living world that we see all around us'. In Ingold's view, architects do not impose their designs on the world as if those two domains were entirely separate; rather they add their 'own impetus to the forces and energies [already] in play'. In relation to climate change and the prospect of future submergence, urban designers must face head on the challenge of designing *with* these future conditions, rather than falling back on the notions of mitigation and containment that continue to characterize mainstream approaches.

Conclusion

As I have demonstrated in this article, it is vital to think through what connects the literary, the pictorial and the architectonic in relation to urban futures and climate change. All three modes of expression are grounded in an imaginative apprehension of the world, and all three disrupt an existing aesthetic field dominated by instrumental thinking in order to create new possibilities that might be sensed and incorporated into an emerging 'real'. Of course, within this generalized purpose, they play themselves out in very different media and to diverse audiences. Yet, it is my belief that they are enriched by a mutual engagement: novelists use architecture as a frame for urban environments disrupted by climate change, drawing out the social and political narratives imagined in those environments; artists create images of urban flooding that complement fiction by visualizing transformed cities that are nevertheless grounded in familiar landmarks or views we already know; while architects work through how to build anew in the submerged urban worlds anticipated through fiction and art. Moreover, as Stephen Graham (2016: 388) has elucidated, these connections between fiction, art and architecture are *already* apparent in our image-saturated contemporary milieu. Thus, there is no clear separation between the fictional cities explored in this article and the material cityscapes that are being constructed, lived in and experienced today. The increasingly complex circuits of information exchange that we inhabit undermine any notion of a 'real' life that exists in isolation of its representation in fiction and

---

7   See http://www.crab-studio.com/soak-city.html for the complete series of renderings of Soak City.

media. Our task therefore is to work through the interactions between the fictive and the real and to see the resulting hybrid aesthetic field as a powerful tool that helps us negotiate the complex range of implications inherent in future urban scenarios. The scientific discourse of climate change may attempt to predict likely outcomes of rising sea levels on cities using empirical evidence, but those predictions are usually stated in bald statistical terms, avoiding engagement with the emotional consequences of presenting such alarming statistics. Climate-change fictions—whether they take the form of texts, images or architectural conjecture—fill the gap here, making room for other kinds of forecasts, not of a predictive nature, but centred on the creation of future narratives—stories we can latch on to in terms of imagining what it would be like to *live* in these possible future urban worlds.

In addition, all of the imagined future cities presented in this article rest on the fundamental assumption that we need to accept the changes resulting from climate change and to adapt to those changes. Of course, these fictions are not suggesting mere resignation in the face of the threat of rising flood waters, or that political, economic and social life should remain as it is; rather, they demonstrate that change—the kind of transformational change that is and will be undoubtedly required of us in the face of a new global climatic order—can only come about by imagining how to *live* that change, rather than merely accepting that it is necessary. This is what underlies Guattari's argument that ecology in its broadest sense is both imaginative and anticipatory. In this sense, the imagination of urban futures is not simply a game to be played—a diversion from life in the real urban world—but rather an essential way in which we can cultivate resilience for ourselves, not in order to wallow in pessimism or justify inaction, but rather the opposite—to nourish mental lives that *resist* the increasingly polarizing political and social discourses that are emerging out of radically uncertain urban futures and the threat of catastrophe. In this understanding, the freedom to imagine the future is not a given—an inviolate inner space—but one that must be seized and protected at all costs. As both Guattari and Rancière have stressed, the cultivation of mental resilience is a fundamentally political act—an assertion of the right to be a free urban citizen. If we agree that our cities really are made and unmade in the imagination as much as in their material spaces—a meld of matter and mind—then imaginative texts, images and designs must mutually inform each other to encourage holistic ways of approaching how we think about the future prospect of urban submergence. This is how we incubate radical responses to it.

Paul Dobraszczyk, Bartlett School of Architecture, 22 Gordon Street, London WC1H 0QB, UK, p.dobraszczyk@ucl.ac.uk

References

Abbott, C. (2016) *Imagining urban futures: cities in science fiction and what we might learn from them*. Wesleyan University Press, Middletown, CT.

Agkathidis, A. (2016) *Biomorphic structures: architecture inspired by nature*. Laurence King, London.

Anderson, D. (2015) *Imaginary cities*. Influx Press, London.

An Inconvenient Truth (2007) Documentary film, directed by D. Guggenheim [WWW document]. URL https://www.youtube.com/watch?v=qvXY-IRY590 (accessed 28 April 2017).

Armstrong, R. (2009) Architecture that repairs itself? Ted talk [WWW document]. URL https://www.ted.com/talks/rachel_armstrong_architecture_that_repairs_itself?language=en (accessed 18 July 2016).

Azzarello, N. (2015) Architecture under water: Francois Ronsiaux imagines man's habitat post ice thaw. *Designboom* 23 January [WWW document]. URL http://www.designboom.com/art/architecture-under-water-francois-ronsiaux-imagines-man-habitat-post-ice-thaw-01-23-2015/ (accessed 18 July 2016).

Bacigalupi, P. (2010) *The windup girl*. Orbit, London.

Bacigalupi, P. (2012) *The drowned cities*. Atom, London.

Baldwin, A. (2015) Premediation and white affect: climate change and migration in cultural perspective. *Transactions of the Institute of British Geographers* 41.1, 78–90.

Ballard, J.G. (2009) Gewalt ohne Ende [Violence without end]. *Die Zeit* 21 April [WWW document]. URL http://www.zeit.de/2005/37/Interview (accessed 18 July 2016).

Ballard, J.G. (2011) *The drowned world*. Fourth Estate/HarperCollins, London.

Barker, R. and R. Coutts (2016) *Aquaterture: buildings designed to live and work with water*. RIBA Publishing, London.

Baxter, J. (2009) *J.G. Ballard's surrealist imagination: spectacular authorship*. Ashgate, Farnham.

Baxter, S. (2008) *Flood*. Gollancz, London.

Beatley, T. (2014) *Blue urbanism: exploring connections between cities and oceans*. Island Press, London.

Bennett-Smith, M. (2013) Nickolay Lamm's sea level rise images depict what U.S. cities could look like in future. *Huffington Post* 4 November [WWW document]. URL http://www.huffingtonpost.com/2013/04/11/nickolay-lamm-sea-level-rise-us-cities-photos_n_3062480.html (accessed 18 July 2016).

Bioshock (2007) Video game, 2K Boston.

Bulkeley, H. (2013) *Cities and climate change*. Routledge, London and New York, NY.

Burnett, J. (2015) Billions spent on flood barriers, but New Orleans still a 'fishbowl' [WWW document]. URL http://www.npr.org/2015/08/28/432059261/billions-spent-on-flood-barriers-but-new-orleans-still-a-fishbowl (accessed 18 July 2016).

Chakrabarty, D. (2009) The climate of history: four theses. *Critical Enquiry* 35 (winter), 197–222.

Cook, P. (2013) Looking and drawing. *Architectural Design* 83.5, 80-87.

Cook, P. (2016) *Architecture workbook: design through motive*. John Wiley, Chichester.

City Under the Sea (2011) Documentary series, National Geographic [WWW document]. URL https://www.youtube.com/watch?v=fgnH5qEBt4U (accessed 28 April 2017).

Cureton, P. (2013) Videre: drawing and evolutionary architectures. *Materials. Architecture. Design. Environment* 7.10, 16-27.

Daily Mail (2011) Our future underwater: terrifying new pictures reveal how Britain's cities could be devastated by flood water. *Mail Online* 9 March 2011 [WWW document]. URL http://www.dailymail.co.uk/sciencetech/article-1363703/Our-future-water-How-devastating-floods-swamp-major-cities.html (accessed 18 July 2016).

Deluge (1933) Film, directed by F.E. Feist.

Dobraszczyk, P. (2017) *The dead city: urban ruins and the spectacle of decay*. IB Tauris, London.

Donnelly, I. (2006) *Atlantis: the antediluvian world*. The Book Tree, San Diego, CA.

Fairs, M. (2008) Flooded London by Squint/Opera. *Dezeen* 18 June [WWW document]. URL http://www.dezeen.com/2008/06/18/flooded-london-by-squintopera (accessed 18 July 2016).

Gandy, M. (2006) *The drowned world*: J.G. Ballard and the politics of catastrophe. *Space and Culture* 9.1, 86-88.

Gandy, M. (2014) *The fabric of space: water, modernity and the urban imagination*. MIT Press, Cambridge, MA.

Garvey, J. (2010) Sub Biosphere 2: designs for a self-sustainable underwater world. *Gizmag* 23 June [WWW document]. URL http://www.gizmag.com/sub-biosphere-2-self-sustainable-underwater-world/15507/ (accessed 18 July 2016).

Gee, M. (2004) *The flood*. Saqi, London.

Graham, S. (2016) Vertical noir: histories of the future in urban science fiction. *City* 20.1, 382-99.

Graves, R. and D. Madoc-Jones (2010) *Postcards from the future*. London Futures 2011 [WWW document]. URL http://www.london-futures.com/2010/10/18/hello-world/ (accessed 18 July 2016).

Guattari, F. (2000) *The three ecologies*. Translated by I. Pindar and P. Sutton, Athlone, London and New Brunswick, NJ.

Harvey, D. (2000) *Spaces of hope*. Edinburgh University Press, Edinburgh.

Hespe, A. and A. Howe (2010) Venice Biennale: Ocean City. *Australian Design Review* 26 October [WWW document]. URL https://www.australiandesignreview.com/features/1719-venice-biennale-ocean-city (accessed 18 July 2016).

Hilbertz, W. (1970) Towards cybertecture. *Progressive Architecture* (May), 98-103.

Hilbertz, W. (1979) Electrodeposition of minerals in sea water: experiments and applications. *IEEE Journal of Oceanic Engineering* 4.3, 94-113.

HM Government (2016) National flood resilience review [WWW document]. URL https://www.gov.uk/government/uploads/system/uploads/attachment_data/file/551137/national-flood-resilience-review.pdf (accessed 18 July 2016).

Holthaus, E. (2016) Our planet's temperature just reached a terrifying milestone. *Future Tense* 12 March 2016 [WWW document]. URL http://www.slate.com/blogs/future_tense/2016/03/01/february_2016_s_shocking_global_warming_temperature_record.html (accessed 18 July 2016).

Hulme, M. (2009) *Why we disagree about climate change: understanding controversy, inaction and opportunity*. Cambridge University Press, Cambridge.

Hutchinson, B. (2011) Port Authority paid architect Santiago Calatrava $500G for bridge plans it didn't ask for or use: report. *New York Daily News* 27 April [WWW document]. URL http://www.nydailynews.com/new-york/port-authority-paid-santiago-calatrava-500g-bridge-plans-didn-report-article-1.1770941 (accessed 18 July 2016).

I am legend (2008) Film, directed by F. Lawrence.

Ingold, T. (2013) *Making: anthropology, archaeology, art and architecture*. Routledge, London.

IPCC (2013) Intergovernmental Panel on Climate Change 2013: the physical science basis, summary for policymakers [WWW document]. URL http://www.ipcc.ch/pdf/assessment-report/ar5/wg1/WGIAR5_SPM_brochure_en.pdf (accessed 18 July 2016).

Jameson, F. (2008) *Archaeologies of the future: the desire called utopia and other science fictions*. Verso, London.

Jefferies, R. (1885) *After London*. Cassell & Co., London.

Jerrold, B. and G. Doré (1872) *London: a pilgrimage*. Grant & Co., London.

Kaji-O'Grady, S. and P. Raisbeck (2005) Prototype cities in the sea. *Journal of Architecture* 10.4, 443-61.

Kearney, R. (1991) *Poetics of imagining: modern to postmodern*. HarperCollins Academic, London.

Levitas, R. (2013) *Utopia as method: the imaginary reconstitution of society*. Palgrave, London.

Linn, J. (2016) Sea level rise maps. *Spatialities* [WWW document]. URL http://spatialities.com/category/sea-level-rise-maps/ (accessed 18 July 2016)

Lynas, M. (2008) *Six degrees: our future on a hotter planet*. Harper Perennial, London.

Machin, A. (2013) *Negotiating climate change: radical democracy and the illusion of consensus*. Zed Books, London and New York, NY.

Miéville, C. (2007) Floating utopias: freedom and unfreedom of the seas. In M. Davis (ed.), *Evil paradises: dreamworlds of neoliberalism*, New Press, New York, NY.

Nead, L. (2000) *Victorian Babylon: people, streets and images in nineteenth-century London*. Yale University Press, London and New York, NY.

Olthus, K. and D. Keuning (2010) *Float! Building on water to combat urban congestion and climate change*. Frame, Amsterdam.

Oreskes, N. (2014) *The collapse of civilization: a view from the future*. Columbia University Press, New York, NY.

Osborne, H. (2015) Sunken city of Igarata begins to emerge as Brazil's drought sees water levels plummet. *International Business Times* 6 February [WWW document]. URL http://www.ibtimes.co.uk/sunken-city-igarata-begins-emerge-brazils-drought-sees-water-levels-plummet-1486951 (accessed 18 July 2016).

Otto-Zimmermann, K. (2014) *Resilient Cities 2: adaptation to climate change. Proceedings of the Global Forum 2011*, Springer, London.

Page, M. (2008) *The city's end: two centuries of fantasies, fears, and premonitions of New York's destruction*. Yale University Press, London and New York, NY.

Pawlyn, M. (2016) *Biomimicry in architecture*. RIBA Publishing, London.

Pelling, M. (2011) *Adaptation to climate change: from resilience to transformation*. Routledge, London and New York, NY.

Rancière, J. (2004) *The politics of aesthetics: the distribution of the sensible*. Translated by G. Rockhill, Continuum, London.

Rockman, A. (2005) *Manifest destiny*. Brooklyn Museum of Art, New York, NY.

Rougerie, J. and E. Rougerie (1974) Habiter la mer [Living in the sea]. *L'Architecture D'Aujourd'hui* 175 (special issue).

Sadler, S. (2005) *Archigram: architecture without architecture*. MIT Press, Cambridge, MA.

Samuel, L. (2007) *The end of the innocence: the 1964–1965 New York World's Fair*. Syracuse University Press, New York, NY.

Self, W. (2007) *The book of Dave*. Penguin, London.

Sellars, S. and D. O'Hara (2014) *Extreme metaphors: collected interviews, J.G. Ballard*. Fourth Estate/HarperCollins, London.

Shimzu Corporation (2014) Ocean spiral. *Shimz* [WWW document]. URL http://www.shimz.co.jp/english/theme/dream/oceanspiral.html (accessed 18 July 2016).

Skilton, D. (2004) Contemplating the ruins of London: Macaulay's New Zealander and others. *Literary London* [WWW document]. URL http://www.literarylondon.org/london-journal/march2004/skilton.html (accessed 18 July 2016).

Skrimshire, S. (2010) Eternal return of apocalypse. In S. Skrimshire (ed.), *Future ethics: climate change and the apocalyptic imagination*, Continuum, London.

Spenhoff, A. (2010) The Biorock process: picturing reef building with electricity. Global Coral Reef Alliance [WWW document]. URL http://www.globalcoral.org/_oldgcra/Biorock%20booklet%20online%20version%201.4.pdf (accessed 28 April 2017).

Suvin, D. (1972) On the poetics of the science fiction genre. *College English* 34.3, 372–82.

Swyngedouw, E. (2010) Apocalypse forever? Post-political popularism and the spectre of climate change. *Theory Culture Society* 27.2/3, 213–32.

Swyngedouw, E. (2013) Apocalypse now! Fear and doomsday pleasure. *Capitalism Nature Socialism* 24.1, 9–18.

The day after tomorrow (2004) Film, directed by R. Emmerich.

The girl with all the gifts (2016) Film, directed by C. McCarthy.

Trexler, A. (2015) *Anthropocene fictions: the novel in a time of climate change*. University of Virginia Press, Charlottesville, VA, and London.

Turner, G. (2013) *The sea and summer*. Gollancz, London.

Vidal R. and I. Cornils (eds.) (2014) *Alternate worlds: blue-sky thinking since 1900*. Peter Lang, Oxford.

Watson, J. and M. Adams (2010) *Design for flooding: architecture, landscape, and urban design for resilience to climate change*. Wiley, London.

Withington, J. (2013) *Flood: nature and culture*. Reaktion, London.

Wyndham, J. (1953) *The kraken wakes*. Michael Joseph, London.

Yusoff K. and J. Gabrys (2011) Climate change and the imagination. *Wiley Interdisciplinary Reviews: Climate Change* 2.4, 516–34.

INTERNATIONAL JOURNAL OF URBAN AND REGIONAL RESEARCH
DOI:10.1111/1468-2427.12582

— **WORLDING WATER SUPPLY:** Thinking Beyond the Network in Jakarta

KATHRYN FURLONG AND MICHELLE KOOY

Abstract

This article draws on scholarship in Southern theory to 'world' the study of water's urbanization. This means complicating scholarship by widening the focus beyond the application of Northern norms to engage with complex and diverse practices in Southern cities. For water's urbanization, this means focusing on what water supply is for the majority: neither the centralized piped-water network nor its absence, but the range of practices and technologies that unite people, nature and artefacts in a complex socio-ecological politics of water. Drawing on scholarship from Southern urbanisms, urban political ecology, and science and technology studies, we illustrate how expanding water's urbanization to include more than networked infrastructure in Jakarta draws attention to the importance of ecological connections between piped water, groundwater, wastewater and floodwater. Thinking beyond the network requires deeper engagement with the ecological connections between the diverse flows of water in and around urban environments. These produce distinct forms of fragmentation that are missed when analysis is limited to piped-water supply. The emphasis on ecological connections between flows of water and power seeks to draw attention back to the importance of the uneven exposure to environmental hazards in cities in which neither water nor nature are wholly contained by infrastructure.

Introduction

Jakarta is sinking, like Manila and New Orleans before it. A coastal city of just under 10 million inhabitants, it sits at the outlet of the Ciliwung River facing north onto the Bay of Java. Several other rivers and streams descend from the highlands to the south, crossing the city, and flowing into the Bay. Jakarta's two private sector water companies draw their piped water supply from reservoirs south of the city. Yet, upwards of 6 million people—more than 60% of Jakarta's inhabitants—rely on groundwater. While the wells of expensive high-rise complexes, businesses and industries extract clean water from the deep aquifer; the wells used by most residents reach only the contaminated water of the shallow aquifer. Groundwater pumping contributes to land subsidence, saltwater intrusion, shallow groundwater salinization, and flooding in the northern coastal areas of the city. Recent tests have shown the shallow aquifer to be contaminated by heavy metals, nitrate and E. coli. Unsurprisingly, the impacts of these interconnected activities are uneven. The city's poorest residents, living on the most marginalized land, experience higher exposure to flooding, have access to poorer quality water, and are less able to invest in household water treatment technologies. At the same time, the self-disconnection of high-income users from the piped network system prevents the cross subsidization upon which service extension to the lower-income areas of the city is based.

In Jakarta, ecological connections between a range of activities that are not contained by networked infrastructure, such as deep aquifer pumping and shallow

This is an open access article under the terms of the Creative Commons Attribution License, which permits use, distribution and reproduction in any medium, provided the original work is properly cited. The research for this article was supported through the project Translating Groundwater Policy to Practice in Jakarta, Indonesia, sponsored by the Netherlands Ministry of Infrastructure and Environment. The authors would like to thank Bosman Batubara for his assistance in producing the map of Jakarta, Prathiwi Putri and Indrawan Prahabaryaka for many discussions on the productive paradoxes of water inequalities in Jakarta, and the three IJURR referees for their constructive comments on the article. All faults in the final article remain with the authors.

aquifer contamination, increase the fragmentation of the urban waterscape. Yet, Jakarta is not alone in this regard. Centralized piped water networks are absent, or very partial, in many cities in the South. In 2014, less than half of the people living in Southern cities could access piped water on their premises, and the figures were even lower in sub-Saharan Africa (WHO/UNICEF, 2014). As Jaglin (2004: 7) points out, focusing on piped water masks the diverse realities of what 'connection' means in Southern cities: 'this seemingly precise and reliable statistic loses its pertinence once the dysfunctional nature of the network, which annihilates the benefit of household or even informal connections' are taken into account.[1] In many Southern cities, water has always been accessed through diverse and multiple means. Importantly, this is not always about an as yet unachieved 'universal infrastructure ideal';[2] urban residents and members of the ICI[3] sector can have a variety of good reasons for choosing not to connect to the network or to retain other supply options in addition to their piped water connection (Bakker *et al.*, 2008; Meehan, 2014). These can be understood as 'contextually creative translations' of dominant technological approaches given particular urban conditions (Monstadt and Schramm, 2017: 109).

These insights are relatively new. Until recently, the focus has tended to remain on formal infrastructure networks. Even where the presence of that network is limited, studies are often concerned with how and why it is limited, and what this says about power and social justice in the city (for a critique, see Jepson, 2014; Lawhon *et al.*, 2014). This conflation of piped water with urban water is increasingly questioned, and work on informal and non-networked water access is growing (e.g. McFarlane, 2008; Liddle *et al.*, 2014). A similar trend can be seen in the natural and applied sciences for which authors are calling for work that goes beyond centralized infrastructure systems in imagining and designing urban water supply (e.g. Srinivasan *et al.*, 2010; Mehta and Movik, 2014). Similarly, advocates of 'water sensitive cities' and urban resilience encourage the development of a diversity of water sources and redundancy in supply systems (Farrelly and Brown, 2014).

On the theoretical side, the past decade has seen the emergence and consolidation of 'decentred' perspectives in urban studies that seek to destabilize the application of Northern norms across diverse contexts. This retheorization of cities—what they are, how they work, and what drives their transformation—has created intellectual space for new ideas that better explain the dynamics of cities across a variety of contexts (Roy and Ong, 2011; Parnell and Oldfield, 2014). This is important, as theories of urbanization based on Northern experiences have proven insufficient and even counterproductive when it comes to understanding life in Southern cities (Roy, 2009; Robinson, 2013; Myers, 2014).

Taking a cue from authors who argue for a 'worlding'—that is, 'decentring' or 'provincializing'—of urban theory, in this article we seek to 'world' water's urbanization. This means putting how water is metabolized and accessed in Southern cities—the majority world (Chatterjee, 2004)—at the centre of theoretical development, on an equal footing with the typical Northern city. In this formulation, water's urbanization refers not only to its metabolization through infrastructure networks, the standard of Northern cities, but also to the range of processes more common to Southern cities—such as private extraction, transportation and sale—that together continually reproduce urban waterscapes. This discounts neither the importance of centralized piped water networks nor the desire of many residents to connect to them. Instead, it underscores the need to look beyond the network for a fuller understanding of water's urbanization and for the development of meaningful policy responses in turn.

---

1   Authors' translation.
2   See Graham and Marvin (2001).
3   Institutional, Commercial, Industrial.

To develop these arguments, we begin by reviewing the concepts of decentring and worlding. We discuss how these interventions challenge our current understanding of urban processes in general and of water's urbanization in particular. We then discuss some of the emerging scholarship in Southern urbanisms, urban political ecology and science and technologies studies (STS) that can help to establish a theoretical basis for engaging with the multiplicity of intersecting pathways through which water is urbanized. Adding to these debates, we argue that understanding these processes requires deeper engagement with the ecological connections between them. Next, we offer a discussion of networked and non-networked water supply in Jakarta to illustrate the importance of the theoretical intervention proposed in the article. This discussion is supported by information and insights accumulated over a decade of academic research and project work in Jakarta, with a specific focus on data gathered through semi-structured interviews from 2015 to 2016. These data are complemented by research in the social and natural sciences documenting Jakarta's groundwater, surface water and piped water flows, enabling us to highlight interactions between Jakarta's unequal water politics and its disproportionate ecological consequences. The study is not exhaustive; it seeks to provide a roadmap for further research by engaging with specific aspects of water supply in Jakarta that can open up debates on water's urbanization to a greater range of processes that are particularly important to Southern cities.

What is worlding? Why world water supply?

–   Southern urbanisms and water supply in Southern cities

The terms 'worlding' and decentring refer to efforts to complicate scholarship by challenging the assumed universality of theories derived from experiences in the North. They follow Chakrabarty's (2000) call for a 'provincializing' of Europe, acknowledging that insights from Europe are reflective of a part of the world but not of the world as a whole. European explanations, like theories from the North, are partial. This is likewise true of urban theory (Roy, 2009). As such, to develop an explanation that better reflects the experiences of a broader range of cities, Northern cities must be displaced from the centre of theorization (Robinson and Parnell, 2011). Indeed, scholars who argue for a decentring of urban theory have identified a disparity between how researchers and practitioners draw on Northern and Southern experiences. This disparity distorts both theory and practice by 'treating places outside the Anglo-American heartland as sources of data rather than as sites of theorization in their own right' (Parnell and Robinson, 2012: 596).[4] As a result, internationally accepted ideas of 'expertise, best practices, models, and technologies related to how best develop and govern cities' are often derived from places where the circumstances are very different (McCann et al., 2013: 582). This creates 'a particular mismatch between current urban theory and the drivers of change that local scholars identify' (Parnell and Robinson, 2012: 597).

To redress this situation, we are called to 'world' urban theory. According to McCann et al. (2013: 584), this requires at least three measures: taking Southern cities as sites of theoretical development, taking the richness of the everyday activities of urban dwellers as the basis for rethinking urban theory, and putting Southern cities on an equal footing with their Northern counterparts in the epistemic imaginaries of researchers and practitioners. Roy (2014: 17–18) offers a set of initiatives to refocus the geography of theoretical development. Here, Southern cities are likewise potential 'worlding nodes' in the creation of 'global connections and global regimes of value', which develop their own 'ambitious experiments'. Experiments that are not necessarily determined by elites but, following Simone, are just as likely to come from 'below', from the everyday practices and complex interactions of people living in cities. Recent work

4   Drawing on Connell (2007).

on water in Southern cities has shown just how much can be gleaned when research engages with Southern experiences as opportunities for knowledge building on par with those of Northern contexts. Such work challenges the North–South binary by engaging with water inequalities—typically thought of as Southern problems—in Northern contexts (Jepson and Vanderwalle, 2015) and by studying Northern and Southern cities comparatively, helping to reconceptualize water access, state engagement and political agency (Ranganathan and Balazs, 2015).

Thus, the idea is not to draw a line between 'North' and 'South' as distinct categories to be theorized independently. As many authors emphasize, the 'South' cannot be understood categorically. Like all spaces, it is relational and exists through a complex network of connections that are always unstable (Comaroff and Comaroff, 2012; Mabin, 2014). In this way, the goal is not to develop a distinct body of theory from and for the South, but to operate on the basis that 'events and ideas in the south are powerful for understanding the world as a whole' (Comaroff and Comaroff, 2012; Mabin, 2014: 24). In this view, building theory from experiences in Southern cities is not only important for improving our understanding of those cities, but for improving our understanding of all cities. It contributes to what Roy (2014: 18) calls a worlding of the disciplines. Worlding, therefore, implies going beyond the development of a specifically Southern theory and the provincializing of Northern concepts. It involves cross pollination and a recognition that we are all working from 'a limited cannon' by virtue of things like language and academic tradition (Mabin, 2014: 27). As Ferguson (2012) states, Southern theory is 'not just thinking-from a place—it is thinking-from more than one place at the same time'. Although innovation in urban development is often occurring in the South, its networks are not simply North–South, but also South–East–North–South, South–South etc. (Mbembe, 2012).

Debates on 'decentring' have also been important in STS. Here, it is the apparent dominance of any particular element in a sociotechnical network that is to be decentred. Researchers seek to supplant the focus on prominent artefacts with analyses that recognize that the power of any artefact is derived from its connections to other 'actants' —human and non-human—that make up the sociotechnical world (Harman, 2009). These two types of decentring—in Southern urbanism and in STS—offer complementary tools to rethink the urbanization of water. While one displaces the centrality of the Northern model, the other displaces the centrality of a particular artefact (like the piped water network) from a position of determinacy. This is important in Southern cities, where centralized networked infrastructure is inadequate for the needs of significant proportions of the population. In this way, focusing on an unmet ideal obfuscates the many ways that water is accessed, urbanized and fragmented. People might access piped water through a variety of 'informal' means, either because they are excluded from the network or because their access is limited due to questions of pressure, reliability or quality. Even households with direct connections may secure most of their water through sources external to the piped-water network, including various raw water sources, like wells and streams, rainwater harvesting, and bottled or sachet water.

It is important to focus on such seemingly supplementary and supposedly temporary processes, not only because of their ubiquity but also because of their role in reproducing and reinforcing inequity. Indeed, there can be as much if not more inequality through the uneven quality, reliability and accessibility of the manifold mechanisms used to meet household needs beyond the piped water network than there is between 'connected' and 'unconnected' households (Kleiman, 2004). In places dependent on rainwater collection in Colombia, for example, some can afford large tanks capable of storing several weeks of water while others can afford only small buckets making them vulnerable to a few days without rainfall. Those who depend on streams may be more or less exposed to contamination, or have access to streams that are more or less reliable during the dry season.

If one is to talk about urban water supply, one must talk about all of these things. Globally, in excess of 1.5 billion urban residents rely on non-centralized groundwater supplies, and it is the most rapidly growing method of meeting basic water needs in cities in sub-Saharan Africa (Foster *et al.*, 2010). Similarly, packaged water—be it bottled or sachet—constitutes an increasingly important source of supply in many Southern cities (Sharma and Bhaduri, 2014). While both groundwater and packaged water suffer contamination and contribute to the contamination of other sources, neither has been the subject of extensive scholarly attention, with a few notable exceptions (e.g. Stoler *et al.*, 2012; Chakava *et al.*, 2014; Srinivasan and Kulkarni, 2014). This oversight, according to Vollmer and Grêt-Regamey (2013), stems from an assumed distance between urban residents and ecological processes when for tens of millions of people in cities, vulnerability to ecological processes is very real.

It is precisely for these reasons that some Southern scholars have recently called for a decentring of infrastructure networks in urban political ecology (UPE). They argue that, given the 'relative paucity' of centralized networks in the South, UPE must broaden its focus to be relevant for Southern cities (Lawhon *et al.*, 2014). The focus on centralized networks is said to produce a cataloguing of 'failed examples' as opposed to real engagement with what is happening in Southern cities (Lawhon *et al.*, 2014: 501); to fail to explore the potential multiplicity of urban infrastructural ideals (Boland, 2007); to overlook the significance of water's biophysical properties (Zérah, 2008); to obfuscate the lack of standardization within the formal system (Gopakumar, 2014); and to neglect a variety of water supply systems beyond the network, at both the household and community levels (Verdeil, 2004). The focus on water networks as defined by Northern theoretical frameworks has also created practical problems for improving service access, increasing spatial segregation (Jaglin, 2008), and limiting the potential to foster a diversity of supply alternatives (Pflieger and Matthieussent, 2008).

While UPE tends to define water's urbanization through its circulation in piped water networks, the original appeal for research was much broader. Swyngedouw (1996: 76) called on scholars to 'reconstruct ... the urbanization process as a political-ecological process with water as the entry point'. Here, the urbanization of water through networked infrastructure became a powerful medium through which to reveal the politics and power guiding the urbanization of nature as a process of uneven development (Gandy, 2002; Kaïka, 2005). Yet, Swyngedouw's call went further, seeking an engagement with the 'multiple temporalities and interpenetrating circulations of water' including the hydrological cycle, climate change and bottled water as well as 'canalization, and distribution networks of all kinds' (Swyngedouw, 1996: 77). Thus moving to a broader engagement with the manifold ways in which water is urbanized, in addition to formal infrastructure, constitutes not a break from the definition of water's urbanization, but a reengagement with its potential breadth.

–   Decentring the piped water network, engaging ecological connection

Theories from STS can help to decentre networked infrastructure, and to bring it and other artefacts into the type of complex social relations with which Southern theorists are concerned. An STS approach, even one that emphasizes the work of technocratic actors, offers something central to the work of 'decentring' by underscoring the contingency of all technical artefacts (Coutard and Guy, 2007), from the seemingly dominant to the apparently insignificant (e.g. Pritchard, 2012). Engaging with contingency, however, is a necessary but insufficient step for the 'worlding' of water's urbanization. Although it may destabilize the apparent 'obduracy' of the centralized infrastructure network, it does not necessarily draw our focus away from it as the central artefact through which to understand urban fragmentation. This is impeded by its imposing material presence as well as its place in a prevailing geographical imaginary about what it is to be a modern city (Dupuy, 2008; Larkin, 2013).

Still, there are tools within STS to help look beyond dominant physical networks to sociotechnical networks of connection. For Latour, the importance of an artefact is not inherent in its properties; it is derived from its connections. In Harnam's reading of Latour's *Irreductions* (2001), nothing is reducible to anything else. *Actants*, Latour's term for the range of living and non-living things that make up the world, 'are not stronger or weaker by virtue of some inherent strength or weakness' (Harman, 2009: 15). Their capacity to shape social relations 'is altered only by their *alliances*'; that is, their connections to other 'actants' (Harman, 2009: 15, emphasis in original).

This same insight that puts an object's connections above its intrinsic properties translates into a necessary decentring of the object and its apparent essence. This speaks directly to the project of decentring the piped water network. Although apparently dominant in its size, 'sunk costs', obduracy and modernist symbolism, it can be decentred if we accept that it is not from such features— but from its connections to a range of actants—that it attains 'dominance' in a given time and space. In this way, the central element of water supply need not be its most imposing or politically pertinent artefact. When water supply is studied through the many *alliances* that structure and mediate the diverse ways in which it is brought into being in the city, the centrality of the piped water network cannot be assumed *a priori* or be held in permanence.

This applies to cities in the North and the South. We need only think of Swyngedouw's (1992) intervention on the role of capital in the production of the 'space/ technology nexus'. He demonstrates the importance of capital mobility in loaning and robbing infrastructures of their importance in the urban landscape. In its wake, capital flight leaves infrastructural landscapes of decay as opposed to dominance. Similarly, Björkman (2015: 19) shows the effects of such capital relations on water infrastructure within a city: in Mumbai, the neoliberal production of a 'world class city' engenders infrastructures of 'water chaos'. At the local and technical scales, moreover, work on water supply has revealed the importance of *mediating technologies* or small-scale technologies in shifting the performance, politics and power dynamics surrounding piped water in a range of contexts (Furlong, 2011; Meehan, 2014; Vandewalle and Jepson, 2015). For Von Schnitzler (2017), such technologies are central in instilling new forms of citizenship in keeping with the neoliberal order of precarious employment. As such, taking Latour's intervention seriously means accounting for proximate relationships as well as the extended connections that can yield the transformation of environments, artefacts and practices within and beyond the piped water network.

Such work has also served to complicate the often-static view of networked infrastructure, revealing it to be dynamic, contingent and interactive. Here, there is no singular network; networks operate differently for different user groups. As such, even households with connections can experience very different levels of service quality and reliability. This may depend on their proximity to a pumping station or treatment plant, their social and political connections, or their capacity to supplement poor services with household treatment devices, storage tanks or different qualities of packaged water (Gopakumar, 2009; Björkman, 2014). Likewise, the practices linking people 'informally' to piped water networks are rife with fragmentation. Informal connections are sometimes tolerated and sometimes penalized by the state, involve unequal relationships with a range of intermediaries, as well as inequitable and unreliable water access (Kooy, 2014; Ranganathan, 2014). The range of activities that occur in response to inadequate piped water provision has led some researchers to call for new infrastructural models that take seriously the integration of other types of supply or of other more sustainable approaches (Pieterse, 2008; Furlong, 2014; Jaglin, 2014; Meehan, 2014). Such thinking is likewise relevant for Northern cities, increasingly concerned with energy consumption and waste cycling (Rutherford, 2008; Coutard, 2010).

Other work in Southern urbanisms, not directly concerned with water supply, takes the decentring of infrastructure a step further. With particular relevance for service provision and access, Simone argues that people themselves act as infrastructure. In many Southern cities, people constitute a central means of insuring material flows, where physical infrastructure is largely absent (Simone, 2004). Reminiscent of Latour's *alliances*, following Simone (2004; 2006), Roy (2009: 827) states that infrastructure 'must be understood not as steel and concrete but rather as fields of action and social networks'. This requires 'spatial literacy' developed through the 'intricate intersections of physical, infrastructural, human and discursive materials', forming a 'collective resourcefulness' which sustains neighbourhoods (Simone, 2014: 1509). With increasing urban segregation, moreover, the spaces of 'relative wealth and impoverishment' must be understood in interaction (Simone, 2014: 1512). For water, these insights are reflected in recent work showing that where and when water flows is a result of 'pressure' applied—socially, technically and above all differentially—affecting the relative flows of water between neighbourhoods. In this framing, infrastructure becomes a dynamic assemblage of actors and artefacts through which citizenship emerges (Anand, 2017).

Building on this work, we emphasize the crucial importance of integrating ecological connections—linking adjacent spaces, but also the seemingly disjointed spaces of 'wealth and impoverishment', through flows of water and contaminants—to better understand the fragmentation of urban waterscapes in Southern cities. This remains an important task despite UPE's many contributions to disrupting the nature–culture binary around water in cities. For Zimmer (2010: 345), even major issues of ecological connection that are common across cities, like wastewater and system losses, 'are hardly ever addressed'. This is not just empirical neglect; it is also ontological. As Braun (2005: 645) states, '[a] great deal is written about water, but nary a word is said about the *properties* of water, and how these might influence the socio-spatial development of cities' (emphasis in original). Thus, while nature is taken as the 'fuel for urbanization', the uncontrollability of hybrids, and their 'lively materiality' is neglected (Braun, 2005: 646).[5] Drawing on the experience of Jakarta, in the section that follows we explore the above issues through the interactions of networked and non-networked flows on water with a particular focus on groundwater abstraction and wastewater flows.

Water's urbanization: engaging ecological connections

– A more than networked phenomenon

In 2003, more than half of the world's megacities, defined as metropolitan areas with over 10 million inhabitants, were groundwater dependent. That is, groundwater constitutes at least a quarter of their water supply (Morris *et al.*, 2003). In sub-Saharan Africa, privately abstracted groundwater is increasing from 1.5% to 5% per year (Foster *et al.*, 2010). On a global level, an estimated 50% of the world's current potable supply is provided by groundwater, with up to '2.8 billion people—nearly half of the world's population—rely[ing] on groundwater as their primary source of drinking water', often accessed through wells, springs and boreholes (Giordano, 2009: 157). Alongside large-scale networked infrastructure, groundwater is urbanized through techniques such as (1) hand-dug shallow wells that supply water to informal housing settlements on the peripheries of cities across Southern Africa and Asia; (2) sophisticated pumping, storage and treatment technologies capable of withdrawing large quantities of groundwater used in industrial production in cities like Dhaka and Jakarta and to fuel urban land transformation for commercial growth in cities like Bangalore; and (3) abstraction, treatment and bottling of groundwater for bottled or packaged drinking water production in cities like Arusha, Dhaka, Jakarta and Mexico City.

Each of these activities is composed of thousands of seemingly separate initiatives that are ecologically connected in ways that are interlaced with power.

5   For an exception, see Robbins (2007).

These processes result in unevenly experienced resource degradation that is compounded—not only by the various forms of abstraction—but also by 'effluent disposal practices in a complex fashion' (Foster, 2001: 185). Aquifers are typically composed of an unconfined or shallow aquifer and a deeper confined aquifer. Between these is a layer of clay or rock of low-hydraulic conductivity called the confining unit or the aquitard. Typically then, it is the unconfined aquifer that faces the most important levels of contamination and that is the most easily and cheaply accessed for abstraction. In addition to a water source, the urban subsurface acts as a sink for wastewater and sanitation flows, leachate from landfills, leakage from municipal infrastructure, pluvial waters and industrial effluents among others. In Foster's (2001) depiction of the relationship between groundwater and urbanization, he underscores the range of flows in cities that are increasing groundwater recharge and contamination, affecting well fields beyond the urban boundary.

In some cities, this means that groundwater levels are increasing despite reduced infiltration due to the proliferation of impermeable surfaces. But in a large number of cities, the increasing reliance on groundwater abstraction for household and ICI use actually means a degradation of water levels despite significant additional flows into the subsurface (Foster, 2001). Contributing to the problem is the dewatering of various sites to make way for construction (Deltares, 2013). These shifts in the subsurface have significant impacts on the built environment and on infrastructure in turn. As soils are drained of water, they can oxidize and compact, leading to land subsidence, compounded by the weight of the built environment. This is particularly problematic in coastal cities, like Jakarta, leading to the further contamination of the unconfined shallow aquifer through salt water intrusion and increased exposure to flooding in low-lying areas (Deltares, 2013).

– Jakarta's waterscape: a product of networked and non-networked flows

Jakarta is defined as a special administrative district, making it simultaneously a province and a megacity with more than 10 million residents living across five municipalities: North Jakarta, South Jakarta, Central Jakarta, East Jakarta and West Jakarta (Figure 1). The megacity is crisscrossed by more than 13 surface waterways, which drain northward into the Bay of Java. Overall, it is estimated that nearly two thirds of the city's water consumption—630 million of 1 billion m³/year—is extracted from groundwater. The remaining third is urbanized through the piped water system, which draws on surface water sources beyond the city boundary (*Kompas*, 2013). Less than 60% of the megacity is covered by piped water infrastructure, while centralized sewage collection and treatment reaches only 2% of the population (BRPAM, 2015). The piped water infrastructure is most densely concentrated in Central Jakarta, while on the edges of North Jakarta, East Jakarta, West Jakarta and South Jakarta the service is absent. The city is served by two separate water supply concessions that bisect the city into Eastern and Western service areas divided by the Ciliwung River. The two 25-year concessions went into effect in 1998. Today two mixed-shareholder companies hold the concessions: Aetra (Eastern) and Palyja (Western).

In Jakarta, as for Southern cities in general (Jaglin, 2014), the water supplied through the centralized system to households and businesses is experienced in highly differentiated ways. While 62% of customers in the Eastern section have 24-hour service, in the Western section this figure drops to 45%. This unreliability within the Western section is further concentrated in the northwestern neighbourhoods of Penjaringan, Kalideres and Cengkareng, which are home to the highest percentage of low-income customers (BRPAM, 2014, 2015). Water pressure is also highly variable across the city. Although the water is potable when it leaves Jakarta's water treatment plants, inadequate pressure throughout the distribution system creates areas of negative pressure leading to wastewater infiltration. Currently just below half of all piped water connections in the

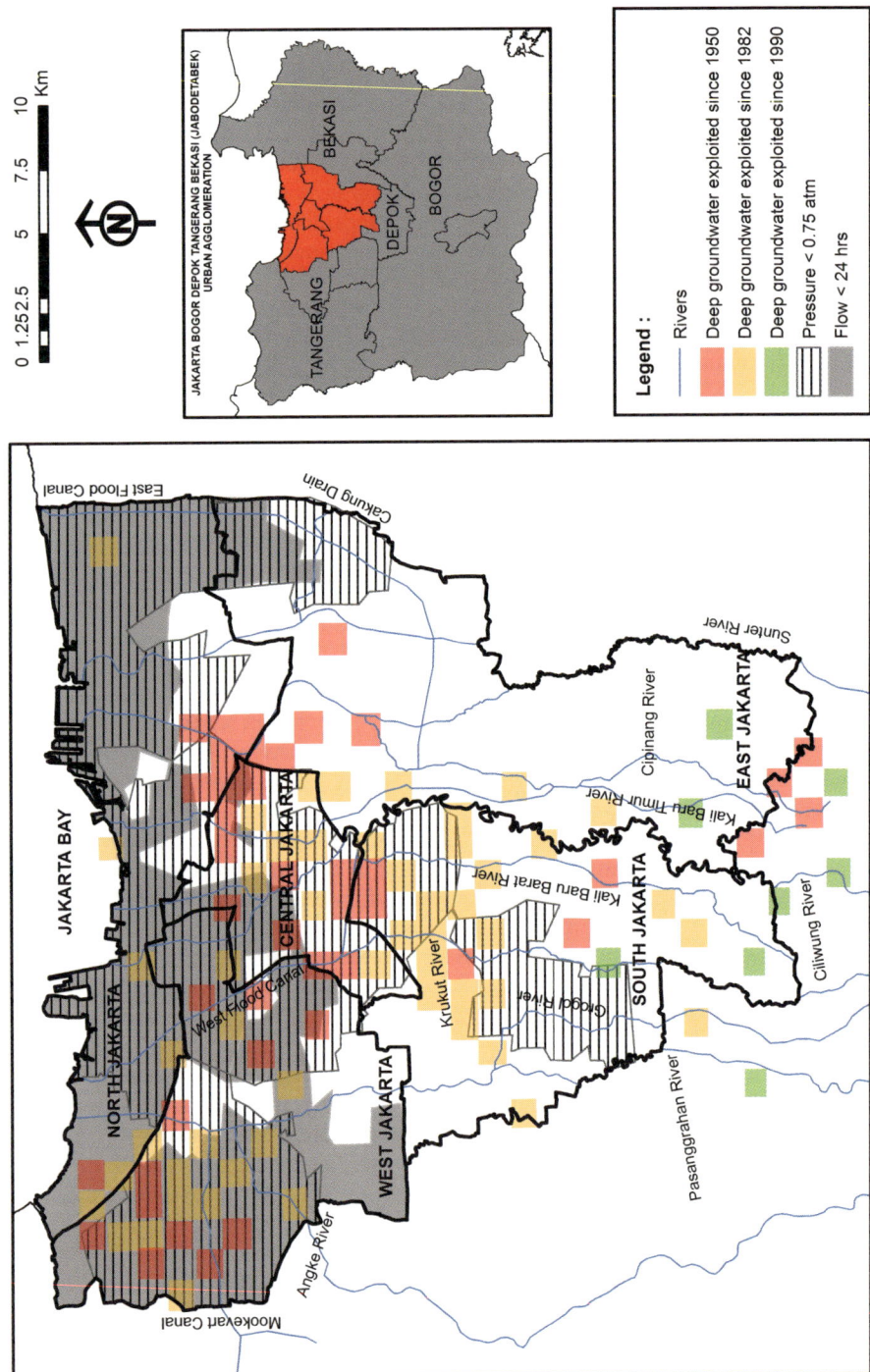

FIGURE 1 Piped water service quality and deep groundwater exploitation in DKI Jakarta (*sources:* 1 km² groundwater cells–Kagabu *et al.*, 2013; (b) hours of provision–BRPAM, 2013; (c) water pressure–BRPAM, 2016)

city meet the standard of 0.75 atmospheric units (atm) of pressure[6] (47% in the Western section and 44% in the Eastern section). Residents, and residential companies for high-income apartment complexes, compensate for low water pressure and infrequent service through rooftop storage tanks. The larger the tank, the more secure the supply.

The widespread unreliability of the centralized piped-water network, its limited reach and the accessibility of groundwater from the confined aquifer have led to a paradoxical situation whereby efforts at service extension are met with high levels of disconnection and neither the very rich nor the very poor are connected to the network. Research commissioned by the Jakarta Water Supply Regulatory Board (BRPAM) shows that between 2008 and 2012, 60% of all new connections aimed at expanding the existing network, were subsequently disconnected for reasons of poor service quality (BRPAM, 2013). Middle-income and lower-middle-income residents represent the largest consumer groups for the Western and Eastern concession areas. In the Eastern sector, middle-income and lower-middle-income households comprise the largest consumer groups, at 21% and 46% respectively. Only 10% are classified in the upper tariff bands (BRPAM, 2014, 2015). The situation is repeated in the Western section, where middle-income and lower-middle-income households comprise 12% and 21% of the consumer base respectively (BRPAM, 2014; 2015). Interestingly, while it is clear that there is no singular network in Jakarta, in keeping with the findings of Gopakumar (2009) and Björkman (2014) for Chennai and Mumbai, those who tend to opt out—with all of the domino effects that this causes—tend to be those with access to the best functioning parts of the network.

For high-income residents living in housing estates and high-rise apartments, better services are available through 'disconnection', a situation common across cities of the South (Jaglin, 2004). These users can afford to opt out in favour of private wells of sufficient depth to pump clean water from the confined aquifer. While such deep wells are common in areas of the city where piped water supply is either absent or very poor, particularly in certain parts of West Jakarta (Figure 1), they are most prevalent where the service is accessible. In a 2015 interview, a special advisor to the Water Supply Directorate in the Ministry of Public Works and former member of the BRPAM stated that most registered deep wells into the confined aquifer are located where piped water supply is adequate; that is, in the shopping complexes, luxury apartment buildings, and business centres of Central Jakarta. This assessment is confirmed by the data in Figure 1. There, the location of registered deep wells in Jakarta is shown according to the period in which their exploitation began (the 1950s, 1980s or the 1990s). Using these data, one can see the consistent increase in the number of registered deep wells in the neighbourhoods of Central and South Jakarta, which are covered by the piped water network, as residential and commercial complexes have spread from the former municipality to the latter since 1990.

Over the decades, groundwater abstraction has continued to increase in Jakarta, especially with population growth. In fact, 60% of the increased access to an improved water source in response to the Millennium Development Goals was met through groundwater abstraction (BPS, 2012). This trend has been actively encouraged by the state, even in areas where piped water is available (Colbran, 2009; Kooy, 2014). While local scientists have been raising the alarm about the impacts of over abstraction from the confined aquifer since the 1980s, it was not until 1998 that such abstraction began to be taxed, with differential tariffs assigned for specific uses. Even then, however, the average price of groundwater remained less than half of that of piped water[7] and the fees

6   The Ministry of Public Works Regulation No. 18/PRT/M/2007 requires a minimum of 1 atm of pressure, yet only 0.75 atm is required in the Cooperation Agreement with the two private operators.

7   The 1998 Local Government Regulation No. 10 levied a 20% tax on groundwater appropriations in Jakarta. The 1999 Jakarta Governor Regulation No. 4554 set a price range for groundwater of US $0.09-0.62/m³, whereas that of piped water was much higher: US $0.13-1.6/m³.

did not apply to state-owned enterprises or to government-owned buildings including offices, schools and hospitals. It was not until 2009 that groundwater abstraction actually came to be priced above piped water for large volume users.[8] Despite these new efforts, groundwater researchers, flood modellers and civil society groups question their impact. They point to continued land subsidence as evidence of thousands of unregistered deep wells across the city and of widespread under-reporting of groundwater consumption by registered users (Wahyono and Wardiat, 2012). Studies estimate that unregistered abstraction constitutes an additional 50–120% of total registered abstraction (CNN Indonesia, 2016). Indeed, the confined aquifer continues to be accessed by those who can afford the costs associated with drilling, maintenance and 'negotiating' the government's official zero abstraction policy for northern parts of Jakarta, where new wells are now illegal but pockets of upper income residential estates require a secure supply in a region of very poor piped water services (Augustinus, 2016).

Private groundwater abstraction in Jakarta does not simply enable access to a source of clean water for those with means; it impacts Jakarta's urban waterscape through its effects on the piped water network and the uneven experience of a range of socio-ecological connections. The ability of wealthy households and businesses to opt out of centralized water supply limits the possibility to cross subsidize either water consumption or water connections for low-income households. This, compounded by various legal and technical restrictions on access, impedes investment in the extension and repair of the network (Kooy and Bakker, 2008). Many residents of Jakarta cannot legally apply for a connection due to questions of residency or land ownership, while the private operators will not extend services to households in low-pressure areas, where they are unable to guarantee service quality. As a result, piped water resale, unregulated connections and water theft are common. Buying piped water from neighbours is an increasingly popular option used by low-income households, especially in areas of North Jakarta (Kooy et al., 2016). Yet, the per-unit price varies widely, averaging more than six times the cost of piped water through a formal connection.[9] Illegal connections and water theft are likewise significant in scale despite years of crackdowns. In a 2014 interview, a Palyja staff member responsible for unaccounted water in the Western sector stated that there were 1,112 known illegal connections there in 2013. In 2015, Jakarta's BRPAM stated that water theft from illegal connections and illegal consumption from registered connections accounted for 34% of daily water loss in Jakarta and up to 50% of all non-revenue water (Kompas, 2014; Aditya, 2015). Unsurprisingly, water theft is most prevalent in areas where piped water services are poorest and where the shallow groundwater is most saline. Where groundwater is saline, it is so because of the effect of the thousands of deep wells that pump water from the confined aquifer located in other parts of the city.

While most deep wells are located in Central Jakarta, the land subsidence of between 10 and 20 cm/year that they engender is concentrated in areas of West and North Jakarta, where such wells are few. This subsidence dramatically increases flood risk, which contaminates shallow wells with mixtures of floodwater and wastewater, and contributes to the progressive salinization of the shallow aquifer. Since the 1960s, groundwater heads in the confined aquifer have dropped by more than 50 m, causing the reversal of vertical flows between the confined and unconfined aquifer layers in the northern half of Jakarta. In those areas, the shallow aquifer now recharges the confined aquifer instead of the reverse (Deltares, 2013). Falling heads have also resulted in the horizontal influx of seawater into the shallow aquifer in North Jakarta, to the point where seawater intrusion now reaches an estimated 3–7 km inland (Delinom, 2008).

---

8 The 2009 Jakarta Governor Regulation No. 37.
9 A survey conducted in North Jakarta showed that resale prices average US $2.20/m³ whereas the price of piped water averages US $0.40/m³ (Kooy et al., 2016).

The associated salinity is dramatically higher in the north, decreasing measurably as one moves inland. Levels of salinity also increase significantly with proximity to surface water, which carries seawater upstream during high tides and flood events (Delinom *et al.*, 2009). In these areas—where neither deep aquifer pumping nor piped water are viable options—the shallow unconfined aquifer has become saline to the point of being unusable even for non-potable purposes (Delinom *et al.*, 2009; Bakr, 2015).

In addition to saltwater intrusion, shallow groundwater is vulnerable to contamination by a range of effluent water flows. In Jakarta, over 90% of residents are dependent on decentralized sanitation systems with inadequate wastewater treatment. Whereas leakage from the piped-water network constitutes the most important source of groundwater recharge in the wealthy areas of cities like Chennai (India), in Jakarta the most important source of recharge for the shallow aquifer is wastewater from leaking septic tanks, unlined soak pits and the direct discharge of black and grey water into open drains (De Vries, 2015). The National Development Planning Agency estimates that 45% of all groundwater in the unconfined aquifer is contaminated with faecal coliform (Detik, 2013), the Provincial Environmental Management Agency doubles that estimate, putting it at 90% (Prabowo, 2011). Leachate from solid waste landfill sites, such as Pulogebang in East Jakarta, further contributes to the contamination of shallow groundwater, as does the dumping of waste into rivers upstream of the city, which overflow during flooding events and contaminate the shallow wells used by residents of the city's informal settlements (Vollmer and Grêt-Regamey, 2013).

Such flooding is exacerbated by groundwater abstraction from the confined aquifer. The land subsidence associated with it is identified as a major cause of heightened flood risk in Jakarta (Deltares, 2013). More than 60% of the city was inundated in 2002, in 2007 and again in 2012, affecting hundreds of thousands of residents through property damage and housing loss (Akmalah and Grigg, 2011). While flood events have affected rich and poor alike, the measures taken to mitigate future flooding have demanded more of the city's most marginalized communities. In 2015 alone, the Institute for Legal Aid in Jakarta reported 113 mass evictions to create space for the widening of river channels, and the development of urban green areas to improve water retention and recharge (LBH-Jakarta, 2016). These evictions affected 8,145 households, particularly low-income residents living along riverbanks and atop polders, and 6,283 informal small businesses. The World Bank funded Jakarta Urgent Flood Management Project also targets low-income households as opposed to confined aquifer pumping or upmarket development in areas reserved for water retention. Specifically, to make way for improvements to the flow of 11 urban rivers and the storage of four reservoirs, the displacement of over 5,000 people is planned (GOI, 2011). Meanwhile, Rukmana (2015) documents the conversion of more than 3,000 hectares of green space, reserved to create zones for recharge and flood retention under the Jakarta Spatial Plan 1985–2005, to commercial development. Many such conversions are even sanctioned by the government. In 2008, Jakarta's governor, Fauzi Bowo, authorized the development of a hotel and a mall in the city centre designated as part of the green area.

Conclusion

Clearly, in Jakarta—as in many other cities—most residents have never relied solely or even primarily on the piped water system to meet their water needs. The various strategies that are employed are neither independent from relations of power nor from each other. The options available, how they are regulated and accessed, the distribution of the associated environmental hazards, and their interactions with other flows of money, power and water—including piped water, different layers of groundwater, seawater, surface water, floodwaters, and effluent waters—all interact to produce Jakarta's water supply. To understand water's urbanization in Jakarta then, one must 'decentre' the piped water network in both the STS sense of not assuming the centrality of a particular artefact and the Southern urbanisms sense of not assuming a particular model of water access. This is what we term as 'worlding' water supply. The former can enable a better understanding of how things work while the latter can open space to think of the potential for new configurations.

Although the vast complexity of the *alliances* and connections that make up Jakarta's waterscape is beyond the scope of a single article, the data above underscore the need for a decentred approach and the importance of an engagement with socio-ecological connections and the 'lively materiality' of the hybrids that result. Bringing together Simone and Roy's call to approach infrastructure as 'fields of action' and Latour's focus on *alliances* helps us to see the piped water network as one element of water's urbanization among others, all of which are mediated by a range of proximate relationships and extended connections. In the case of Jakarta, the *alliances* between the law, income inequality, aging piped water infrastructure, an inadequate revenue model, under investment, accessible groundwater and established practice connect to promote and maintain private groundwater abstraction—as a central network of artefacts and the key model of water access for upper-middle-income and high-income residents, affecting the model of water access for everyone else in the city.

This network of artefacts is not linked primarily by 'steel and concrete' but by 'fields of action' and socio-ecological connection. The 'fields of action' that bring together the work of real estate developers, upper-middle and high-income residents, and groundwater resource regulators serve to limit investment in and the extension of the piped water network and thus in turn contribute to increased groundwater abstraction. They link spaces of 'relative wealth and impoverishment' through their impacts on the extension of the piped water network as well as through the ecological connections set in motion. They foment other 'fields of action' and alliances to make water flow through water resale, illicit connections and extensive shallow groundwater and surface water reliance. The latter tie Central and South Jakarta to West and North Jakarta through land subsidence, shallow groundwater salinization, flooding and floodwater contamination. Such ecological connections are important in many cities, where the highest rates of bacterial and viral contamination are found in the groundwater and surface water most accessible to the lowest-income residents and thus the water most important in meeting their water needs (Graham and Polizzotto, 2013; Chakava *et al.*, 2014).

In many Southern cities, built infrastructure never completely replaced nor did it completely contain the ecological flows upon which residents depend and from which they need shelter. In fact, the more dependent residents are on water-related environmental services (unmediated by infrastructure), the more elevated their exposure to water-related hazards (Vollmer and Grêt-Regamey, 2013). When one is dependent on streams, rainwater collection or shallow wells that are declining in yield or are degraded by distant uses, one's direct dependence on the ecological world remains a daily reality and a daily struggle. As such, in addition to asking how people make water flow when infrastructure is absent or unreliable—how they act as infrastructure, we call for a focus on how these and other 'pressures' to make water flow overlap and intersect ecologically in ways that escape both infrastructural containment and technical control. These ecological connections— mediated by socio-technical practices and power—are important because making water flow in one area easily leads to the degradation of flows in other parts of the city.

In this article, we sought to 'world' water supply by developing theoretical tools for conceptualizing what water supply is for the majority—not just the network or its absence, but the range of practices and technologies that unite people, nature and artefacts in a complex socio-politics of water supply. In particular, we highlighted the need to pay more attention to ecological connections in shaping urban livelihood possibilities. To do so, we built on scholarship in Southern urbanisms and STS that calls on researchers to decentre theory and dominant artefacts by paying attention to connections and recent work on water supply in Southern cities. Analyses of water supply in Southern cities that do not pay attention to processes beyond the network can obscure deep inequalities grounded in conditions of ecological vulnerability. Looking beyond the network lends greater complexity to discussions of water's urbanization. These arguments are illustrated through the examples of the interacting flows of piped water, groundwater, wastewater and floodwater in Jakarta. Although these cannot account for the fullness of water's urbanization, they demonstrate its importance beyond the network and the need for research in Southern urbanisms and in UPE to engage seriously with networks that are not only multiple and unstable, but that are constantly remaking and being remade through the intersections of inequality, technology and ecology.

Kathryn Furlong, Département de Géographie, Université de Montréal, Chaire de recherche du Canada en Eau et urbanisation, C.P. 6128, Succursale Centre-ville, Montréal, Québec H3C 3J7, Canada, kathryn.furlong@umontreal.ca

Michelle Kooy, Department of Integrated Water Systems and Governance, IHE-Delft Institute for Water Education, Westvest 7, Delft 2611 AX, The Netherlands, m.kooy@un-ihe.org

References

Aditya, R. (2015) Berbincang santai dengan dirut PAM Jaya, sriwidayanto kaderi [Casual Conversation with the Director of PAM Jaya]. Indopos, Jakarta.

Akmalah, E. and N.S. Grigg (2011) Jakarta flooding: systems study of socio-technical forces. *Water International* 36.6, 733–47.

Anand, N. (2017) *Hydraulic city: water and the infrastructure of citizenship in Mumbai*. Duke University Press, Durham, NC.

Augustinus, R.B. (2016) Understanding the implementation of groundwater regulations and policies for the commercial deep well users in Jakarta, Indonesia. Master's, UNESCO-IHE Institute of Water Education.

Bakker, K., M. Kooy, N.E. Shofiani and E-J. Martijn (2008) Governance failure: rethinking the institutional dimensions of urban water supply to poor households. *World Development* 36.10, 1891–915.

Bakr, M. (2015) Influence of groundwater management on land subsidence in deltas. *Water Resources Management* 29.5, 1541–55.

Björkman, L. (2014) Un/known waters: navigating everyday risks of infrastructural breakdown in Mumbai. *Comparative Studies of South Asia, Africa and the Middle East* 34.3, 497–517.

Björkman, L. (2015) *Pipe politics, contested waters: embedded infrastructures of millennial Mumbai*. Duke University Press, Durham and London.

Boland, A. (2007) The trickle-down effect: ideology and the development of premium water networks in China's cities. *International Journal of Urban and Regional Research* 31.1, 21–40.

BPS (2012) Survey sosio-ekonomi nasional 2012 [National socio-economic survey]. Direktorat Statistik Kesejahteraan Rakyat dan Direktorat Statistik Harga—Badan Pusat Statistik, Jakarta.

Braun, B. (2005) Environmental issues: writing a more-than-human urban geography. *Progress in Human Geography* 29.5, 635–50.

BRPAM (2013) *Jam pelayanan sebagai implementasi, pemantuan kontinuitas pelayanan di DKI* [Jakarta, Final report of assessment survey]. Badan Regulator Penyediaan Air Minum DKI, Jakarta.

BRPAM (2014) *Knowledge base: sistem penyediaan air minum di DKI Jakarta* [The drinking water supply system in DKI Jakarta]. Badan Regulator Penyediaan Air Minum, Jakarta.

BRPAM (2015) *Evaluasi kinerja pelayanan air minum tahun 2014* [Evaluation of the performance of the service of drinking water by 2014]. Badan Regulator Penyediaan Air Minum, Jakarta.

BRPAM (2016) *Evaluasi triwula –II/2016 Perjanjian kerjasama Pam Jaya dengan Palyja dan Aetra: Aspek keuangan, teknik dan humas* [Evaluation of quarter II/2016 cooperation agreement with Pam Jaya, Palyja and Aetra: financial aspects, engineering and public relations]. Badan Regulator Penyediaan Air Minum, Jakarta.

Chakava, Y., R. Franceys and A. Parker (2014) Private boreholes for Nairobi's urban poor: the stop-gap or the solution? *Habitat International* 43 (July), 108–16.

Chakrabarty, D. (2000) *Provincializing Europe: postcolonial thought and historical difference*. Princeton University Press, Princeton, NJ.

Chatterjee, P. (2004) *The politics of the governed: reflections on popular politics in most of the world*. Columbia University Press, New York.

CNN Indonesia (2016) Darurat air tanah Jakarta [Jakarta's Groundwater Emergency] [WWW document]. URL http://www.cnnindonesia.com/nasional/focus/darurat-air-tanah-jakarta-3085/berita (accessed 29 October 2016).

Colbran, N. (2009) Will Jakarta be the next Atlantis? Excessive groundwater use resulting from a failing piped water network. *Law, Environment and Development Journal* 5.1, 18–37.

Comaroff, J. and J.L. Comaroff (2012) *Theory from the South: or, how Euro-America is evolving toward Africa*. Paradigm Publishers, Boulder, CO and London.

Connell, R.W. (2007) *Southern theory: social science and the global dynamics of knowledge*. Polity, Cambridge.

Coutard, O. (2010) Services urbains: la fin des grands réseaux? [Urban services: the end of the big networks?] In O. Coutard and J-P. Lévy (eds.), *Écologies urbaines* [Urban Ecologies], Économica, Anthropos, Paris.

Coutard, O. and S. Guy (2007) STS and the city: politics and practices of hope. *Science Technology and Human Values* 32.6, 713–34.

Delinom, R.M. (2008) Groundwater management issues in the greater Jakarta area, Indonesia. International Workshop on Integrated Watershed Management for Sustainable Water Use in a Humid Tropical Region,

JSPS-DGHE Joint Research Project, 2008. University of Tsukuba, Tsukuba.

Delinom, R.M., A. Assegaf, H.Z. Abidin, M. Taniguchi, D. Suherman, R.F. Lubis and E. Yulianto (2009) The contribution of human activities to subsurface environment degradation in Greater Jakarta Area, Indonesia. *Science of the Total Environment* 407.9, 3129–41.

Deltares (2013) *Sinking cities: an integrated approach towards solutions*. Deltares, Delft, The Netherlands.

Detik (2013) 45% air tanah Jakarta tercemar e-coli [45% of Jakarta's ground water contaminated with E. coli] [WWW document]. URL http://news.detik.com/berita/2411711/45-persen-air-tanah-jakarta-tercemar-bakterie-coli (accessed 29 October 2016).

De Vries, S. (2015) Groundwater use in DKI Jakarta and the impact of its use on the subsurface of Jakarta. Technical University of Delft, Delft, The Netherlands.

Dupuy, G. (2008) *Urban networks—network urbanism*. Techne Press, Amsterdam.

Farrelly, M.A. and R.R. Brown (2014) Making the implicit, explicit: time for renegotiating the urban water supply hydrosocial contract? *Urban Water Journal* 11.5, 392–404.

Ferguson, J. (2012) Theory from the comaroffs, or how to know the world up, down, backwards and forwards. *Cultural Anthropology* [WWW document]. URL: https://culanth.org/fieldsights/271-theory-from-the-comaroffs-or-how-to-know-the-world-up-down-backwards-and-forwards (accessed 7 November 2017).

Foster, S., R. Hirata, H. Garduno and C. Tovey (2010) *Urban groundwater use policy—balancing benefits and risks. GW-MATE strategic overview series*. World Bank, Washington DC.

Foster, S.S.D. (2001) The interdependence of groundwater and urbanisation in rapidly developing cities. *Urban Water* 3.3, 185–92.

Furlong, K. (2011) Small technologies, big change: rethinking infrastructure through STS and geography. *Progress in Human Geography* 35.4, 460–82.

Furlong, K. (2014) STS beyond the 'modern infrastructure ideal': extending theory by engaging with infrastructure challenges in the South. *Technology in Society* 38 (August), 139–47.

Gandy, M. (2002) *Concrete and clay: reworking nature in New York City*. MIT Press, Cambridge, MA.

Giordano, M. (2009) Global groundwater? Issues and solutions. *Annual Review of Environment and Resources* 34.1, 153–78.

GOI (2011) Consolidated summary of the environmental impact assessment [Draft: Jakarta Urgent Flood Mitigation Project/JUFMP]. Ministry of Public Works, Directorate General of Water Resources, Jakarta.

Gopakumar, G. (2009) Investigating degenerated peripheralization in urban India: the case of water supply infrastructure and urban governance in Chennai. *Public Works Management & Policy* 14.2, 109–29.

Gopakumar, G. (2014) Experiments and counter-experiments in the urban laboratory of water-supply partnerships in India. *International Journal of Urban and Regional Research* 38.2, 393–412.

Graham, J.P. and M.L. Polizzotto (2013) Pit latrines and their impacts on groundwater quality: a systematic review. *Environmental Health Perspectives* 121.5, 521–30.

Graham, S. and S. Marvin (2001) *Splintering urbanism: networked infrastructures, technological mobilities, and the urban condition*. Routledge, New York.

Harman, G. (2009) *Prince of networks: Bruno Latour and metaphysics*. re.press, Melbourne.

Jaglin, S. (2004) Être branché ou pas: les entre-deux des villes du sud [Being connected or not: the in-between of the cities of the South]. *Flux* 56/57.2, 4–12.

Jaglin, S. (2008) Differentiating networked services in Cape Town: echoes of splintering urbanism? *Geoforum* 39.6, 1897–906.

Jaglin, S. (2014) Regulating service delivery in Southern cities: rethinking urban heterogeneity. In S. Parnell and S. Oldfield (eds.), *The Routledge handbook on cities of the global South*, Routledge, London and New York.

Jepson, W. (2014) Measuring 'no-win' waterscapes: experience-based scales and classification approaches to assess household water security in colonias on the US-Mexico border. *Geoforum* 51 (January), 107–20.

Jepson, W. and E. Vanderwalle (2015) Household water insecurity in the global North: a study of rural and periurban settlements on the Texas-Mexico border. *The Professional Geographer* 68.1, 66–81.

Kagabu, M., J. Shimada, R. Delinom, T. Nakamura and M. Taniguchi (2013) Groundwater age rejuvenation caused by excessive urban pumping in Jakarta area, Indonesia. *Hydrological Processes* 27.18, 2594–604.

Kaïka, M. (2005) *City of flows: modernity, nature, and the city*. Routledge, New York and London.

Kleiman, M. (2004) Pratiques quotidiennes des communautés populaires mal branchées aux réseaux d'eau et d'assainissement dans les métropoles brésiliennes: les cas de Rio de Janeiro et Salvador [Daily practices of popular communities badly connected to the networks of water and sanitation in the Brazilian metropolises: the case of Rio de Janeiro and Salvador]. *Flux* 56/57.2, 44–56.

Kompas (2013) Terlalu lama Jakarta menahan dahaga [Jakarta withstands thirst too long]. Kompas.com 26 December. [WWW document] URL: http://megapolitan.kompas.com/read/2013/12/26/0808560/Terlalu.Lama.Jakarta.Menahan.Dahaga (accessed 14 March 2014)

Kompas (2014) Jakarta utara dominasi kasus pencurian air [North Jakarta dominates in cases of water theft]. Kompas.com 23 December [WWW document] URL: http://megapolitan.kompas.com/read/2014/12/23/20320851/Jakarta.Utara.Dominasi.Kasus.Pencurian.Air (accessed 5 January 2015).

Kooy, M. (2014) Developing informality: the production of Jakarta's urban waterscape. *Water Alternatives* 7.1, 35–53.

Kooy, M. and K. Bakker (2008) Technologies of government: constituting subjectivities, spaces, and infrastructures in colonial and contemporary Jakarta. *International Journal of Urban and Regional Research* 32.2, 375–91.

Kooy, M., C.T. Walter and I. Prabaharyaka (2016) Inclusive development of urban water services in Jakarta: the role of groundwater. *Habitat International*. https://doi.org/10.1016/j.habitatint.2016.10.006

Larkin, B. (2013) The politics and poetics of infrastructure. *Annual Review of Anthropology* 42.1, 327–43.

Latour, B. (2001) *Pasteur: guerre et paix des microbes, suivi de irréductions* [Pasteur: the war and peace of microbes, followed by Irreductions]. La Découverte & Syros, Paris (first published in 1984 as Microbes: guerre et paix by Éditions Anne-Marie Métailié).

Lawhon, M., H. Ernstson and J. Silver (2014) Provincializing urban political ecology: towards a situated UPE through African urbanism. *Antipode* 46.2, 497–516.

LBH-Jakarta (2016) *Atas nama pembangunan: laporan penggusuran paksa di wilayah DKI Jakarta tahun 2015* [In the name of development: report of the evictions in Jakarta region by 2015] *LBH-Jakarta* [WWW document] URL: https://www.bantuanhukum.or.id/web/seperti-puing-laporan-penggusuran-paksa-di-wilayah-dki-jakarta-tahun-2016/ (accessed 21 January 2017).

Liddle, E.S., S.M. Mager and E.L. Nel (2014) The importance of community-based informal water supply systems in the developing world and the need for formal sector support. *The Geographical Journal* 182.1, 85–96.

Mabin, A. (2014) Grounding Southern city theory in time and place. In S. Parnell and S. Oldfield (eds.), *The Routledge handbook on cities of the global South*, Routledge, London and New York.

Mbembe, A. (2012) Theory from the antipodes: notes on Jean & John Comaroffs' TFS. *Cultural Anthropology* 25 February [WWW document]. URL: https://culanth.org/fieldsights/272-theory-from-the-antipodes-notes-on-jean-john-comaroffs-tfs (accessed 7 November 2017).

McCann, E., A. Roy and K. Ward (2013) Assembling/worlding cities. *Urban Geography* 34.5, 581–89.

McFarlane, C. (2008) Sanitation in Mumbai's informal settlements: state, 'slum', and infrastructure. *Environment and Planning A* 40.1, 88–107.

Meehan, K. (2014) Tool-power: water infrastructure as wellsprings of state power. *Geoforum* 57.1, 215–24.

Mehta, L. and S. Movik (2014) Liquid dynamics: challenges for sustainability in the water domain. *WIREs Water* 1.4, 369–84.

Monstadt, J. and S. Schramm (2017) Toward the networked city? Translating technological ideals and planning models in water and sanitation systems in Dar es Salaam. *International Journal of Urban and Regional Research* 41.1, 104–25.

Morris, B.L., A.R.L. Lawrence, P.J.C. Chilton, B. Adams, R.C. Calow and B.A. Klinck (2003) *Groundwater and its susceptibility to degradation: a global assessment of the problem and options for management.* UNEP, Nairobi, Kenya.

Myers, G. (2014) From expected to unexpected comparisons: changing the flows of ideas about cities in a postcolonial urban world. *Singapore Journal of Tropical Geography* 35.1, 104–18.

Parnell, S. and S. Oldfield (2014) *The Routledge handbook on cities of the global South.* Routledge, London and New York.

Parnell, S. and J. Robinson (2012) (Re)theorizing cities from the global South: looking beyond neoliberalism. *Urban Geography* 33.4, 593–617.

Pflieger, G. and S. Matthieussent (2008) Water and power in Santiago de Chile: socio-spatial segregation through network integration. *Geoforum* 39.6, 1907–21.

Pieterse, E. (2008) *City futures: confronting the crisis of urban development.* Zed Books and UCT Press, London, New York and Cape Town.

Prabowo, D.S. (2011) 90 persen air tanah Jakarta mengandung bakteri e-coli [90 percent of Jakarta's groundwater contains e-coli bacteria]. *Tribunnews* 7 June [WWW document]. URL: http://www.tribunnews.com/metropolitan/2011/06/07/90-persen-air-tanah-jakarta-mengandung-bakteri-e-coli (accessed 7 March 2014).

Pritchard, S.B. (2012) From hydroimperialism to hydrocapitalism: 'French' hydraulics in France, North Africa, and beyond. *Social Studies of Science* 42.4, 591–615.

Ranganathan, M. (2014) 'Mafias' in the waterscape: urban informality and everyday public authority in Bangalore. *Water Alternatives* 7.1, 89–105.

Ranganathan, M. and C. Balazs (2015) Water marginalization at the urban fringe: environmental justice and urban political ecology across the north–south divide. *Urban Geography* 36.3, 403–23.

Robbins, P. (2007) *Lawn people: how grasses, weeds, and chemicals make us who we are.* Temple University Press, Philadelphia, PA.

Robinson, J. (2013) The urban now: theorising cities beyond the new. *European Journal of Cultural Studies* 16.6, 659–77.

Robinson, J. and S. Parnell (2011) Traveling theory: embracing post-neoliberalism through Southern cities. In G. Bridge and S. Watson (eds.), *The new Blackwell companion to the city,* Wiley-Blackwell, Oxford.

Roy, A. (2009) The 21st-century metropolis: new geographies of theory. *Regional Studies* 43.6, 819–30.

Roy, A. (2014) Worlding the South: towards a post-colonial urban theory. In S. Parnell and S. Oldfield (eds.), *The Routledge handbook on cities of the global South.* Routledge, London and New York.

Roy, A. and A. Ong (eds.) (2011) *Worlding cities: Asian experiments and the art of being global.* Studies in Urban and Social Change series, Wiley-Blackwell, Oxford.

Rukmana, D. (2015) The change and transformation of Indonesian spatial planning after Suharto's new order regime: the case of the Jakarta metropolitan area. *International Planning Studies* 20.4, 350–70.

Rutherford, J. (2008) Unbundling Stockholm: the networks, planning and social welfare nexus beyond the unitary city. *Geoforum* 39.6, 1871–83.

Sharma, A. and S. Bhaduri (2014) Consumption conundrum of bottled water in India: an STS perspective. *Bulletin of Science, Technology & Society* 33.5/6, 172–81.

Simone, A. (2004) People as infrastructure: intersecting fragments in Johannesburg. *Public Culture* 16.3, 407–29.

Simone, A. (2006) Pirate towns: reworking social and symbolic infrastructures in Johannesburg and Douala. *Urban Studies* 43.2, 357–70.

Simone, A. (2014) 'We are here alone': the ironic potentials and vulnerabilities of mixed (up) districts in central Jakarta. *International Journal of Urban and Regional Research* 38.4, 1509–24.

Srinivasan, V., S.M. Gorelick and L. Goulder (2010) A hydrologic-economic modeling approach for analysis of urban water supply dynamics in Chennai, India. *Water Resources Research* 46.7, 1–19.

Srinivasan, V. and S. Kulkarni (2014) Examining the emerging role of groundwater in water inequity in India. *Water International* 39.2, 172–86.

Stoler, J., G. Fink, J.R. Weeks, R.A. Otoo, J.A. Ampofo and A.G. Hill (2012) When urban taps run dry: sachet water consumption and health effects in low income neighborhoods of Accra, Ghana. *Health & Place* 18.2, 250–62.

Swyngedouw, E. (1992) Territorial organization and the space/technology nexus. *Transactions of the Institute of British Geographers* 17.4, 417–33.

Swyngedouw, E. (1996) The city as a hybrid: on nature, society and cyborg urbanization. *Capitalism Nature Socialism* 7.1, 65–80.

Vandewalle, E. and W. Jepson (2015) Mediating water governance: point-of-use water filtration devices for low-income communities along the US–Mexico border. *Geo: Geography and Environment* 2.2, 107–21.

Verdeil, V. (2004) Branchements collectifs et pratiques sociales à Metro Cebu, Philippines: des services d'eau en quête de legitimation [Collective connections and social practices in Metro Cebu, Philippines: water services in search of legitimacy]. *Flux* 56/7.2, 57–70.

Vollmer, D. and A. Grêt-Regamey (2013) Rivers as municipal infrastructure: demand for environmental services in informal settlements along an Indonesian river. *Global Environmental Change* 23.6, 1542–55.

Von Schnitzler, A. (2017) *Democracy's infrastructure: techno-politics and protest after apartheid.* Princeton University Press, Princeton, NJ.

Wahyono, A. and D. Wardiat (2012) Integritas pelayanan publik dalam perizinan pemanfaatan air bawah tanah di DKI Jakarta [Integrity of the public service in licensing groundwater use in DKI Jakarta]. *Jurnal Masyarakat dan Budaya* 14.1, 99–126.

WHO/UNICEF (2014) *Progress on sanitation and drinking water: 2014 update.* World Health Organization and UNICEF, Geneva.

Zérah, M-H. (2008) Splintering urbanism in Mumbai: contrasting trends in a multilayered society. *Geoforum* 39.6, 1922–32.

Zimmer, A. (2010) Urban political ecology: theoretical concepts, challenges, and suggested future directions. *Erdkunde* 64.4, 343–54.

INTERNATIONAL JOURNAL OF URBAN AND REGIONAL RESEARCH
DOI:10.1111/1468-2427.12546

— URBAN WARFARE ECOLOGY: A Study of Water Supply in Basrah

MARK ZEITOUN, HEATHER ELAYDI, JEAN-PHILIPPE DROSS, MICHAEL TALHAMI, EVARISTO DE PINHO-OLIVEIRA AND JAVIER CORDOBA

Abstract

This article assesses the impact of armed conflict on the drinking water service of Basrah from 1978 to 2013 through an 'urban warfare ecology' lens in order to draw out the implications for relief programming and relevance to urban studies. It interprets an extensive range of unpublished literature through a frame that incorporates the accumulation of direct and indirect impacts upon the hardware, consumables and people upon which urban services rely. The analysis attributes a step-wise decline in service quality to the lack of water treatment chemicals, lack of spare parts, and, primarily, an extended 'brain-drain' of qualified water service staff. The service is found to have been vulnerable to dependence upon foreign parts and people, 'vicious cycles' of impact, and the politics of aid and of reconstruction. It follows that practitioners and donors eschew ideas of relief–rehabilitation–development (RRD) for an appreciation of the needs particular to complex urban warfare biospheres, where armed conflict and sanctions permeate all aspects of service provision through altered biological and social processes. The urban warfare ecology lens is found to be a useful complement to 'infrastructural warfare' research, suggesting the study of protracted armed conflict upon all aspects of urban life be both deepened technically and broadened to other cases.

Introduction

This article assesses the impact of over three decades of armed conflict on the drinking water service of Basrah in order to draw out both its implications for emergency relief programming and its relevance to urban studies. Both aims are important because classical relief interventions, originally designed for acute rural conflicts, are increasingly found by practitioners to be inappropriate for chronic conflict occurring in urban settings, yet there is a lack of critical thought and research dedicated to supporting any progress in that direction (ICRC, 2015a). The roughly 50 million urban residents currently living in such contexts (Dross *et al.*, 2016) stand to gain from even incremental improvements in programming and research.

A discussion on the development of urban warfare ecology is followed by the identification of data gaps and conceptual shortcomings in policy and academic writing on urban infrastructure and armed conflict. A novel frame for gauging impact is developed with the understanding that armed conflict and sanctions permeate all aspects of social and biological ecosystems, with a focus on drinking water services. The frame serves to interpret an extensive set of empirical data found in public and unpublished reports and research articles (from 1978 to 2013), as well as interviews with long-standing Iraqi and expatriate water engineers.[1] The sources of vulnerability of the service are then identified, and practical and theoretical implications discussed.

Special thanks are due to Adel al Attar, Andrea Buletti, Abdoule-Karim Dioumande, David Kaelin, Guillaume Pierrehumbert, Stephanie Hawkins, Charlie Thompson and Ruth MacDougall.

1   The limits of this article's analysis are bounded primarily by the extensive empirical data analysed. The bulk of this derives from unpublished reports from relief agencies active in the sector in Iraq, and individual or group interviews with employees of the same agencies (but not those on recent, direct fieldwork). Among the many important issues and methods thus excluded are the coping mechanisms developed by people; the intent of the belligerents; and ballistics analysis of damage. Anonymized internal reports and other documents cited within this article are referred to by the abbreviation Int. Doc.

The analysis finds that a step-wise drop in water service quality 'from world class to worst class' has many facets, including lack of water treatment chemicals (chlorine and aluminium sulfate), lack of spare parts (e.g. alum dosing pumps), and, primarily, an extended 'brain-drain' of qualified water service staff. The service is found to be vulnerable to dependence upon foreign parts and people, vicious cycles of direct and indirect impact, and the politics of aid and of reconstruction. The analysis also asserts that, where an urban warfare biosphere has developed, the design of relief programming should replace its assumptions about progress through an RRD model with an acceptance that reality is more accurately described as exacerbations within a chronic conflict. It thus emphasizes sustained and integrated support to local water service operators, for example, and an immediate and minimal goal of avoiding the vicious cycles identified.

In pegging the degradation of the service directly to military or political events, the analysis breaks from the macro-scale journalistic approach that sees cities simply as 'impact points' of warfare (see discussion in Graham, 2006: 263). Apart from the practical relevance of an urban warfare ecology reading, then, the detailed 'bottom-up' analysis of *impact* and *services* is also found to be a useful and more focused complement to the 'top-down' 'infrastructural warfare' work (e.g. Agre, 2001; Graham, 2005) that emphasizes the intent of belligerents. For reasons discussed herein, furthermore, the urban warfare ecology approach may be considered a political engineering equivalent to 'forensic architecture' work (Weizman, 2007; 2011).

Urban ecology of war and critical urban research

In their study of the impact of protracted war and sanctions in Syria and Iraq, Dewachi *et al.* (2014) found that the health care systems had been both regionalized and militarized, thereby complicating any potential reconstruction—if ever there were to be an end to the conflict. In pressing the point about these changed 'therapeutic geographies', and also tracing the development pathways of multi-drug-resistant organisms in war-wounded in Iraq, Syria and Lebanon (Dewachi *et al.*, 2016; Sahli *et al.*, 2016), Abu Sitta, Dewachi and others (2016) suggest the dynamics be interpreted through interdisciplinary analysis referred to as the 'ecology of war'.

The assertion is that a complex biosphere of war develops when armed conflicts alter every element of life-sustaining processes, notably the 'physical infrastructure, and the biological and social environments' (Abu Sitta *et al.*, 2016: 2). A particular set of health needs are generated by the complex interactions that develop as warfare (in all of its forms) incessantly ravages or wears down hospital staff, equipment and infrastructure, and injures and re-injures the bodies and psyches of patients. The authors argue that the discipline of war surgery is ill-equipped to meet such needs, for having grown as a response to acute (and largely rural) conflicts, and any effective 'relief' or 'development' intervention undertaken in such contexts will be done with the understanding that there is no crisis. There is, instead, an enduring and particular biosphere shaped by the protracted armed conflict. As this determines the victims' needs, it should shape a range of interventions that are likely to be distinct from those developed for temporary emergencies (Abu Sitta and Dewachi, 2016; Abu Sitta, *et al.*, 2016).

The environmental conservation scientific community has also outlined warfare ecology as a field of study that applies ecological theory, methods and empirical studies to the destruction of habitat and disorganization of social systems (Machlis and Hanson, 2008: 730). In a less purely ecological and more politically aware form, warfare ecology has served to assess the 'pervasive and often diffuse effects' of the Israeli occupation of Palestinian territory (Mason, 2011: 11).

Urban warfare ecology, then, is interpreted as the interdisciplinary study of the set of interacting biophysical and social ecosystems that shape all urban space—otherwise known as the 'urban biosphere'. More specifically, urban warfare ecology employs a range of disciplines—from engineering to medical, environmental and political science—to study the myriad of interdependent institutions, transportation systems, disease transmission routes, ICT flows, social networks and urban services that support life in a city. As the study of Basrah will show, drinking water services are seen as a particularly significant urban ecosystem within the urban warfare biosphere, because of their important connection to so many other services and processes.

Loosely applied as it is here, urban warfare ecology both challenges and builds neatly on programming and academic urban research. Though the current fighting in cities throughout the Middle East is less a novel than a recurrent phenomenon (see e.g. Davis, 2003), the protracted nature of these conflicts has caught the relief industry off-guard, and is eliciting collective reflection on its programming. Perhaps the most blatant deficiency is the enduring assumption that the fighting will end at some point, allowing progression from relief interventions to rehabilitation projects and 'development'[2] programmes (see the 'RRD' work of e.g. Duffield, 1994; Keen, 2007; Mosel and Levine, 2014), with agencies specialized in each phase passing an imaginary baton on to the others.

A number of projects (e.g. *Villes en guerre* (Groupe URD), *Conflict in Cities* (the Centre for Urban Conflicts Research, Cambridge University), *Urbanization and Emergencies* (Harvard Humanitarian Initiative), and *Understanding the Tipping Point of Urban Conflict* (University of Manchester) are taking a problem-solving approach to the longer-term urban challenges. These typically consider the influence of basic urban characteristics (such as the large spatial scale of challenges, density of populations, etc. (e.g. BRC, 2013; USAID, 2013) upon different sectors such as wastewater (Bastable and Russell, 2013), energy (Lahn and Grafham, 2015), shelter (Skat-IFRC, 2012) and public health (Rouhani *et al.*, 2011; Patel and Burke, 2012). This body of knowledge recognizes the fundamentally political nature of the challenge, but generally avoids confronting it.

Academic research that has examined interdependent urban infrastructure from a technical perspective of complex adaptive systems has concentrated on understanding different modes of infrastructure failure. The term 'cascading failure' is of particular relevance to the case studied here, as this is defined as occurring 'when a disruption in one infrastructure causes the failure of a component in a second infrastructure, which subsequently causes a disruption in the second infrastructure' (Rinaldi *et al.*, 2001: 22). Efforts at controlling cascading failure emphasize solutions deriving from information technology (Zimmerman and Restrepo, 2009) or risk analysis (Little, 2002), and note the particularly challenging complexity of water and wastewater infrastructure (Gillette *et al.*, 2002).

Critical thought and politics are also sidestepped in the otherwise considered body of work on disaster preparedness. Most of this is designed for stable political and institutional situations like the US (AWWA, 2001; CDCP-AWWA, 2012), and is at best tangential to urban areas in the current Middle East. The much more complex hybrid governance arrangements observed in the degrading cities of Iraq, at least, obliges a frame that can test the extent to which armed conflict has distorted pre-conflict urban life, possibly into a significantly different biosphere.

In contrast, critical academic urban studies research often begins with the inherent vulnerabilities of people in densely populated areas to a wide range of issues, including social conflict, predatory governance systems, climate change, and natural disasters (e.g. Pelling, 2003; Loftus and Lumsden, 2007; Satterthwaite, 2013; Shapely, 2013). Urban scholars have recognized technological networks and networked infrastructure to be a constitutive feature of life in cities (Kaika and Swyngedouw, 2000; Graham and Marvin, 2001; Coward, 2009), a source of political power in and

---

2   The corresponding limitations of capacities and operational modes developed for much smaller-scale and less complex rural settings has been well noted (see Janneck, *et al.*, 2012; Sanderson, *et al.*, 2012; Lucchi, 2013; Bryant and Campbell, 2014).

of themselves (Meehan, 2014) or a determining element of social control (Mayntz and Hughes, 1988). While the focus has been primarily on traditional infrastructure systems such as water, energy, and public health, the crucial importance of the people who operate those systems has also been acknowledged (see e.g. Anand, 2005; Barnes and Newbold, 2005). McFarlane and Rutherford (2008: 363), for example, refer to the 'inherently political nature of networked urban infrastructure' to describe the complexities in the web of people employing the same arrangement of systems.

Much of the discussion of disruption of urban infrastructure networks focuses on structural inequalities in terms of access to it (such as McFarlane, 2010), including examination through the concept of metabolism (Silver, 2016), or disruptions induced by natural disasters, or by privatization and neoliberalism (Graham and Marvin, 2001). Disruptions due to armed conflict have generated only a fraction of the critical attention paid to both the political economic driving forces of war and the effect of the militarization of urban life and 'space' (e.g. Herold, 2002; Graham, 2006; 2012).

The critical urban studies work most relevant to warfare ecology may be that concerned with investigation of the motives of belligerents active in urban areas, namely within thinking on 'infrastructural warfare' (Agre, 2001; Graham, 2005), 'place annihilation' (Hewitt, 1983), and 'urbicide' (Coward, 2008). The research sheds light on how belligerents use urban space to further their military objectives. The US Army's (2008) classified field manual *Intelligence Support for Urban Operations* asserts, for instance, that the selection of targets, objectives and weaponry rely upon solid understanding of networked urban infrastructure and transportation patterns (see also Patterson, 2000).

The work has been built on by studies of 'infrastructural violence' (Jabary Salamanca, 2011; 2015), and 'network-centric violence' (Coward, 2009) in the context of armed conflict. Collectively, this 'infrastructural warfare' body of work examines the intentional manipulation, disconnection, and destruction of critical infrastructure as a means of control, repression and demodernization. The top-down approach does not detail the impact, however, on urban *services,* which include people and consumables, as well as infrastructure and other forms of hardware. On the whole, furthermore, the research field of urban studies has tended to view infrastructure as a technological black box, or as dominated by technical and professional discourses. There thus remains an acknowledged need to 'break down the barriers between a range of largely separated debates about cities, technologies and infrastructure networks' (Graham and Marvin, 2001: 33). There is considerable merit, in other words, in blending the technical and political understanding of urban warfare ecology with the body of critical urban research—in very much the way that the profession of architecture has contributed to the discussion through its bottom-up 'forensic' exploration of destruction (Segal, 2003; Weizman, 2007; 2011).

The cumulative and cyclical impact of armed conflict on urban services

'With the changes in military technology and the strategy of warfare, including the capacity to target precisely and destroy a country's infrastructure, there may be many more indirect than direct injuries and deaths.'
Harvard Study Team (1991: 980)

It is perhaps the complexity of war in cities more than any other feature that calls classic relief efforts into question in urban warfare ecology. Particularly where there is endemic violence and a lack of collaborative (or existence of coercive) central control—as in IDP camps, or slums—armed conflict can contribute to the tensions, and possibly fuel the wider war (Norton, 1993; Keen, 2007; IASC, 2011; Pullan, 2011; Moser and McIlwaine, 2014). Tensions can be exacerbated by the allure that cities hold for warring factions on account of their high concentration of valuable economic and political targets (see Gregory, 2010; Pinera, 2011: 92), the advantage of the psychological impact of attacks (Graham, 2004), and the preference of irregular forces engaged in 'asymmetric warfare'. The proximity of urban residents to each other further increases social tensions, by putting the entire population at greater risk of communicable diseases—as with the cholera epidemic in Syria in 2013 (Luff, 2014) and Iraq in 2015 (WHO, 2015), as well as the outbreaks predicted in Iran (Medact, 2014).

The public health risks are compounded by the large movements of people into cities, as outward fluxes of people fleeing armed combat can occur just before an inward movement of people seeking shelter from fighting in other cities. Both movements can follow years of rural-to-urban migration driven by changes in the national economy (for the case of the war in Syria, see De Châtel, 2014; Selby *et al.*, 2017). The resultant informal settlements are not usually served (or well-served) by the public services typically provided by local government departments, and so the communities self-organize to provide these. As a result, people in different parts of the same urban area have very different levels of service, and the social inequities arising from urban fragmentation, particularly for drinking water services, can increase the chance of tensions with the local authorities or neighbours (Gandy, 2008; MacKillop and Boudreau, 2008).

Such inherent 'urban' complexities are compounded by the previously discussed multiple facets and interdependencies of the services themselves. The treatment and delivery of drinking water, for instance, requires a power supply to run the pumps, chemicals to cleanse the unsafe water, and the people and institutions that manage it all. As will be shown, the 'inherently political nature' (to return to McFarlane and Rutherford's term) of the water service in Basrah is certainly apparent in the construction, reconstruction and re-reconstruction efforts, even if it is not militarized and reorganized to the same extent as public health services in Syria and Iraq.

Those who wage wars clearly do not feel obliged to support the theory that progress develops along the RRD continuum (see Perrin, 2001: p x). Different parts of Beirut suffered continuously from 1982 to 1990 (World Bank, 1983; Nembrini, 1994), for instance, and again in 2006 (GOL, 2006; UNEP, 2007), even if these most recent attacks are sometimes treated in isolation (e.g. Hamieh and Mac Ginty, 2010; Fawaz, 2014; Zeitoun *et al.*, 2014). In Iraq, the experience of prolonged conflict was compounded by the trade embargo imposed on the government by the UN in 1990. Trade sanctions are so common in protracted armed conflict that they should be considered an integral (not distinct) part of them.[3] The enduring effect of economic sanctions in Burundi, for instance, has emphasized that problems with electricity and water services 'continue to this day, long outliving the sanctions regime itself' (Bossuyt, 2000: para 79). The impact is felt most directly through restricting the flow of consumables and parts required for routine operations and maintenance, or repairs (see also Hoskins and Nutt, 1997). Cuba's general work-around of US sanctions was similarly challenged when these bit harder in the early 1990s, with a clear impact of reduced funding for water supply, treatment, and sanitation (AAWH, 1997).

'Dual-use' restrictions are particularly problematic for restoring water services. The impact in Gaza of the Israeli denial of a vast range of material deemed to serve military as well as civilian purposes is well-known to those agencies attempting emergency and development efforts there (OGB, 2017). There are other, less considered, effects of sanctions necessitated by an assessment of an urban water system's vulnerability. These include the degradation associated with the very poor quality of those commodities that do make it past the sanctions, and the discouragement

---

3   It is next to impossible to separate the impact of the sanctions from the impact of armed conflict and neglect. The visible results in Iraq have been cumulative, a combined effect on a time continuum over 30 years of multiple crises and bad management (ICRC Focus Group, 2014).

of creative coping mechanisms by the brakes put onto private commerce (personal communication from Jeremy Loveless, 13 December 2013). For example, traders of higher-quality goods (and lending banks such as Barclays)[4] that break embargoes were fined a total of US$1.7 billion between 2008 and 2012 (*Standard Bulletin*, 2012).

Because of increased exposure to hazards, death and disability due to the 'indirect and lingering effects' of armed conflict can be greater than exposure caused directly by hostilities or immediately after their cessation (Ghobarah et al., 2003; see also Butala et al., 2010). Yet, distinguishing between these types of effects and more direct impact is not straightforward. In developing a basic 'skeleton' framework with which to examine different types of impact for an early Basrah case study, for instance, Barakat (1993: 33) acknowledged that 'there is no clear distinction between the immediate impact of war, the side-effects of that impact and the long-term effects', suggesting attempts to develop a comprehensive frame would be futile.

In order to define the distinction, the *direct impact* of protracted armed conflict here refers to immediate and (usually) physical impact directly from the armed conflict, such as the deaths of water workers or looting of spares stores. *Indirect impact* is understood to mean the impact upon an associated component of a system, usually in the short to medium term, such as the 'brain-drain' that occurs following demotivation of staff, or shortages in spares due to a lack of funds to replace them. Borrowed from thinking on environmental impact assessments, *cumulative impact* is that 'which results from the incremental impact of the action when added to other past, present, and reasonably foreseeable future actions' (Canter and Sadler, 1997: 69). This includes the lack of planning that results from insufficient staff over the long term, or the damaging 'repairs' made to machinery running with poorly calibrated or poorly fitting parts.

While there is considerable literature on the direct impact of armed conflict upon water infrastructure (see e.g. Nembrini, 1994; Nembrini et al., 2003; Nembrini and Moreau, 2009; Pinera and Reed, 2011; Pinera, 2012), indirect and cumulative impacts remain wholly understudied. Any combination of direct, indirect or cumulative impacts may affect any of the people, hardware, or consumables that make up the water service, yet this remains insufficiently conceptualized. In much the same way that interdependent or networked infrastructure is prone to 'cascading failure' (to return to Little, 2002; Zimmerman and Restrepo, 2009), the links that exist between the different types of impact can in some urban warfare biospheres create effects that are irreversible. The economic sanctions on Gaza, Iraq and Cuba, for instance, have led to a reduction of funds being transferred from the central government to the water and sanitation sectors (US DIA, 1991; AAWH, 1997; Doyle, 2003; COHRE, 2008). Insufficient funding leads to lack of infrastructure maintenance, which, in turn, leads to more water leaks and lower pressure in the distribution networks—and so higher public health risks associated with the cross-contamination with sewage (EWASH 2012). Considered alongside the interdependencies that exist between the different components of drinking water services, this interdependent pathway can be conceptualized as a vicious cycle of cumulative impact—as in Figure 1.

Based on cases documented in Dushanbe (Roberts, 2000) and various Afghani cities (Pinera and Reed, 2011), the figure demonstrates how direct and indirect impact can become nearly permanent. A reduction in staff levels followed attacks upon several members, making follow-up of unlicensed tapping into the water network difficult. This results in reduced cost recovery by the municipality (and may be exacerbated by reduced funding from the central authorities), leading to shortages in spare parts. The resultant reduced pressure in the network leads people to install household-level booster pumps—a negative coping mechanism that could result in serious health problems

---

4   Other banks and companies include ABN Amro, Lloyds TSB, Chevron and DHL (for trading with Iran, Libya, Syria, Sudan, Cuba, Burma, Liberia).

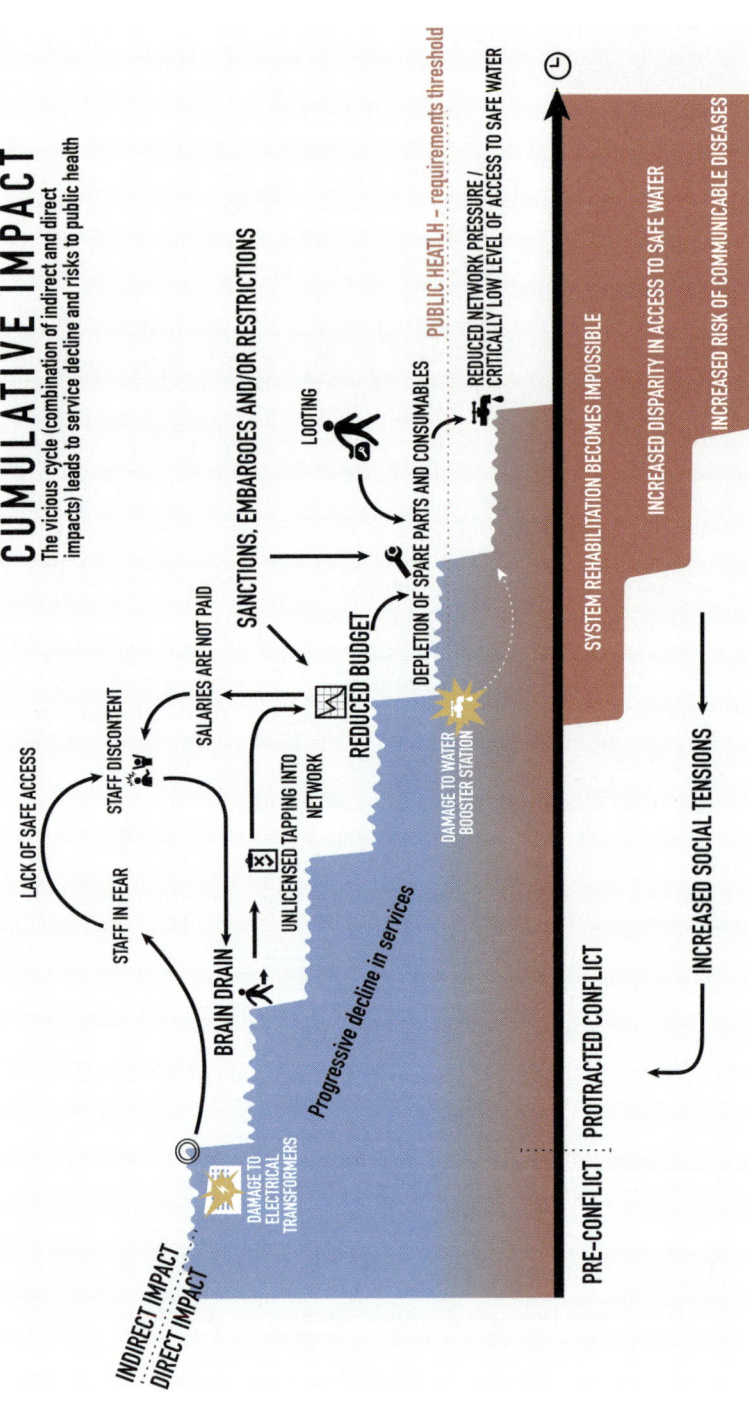

FIGURE 1 A vicious cycle of cumulative impact in drinking water service (*sources:* ICRC, 2015a: Figure 3, showing examples from cases documented in Dushanbe [Roberts, 2000], and various Afghan cities [Pinera, 2011]; reprinted with permission of the ICRC).

NOTE: The cumulative impact of incremental direct and indirect impacts of protracted armed conflict on the people, hardware and consumables that make up the service ultimately affects public health and may contribute to the very conflict which created it. The cycle of impact, therefore, sits within the cycles of conflict that characterize complex emergencies.

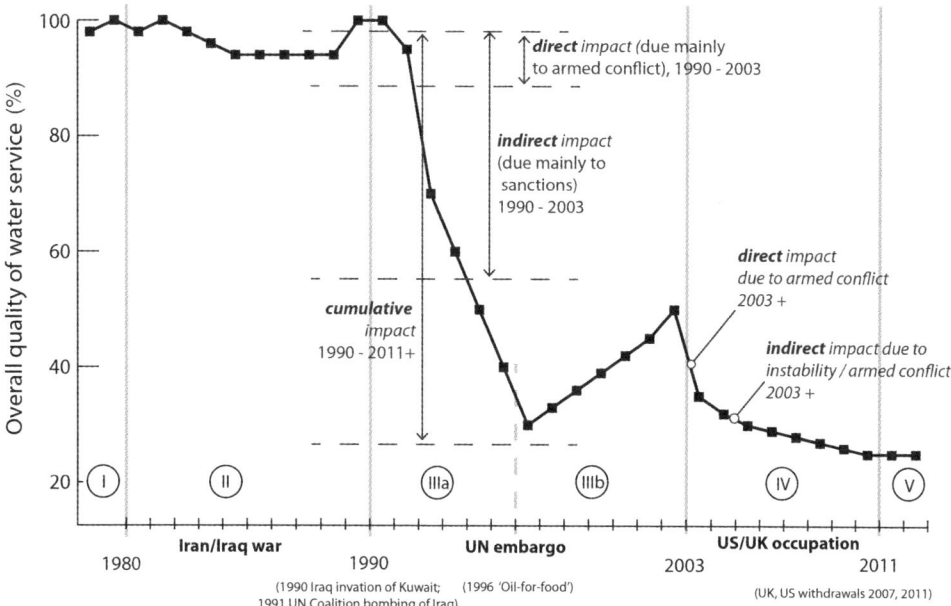

NOTE: The step-wise decline in relative quality reflects the significant political or military events shown, and is attributed to direct, indirect and cumulative impact upon staff, consumables and hardware. The overall quality of water service is a composite of quantity and quality of water provided, and so indicative rather than absolute.

FIGURE 2   The relative quality of water service delivery in Basrah from 1978 to 2013 (*source*: authors).

due to the risk of cross-contamination of the drinking water with contaminated soil water. The decline in service also reduces the bill-collection rates, and dashes hopes of relatively straightforward network repairs, if and when the fighting stops. After some (undefined) point, the cumulative impact is thus not readily reversible, and may, furthermore, increase social tensions leading to the urban violence and armed conflict that originally drove it (though this issue is not considered further here).

The impact of protracted armed conflict and sanctions on the drinking water service ecosystem in Basrah

The impact of protracted armed conflict and sanctions upon drinking water services in Basrah[5] over the 36-year period from 1978 to 2013 is presented in Figure 2. The assessment of quality of service is a composite of the quantity and quality of the water provided, and interpreted within the frame of direct, indirect, and cumulative impact upon hardware, consumables, and people.

The state of drinking water services throughout the period under consideration was very closely pegged to the military and political events shown in Figure 2. The phases defined by the events start with the 'baseline' period prior to the Iran–Iraq war (Phase I); and are followed by the 1980–1988 Iran–Iraq war (II); the UN Security Council-imposed sanctions ('the embargo') from 1990 to 1996, beginning just after the

---

5   The experience of Basrah is considered to be broadly representative of large urban centres throughout Iraq, with the notable exceptions of Baghdad and cities in the northern Kurdish parts of the country during the sanctions period (1990-2003). Both sets of urban centres fared better than Basrah during this period, the former because the Iraqi government favoured it, and the latter because it was beyond its reach. The population of the city of Basrah was roughly 2.7 million in the 1980s, and 3.4 million by 2015.

Iraqi invasion of Kuwait in August 1990 and before the UN Coalition attacks on Iraq (Janurary–Februrary 1991) (IIIa); UN Security Council Resolution 986 (the 'Oil-for-food' programme), from 1996 to 2003 (IIIb); the US/UK invasion and occupation 2003–2011 (IV); and the ongoing internationalized civil unrest (V).

The baseline used for this analysis is the latter part of the period of political stability (and political oppression), from 1968 to the start of the Iran/Iraq war, in 1980. Numerous reports depict a country that had essentially completed at least the urban parts of its 'hydraulic mission' (see e.g. Swyngedouw, 1999; Allan, 2001), to deliver water to all of its citizens. Drinking water meeting international quality standards was available throughout most cities at a rate ranging from 250 to 450 litres/person/day (Harvard Study Team, 1991; WHO/UNICEF, 1991: 17; Khogali et al., 1996: 3; SIGIR, 2010: 7).

The type and magnitude of the impact of the conflict upon the quality of drinking water services is expected to reflect the nature of each military and political phase. Standing armies faced each other during Phase II through aircraft, surface-to-air and surface-to-surface missiles (and, earlier, tank battles and hand-to-hand combat), with the bulk of the fighting and damage suffered in Iran. The UN Coalition bombing of Iraqi forces at the start of the embargo period was focused on southern Iraq. Though the bombing did not directly affect Basrah, the 1991 uprisings against the government there elicited first violent then negligent responses from the Ba'ath government until its downfall in 2003. The UN trade embargo outlawing the import of anything other than 'essential needs' was imposed in 1990, and purportedly eased in 1996 under the 'Oil for food' programme (UNSC Resolution 986). International armed conflict during the embargo period comprised primarily one US bombing campaign of Baghdad in 1998. The US/UK-led 2003 invasion was conducted initially through aircraft, surface-to-air and long-range surface-to-surface missiles, and the ensuing occupation was shaped by the rule of the Coalition Provisional Authority (CPA). At some point prior to the UK withdrawal from Basrah in 2007 and the US withdrawal from Iraq in 2011, the violence turned to asymmetric warfare between US, UK, Iraqi army and other troops, and Iraqi insurgents. The internationalized armed conflict continues to this day, with the rise of ISIS and other militant groups.

The impact of the sustained violence upon the drinking water system itself is but an indicator of the extent the people suffered from the degraded service.[6] The US Defense Intelligence Agency (1991) and Harvard Study Team (1991) both reported concern, for instance, about outbreaks of water-quality-related cholera, typhoid and hepatitis. While the effect of the Iraqi conflict on health is better documented in medical research journals (Pellett, 2000; Salvage, 2002: Table 2; Medact, 2003; WHO, 2003; Al-Naseri et al., 2008), it is notoriously difficult to isolate associations solely with water quality issues induced by disrupted services. As Hunter (2009) shows, a single short disruption in drinking water service (lasting, say, a day or week), can greatly increase the probability of infection with endemic diseases, if the quality of the service was previously reliable. The concern of the US DIA report may be overstated (or underinformed) in this regard, in the sense that it gives little credence to the capacity of Iraqi people to cope[7] (see Int. Doc. 006, 1991). In any case, by 2005 less than one quarter of the people in Basrah governorate rated their water or wastewater services as 'good to very good' (US GAO, 2005: 18). By 2014 the figure had dropped to 6% (Takechi, 2014), and a genuine outbreak of cholera (with at least 60 cases confirmed in Basrah governorate) came in 2015 (WHO, 2015).

---

6   This article's analysis remains focused on disruptions to services, and so does not seek to gauge the impact of the war directly upon people.
7   Coping mechanisms are not discussed further here, but have been identified by the ICRC Focus Group as including: illegal connections; installation of household booster pumps (at least 1.5 million around Iraq!); compact-unit water treatment plants; bottled water; private, neighbourhood-level reverse osmosis (desalination) plants; imports from Kuwait; generators at household or neighbourhood level; leaving the country; rooftop storage reservoirs.

–   Impact on staff: the 'natural brain drain'
Iraq was, of course, not spared the 'brain drain' so commonly seen in war economies (see Burnham *et al.*, 2009). Many skilled workers critical to the drinking water supply services left immediately after the start of embargo in 1991, and often those with 'middle'-qualifications (e.g. water maintenance technicians), joined the private sector for the better wages offered (ICRC Focus Group, 2014).

The shortage of skilled staff was most acute in the smaller urban centres and villages—where it was not uncommon to have no maintenance staff whatsoever (Int. Doc. 063, 1996)—though it became noticeable in the larger governorates by 1995, and was felt across most water boards by 1997 (ICRC Focus Group, 2014: 13). Even during the time of the UN's Oil for Food Programme, the lack of (or very low) salaries of service workers remained an issue, with public sector water technicians earning US $5 per month (Int. Doc. 053, 1996: 2), and fewer (though unquantified) staff reporting to work (Int. Doc. 052, 1991; Int. Doc. 071, 1993: 15; Khogali, *et al.* 1996: 6; Nembrini *et al.*, 2003: 26). There were only seven engineering staff in Basrah's Department of Water in 2001, for instance, down from hundreds before (Remote interview with Basrah water engineer, December 2013). By 2008 there were approximately 70 engineers earning US $300 per month, though with fewer qualifications (Int. Doc. 158, 2008: 8).

The lack of qualified staff has been exacerbated by what has been called a '*natural* brain drain' (ICRC Focus Group, 2014: 14) over the two and half decades under consideration, as the qualified people who remained in service eventually reach their retirement age. The intricate knowledge these skilled workers had of the patchy systems that had been created is not replaceable, or easily transferrable to younger, less well formally trained staff (*ibid.*).

As was the case for retrofitting the sewage-lifting stations of Basrah (Int. Doc. 053, 1996), the effect of poorly trained or motivated or overworked staff meant that, in some cases, there were no staff on hand to install the new equipment that did make it through the embargo. Equipment and spares imported into Basrah were just as easily misused or mistakenly broken (Int. Doc. 039, 1992; Int. Doc. 099, 1992: 3; Int. Doc. 132, 2003; Int. Doc. 142, 2004). Irregular payment of the salaries of technicians and other support staff continued through 2003 (Int. Doc. 122, 2003; Int. Doc. 134, 2003; US GAO, 2005: 27), at least through 2010 (Int. Doc. 158, 2008; SOCMD, 2010: 9). The CPA's policy of exchanging the Iraqi civil service ('de-Ba'athification'), furthermore, compounded the exodus at a point when it might have been slowed.

The impact of such personnel issues throughout Iraq is confirmed in an internal ICRC assessment of 92 of its water projects from 2011 to 2014 (ICRC, 2014). The extent of the influence of the personnel issues is difficult to untangle from those related to consumables and hardware, because of the importance of adequate maintenance. Underqualified or inexperienced staff would often order parts through the embargo with incorrect dimensioning, or were unable to properly install the spares, and it is generally felt that the majority of the problems related to spare parts stems from their improper installation (ICRC Focus Group, 2014: 24.).

–   Impact on hardware: problems with spare parts
The water treatment plants within Basrah have long relied on a single source over 200 km away on the Euphrates River (Etienne and Nembrini, 1995; Nembrini *et al.*, 2003). The UN coalition bombing in early 1991 targeting national electrical power production thus had an indirect and immediate impact on water treatment (and, so, drinking water quality) and distribution particularly in Basrah (as well as Baghdad) (Int. Doc., 025 1991: 3; WHO/UNICEF, 1991: 17; SIGIR, 2010: 10). Some disruptions to water services (at al-Qurna and Basrah city) were also attributed to damage to bridges in 1991 and in 2003, which prevented the access of maintenance staff (Int. Doc. 039, 1992: 4; Nembrini *et al.*, 2003: 7).

The 2003 US/UK invasion also resulted in hundreds of leaks in the distribution pipes of Basrah's water network (direct impact), hundreds of illegal household connections (indirect impact), and the reduction of water produced for some neighbourhoods to 30–40% of full capacity (Nembrini *et al.*, 2003: 14–20). Meanwhile, over 1,000 water tankers and wastewater evacuation trucks were denied entry into Iraq, on the grounds that their stainless steel linings might have 'dual use' (Gordon, 2010: 71), as was the stainless steel required for wastewater treatment plants (Remote interview with Basrah water engineer, December 2013).

Though diesel fuel and petrol remained readily available for electrical generators to run water treatment plants, booster stations, and sewage lifting stations, difficulties importing spare parts for these made water treatment and supply throughout the rest of the 1990s intermittent and unreliable, at best (Int. Doc. 025, 1991; Int. Doc. 044, 1992; Etienne and Nembrini, 1995). In hindsight, most hardware-related disruptions to the service were caused by the lack of availability of spares, due to the embargo and/or looting. In particular, shortages of aluminium-sulfate dosing equipment[8] reduced the quality of water treatment (Int. Doc. 025, 1991, Int. Doc. 032, 1992; Etienne and Nembrini, 1995), and broken chlorination pumps led to 'haphazard' treatment (Int. Doc. 032, 1992: 17).

The poor quality of spares that the ministries, municipalities and international organizations managed to get through the embargo may have been as much a problem as their lack of availability. From very small chlorine- and alum-dosing pumps to very large water booster pumps, reliable treatment and delivery of drinking water requires equipment that is designed and built to standards that fit the rest of the system that they are part of. The pre-1990 heavy reliance of the Iraqi water authorities upon top-quality European parts (filters from the Netherlands, for example, or pumps from Germany and Scotland [Int. Doc. 061, 1991]), thus ensured they were vulnerable to the embargo (Int. Doc. 059, 1998). Chinese and Iranian companies proved more willing than their European counterparts to supply parts that others could bring in around the embargo, but the host of spares available in these markets (sometimes at one-thirtieth the cost) would rarely match the micromillimetre tolerances required of finely machined parts, and so could not be finely calibrated (Remote interview with Basrah water engineer, December 2013; ICRC Focus Group, 2014).

Though over 100 European chlorine-dosing devices were repaired to high standards in Baghdad (and at a much lower cost than imports) (ICRC 029, 2000), the once sizeable local manufacturing industry is considered to have been 'on its knees' by the mid-1990s (ICRC Focus Group, 2014: 15). This poor situation with spare parts also led to their 'cannibalization', a term used to describe the removal of functional equipment from a lower-priority part of a water system to a higher-priority part. Predicted to occur early on (US DIA, 1991), the practice ensured sustained water supply to hospitals and health centres in Basrah and elsewhere, at least through 1991 (Int. Doc. 025, 1991). Cannibalization of equipment was compounded by looting immediately after the 2003 invasion (Int. Doc. 134, 2003: 4; Nembrini *et al.*, 2003: 26), and beyond (Int. Doc. 147, 2004; Int. Doc. 158, 2008; Remote interview with Basrah water engineer, November 2015), leading to further deterioration of the electrical power supply, and a renewed reliance on electrical generators (Int. Doc. 128, 2003). Though revenues from oil began flowing to the CPA in the years that followed, spending remained unevenly distributed throughout the country. International donors began to fund hardware for new projects, but not always its installation, or its operation and maintenance costs (ICRC Focus Group, 2014: 6–7). British authorities installed many short-lived Compact Units[9] in the

---

8   The equipment is used to deliver the alum, which facilitates the removal of sediment suspended in the muddy river water

9   These self-contained compact water treatment plants, which can be dropped in by trailer and so appear to be quick-fix solutions, were very popular as a relief intervention (there were 91 compact units around Basrah in 1991, and 430 by 2015 (Al Janoob, 2015). Because of their sophisticated technology, reliance on chemicals, and poor ability to deal with turbid water, these compact units have proven very ill suited for southern Iraqi villages.

villages, for example, while US plans to replace the main canal feeding Basrah with a large-diameter transmission pipe never materialized (Remote interview with Basrah water engineer, November 2015).

–   Impact on consumables: alum, chlorine, cholera
The relative importance of hardware and consumables is put firmly into perspective in the Harvard Team's report: 'Direct physical damage, either from the bombing or looting during the civil uprisings, was found to be only a minor factor in the impairment of water and wastewater systems. The primary rate-limiting factors are lack of spare parts and supplies of chlorine and erratic electric supply' (Doleh and Piper, 1991: 1). The consumables most directly affected by the protracted conflict and embargo in Iraq were the chlorine and aluminium sulphate (more commonly referred to as 'alum') required for water treatment, particularly in Baghdad and Basrah. There was an acute shortage of these following the imposition of the embargo (Int. Doc. 043, 1991; CARE International, 1997) and they were recognized as a major limiting factor shortly after the UN Coalition's bombing (Int. Doc. 041, 1991; Int. Doc. 032, 1992; Int. Doc. 044, 1992).

Iraqi-produced alum was low in quality (CARE International, 1997; ICRC Focus Group, 2014: 25), meaning the sediment suspended in the muddy water of the Tigris, Euphrates or Shatt al Arab rivers could only be poorly flocculated, making the water much more difficult to disinfect effectively with chlorine. The good-quality chlorine produced in Basrah that once supplied the entire country was in severe shortage by 1993 (Int. Doc. 031, 1996; Remote interview with Basrah water engineer, November 2015). The Chinese-imported chlorine supplied by the Iraqi water authorities throughout the country contained impurities, leading to blockage of the chlorine-dosing pipes and thus further increasing the need for the ever-decreasing maintenance or replacement of the pipe (CARE International, 1997).

In a somewhat perverse beneficial relationship, there were no chlorine shortages during the worst periods of armed conflict, as very few water treatment plants still operated, creating little demand for it (Doleh and Piper, 1991). Shortages in chlorine dioxide gas began soon afterwards, however, with treatment plant operators in Basrah obliged to replace chlorine with bleaching powder, a practice also observed in Nassiriah, Najaf and Kerbalah (Int. Doc. 114, 1991). As neither the operators nor the treatment plants were prepared to work with bleaching powder, any improvements in water quality are judged as marginal (Int. Doc. 025, 1991; Int. Doc. 032, 1992).[10]

The resumption of chlorine gas delivery to Basrah in 1992 is credited with a general improvement in the level of domestic water services (in contrast to the situation in Baghdad [CARE International, 1997: 8]). Along with alum and alum-dosing equipment, higher-quality chlorine was one of the first requests made by the various water boards under Resolution 986 (Int. Doc. 020, 1997). As a result, chlorine shortages appeared to subside from 1998, even if the gas cylinders were not handled safely on site by underqualified staff (ICRC Focus Group, 2014: 24).

Chlorine and alum shortages re-emerged following the US/UK invasion (Int. Doc. 122, 2003, Int. Doc. 134, 2003), and reliable and quality supplies were still wanting in 2008 (Int. Doc. 158, 2008). By 2015 there was essentially no chlorine treatment of any of Basrah's piped drinking water, meaning the overall microbiological quality of the drinking water (and, by extension, the service) was lower than the previous low at the start of the embargo period (Remote interview with Basrah water engineer, November 2015). While the quantity of water produced in 2015 was generally sufficient, its high salinity meant that all those who could afford to purchased bottled water. Those who could not afford bottled water continued to rely on the unchlorinated piped water,

10   In some cases (e.g. Ninevah), there was a shortage even of bleaching powder (CARE International, 1997).

which, when cross-contaminated with sewage water, was blamed in part for the 2015 cholera outbreak (WHO, 2015).

Vulnerabilities of the drinking water service ecosystem in Basrah

Though the perseverance of Iraqi water workers at times slowed or reversed the step-wise decline of the Basrah drinking water service, every improvement was curtailed by the enduring effect of the trade embargo or renewed fighting. Any relapse into overt violence—or return to a sanctions regime—is likely to quickly reverse any gains made in what appears to be a substantially altered urban biosphere. The precariousness of the drinking water ecosystem is credited to at least three vulnerabilities: dependence on foreign parts and people, the accumulation of impact, and the politics of aid and reconstruction.[11]

–   Vulnerability induced by dependence upon foreign parts and people
The technical qualifications of engineers in ministries, consulting bureaus and construction firms throughout Iraq was very high in the 1980s, yet most of the large water treatment stations had been constructed, operated and maintained with considerable involvement of foreign expertise. This left drinking water systems particularly vulnerable to the predictable departure of such staff, as, for instance, during the 1991 UN bombing campaign (Int. Doc. 032, 1992, Int. Doc. 044, 1992). Water treatment plants built at the end of the 1980s were fitted with high-technology equipment (Int. Doc. 025, 1991), which, furthermore, required highly skilled foreign operators who were in short supply even before the Iraqi invasion of Kuwait. Always a disadvantage to a country suffering a war, the phenomenon affected the modern, tertiary-level Basrah sewage treatment plant, a planned upgrade of which was 90% complete at the start of the fighting—at which point the (Indian) contractors fled. The dependence continues, with a Turkish company taking over the upgrade in 2009 but unable to complete its work due to mismanagement (Remote interview with Basrah water engineer, November 2015), which led to the Japanese International Cooperation Agency's plans to rehabilitate the city's entire drinking water system (Takechi, 2014).

Apart from the effect of abandoning projects during bombing campaigns, Iraq's reliance on foreign expertise also created a 'technological dependence' which became difficult to escape (Int. Doc. 044, 1992: 13). It was rarely possible to bring enough foreign technical know-how into Iraq to tackle complex technical difficulties, and training programmes only ever managed to reach dozens of the thousands required (Int. Doc. 132, 2003; US GAO, 2005: 26). New projects or repairs that required such expertise were typically abandoned (Int. Doc. 032, 1992), at least during the early phases under consideration here. The ability of the occupying forces or international organizations and NGOs to help fill this gap proved very limited indeed, in part because expatriate engineers were never committed to long missions (Int. Doc. 027, 1996; WICRC 024, 1998).

–   Vulnerability induced by *cumulative* impact
The step-wise decline in the quality of the drinking water service in Basrah has been read as the result of an accumulation of combined, incremental direct and indirect impacts of war and embargo on service people, hardware and consumables. Much of this is related to the degraded electrical power system (Int. Doc. 059, 1998) and failing

---

11   A fourth source of vulnerability may derive from interdependence with other systems. The internal documentation demonstrates the clear relation between electricity and water (without the former there is none of the latter). With the failure of the national electricity grid and very low cost of diesel fuels, most water systems became reliant upon electrical generators, though these have proven very difficult to maintain (Int. Doc. 059, 1998). Transportation (e.g. of treatment chemicals) and the reaction of some international companies fearing the consequences of breaking the embargo are further sources of vulnerability arising from interdependence.

economy, and is evident in the demotivation and other opaque manifestations that occurred in step with the degradation of the general warfare ecology. At some point during the protracted conflict, water service staff were caught in emergency or response mode and stopped planning altogether. With most of the qualified people who had not left the country now retired, the messy patchwork of systems that made up the water service proved too complicated to operate or upgrade. Though water still filled the distribution pipes in 2015, its very poor microbiological quality meant that it was drunk only by those who could not afford to purchase bottled water (Remote interview with Basrah water engineer, December 2013). The published advice on disaster preparedness is of little use when a system has been transformed so completely from world-class to worst-class, and from safe to dangerous.

A large part of this system's vulnerability stems from the predictable and justifiable responses of the service operators, such as the cannibalization of parts. In situations where good-quality spares are impossible or very lengthy to procure, however, the activity is the first step down a slippery path. Not only are the systems that the parts are cannibalized from never likely to operate again, released relaxation of the pressure to render the higher-priority system operational can tend to reduce efforts to seek replacements—and thus lead to an inevitable repeated failure of the more important system. Throughout Iraq, the accumulating impact of the war and sanctions ultimately led to a drop in design criteria from national standards (based on British Standards) under a new operating logic of 'semi-sustainability' (Etienne and Nembrini, 1995). The rationale for this suboptimal design was based on an acknowledgement that the regular delivery and installation of spares required by any complex system were not achievable. It may thus have appeared more pragmatic to maintain minimal operations capacity for an interim period in the hope that a return to 'normal' was imminent, i.e. that the embargo would be lifted (Int. Doc. 044, 1992: 7; ICRC Focus Group, 2014: 7). In situations where sanctions are not lifted or that are, in effect, just a return to chronic crisis within a warfare biosphere, however, pragmatic efforts can have little enduring positive effect.

Vulnerabilities related to the cumulative impact upon the people running the service stem from both the brain-drain and the reliance on foreign workers. It would be difficult to exaggerate the benefit of the constant presence of devoted local staff who are intimate with the particularities and idiosyncrasies of any service, particularly one that has been patched up as often as that of Basrah. The retirement of such staff over the duration of prolonged conflicts (the so-called 'natural' brain-drain) may be even more damaging than the exodus of skilled labour out of the country, in the sense that their knowledge is irreplaceable and cannot be recovered by a sudden influx of skilled Iraqi (or foreign) labour, or the typical capacity-development programmes discussed in the previous section.

–   Vulnerability enhanced by the politics of aid and reconstruction
Just as the impacts of the protracted conflict have been shown to reflect the conflict's nature across different phases, reconstruction efforts very much reflect the preferences and commitment of the ruling authorities of the time. This is the 'inherently political' side of interdependencies of urban infrastructure during wartime (McFarlane and Rutherford, 2008) and arguably present in any urban warfare biosphere. The Ba'ath government's response to the UN-imposed embargo, for instance, clearly privileged certain cities and regions over others (generally disadvantaging Basrah city and governorate). Reconstruction efforts by the Coalition Provisional Authority were also asymmetrically distributed, as the poor security situation disfavoured areas in the centre and south of the county (US GAO, 2005), and favoured the predominantly Kurdish areas in the north. Nearly two billion dollars targeted by the US authorities for water and sanitation was later reallocated to security, justice, and employment-development

sectors (US GAO, 2005; SIGIR, 2013: 59), furthermore, the bulk of the US $500 million of water projects implemented during the occupation were judged to have had major or minor deficiencies (SIGIR, 2013: Fig 1.2).

While it is clearly difficult to gauge reconstruction needs at any particular point in an extended armed conflict, knowledge of the context certainly helps. A 2003 US government strategy document heaps all of the blame for the 'outdated … and badly dilapidated' state of Iraq's drinking water systems on the Ba'ath government, for example, and none for the effects of the UN embargo (USAID, 2003: 1). Convinced that progress passes through phases of relief, rehabilitation and development, the same report and other needs assessments (e.g. UN-World Bank, 2003; US GAO, 2005; Baker and Hamilton, 2006) suggest that the reconstruction phase was to shift into long-term development planning in 2004. But in many parts of the country a 'recovery' phase was certainly delayed, and arguably never really entered into. The British armed forces in Basrah left little more behind than dozens of short-lived Compact Units, and new village water networks that are still waiting for an adequate water source (Remote interview with Basrah water engineer, November 2015). An ICRC report of the same time was more realistic, foreseeing a lag before the re-activation of the former Oil-for-Food supply pipeline would be possible, and expecting that lack of quality spare parts would remain an issue until the reconstruction funds that had been committed began to flow (Int. Doc. 122, 2003: 6).

The glut of implementing agencies following the 2003 US invasion exposes the opportunistic character of some actors in the industry, with very few NGOs active towards what turned out to be the end of the sanctions period. The general failure of the UN's Oil for Food Programme to reduce the suffering of people throughout Iraq (particularly those punished by the contemporary Iraqi government (Joyner, 2003) furthermore exposes the invalidity of the self-financing assumptions upon which Iraqi 'reconstruction' efforts were based. The same may be said for the dashed US hopes that a combination of oil wealth and a more open marketplace would help the country's systems off their knees (as early as 2004, in some estimates) (ICRC Focus Group, 2014). Despite the wealth, the country generally has not managed to return to pre-1980 conditions, and neither, certainly, has the drinking water service in Basrah.

Learning from the urban warfare ecology reading

To summarize the urban warfare ecology reading of the impact of armed conflict on the drinking water service of Basrah: the degradation may be traced to the brain-drain (in the immediate, short and long-term), the lack of good-quality spare parts (where cannibalization of parts eventually led to a deterioration in planning, and poor-quality spares led to a patchwork system), and the limited availability of the treatment chemicals alum and chlorine. The evidence clearly shows that the poor quality of drinking water service that residents currently receive has its roots in the previous decades of armed conflict and sanctions (see ICRC, 2014). Conceived as a slide down the vicious cycle of cumulative impact, the main initiating factor was the indirect impact caused by the violent conflict and the UN trade sanctions, and chiefly the economic aspects of the latter. The service has been shown to be vulnerable to dependence upon foreign parts and people, sensitivity to vicious cycles of direct and indirect impact, and the politics of aid and of reconstruction.

–   Implications for relief programming

The analysis implies that relief programming in urban warfare biospheres should seek first and foremost to avoid the predictable vicious cycles. One path towards this is the reduction of vulnerabilities induced by reliance on foreign parts and people, or by the politics of aid and reconstruction. Most relevant to local municipalities, agencies and ministries, the former suggests that strengthening national capacity in all regards (e.g. technical or social knowledge, industrial production, construction capacity, etc.) will render urban services more resilient. This is, of course, much easier said than done for communities and institutions beset by protracted conflict, but highlights the importance of low-risk capacity-building and training programmes.

Addressing the vulnerability induced by the politics of aid and reconstruction in urban warfare biospheres obliges us to question the way that the relief industry is structured, including the duration of its commitment and its founding assumptions (see e.g. ICRC, 2016). Even the few international organizations that have maintained a long-term presence in Iraq (e.g. Unicef and the ICRC) have not been able to plan more than one year ahead, and this has also been the case for those that rushed in after 2003. Short-term planning reflects the donor preference (or industry standard) for distinguishing between emergency and 'development' assistance—the 'post-war' thinking based on a hope that the armed conflict will end within a predictable and manageable period of time. The classic humanitarian time-bound funding sources which limit the NGOs dependent on them to six-month funding cycles (see e.g. Olsen *et al.*, 2003) seems excessively and myopically short, in this regard. Using such funding models to address the challenges of urban warfare biospheres can be read as negligent of so-called humanitarian ideals, and the people most affected. Longer-term and more flexible funding (as by the UK's Department for International Development (DFID) in Yemen—see McElhinney, 2014) will likely support better programming, though it would necessarily entail less stringent monitoring of spending.

Rethinking the RRD paradigm in urban ecologies of war is key for operational staff, as well. In their call for a shift from that paradigm, the ICRC (2015) suggested that international agencies improve their logistical and technical capacity in order to better support local water service operators—a point made by several others, on different foundations (e.g. Duffield, 1994; Smirl, 2009; Mosel and Levine, 2014). That capacity is typically constrained by short-term contracts and staff with managerial—rather than technical—experience and expertise. Effective long-term programming throughout the exacerbations of chronic crises obliges external relief workers to get into the full detail of proper service delivery, beyond disaster preparedness and prepositioning of stocks, to understanding and addressing the classic 'development' issues of; for example, financing, innovative technology and asset management (see e.g. Verhoeven *et al.*, 2015), and technical support to the very large and complex systems that the local operators manage.

–   Relevance to urban studies

More effective relief programming will also benefit from pushing the envelope that constrains our collective understanding—through a more appropriate research base, for instance. In short, this means more critical and innovative policy-oriented research to support the shift in paradigm, as well as critical research that is more engaged with those delivering and funding the service.

The evidence reviewed through the urban warfare ecology approach suggests ways in which the degradation of services may be linked with 'infrastructural warfare' research into the intentional destruction of infrastructure as a means of social control. The motives of those who created the direct (and, also, the indirect and cumulative) impacts were not examined, however, and the effects not gauged in terms of repression. The analysis has emphasized that it is the *cumulative* impact of the UN trade sanctions that is most concerning, suggesting that the drinking water services are more a victim than a target of conflict (in the case of Basrah, at least). The point requires contextualization, first because conclusions drawn about the drinking water services of one city (Basrah) do not hold for the interdependent infrastructure in the same city, or in other cities. Second, and perhaps more importantly, the devastating consequences of the degradation of the service are similar, whether the damage is intentional or not. The findings thereby oblige consideration of the drivers of the violence that initiated the degradation. Targeted research into the geopolitics of the sanctions would help situate this article's analysis more accurately, as would investigation of the awareness and intent of the belligerents involved. The way that water services may serve as a tool of conflict (Jaubert *et al.*, 2014) or contribute to existing tensions (as in Figure 2, and CinC, 2012) would be especially useful, in this regard.

In Basrah, the alteration of the social and biological processes that make up the drinking water service has led to the development of short-term coping mechanisms and long-term adaptive practices, and, likely, an increased incidence of communicable diseases (though that has not been studied here). But there are also distinctions to be made with the 'changing therapeutic geographies' that Dewachi *et al.* (2014) noted with respect to the public health services in Iraq and Syria. Within Basrah's warfare biosphere, the protracted armed conflict and trade sanctions have transformed the drinking water service ecosystem in a number of ways. Internal and transnational supply lines have been established, interrupted, dissolved, and created anew; much less qualified staff deal with a much more complex and complicated system; and coping mechanisms at every level have altered the once highly central and hierarchical management of the sector to one of overlapping hybrid governance (see e.g. Shapely, 2013). On the whole, however, the drinking water service of Basrah has not been militarized or reorganized to the extent that public health services have been, for reasons that merit further investigation.

There are parallels to be drawn between this insight into damage to complex engineering systems and the ballistics analysis of the damage—as in 'forensic architecture' work (Weizman, 2011). It follows that a blend of technical engineering awareness of the functioning of water services with ballistics expertise and sharp social/political science will serve to move us closer to the roots of the problem.

The analysis's focus on indirect and cumulative impact further draws attention to the extension in space and in time of armed conflict. Even relatively precise attacks on military targets can cause knock-on effects along the vicious cycle identified here, well beyond the direct impact zone of the explosive and long after the dust has settled. Such 'reverberating effects' of weaponry are the subject of debates about military targeting and proportionality in International Humanitarian Law (ICRC, 2015b: 5; Robinson and Nohle, 2017; Zeitoun and Talhami, 2017), and are attracting campaigns against the use of wide-area explosives in populated areas (e.g. Brehm and Borrie, 2010; Rappert *et al.*, 2012).

Examination of the impact of armed conflict through interdisciplinary urban warfare ecology has not only allowed sight of the extent of one aspect of a greater urban transformation, it also shines a spotlight on the very mechanisms of the transformation itself. Application of the frame to other services (e.g. solid waste, energy, health) and other urban warfare biospheres (e.g. Aleppo, Beirut, Donetsk, Gaza, Ta'iz) will reveal yet more of the enduring and otherwise hidden impacts of war.

Mark Zeitoun, School of International Development and UEA Water Security Research Centre, University of East Anglia, Norwich NR4 7TJ, UK, m.zeitoun@uea.ac.uk

Heather Elaydi, Arab Group for the Protection of Nature, Amman, Jordan, heather. elaydi@gmail.com

Jean-Philippe Dross, Water and Habitat Unit, International Committee of the Red Cross, 19 Avenue de la paix, 1202 Geneva, Switzerland, pdross@icrc.org

Michael Talhami, Water and Habitat Unit, International Committee of the Red Cross, 19 Avenue de la paix, 1202 Geneva, Switzerland, m.talhami@icrc.org

Evaristo de Pinho-Oliveira, Water and Habitat Unit, International Committee of the Red Cross, 19 Avenue de la paix, 1202 Geneva, Switzerland, eoliveira@icrc.org

Javier Cordoba, Water and Habitat Unit, International Committee of the Red Cross, 19 Avenue de la paix, 1202 Geneva, Switzerland, jcordoba@icrc.org

References

AAWH (American Association for World Health) (1997) *Denial of food and medicine: the impact of the U.S. embargo on health & nutrition in Cuba*. American Association for World Health, Washington, DC.

Abu Sitta, G. and O. Dewachi (2016) *Conflict medicine program at the American University of Beirut*. American University of Beirut, Beirut, Lebanon.

Abu Sitta, G., O. Dewachi, V-K. Nguyen and J. Whittall (2016) Conflict medicince—a manifesto. *MSF Analysis: Reflections on Humanitarian Action* [WWW document]. URL msf-analysis.org/conflict-medicine-manifesto/ (accessed 8 September 2017).

Agre, P. (2001) Imagining the next war: infrastructural warfare and the conditions of democracy. *Radical Urban Theory* 15 September 2001 [WWW document]. URL http://polaris.gseis.ucla.edu/pagre/war.htm.

Al-Naseri, H., M. Birch, J. Cook, J. Piachaud, J. Salvage and S. Sharma (2008) *Rehabilitation under fire: health care in Iraq 2003-7* Medact, London [WWW document]. URL http://www.ippnw.org/pdf/medact-iraq-2008.pdf (accessed 8 September 2017).

Allan, J.A. (2001) *The Middle East water question: hydropolitics and the global economy*. I.B. Tauris, London.

Anand, P.B (2005) *Getting infrastructure priorities right in post-conflict reconstruction*. UNU-WIDER Research Paper 2005/42 [WWW document]. URL https://www.wider.unu.edu/publication/getting-infrastructure-priorities-right-post-conflict-reconstruction (accessed 8 September 2017).

AWWA (American Water Works Association) (2001) *Emergency planning for water utility management. Manual of water supply practices—M19*, Fourth edition, AWWA, Denver, CO.

Baker, J.A., III and L.H. Hamilton (2006) *The Iraq study group report*. Vintage Books/Random House, New York, NY.

Barakat, S. (1993). Reviving war-damaged settlements: towards an international charter for reconstruction after war. Doctoral dissertation, Institute of Advanced Architectural Studies, University of York, York.

Barnes, J. and K. Newbold (2005) Humans as a critical infrastructure: public-private partnerships essential to resiliency and response. Paper presented at the First IEEE International Workshop on Critical Infrastructure Protection, 3-4 November, Darmstadt, Germany.

Bastable, A. and L. Russell (2013) *Gap analysis in emergency water, sanitation and hygiene promotion*. Humanitarian Innovation Fund, London.

Bossuyt, M. (2000) *The adverse consequences of economic sanctions on the enjoyment of human rights*. United Nations, Geneva [WWW document]. URL http://www.ohchr.org/Documents/Events/WCM/MarcBossuyt_WorkshopUnilateralCoerciveSeminar.pdf (accessed 8 September 2017).

BRC (British Red Cross) (2013) *Learning from the city: British Red Cross urban learning project scoping study*. British Red Cross Society, London.

Brehm, M. and J. Borrie (2010) Explosive weapons: framing the problem. Background Paper No. 1 of the Discourse on Explosive Weapons project. UN Institute for Disarmament Research, Genenva.

Bryant, J. and L. Campbell (2014) *Urban WASH in emergencies*. ALNAP Learning Report. ALNAP and Registered Engineers for Disaster Relief, London.

Burnham, G.M., R. Lafta and S. Doocy (2009) Doctors leaving 12 tertiary hospitals in Iraq, 2004-2007. *Social Science & Medicine* 69.2, 172-77.

Butala, N.M., M.J. VanRooyen and R.B. Patel (2010) Improved health outcomes in urban slums through infrastructure upgrading. *Social Science & Medicine* 71.5, 935-40.

Canter, L. and B. Sadler (1997) *A tool kit for effective EIA practice—review of methods and perspectives on their application*. A supplementary report of the International Study of the Effectiveness of Environmental Assessment. Environmental and Ground Water Institute, University of Oklahoma, and Institute of Environmental Assessment, UK, and International Association for Impact Assessment [WWW document]. URL http://www.iaia.org/pdf/Training/SRPEASEIS01.pdf (accessed 8 September 2017).

CARE International (1997) *Watsan project report—September 1997*. Internal communication of CARE International classified as ICRC file no 022.

CDCP-AWWA (Centers for Disease Control and Prevention, and American Water Works Association) (2012) *Emergency water supply planning guide for hospitals and health care facilities*. US Department of Health and Human Services, Atlanta, GA.

CinC (Conflict in Cities) (2012) Rethinking conflict infrastructure: how the built environment sustains divisions in contested cities. Conflict in Cities and the Contested State—Briefing Paper 2 [WWW document]. URL https://www.urbanconflicts.arct.cam.ac.uk/downloads/briefing-paper-2 (accessed 8 September 2017).

COHRE (Centre on Housing Rights and Evictions) (2008) *Policies of denial: lack of access to water in the West Bank*. The Centre on Housing Rights and Evictions, Geneva, Switzerland.

Coward, M. (2008) *Urbicide: the politics of urban destruction*. Routledge, London.

Coward, M. (2009) Network-centred violence, critical infrastructure and the urbanization of security. *Security Dialogue* 40.4/5, 399-418.

Davis, P.K. (2003) *Besieged: 100 great sieges from Jericho to Sarajevo*. Oxford University Press, Oxford.

De Châtel, F. (2014) The role of drought and climate change in the Syrian uprising: untangling the triggers of the revolution. *Middle Eastern Studies* 50.4, 521-35.

Dewachi, O., M. Skelton, V-K. Nguyen, F.M. Fouad, G. Abu Sitta, Z. Maasri and R. Giacaman (2014) Changing therapeutic geographies of the Iraqi and Syrian wars. *The Lancet* 383.9915, 449-57.

Dewachi, O., J. Whittall, S. Kassamali and T. Zreik (2016) *The changing ecologies of war and humanitarianism—Conference report*. The Changing Ecologies of War and Humanitarianism, May 2016, Beirut, Issam Fares Institute for Public Policy and International Affairs, and Faculty of Health Sciences, American University of Beirut.

Doleh, W. and W. Piper (1991) *Harvard team's report on the water and wastewater systems of Iraq*. Int. Doc. 026, 11 November, Baghdad.

Doyle, B. (2003) *Water and environmental sanitation*. Iraq Watching Briefs, UNICEF, New York, NY.

Dross, P., M. Talhami, E. de Pinha-Oliveira, J. Cordoba and M. Zeitoun (2016) Urban services in protracted armed conflict. *Crisis Response Journal* 11.3 [WWW document]. URL https://www.crisis-response.com/archive/article_pdf.php?num=1020 (accessed 8 September 2017).

Duffield, M. (1994) Complex emergencies and the crisis of developmentalism. *IDS Bulletin* 25.4 [WWW document]. URL https://www.ids.ac.uk/files/dmfile/duffield254.pdf (accessed 8 September 2017).

Etienne, Y. and P.G. Nembrini (1995) Establishing water and sanitation programmes in conflict situations: the case of Iraq during the Gulf War. *International Journal of Public Health* 40.1, 18-26.

EWASH (Emergency Water Sanitation and Hygiene) (2012) *Thirsting for Justice campaign: Palestinian rights to water & sanitation*, Emergency Water Sanitation and Hygiene in the occupied Palestinian territory. [WWW document]. URL http://reliefweb.int/report/occupied-palestinian-territory/thirsting-justice-palestinian-rights-water-and-sanitation (accessed 8 September 2017).

Fawaz, M. (2014) The politics of property in planning: Hezbollah's reconstruction of Haret Hreik (Beirut, Lebanon) as case study. *International Journal of Urban and Regional Research* 38.3, 922-34.

Gandy, M. (2008) Landscapes of disaster: water, modernity, and urban fragmentation in Mumbai. *Environment and Planning A* 40.1, 108–30.

Ghobarah, H.A., P. Huth and B. Russett (2003) Civil wars kill and maim people—long after the shooting stops. *American Political Science Review* 97.2, 189–202.

Gillette, J., R. Fisher, J. Peerenboom and R. Whitfield (2002) Analyzing water/wastewater infrastructure interdependencies. Paper presented to the 6th International conference on probabilistic safety assessment and management (PSAM6) [WWW document]. URL http://www.ipd.anl.gov/anlpubs/2002/03/42598.pdf (accessed 8 September 2017).

GOL (Government of Lebanon) (2006) *Lebanon: on the road to reconstruction and recovery, a periodic report published by the Presidency of the Council of Ministers on the post-July 2006 recovery & reconstruction activities 2006* [WWW document]. URL http://www.pcm.gov.lb/Admin/DynamicFile.aspx?PHName=Document&PageID=3916&published=1 (accessed 8 September 2017).

Gordon, J. (2010) *Invisible war: the United States and the Iraq sanctions.* Harvard University Press, Cambridge, MA.

Graham, S. and S. Marvin (2001) *Splintering urbanism: networked infrastructures, technological mobilities and the urban condition.* Routledge, London.

Graham, S. (2004) Postmortem city: towards an urban geopolitics. *City* 8.2, 165–96.

Graham, S. (2005) Switching cities off. *City* 9.2, 169–94.

Graham, S. (2006) Cities and the 'War on Terror'. *International Journal of Urban and Regional Research* 30.2, 255–76.

Graham, S. (2012) When life itself is war: on the urbanization of military and security doctrine. *International Journal of Urban and Regional Research* 36.1, 136–55.

Gregory, D. (2010) War and peace. *Transactions of the Institute of British Geographers* 35.2, 154–86.

Hamieh, C.S. and R. Mac Ginty (2010) A very political reconstruction: governance and reconstruction in Lebanon after the 2006 war. *Disasters* 34.S1, S103–S123.

Harvard Study Team (1991) The effect of the Gulf Crisis on the children of Iraq. *The New England Journal of Medicine* 325.13, 977–80.

Herold, M.W. (2002) US bombing and Afghan civilian deaths: the official neglect of 'unworthy' bodies. *International Journal of Urban and Regional Research* 26.3, 626–34.

Hewitt, K. (1983) Place annihilation: area bombing and the fate of urban places. *Annals of the Association of American Geographers* 73.2, 257–84.

Hoskins, E. and S. Nutt (1997) *The humanitarian impacts of economic sanctions on Burundi.* The Thomas J. Watson Jr. Institute for International Studies, Providence, RI.

Hunter, P.R., D. Zmirou-Navier and P. Hartemann (2009) Estimating the impact on health of poor reliability of drinking water interventions in developing countries. *Science of the Total Environment* 407.8, 2621–24.

IASC (Inter-Agency Standing Committee) (2011) *Report on Reference Group for Meeting Humanitarian Challenges in Urban Areas—Activities in 2011.* Inter-Agency Standing Committee Working Group [WWW document]. URL http://www.alnap.org/resource/6589 (accessed 11 October 2017).

ICRC (International Committee of the Red Cross) (2000) *Water treatment.* ICRC News Bulletin, ICRC Iraq-No. 7, March, Baghdad.

ICRC (2014) *Cumulative impact of armed conflict on essential services. Part I: report on findings.* International Committee of the Red Cross, Geneva, Switzerland.

ICRC (2015a) *Urban services during protracted armed conflict: a call for a better approach to assisting affected people.* International Committee of the Red Cross, Geneva, Switzerland.

ICRC (2015b) *Explosive weapons in populated areas: humanitarian, legal, technical, and military aspects.* Report of the ICRC Expert Meeting in Chavannes-de-Bogis, Switzerland, 24 to 25 February 2015. International Committee of the Red Cross, Geneva, Switzerland.

ICRC (2016) *Protracted conflict and humanitarian action: some recent ICRC experiences.* International Committee of the Red Cross, Geneva, Switzerland.

ICRC Focus Group (2014) *Interview with ICRC Focus Group, Geneva, 24 March 2014.*

Int. Doc. 006 (1991a) *Résumé et critique des resultats des missions d'evaluation en Irak, fevrier à octobre 1991.* [Summary and critique of the results of the evaluation missions in Iraq, February to October 1991]. ICRC internal technical document, Geneva, 18 November 1991.

Int. Doc. 020 (1997) *Follow up on ICRC Watsan programmes in Iraq.* OP/SAN/OP 97/69. ICRC internal technical document, Geneva, 11 March 1997.

Int. Doc. 025 (1991b) *Final report of water and sanitation activities in Bassra [sic].* ICRC internal technical document, Basrah, 13 June.

Int. Doc. 027 (1996a) *Activités WATSAN mesuelles (octobre)* [Monthly WATSAN activities (October)]. BAG96/424. ICRC internal technical document, Baghdad, 4 November.

Int. Doc. 031 (1996b) *Rapport synthétique du rapport de mission de l'OMS intitulé: Water and Environmental Assessment (Iraq 26 dec. 95 - 09 jan. 96)* [Summary of mission report entitled: Water and Environmental Assessment]. ICRC internal technical document OP/MED 92/205, Geneva, 22 May.

Int. Doc. 032 (1992a) *Short and long-term approach for restoring water supplies for the civilian population of Iraq during the Gulf War.* ICRC internal technical document (Manuscript submitted for publication to the American Medical Association).

Int. Doc. 039 (1992b) *Report on sanitation activities in Basrah.* ICRC internal technical document, Baghdad, 23 June.

Int. Doc. 041 (1991c) *Water and sanitation survey in Dashtan refugee area.* ICRC internal technical document, Baghdad, 9 May.

Int. Doc. 043 (1991d) *Mission report.* OP/MED 91/231. ICRC internal technical document, Geneva, 10 June 1991.

Int. Doc. 044 (1992c) *Situation report concerning water and sanitation in Irak. ICRC activities since April 1991 and future prospects.* OP/MED 92/205. ICRC internal technical document, Geneva, 22 May.

Int. Doc. 052 (1991e) *General situation—effect of embargo.* BAS 91/1. ICRC internal technical document, Basrah, 5 June.

Int. Doc. 053 (1996c) *Implementation of Watsan Programmes in Iraq.* BAG 96/337. ICRC internal technical document, Geneva, 2 September.

Int. Doc. 059 (1998) *Rapport mensuel: activités Wat/San mensuelles de Juin-98* [Monthly report: monthly WATSAN activities, June 1998]. BAG 98/276. ICRC internal technical document, Baghdad, 30 June.

Int. Doc. 061 (1991f) *Visit report to Al-Hindya water supply, in Kerbala.* BAG 91-GVA 253, ICRC internal technical document, Bagdad, 19 August.

Int. Doc. 063 (1996d) *Rapport fin de mission* [End of mission report]. BAG 963. ICRC internal technical document, Baghdad, 7 January.

Int. Doc. 071 (1993) *Situation report on field trip to South.* BAG 93-R113. ICRC internal technical document, Baghdad, 29 October.

Int. Doc. 099 (1992d) *ICRC sanitation activities in Basrah area.* BAG 92-R/9. ICRC internal technical document, Baghdad, 29 January.

Int. Doc. 114 (1991g) *Rapport général d'activités dans le domaine de l'eau et de l'assainissement en Irak* [General report on activities in the domain of water and sanitation in Iraq]. BAG 91-GVA 181. ICRC internal technical document, Baghdad, 30 June.

Int. Doc. 122 (2003a) *WatHab Programme Iraq—progress report April/May 2003.* BAG 0653. ICRC internal technical document, Baghdad, 13 June.

Int. Doc. 128 (2003b) *Mission CICR à Rutba* [CIRC mission to Rutba]. AMM 03-E1100. ICRC internal technical document, Amman, 25 April.

Int. Doc. 132 (2003c) *IQ DP initial proposal no 5—WatHab training. BAG 04-E2348*. ICRC internal technical document, Baghdad, 10 July.

Int. Doc. 134 (2003d) *WatHab Programme Iraq - Progress Reports for Sept-Oct. 2003*. ICRC internal technical document, Baghdad, November 2003.

Int. Doc. 142 (2004a) *WatHab General meetin [sic], on 23.03.2004. BAS 04-E32*. ICRC internal technical document, Baghdad, 6 April.

Int. Doc. 147 (2004b) *Urgent—response to your message 04-E1054 dated 15.04.04. 04-E1326*. ICRC internal technical document, Baghdad, 16.04.2004.

Int. Doc. 158 (2008) *Reconstruction and rehabilitation of public infrastructure in Iraq—EOM report Co-WatHab. Iraq/IQS 08-E8496*. ICRC internal technical document, Baghdad, 17 December.

Jabary Salamanca, O. (2011) Unplug and play: manufacturing collapse in Gaza. *Human Geography* 4.1, 22-37.

Jabary Salamanca, O. (2015). Road 443: cementing dispossession, normalizing segregation and disrupting everyday life in Palestine. In S. Graham and C. McFarlane (eds.), *Infrastructural lives: urban infrastructure in context*, Routledge, New York, NY.

Janneck, L., R. Patel, S.A. Rouhani and F.M. Burkle (2012) Urbanization and humanitarian access working group: towards guidelines for humanitarian standards and operations in urban settings. *Prehospital and Disaster Medicine* 26.6, 464-69.

Jaubert, R., F. Münger and C. Bösch (2014) *Syria: the impact of the conflict on population displacement, water and agriculture in the Orontes River basin*. Water Security in the Middle East, Swiss Agency for Development and Cooperation, and Graduate Institute of International and Development Studies, Geneva, Switzerland.

Joyner, C.C. (2003) United Nations sanctions after Iraq: looking back to see ahead. *Chicago Journal of International Law* 4.2, 329-54.

Kaika, M. and E. Swyngedouw (2000) Fetishizing the modern city: the phantasmagoria of urban technological networks. *International Journal of Urban and Regional Research* 24.1, 120-38.

Keen, D. (2007) *Complex emergencies*. Polity Press, Bristol.

Khogali A., K.A. Rahman, F. Baba and M. Khalil (1996) *Environmental health mission-Iraq 26 December 1995-9 January 1996*. World Health Organization-Regional Office for the Eastern Mediterranean, Cairo, Egypt.

Lahn, G. and O. Grafham (2015) *Heat, light and power for refugees: saving lives, reducing costs*. Chatham House, Royal Institute of International Affairs, London [WWW document]. URL https://www.chathamhouse.org/sites/files/chathamhouse/publications/research/20151117HeatLightPowerRefugeesMEILahnGrafhamExecSummary.pdf (accessed 8 September 2017).

Little, R. (2002) Controlling cascading failure: understanding the vulnerabilities of interconnected infrastructures. *Journal of Urban Technology* 9.1, 109-23.

Loftus, A. and F. Lumsden (2007) Reworking hegemony in the urban waterscape. *Transactions of the Institute of British Geographers* 33.3, 109-26.

Lucchi, E. (2013) Humanitarian interventions in situations of urban violence. ALNAP Lessons Paper, Active Learning Network for Accountability and Performance/Overseas Development Institute, London.

Luff, R. (2014) Review of humanitarian WASH preparedness and response in urban and peri urban areas. Unpublished document. Registered Engineers for Disaster Relief, London.

Machlis, G.E. and T. Hanson (2008) Warfare ecology. *Bioscience* 58.8, 729-36.

MacKillop, F. and J-A. Boudreau (2008) Water and power networks and urban fragmentation in Los Angeles: rethinking assumed mechanisms. *Geoforum* 39.6, 1833-1842.

Mason, M. (2011) The application of warfare ecology to belligerent occupations. In G. Machlis, T. Hanson, Š. Zdravko and J.E. McKendry (eds.), *Warfare ecology: a new synthesis for peace and security*, Springer, Dordrecht.

Mayntz, R. and T.P. Hughes (1988) *The development of large technical systems*. Campus Verlag, Frankfurt-am-Main, Germany.

McElhinney, H. (2014) The evolution of DFID's humanitarian financing in Yemen. *Humanitarian Exchange Magazine* Issue 61 (May), Humanitarian Practice Network, London [WWW document]. URL http://odihpn.org/magazine/the-evolution-of-dfid%C2%92s-humanitarian-financing-in-yemen/ (accessed 30 June 2014).

McFarlane, C. (2010) Infrastructure, interruption, and inequality: urban life in the global South. In S. Graham, (ed.), *Disrupted cities: when infrastructure fails*, Routledge, New York, NY.

McFarlane, C. and J. Rutherford (2008) Political infrastructures: governing and experiencing the fabric of the city. *International Journal of Urban and Regional Research* 32.2, 363-74.

Medact (2003) *Continuing collateral damage—the health and environmental costs of war on Iraq 2003*. Medact, London.

Medact (2014) *Health impact assessment and conflict: a case study to assess the potential health consequences of military action against Iran*. Medact, London.

Meehan, K.M. (2014) Tool-power: water infrastructure as wellsprings of state power. *Geoforum* 57 (November), 215-24.

Mosel, I. and S. Levine (2014) *Remaking the case for linking relief, rehabilitation and development*. HPG Commissioned Report, Humanitarian Policy Group, Overseas Development Institute, London.

Moser, C.O.N. and C. McIlwaine (2014) Editorial: new frontiers in twenty-first century urban conflict and violence. *Environment and Urbanization* 26.2, 331-44.

Nembrini, P.G. (1994) Lebanon: water supply problems during the 1989 and 1990 wars. Paper presented at Water and War: Symposium on Water in Armed Conflict, 21-23 November, Montreux. .

Nembrini, P.G., C. Generelli, A. Al-Attar, M.A. Graf, A.M. Yousif, N.S. Karomy, H.M. Al Al-Fakhri, J. Abdul-Zehra, N.S. Alyas and K.H. Al-Shakarchi (2003) *Basrah water supply during the war on Iraq*. International Committee of the Red Cross, Geneva.

Nembrini, P.G. and A. Moreau (2009) The Gaza strip: the last 'ghetto'. An organized deprivation and a denied urban development. Occasional paper no. 9 [WWW document]. URL http://www.thirstycitiesinwar.com/wp-content/uploads/2013/03/the_gaza_strip_version_5_footnotes_ref.pdf (accessed 19 September 2017).

Norton, R.J. (1993) Feral cities. *Naval War College Review* 56.4, 97-106.

OGB (Oxfam, Great Britain) (2017) Treading water: the worsening water crisis and the Gaza Reconstruction Mechanism. Oxfam Briefing Paper, March 2017 [WWW document]. URL https://www.oxfam.org/sites/www.oxfam.org/files/bp-treading-water-gaza-reconstruction-mechanism-220317-en.pdf (accessed 19 September 2017).

Olsen, G.R., N. Carstensen and K. Hoyen (2003) Humanitarian crises: what determines the level of emergency assistance? Media coverage, donor interests and the aid business. *Disasters* 27.2, 109-26.

Patel, R.B. and T.F. Burke (2012) Urbanization—an emerging humanitarian disaster. *The New England Journal of Medicine* 361.8, 741-42.

Patterson, C.M. (2000) *Lights out and gridlock: the impact of urban infrastructure disruptions on military operations and non-combatants*. No. IDA/HQ-D-2511, Institute for Defense Analyses. Alexandria, VA.

Pellett, P. (2000) Sanctions, food, nutrition and health in Iraq. In A. Arnove (ed.), *Iraq under siege: the deadly impact of sanctions and war*, South End Press, Cambridge.

Pelling, M. (2003) *The vulnerability of cities: natural disasters and social resilience*. Earthscan, London.

Perrin, P. (2001) *Health emergencies in large populations: public health course in the management of humanitarian aid*. International Committee of the Red Cross, Geneva.

Pinera, J-F. (2011) *Cities, water and war: looking at how water utilities and aid agencies collaborate in cities affected by armed conflicts*. LAP LAMBERT Academic Publishing, Loughborough.

Pinera, J-F. (2012) Urban armed conflicts and water services. *Waterlines* 31.1/2, 105-21.

Pinera, J-F. and R. Reed (2011) Restoring services, rebuilding peace: urban water in post-conflict Kabul and Monrovia. *Water International* 36.2, 222-31.

Pullan, W. (2011) Frontier urbanism: the periphery at the centre of contested cities. *The Journal of Architecture* 16.1, 15-31.

Rappert, B., R. Moyes and I. Lang (2012) The case for addressing explosive weapons: conflict, violence and health. *Social Science & Medicine* 75.11, 2047-54.

Rinaldi, S.M., J.P. Peerenboom and T.K. Kelly (2001) Identifying, understanding, and analyzing critical infrastructure interdependencies. *IEEE Control Systems* 21.6, 11-25.

Roberts, L. (2000) The Achilles heel of modern water systems. In ICRC Forum, *War and Water*, International Committee of the Red Cross, Geneva.

Robinson, I. and E. Nohle (2017) Proportionality and precautions in attack: the reverberating effects of using explosive weapons in populated areas. *International Review of the Red Cross* 98.1, 1-39.

Rouhani, S.A., R.B. Patel, L.M. Janneck, A. Prasad, J. Lapitan and F.M. Burkle (2011) Urbanization and Humanitarian Access Working Group: a blueprint for the development of prevention and preparedness indicators for urban humanitarian crises. *Prehospital and Disaster Medicine* 26.6, 460-63.

Sahli, Z., A.R. Bizri and G.A. Sitta (2016) Microbiology and risk factors associated with war-related wound infections in the Middle East: the experience of a regional tertiary medical centre. *Epidemiological Infections* 144.13, 2848-57.

Salvage, J. (2002) *Collateral damage: the health and environmental costs of war on Iraq*. MedAct, Washington, DC.

Sanderson, D., P. Knox-Clarke and L. Campbell (2012) *Responding to urban disasters: learning from previous relief and recovery operations*. ALNAP Lessons Paper, Active Learning Network for Accountability and Performance/Overseas Development Institute, London.

Satterthwaite, D. (2013) The political underpinnings of cities' accumulated resilience to climate change. *Environment and Urbanization* 25.2, 381-91.

Segal, R. and E. Weizman (2003) *A civilian occupation: the politics of Israeli architecture*. Babel, Tel Aviv, Israel.

Selby, J., O.S. Dahi, C. Frölich and M. Hulme (2017) Climate change and the Syrian civil war revisited. *Political Geography* 60 (September), 232-44.

Shapely, P. (2013) Governance in the post-war city: historical reflections on public-private partnerships in the UK. *International Journal of Urban and Regional Research* 37.4, 1288-304.

SIGIR (Special Interest Group on Information Retrieval) (2010) *Review of major U.S. government infrastructure projects in Iraq: Nassiriya and Ifraz water treatment plants*. SIGIR, New York, NY.

SIGIR (Special Interest Group on Information Retrieval) (2013) *Learning from Iraq*. SIGIR, New York, NY.

Silver, J. (2016) Disrupted infrastructures: an urban political ecology of interrupted electricity in Accra. *International Journal of Urban and Regional Research* 39.5, 984-1003.

Skat-IFRC (2012) *Sustainable reconstruction in urban areas: a handbook*. Skat-Swiss Resource Centre and Consultancies for Development, and International Federation of the Red Cross and Red Crescent Societies, Geneva.

Smirl, L. (2009) Plain tales from the reconstruction site: spatial continuities in contemporary humanitarian practice. In M. Duffield and V. Hewitt (eds.), *Empire, development and colonialism: the past in the present*, James Currey, London.

SOCMD (Stars Orbit Consultants and Management Development) (2010) *Rehabilitation of sewerage facilities in select facilities in Basrah City E3-13a*. External evaluation report submitted to the United Nations Children's Fund by Stars Orbit Consultants and

Management Development [WWW document]. URL https://www.unicef.org/evaldatabase/index_67817.html (accessed 7 September, 2017).

Standard Bulletin (2012) Special edition: sanctions. *The Standard Bulletin* [WWW document]. URL http://www.standard-club.com/media/1557763/introduction-to-standard-bulletin-special-edition-sanctions-august-2012.pdf (accessed 11 October 2017).

Swyngedouw, E. (1999) Modernity and hybridity: nature, regeneracionismo, and the production of the Spanish waterscape, 1890-1930. *Annals of the Association of American Geographers* 89.3, 443-65.

Takechi, A. (2014) *Basrah water supply from viewpoint of its water sources*. Tokyo Engineering Consultants Co., Ltd, Tokyo.

UNEP (2007) *Lebanon: post-conflict environmental assessment*. United Nations Environment Programme, Nairobi.

UN-World Bank (2003) *United Nations/World Bank joint Iraq needs assessment*. United Nations Development Group/World Bank [WWW document]. URL http://siteresources.worldbank.org/IRFFI/Resources/Joint+Needs+Assessment.pdf (accessed 11 October, 2017).

USAID (2003) *Strategy for U.S. government activities in water supply and sanitation in Iraq—draft for discussion (rev. 3) May 2, 2003*. USAID, OFDA/DART, HOC Engineering Liaison, Kuwait.

USAID (2013) *Sustainable service delivery in an increasingly urbanized world*. USAID, Washington, DC.

US Army (2008) *Intelligence support to urban operations*. Field Manual FM 2-91.4, Headquarters, Department of the Army, US Army Intelligence Center and School for the US Training and Doctrine Command, Washington, DC.

US DIA (1991) *Iraq water treatment vulnerabilities*. 5111rept.91, US Defense Intelligence Agency, to CENTCOM, Washington DC.

US GAO (2005) *Rebuilding Iraq—U.S. water and sanitation efforts need improved measures for assessing impact and sustained resources for maintaining facilities*. Report to Congressional Committees United States Government Accountability Office [WWW document]. URL http://www.gao.gov/new.items/d05872.pdf (accessed 20 September 2017).

Verhoeven, J., E. Uijtewall and T. Schouten (2015) *Experiences with sustainability instruments: clauses, checks and compacts for ensuring WASH services. Supporting water sanitation and hygiene services for life*, IRC International Water and Sanitation Centre, The Hague, Netherlands.

Weizman, E. (2007) *Hollow land: Israel's architecture of occupation*. Verso, London.

Weizman, E. (2011) *The least of all possible evils*. Verso, London.

WHO (2003) Briefing note on the potential impact of conflict on health in Iraq: March 2003. WHO, Geneva.

WHO (2015) Cholera-Iraq. World Health Organization—Disease Outbreak News, 12 October 2015 [WWW document]. URL http://www.who.int/csr/don/12-october-2015-cholera/en/ (accessed 11 October 2017).

WHO/UNICEF (1991) *Special mission to Iraq*. S/22328 Joint WHO/UNICEF Team Report—A visit to Iraq, 16-21 February 1991 [WWW document]. URL https://digitallibrary.un.org/record/109174/files/S_22328-EN.pdf (accessed 11 October 2017).

WICRC 024 (1998) *Compilation report from Wat-San activities in Iraq*. BAG 335, Baghdad, 30 August 1998. Internal communication of the International Committee of the Red Cross, Geneva.

World Bank (1983) *Lebanon: reconstruction assessment report*. Report No. 4434-LE, World Bank, Beirut.

Zeitoun, M., K. Eid-Sabbagh and J. Loveless (2014) The analytical framework of water and armed conflict: a focus on the 2006 Summer War between Israel and Lebanon. *Disasters* 38.1, 22-44.

Zeitoun, M. and M. Talhami (2017) The impact of explosive weapons on urban services: direct and reverberating effects across space and time. Special Issue on War in Cities, *International Review of the Red Cross* 98.1, 53-70.

Zimmerman, R. and C.E. Restrepo (2009) Analysing cascading effects within infrastructure sectors for consequence reduction. *Proceedings of the HST 2009 IEEE Conference on Technologies for Homeland Security*, Waltham, MA [WWW document]. URL http://research.create.usc.edu/cgi/viewcontent.cgi?article=1146&context=nonpublished_reports (accessed 7 September 2017).

DOI:10.1111/1468-2427.12549

SPATIAL PRACTICES AND THE INSTITUTIONALIZATION OF WATER SANITATION SERVICES IN SOUTHERN METROPOLISES: The case of Jakarta and its Kampung Kojan

PRATHIWI W. PUTRI AND FRANK MOULAERT

Abstract

This article examines the spatial practices and forms of institutionalization in the water and water sanitation sector in Jakarta, capital of Indonesia, and especially in Kampung Kojan in the Kalideres subdistrict of Jakarta. To this end, it develops a three-layered analytical framework viewing the city as a multi-scalar socio-ecological system in which different forms of human–water relations and their institutionalization are found. Particular attention is given to informality in this system and how it interacts with 'regular' state and corporate market sector practices. Within these interactive dynamics, informality is not only understood as a survival strategy but also as a creative practice connecting various social-ecological opportunities, traditional and contemporary technologies and modes of institutionalization to each other. Ongoing institutionalization processes in the formal and informal economy, as well as between them, are analysed. Opportunities to integrate and regularize the diverse water sanitation services into community-led closed water–wastewater cycles capable of ensuring public health and sustaining a bio-hydrological balance at the local level are explored.

Introduction

This article works with a triple-layered analytical framework to study different water and sanitation services and their multiple forms of institutionalization in cities of the global South. It centres on the analytical concept of informality and applies it to Jakarta and one of its kampungs, namely Kampung Kojan.

Two main analytical concerns lie at the basis of the design of this framework. First, the framework is intended to explain the (re)production of agency and institutions within overlapping and scalarly articulated territories for water-related services that embed various forms of informality. Informal practices and processes are not only impregnated by local dynamics, they also articulate with the multi-scalar socio-economic system (Castells and Portes, 1989; Mingione, 1991; Kesteloot and Meert, 1999) and the complex socio-ecological system in which the latter is embedded (Walker, 2014). Echoing Mingione (1991), Kesteloot and Meert (1999) argue that through such articulation, variation in the informalization of economic relations increases at the local scale.

The concept of 'informality' as a mode of economic production and allocation has been widely accepted in the analysis of urbanization processes in the global South (for reviews see Roy, 2005; 2010). Contemporary studies of urban informality are in line with the critical perspective introduced by Mingione in 1991, regarding it as practices of valuation and negotiation rooted in a broader socio-economic and socio-political

The research for this article was made possible by generous support from the Vlaamse Interuniversitaire Raad/ University Development Cooperation (VLIR-UOS), and by Dr Teti Argo and Dr Ibnu Syabri who hosted our fieldwork at the Regions and Infrastructure Research Center, Institut Teknologi Bandung, Indonesia. The authors also thank the various respondents who took part in interviews and Setiaji Wibowo who assisted the fieldwork. Seminar discussions within the Planning and Development Unit, KU Leuven, have shaped the arguments in this article; sincere gratitude goes to our colleagues within the Unit. The authors also thank Erik Swyngedouw, Adriana Allen and the anonymous IJURR referees for their valuable suggestions. The content of the article and any shortcomings are, of course, the authors' responsibility.

metabolism involving statutory and non-statutory institutionalization processes (see Roy, 2005; McFarlane, 2012).

The world of water and sanitation services in Southern metropolises expresses the features of informality cogently (see also Kooy, 2014). Accordingly, studying the fluid urban water sector in Jakarta requires a comprehensive examination of its agency and institutionalization as part of the waterscape—a metaphor for the overall socio-hydrological system. Households and neighbourhood communities have a prominent role in water sanitation services and address more than local needs. As has been argued by Miraftab (2004), the involvement of household members in managing neighbourhood sanitary conditions, very often in informal ways, also germinates new discourses and practices fitting the ambitions of neoliberal agendas in reducing state expenditures for environmental protection.

Second, the analytical framework should embrace the water and sanitation problematic in an integrated way. The socio-economic and socio-political metabolism metaphor should include the entire multifaceted bio-geochemical cycle of water (from precipitation to evaporation) as embedded in the overall socio-ecological metabolism of the urban system. As part of these dynamics, the framework should seek to induct socio-political dynamics into the modernist perspective, which reductively links improved socio-ecological conditions to advances in technology and organization.

Yet modernist logic still dominates major infrastructure works in the water and sanitation sector and remains current in its institutionalization discourse and practice. This logic is built on a functionalist conception of the water system that breaks up the loop of water into sections, thus separating 'clean water' from other forms. Accordingly, practices are prescribed that encourage broader private-sector supply of sectionalized services to fill lacunae in public service provision (see Bakker, 2003; Braadbaart, 2005). These prescriptions do not recognize the unevenness in opportunities for households and small enterprises to access 'formal' service provision; they deny the existence of different levels of community vulnerability in the fast deteriorating urban environment; nor do they discern the holistic character of the metabolic processes interconnecting a diversity of water-based need satisfaction practices and their intrinsic interconnection.

Combining both analytical concerns has significant consequences for the way the roles, agencies and the institutionalization of different water service relationships are addressed in the analytical framework. Considering that neither the state nor the corporate market sector alone can meet, or even properly identify, the needs and institutional relations among the urban poor in the global South, desperately needed institutional reforms to solve water-related problems should also involve so-called informal actors and their networks. The study and design of 'new' agencies ought to take into account the bio-geochemical conditions under which water sanitation services 'naturally' occur, offering alternatives for the conventional technologies and modes of governance that modernist infrastructure systems have failed to provide.

In the light of these analytical concerns, this article disentangles the varying informalities embedded in the urban water and water sanitation sector using a framework with three interrelated layers of explanation. The framework directly or indirectly makes use of theories in political economy (Bakker, 2007; Walker, 2014), political ecology (Swyngedouw et al., 2002; Swyngedouw, 2004), scalar geography (Swyngedouw, 1997; Brenner, 2001; Jonas, 2006) and territorial development (Moulaert and Nussbaumer, 2008) as well as the institutional and cultural turns these theories have adopted (Moulaert *et al.*, 2016).

Scholars within Political Ecology stress the critical role of 'scale' in understanding urbanization as social-ecological processes with varying dialectical relations among different ecological and social entities that are socially constructed (Rangan and Kull, 2009; Angelo and Wachsmuth, 2015). They view cities not just as types of settlement or forms of physical container, but as signifiers of greater urbanizing metabolisms with diverse relations of political actions for socio-ecological change. Territorial development analysts consider 'territories'—mainly neighbourhoods or kampungs and their surroundings in this article—as places of social relationality, collective agency and deployment of resources embedded within these interscalar dynamics (Moulaert and Nussbaumer, 2008: 47).

The first layer unravels the production of the contemporary waterscape in cities of the global South as a *multi-stage geographical-historical transformation process* through which a variety of agencies embedded in different socio-ecological spaces operate. The second layer explains water and sanitation development practices and processes *at the neighbourhood level*. In many cases, these dynamics can be attributed to uneven economic development resulting from ongoing economic restructuring and asymmetric institutionalization processes that involve (global) firms and state agencies as well as enterprises from the informal sector. The third layer analyses the reproduction of the uneven development of the water sanitation sector and inequalities in access to services *across neighbourhoods*. It examines different modes of institutionalization of collective spatial practices, and how they interact and hybridize.

This three-layered analytical framework has guided our analytical movements (*cf.* Lund, 2014), between empirically researching and conceptually summarizing water and sanitation practices and their institutionalization in Jakarta and in Kampung Kojan in the Kalideres subdistrict. In the colonial period, the indigenous word 'kampung' was used to label non-European and non-Chinese settlements. Today an urban kampung is a typical spatial enclave in Indonesian cities in which informality takes on different yet articulated institutional and spatial forms. Kampung Kojan is representative of the peripheral kampungs in Jakarta, surrounded by housing estates and industrial districts. Its historical-geographical trajectory goes back to the original ethnicity of Jakarta, the Betawi people. It is a nexus of the struggle over water and has been the 'laboratory' of development initiatives by (multinational) water companies and NGOs for the last decade.

Fieldwork was conducted between May and December 2011, by way of participatory observation and interviewing household representatives and owners of rental rooms for workers who have benefited from a sanitation development project delivered by Mercy Corps, an international NGO. Key officers of the NGO and some local leaders were also interviewed. To learn about urban dynamics beyond the Kampung, several government officials and corporate leaders were interviewed between August 2010 and October 2012. Data from the interviews used in the analysis are acknowledged in footnotes. Information about planning procedures and projects in Jakarta was updated to 2015.

Five sections follow this introduction. The first explains the three-layered framework and how it addresses the analytical concerns. The next three sections are devoted to the empirical analysis of Jakarta and Kampung Kojan. Each of these sections focuses on one analytical layer, yet accounts for the connections between all layers. Section six wraps up the findings of the analysis and volunteers some prospects for integrated governance of the diverse practices of water and water sanitation services.

A three-layered analytical framework

Figure 1 summarizes the role of each layer in the analytical framework as well as the connections among them. The common principle binding the analytical framework is that water as a natural element is also a product of complex social dynamics. Securing water supply is part of a greater (conflictive) socio-ecological process inside and outside the city (see Swyngedouw, 2004). The city itself consists of different yet connected socio-ecological environments that are 'actively and historically produced' by multiple actors (agents), with different capabilities to influence the urban metabolism processes (Swyngedouw et al., 2002) and the institutionalization of spatial practices in the city (Lambooy and Moulaert, 1996).

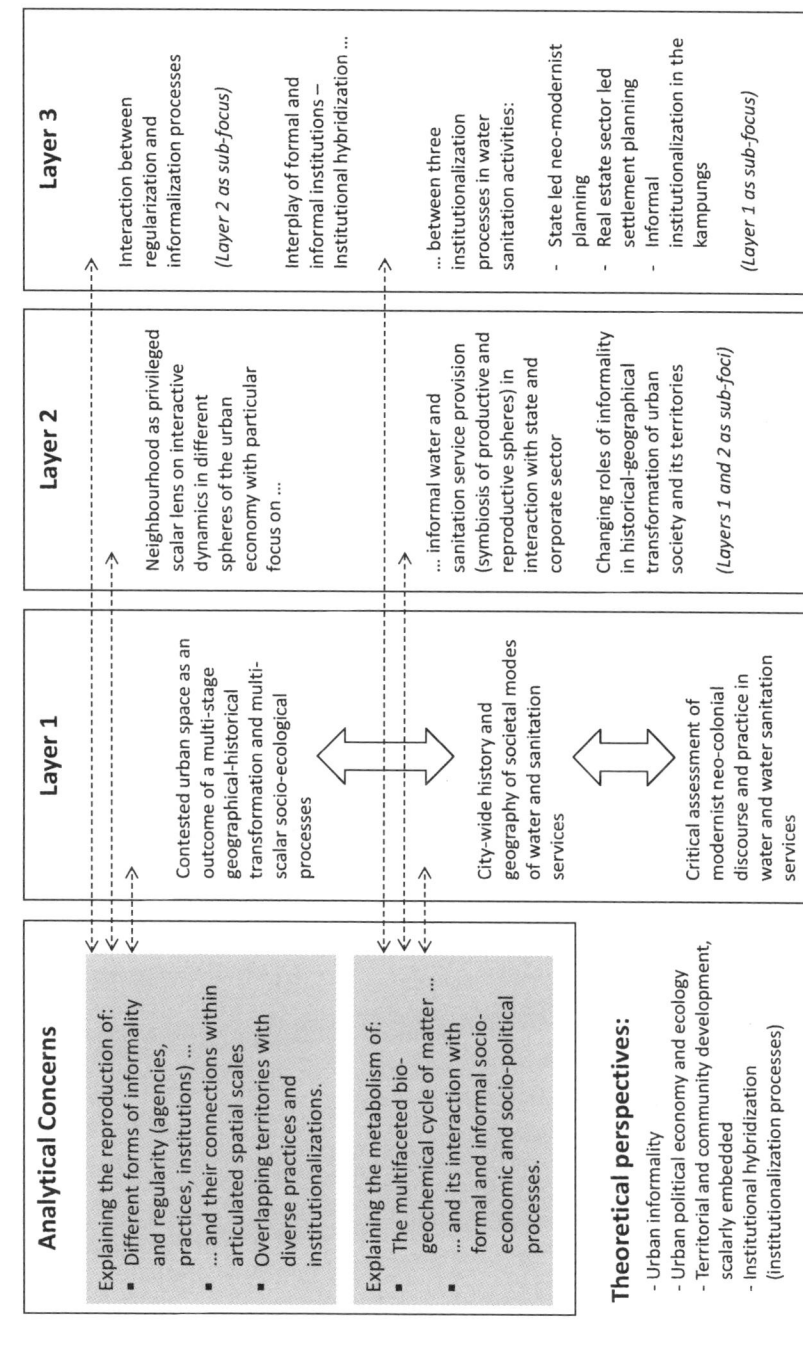

FIGURE 1   The analytical framework (*source*: the authors)

Layer one of the analysis is built on the existential assertion that communities in the city use water within a contested and fragmented urban space. As an epistemological premise to the two other analytical layers, the first layer unfolds dual complexities in the water and sanitation sector as the expression of relationships between human and non-human actors through time and space. Appropriation and uses of urban space are determined by human–human and human–nature relations in which informal practices are ubiquitous. The contested urban space is the outcome of intertemporal and territorial articulations of these social-ecological configurations. Intertemporal dynamics refer to the multiplicity of temporal dimensions with different yet interconnected institutional settings arising across time and often operating at the same time (Massey, 2005).

In water sanitation services, different corporate-, state- or community-led infrastructure networks have their own temporal cycles of institutionalization to keep them functioning within or beyond their technical ambitions (Ranganathan, 2014; Putri, 2017). While in pre-industrial societies the production and reproduction spheres formed a unity, with industrialization they became increasingly separated. But industrialization indirectly also triggered a new rapprochement between the two spheres. Irregular household income structures resulting from uneven industrialization forced people to turn to more traditional systems of 'self-service' water sanitation provision or to live in cheaper areas where only such servicing was available.

From time–space analysis of urban development, we learn that the modernity approach focusing on large-scale technology and centralized management has significantly shaped the configuration of both the colonial and postcolonial city and their waterscape (Gandy, 2008; Kooy and Bakker, 2008). When interpreted and applied linearly, the modernist vision considers the water-related problems and practices in the global South as inherent to a development stage that is far behind that of advanced-industrialized Northern countries. Repeatedly resonated by international organizations and corporate enterprises, this misunderstanding keeps policymakers in Southern countries adopting the modernist urban ideals of advanced industrialized countries and corporations, despite the failure of corporatization, privatization and commodification schemes (see also Bakker, 2007; Dagdeviren, 2008). Thus the belief persists that uncontextualized transfers of the Northern institutional and technological models to the global South will drive its development forward. This kind of transfer reserves a lead role for corporate market players in building the infrastructures for water and water sanitation services, in which a commodification—often tantamount to an annihilation—is taking place of nature and community-based relationships that traditionally matter for protecting the neighbourhood socio-ecological environment (see also Miraftab, 2005).

Grounded in the time–space dialectics of modernist versus traditional, productive versus reproductive, informal versus regular activities, the *second layer* highlights the characteristics of the informal water and sanitation sector and emphasizes its internal differentiation within the urban socio-ecological system, especially by reflecting on the role of informality. It scrutinizes the symbiosis between the formal and informal economies as well as between the productive and reproductive spheres. It explains the actual meaning of the interplay between informality and formality in water and water sanitation services that determines household strategies in meeting basic sanitation needs.

Enzo Mingione (1991) laid the foundations for analysing 'informality', situating it within the interactive dynamics of different sectors in the economy and society as a whole. Commencing with a theoretical discussion of the broad concept of *work* through which humans fulfil the needs of material survival, he explains how industrialization, as it determines societal transformations today, requires a broad range of associative regulatory processes. Together with 'regulatory' ones, 'informalization' processes are also active within industrial transformations. 'Informalization' processes materialize through the diffusion of informal activities, such as reciprocal arrangements that respond to economic tensions stemming from industrialization. Informal practices are not only survival strategies for families and communities, they also constitute a pool of practices promoted by global agents pursuing neoliberal agendas at the local level (Swyngedouw, 1997; Roy, 2005).

Mingione avoids putting the formal and informal economies into binary opposition, and does not refer to 'regulatory processes' as 'formalization'; he argues that 'regulatory processes' are connected and developed along the same lines as 'informalization' (Mingione, 1991: 85). Both types of process form part of 'a cycle of successive adjustments' pushed by interest groups, mainly to reduce or effectively remove obstacles (*ibid.*: 116–17). Thus, 'informality' is not a static condition, and the distinction between formal and informal is possible only when and where the economy is subjected to a relatively high degree of regulation by the state, business corporations and the associated institutional regulatory system (*ibid.*: 84–86, 108, 118).

The strict division of work types generated by the modern industrialization process has 'brought about a variable and changing degree of separation of productive human behaviour from an originally unified productive-reproductive collective organization based on reciprocity' (*ibid.*: 190). The informal economy, in contrast, maintains the interwoven nature of productive and reproductive activities. As regular services become unaffordable, inaccessible or dependent on the low-cost structure of informal inputs, informality and symbiosis between productive and reproductive spheres intensify. Very often unreliable (formal) incomes have been a main factor in growing informal economy networks (Castells and Portes, 1989). As discussed by, among others, Kesteloot and Meert (1999) and Mingione (1991: 185–90), there exists a diffuse and variable form of reciprocity in informal service relations that does not fit economic regularization processes but sustains various modes of community service provision with their specific institutionalization processes.

In urban Indonesia, informal specialized community services have flourished in parallel with rapid population growth to provide inhabitants in kampungs with cheap catering, laundry and cleaning services. Many of these services contribute to ease the burden of domestic work of middle- and high-income classes while offering additional income to low-income groups. In the field of water and water sanitation, informal provision includes services that emerge either outside or in interaction with the state/market provision systems. In Jakarta's kampungs, community services are accessed to a large extent through (informal) redistribution and non-monetary exchange as via the solidarity and self-help networks often advocated or coordinated by civil society organizations. However, such solutions for meeting day-to-day sanitary needs are exposed to external pressures stemming from ambiguous market regularization ambitions and ambivalent state performance.

Focusing in on the dialectics between regularity and informality embodying diverse institutionalization processes, *layer three* of the analytical framework addresses the hybrid institutionalization of spatial practices in accessing water and sanitation services. It recognizes different spatial scales (i.e. the Kampung, neighbourhood, urban Jakarta) as well as the articulation between them (e.g. spatial practices and agreements to connect informal on-site services to the city-wide state-controlled infrastructure networks).

In line with Loftus (2009), it can be argued that everyday struggles for water fuel the urban territorial processes in which localized yet scalarly embedded social relations and institutionalizations often materialize in place-linked communities (Moulaert and Nussbaumer, 2008). It is within the everyday practices of everyday agency that spatial knowledge is materialized, thus fuelling and creatively transforming the institutionalization of water and sanitation practices (see Loftus, 2007). By focusing on the hybridization among various territorially rooted and scalarly connected institutionalization forms, layer three reveals how regular and informal spatial practices engage with the socio-ecological system of an urban region and how institutions arise from this engagement; how institutionalization processes give rise to different spatially articulated, often hybridized governance institutions.

After a long history of 'decentralized' water sanitation systems established at the traditional kampung level, massive investment in water and sanitation infrastructure in urban Jakarta produced a new arena of capital accumulation. This accumulation supported by centralized land-use planning took place without engaging with the complexity of the social and cultural institutions embedded in the kampungs and their communities. Water utilities that once were regulated centrally by the colonial and post-colonial state were turned over to the private sector, thus stimulating the creation of 'premium networked spaces' at the expense of areas falling beyond the reach of the state and corporate spatial planning (Graham, 2000; 2002). At the same time 'decentralized' traditional and new small-scale sanitation infrastructures have (re)discovered the way to the kampungs. Fragmented urban spatial patterns, including the uneven geographical distribution of basic sanitation services are (re)produced through continuous negotiation between multiple forms of regularization and informalization among a diversity of actors.

Thus three main modes of institutionalization and their interaction conceptually underpin layer three: the state spatial planning system in the modernist tradition that exists in advanced symbiosis with the corporate market sector; the procedures applied by real estate developers; the institutionalization in kampungs situated in the grey area between regularization and informality. These modes of institutionalization interactively affect the development and the potential of integrated governance of the water and sanitation services in the urban territories of Jakarta.

Space-time dynamics of Jakarta's waterscape

Guided by the first analytical layer (time–space analysis), this section elucidates the history of Jakarta's waterscape as a metabolic socio-ecological system shaping and shaped by the fragmented yet intertwined territories of various water and water sanitation practices.

In the mid-eighteenth century, while the colonial port-city of Batavia was dominated by the Europeans and Chinese, kampungs in the southern areas were mainly occupied by indigenous communities with a traditional economy based on subsistence agriculture and commerce (Abeyasekere, 1989). These traditional communities, individually or collectively and through a diversity of means, had access to water and sanitation being part of a closed water circuit. But the nineteenth–century development of the inland town led to land shortages and forced communities to abandon their subsistence agriculture system (Elson, 1986). The changing relationship between communities and their lands affected the domestic water cycle; modern water infrastructures were introduced and interfered with the traditional water-cycle logic in community gardens and fishponds, through which ground water flowed into traditional wells. Such socio-ecological transformations have affected Jakarta's contemporary urban waterscape. Figure 2 shows the overlapping and conflictive networks of rivers, canals, water pipes and roads that are sustaining different, yet interdependent, sets of socio-ecological relations in Jakarta.

Today, for many of Jakarta's kampung communities, the thirteen rivers flowing across the low lands remain crucial resources for living, cultivation and transportation. However, the quality of their activities keeps decreasing because the rivers also function as open sewers. The 'centralized' sewerage system began to operate in 1983 and up to now covers a mere 2% of the Jakarta area. Septic tanks form the backbone of the decentralized sewerage system for waste water collection. But there are only about 2 million septic tanks in the urban area for a population of about 13 million; and they often leak, thus polluting the soil and water bodies (Miller, 2006; Yachiko Engineering, 2012). The municipality and licensed private enterprises operate around 188 trucks to empty these septic tanks and haul the sludge to two dedicated treatment plants.

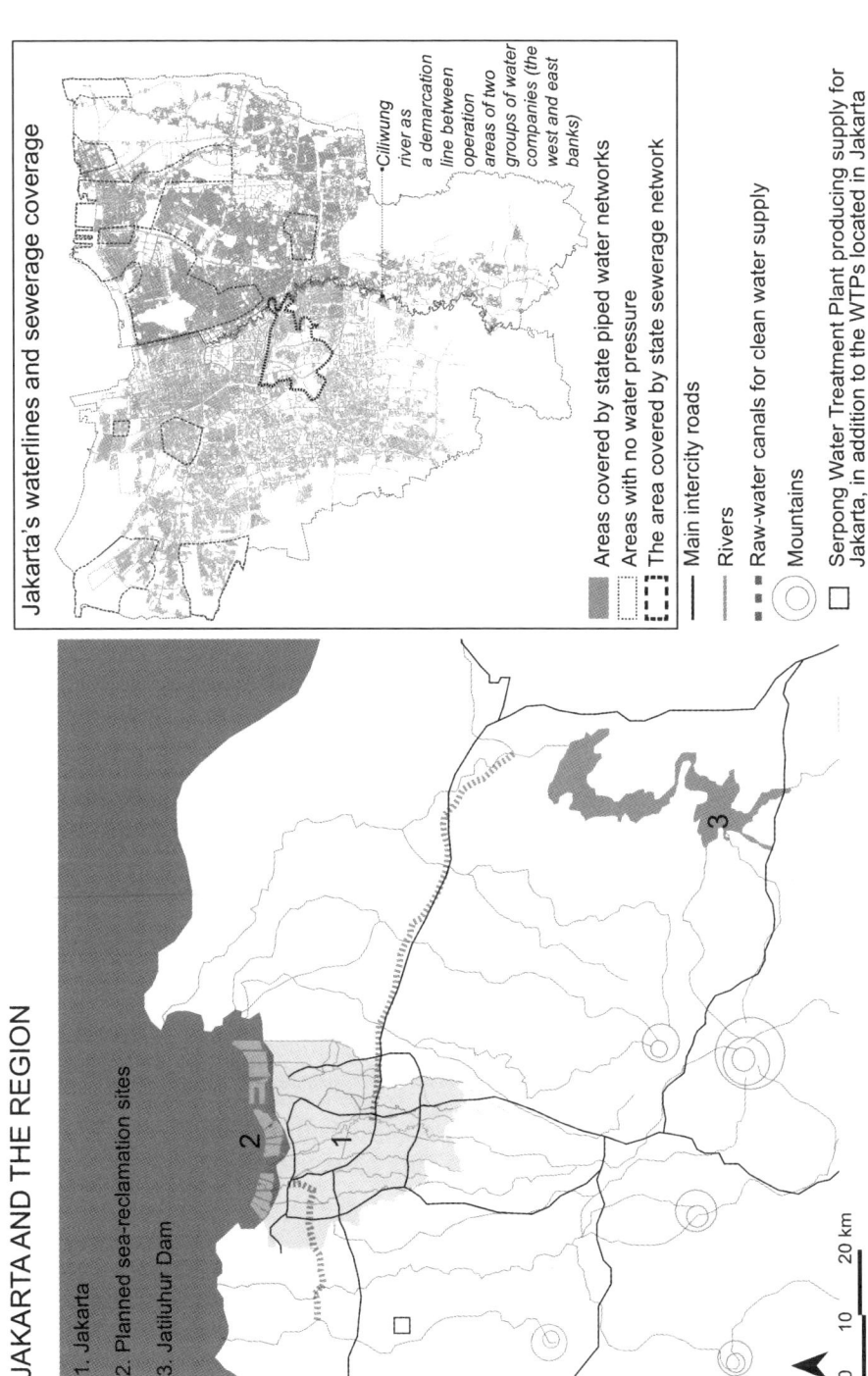

FIGURE 2 The socio-ecological networks of Jakarta (sources: compiled and redrawn by the main author based on data and maps issued by PAM Jaya, the provincial-state water company, and maps issued in the Jakarta Master Plan 2030)

There is frequent illegal discharge of sludge into nearby open water bodies, as many operators—including the informally subcontracted and non-registered ones—prefer to keep transportation costs low by avoiding remote septage treatment plants.[1]

The polluted rivers, charged by the history of uneven modernization, not only bring calamities to poor communities, especially during the driest days and the beginning of the rainy season, but also exacerbate the problems of water resource management for the two piped water companies in Jakarta. Production costs for clean water provision keep increasing, leading to higher water tariffs.[2] In fact, providing water to the urban population in the low lands of Jakarta has been socially conflictive since the colonial era. In 1873, water provision was organized collectively for the first time when the state constructed artesian hydrants that were individually connected to European houses through local pipe networks (Kooy and Bakker, 2008). Following an insufficient supply of clean water, twentieth-century Batavia was served with spring water from the southern mountains via 50 kilometres of iron pipes, especially to still the thirst of its wealthy families.

After independence, in the period from the 1950s to the 1990s, the water provision system was further modernized with the construction of seven water treatment plants through which every second nearly 18,000 litres of surface water are channelled for purification. Around 80% of this volume comes from the Jatiluhur Reservoir, transported through the 70-kilometre West Tarum Canal by means of 17 hydraulic pumps (IndII, 2010). But the political and technological efforts to pump, treat and distribute water could not meet the challenge of bringing water to the entire urban population. Currently, the piped water networks cover about 62% of the Jakarta area, but only around 800,000 households are listed as subscribers of the state water company.[3]

Thus Jakarta's waterscape with its water and sanitation infrastructure is a result of the historical-geographical articulation of traditional, colonial and modernist modes of development. Today, it is formed by diverse spatial practices with their own technologies and modes of institutionalization, all of which have a certain level of permeability. For example, state networks are illegally connected to many (informal) settlements and non-revenue water 'leaks' to benefit not only poor households but also to corrupt bureaucrats who levy a commission on such connections. At the same time, pollutants contaminate the water supply due to technically failing pipe networks, and untreated wastewater cannot be stopped from penetrating the open canals that convey raw water to water supply treatment plants. In addition to the bio-geochemical permeability, a variety of institutional logics diffuse across different water infrastructure systems.

In this symbiotic urban socio-ecological system of Jakarta, distinctions and connections between formal and informal water and sanitation service provision cannot solely be mirrored onto piped versus non-piped or centralized versus decentralized technological systems (see also Kooy, 2014). Such dual categorizing flouts the fact that the popular use of non-piped technologies such as individual household septic tanks or the widespread consumption of bottled drinking water has always been encouraged by formal policies and legal regulations. While the grand policy discourse on Jakarta wastewater management mainly resonates the 'centralized–decentralized' dualism of technological systems and not so much the 'formal–informal',[4] institutionalization practices on the ground in contrast tend to recognize the vital roles of informality and its connections with the regular services.

---

1   An official of PDPAL Jaya during interviews on 7 and 20 January 2011 and an official of Jakarta Cleansing Agency in an interview on 27 March 2012.
2   A technical expert of PALYJA, interviewed on 8 November 2010.
3   Official presentation of the chief director of PAM Jaya, 30 June 2011.
4   Several government officials during interviews, as well as sessions and discussions during the national conference on water and sanitation, 18 January 2011.

Water sanitation and informality in Kampung Kojan, Jakarta

Following the logic of the *second analytical layer* that stresses individual and community practices in water and sanitation services within the informal economy, the highly permeable membranes of the so called 'productive' and 'reproductive' spheres of the informal economy not only mould the modes of community service production, but also the service relation patterns in both the formal and informal provision systems. Regular (market, state) service suppliers who become active in the Kampung therefore have to attune themselves to a diversity of mainly informal, small-scale, yet interconnected initiatives that are predominant there.

Kampung Kojan is surrounded by factories, warehouses, logistics providers and supply chain industries, but also by gated housing estates that began to grow in the late 1970s. The Betawi people, acknowledged as the original ethnic group of Jakarta, dominate the kampung's cultural-political constellation, with most neighbourhood leaders and landowners being Betawi. The actual population covers at least four generations and, according to witness reports, some community members moved into the area after being evicted from other areas in Jakarta.[5]

Around 6,000 people or between 1,500 and 1,700 families live in Kampung Kojan.[6] Many households have irregular employment relations with national and international companies; and others have no proper occupation in the formal job market but work as petty traders or in the informal economy in various service activities. Regular employment (blue collar workers and low-level employees) accounts for only around 16% of the population. Partly in parallel with the more frequent circular migrations, the level of informal employment is high.

There are intimate links between the (informal) job and the (informal) housing markets. For a large part of the population, fragile income conditions impede access to land and home ownership. Some 41% of the households in Kampung Kojan rent a house or room (SUEZ Environment and Mercy Corps, 2010). Many Betawi people have constructed rooms to be rented out, to respond to a high demand for cheap housing for the workers. These rooms are located on former agricultural land. The number of rental rooms built by and managed under the same owner or operator varies, but most estates are small-scale, probably because the agricultural lands have been divided among family members or sold parcel-wise to migrants.[7]

Built on relatively small plots of land, not all housing units provide latrines and bathrooms for the tenants. If available, these facilities are used collectively by tenants and sometimes shared also with the owners. Meeting the high demand for sanitation facilities, four public latrines in Kampung Kojan have been operating satisfactorily until recently but are now in decline. Manifestly, unequal income structures have led to different levels of investment by landlords and tenants in water and sanitation infrastructures. Because members of low-income groups frequently have to change jobs and homes, many landlords in the Kampung are reluctant to upgrade the sleeping shelters, not to mention spending resources on improving water and sanitation facilities, even for themselves.

In general, the inhabitants living in individually owned houses or rental rooms have limited access to piped water or proper sewage collection services. This situation will not improve as Kampung Kojan is excluded from the future sewerage infrastructure expansion projects. Water and sewerage companies tend to prioritize communities with stable land tenure status, and inhabitants with reliable purchasing power like those living in regular housing estates outside the kampung. The state has taken some initiatives to integrate the urban poor in the state- and market-led water and

---

5   As witnessed by some community members in several interviews.
6   Data from RW 6 leader, October 2011.
7   In the Kampung, of the 34 landlords listed as beneficiaries of Mercy Corps, 29 own fewer than 10 rooms (the Program of Urban Sanitation and Hygiene Promotion, Mercy Corps 2010).

sanitation service provision systems. But as they have been designed to address mainly the technological infrastructure problems of service provision, these initiatives require institutional reforms which are hard to accomplish in the Indonesian context.

In early 2008, one of the private water operators PALYJA launched a project as part of the World Bank Global Partnership on Output Based Aid (GPOBA) programme. Preceded by a socio-demographic research conducted by Mercy Corps for the GPOBA, this project has extended the city water pipe network to some kampungs. Piped water now reaches 58% of the households in Kampung Kojan. The project has also regularized the connections to the piped-water network of those who had previously been 'illegally' channelling water from the network to their houses.[8]

However, due to the lack of water pressure, the GPOBA water subscribers suffer from intermittent supply and often have no alternative but to draw on shallow wells for their water provision. Topography plays a significant role in this; Jakarta is a coastal city located just above sea level, with several areas, including Kampung Kojan, having low or often no water pressure in their piped-water network. The water company PALYJA thus has difficulty delivering water to these places via the centralized system.

While corporate market providers consider clean water as a market-worthy commodity, they find investing in the water sanitation sector unprofitable. For many decades the responsibility for wastewater management had been left to individual households, thus causing urban environmental decay and increasing sanitation costs in general. The state recently changed its position towards urban wastewater management and began to speed up the pace of sanitation infrastructure development. So-called state-facilitated decentralized wastewater treatment has become a key plank of sanitation development in Indonesia (*Percepatan Pembangunan Sanitasi Permukiman*, the 2009 national acceleration program for urban sanitation development).

The state strategy of decentralizing wastewater management can be seen as a way to accommodate the heterogeneity of environmental problems within the fragmented urban fabric. Nevertheless, state involvement remains insufficient and communities are burdened with responsibilities of environmental management which they are seldom up to (see Miraftab, 2005). This brings about a real challenge for the households who, after having paid for the water to private suppliers, are faced with insufficient purchasing power to cover public or private environmental protection costs. Still they are expected to keep their wastewater from polluting the wider urban ecological landscape and troubling piped-water production by their own efforts. This ambiguous relationship between affordability and necessity pushes them even further into informality.

–   Asymmetric permeability and weakening reciprocity

A neighbourhood with high population density definitely needs a collective water management system to keep up its waterscape. As well as being polluted, wells are drying up, and the engineering of ground water recharge is beyond the capability of individual households and needs a collective venture.

But the kampungs do not have access to the assets required to build a cohesive community-driven water provision and sanitation infrastructure which they could govern collectively. Hence, many types of informal community water and sanitation service keep growing as short-term survival tactics of individual households. These services are supported by overlapping reciprocity-based networks involving households and communities. Kinship and friendship, among others, are fundamental social relations for households' survival strategies. Many inhabitants in the Kampung are still relatives, living in sufficiently close social proximity to share water and sanitation facilities, as the following example illustrates.

8   The leader of a compound administrative unit *Rukun Tetangga* 7 (RT 7), in an interview on 5 October 2011.

Sn, a 30 year-old female, lives with Sr, a widow, in a household of three generations with five breadwinners and three children. She explains:

> We are using a manual pump … we are also connected to the piped water of our relatives' house. When the pump is not working, the water from the next house is channelled to this house … If the [piped] water is not running, they come to us. [With the new latrine supported by Mercy Corps] we don't have to defecate in the canal anymore … sometimes other relatives stop by to use [the latrine].[9]

Sharing facilities among neighbouring households is common. This tradition of resource sharing has now been valorized by the water company, but on its own terms and for its own benefit; the strategy of expanding the piped-water network in Kampung Kojan involves the utilization of shared meters. But sharing water meters does not motivate households to join forces to gain improved general access to water service provision. When facing an intermittent supply, households still rely on filthy water from the canal for laundry and cleaning as the only available alternative.

Drinking water is prepared by boiling water or purchasing it as ready-to-drink water in refillable containers provided by small local vending stations that have been operating in Jakarta for decades. Among 14 respondents,[10] six families fully rely on this source of drinking water, two families use it in addition to boiling water from the state network, and three families drink it in addition to boiling water from wells and mobile vendors. In interviews with the respondents, five families claimed to spend 7–10% of their family income on water. This is a relatively high proportion, compared to the standards set by some international organizations, suggesting that a household should not spend more than 3% of its income on water (Dagdeviren, 2008).

The widespread informality in the water and sanitation sector is a clear example of what Miraftab (2005) has termed 'informalizing social reproduction'. Diffuse reciprocity infiltrates the domain of public welfare services, thus keeping social reproduction costs of workers in both the formal and informal economic sectors low.

The informalization of water and sanitation services does not necessarily lead to improved sanitary conditions in the kampungs, nor does it reinforce traditional reciprocities as a key to alternative collective provision modes. Without a collective infrastructure to recycle wastewater and protect their traditional water sources, this ambivalent situation will persist. The implementation of PUSH, the Program of Urban Sanitation and Hygiene Promotion, by the NGO Mercy Corps in 2009–2010 with the construction of better quality septic tanks for 219 households has reduced faecal pollution in Kampung Kojan. The NGO continued PUSH and made funding available to initiate the community business of septage desludging and established a revolving fund in other kampungs to self-finance the construction of higher-quality septic tanks. The NGO also introduced small vehicles fit to pass through the small alleys in the kampungs.

It was Mercy Corps' great concern to adapt the septage hauling services to diverse socio-economic conditions of households. However, the experiences of PELITA,[11] the community desludging enterprise founded by Mercy Corps, show that these services are economically poorly sustainable. Mh, the coordinator, explains:

> If it is only one call [to desludge a septic tank], we don't go [this is often the case] … the operational cost would be too high. We have to pay for two workers and their food … the fuel [to operate the machine] and [a fee for] the municipal truck [hauling the sludge to the final treatment plant].[12]

---

9   Sn and Sr were interviewed on 22 September and 22 October 2011.
10   These respondents were selected from project beneficiaries of Mercy Corps.
11   An abbreviation for Pengolahan *Limbah Tinja* or faecal waste treatment, but, as an Indonesian word, *pelita* means 'sources of lights'
12   In an interview on 21 December 2011.

In sum, the decentralized formal and informal service provision initiatives for drinking and clean water as well as public latrines and septage hauling in Kampung Kojan have only small roles in the multi-scalar yet heavily territorialized waterscape. Reciprocal relations involving small numbers of households, sometimes with, sometimes without NGO or state partners, support these small-scale provision systems; but these particular networks of social relations are fragilized by the regular market economy that treats water as a commodity and continuously reimposes cost and profit criteria. Having a high level of porosity, the community productive-reproductive membranes are easily penetrated by 'solidly fluid' pro-market institutional mechanisms reinforced by a market-oriented state planning system, thus mutating many forms of affective and nurturing activities within communities into day-to-day survival strategies.

Spatially diversified institutionalization in the waterscape of Jakarta

Layer three of the analytical framework addresses modes of scalarly articulated institutionalization in the water sanitation sector and how they influence each other. For the water provision and sanitation sector in Jakarta, the three following institutionalization processes should be considered: (1) the state-led neomodernist planning system in which the global corporate sector has a significant role; (2) the procedures applied by real estate developers and tolerated by the state to unbundle infrastructure development in the (new) middle-class settlements; (3) the informal institutionalization of water sanitation services in the territorially marginalized kampung communities. As part of the dynamics of the urban socio-ecological system, these institutionalization processes are porous and counteract, destroy, co-evolve with or reinforce each other—or evolve towards an integrated governance system.

–   State spatial planning: corporate logic and a failing delivery system

Jakarta's first wastewater plan was devised in 1977 and followed in the tracks of the neomodernist waste water treatment systems of both the colonial and postcolonial period: centralized, technology-driven and built by or in close cooperation with the corporate sector. Only a small part of the plan was implemented. Its spatial coverage coincides with the existent state sewerage system that serves only 2% of the Jakarta urban area. Indeed, the sewerage company PDPAL Jaya tends to prioritize communities with stable purchasing power and land tenure status, leading to exclusion of many urban kampungs from the development plan.

The most recent master plan (2012) in which the national government, the provincial administration, the national public works agency and Japanese consulting firms were involved starts from the observation that Jakarta cannot be served by a single centralized system, but should be divided into fifteen zones of sewerage networks with separate wastewater treatment plants. The 2012 Master plan advocates local, individual or communal systems and incorporates institutional guidance for sustaining infrastructures (Yachiko Engineering, 2012).

However, despite these realistic starting points, major flaws in planning and implementation persist: the plan counts on the private sector to build the new infrastructures; it pays only lip service to the integration of the diversity of on-site treatment technologies and favours the building of centralized networks; it misperceives both the geological structure and spatial structure of the local communities, in particular those in the slums; it offers no concrete strategies to improve the on-site or smaller network systems that would work better in these areas; and, last but not least, no legal frameworks, administrative regulations or financial resources have been provided to implement the plan. The most explicit expression of this policy vacuum is that until today no agency is responsible, or has the resources necessary, for implementing the sanitation development policies in the whole of Jakarta. As a consequence, communities keep developing informal, fragmented, small-scale service facilities, often in cooperation with local (district) authorities and NGOs.

Completely overlooking the urgent need to reinstate small-scale closed water cycles serving both water and sanitation services, the Government has proposed the controversial 2,700-hectare land reclamation project in Jakarta Bay, claiming it would also support the latest national development policy on coastal development (the National Capital Integrated Coastal Development or NCICD). A small part of the project has been implemented at tremendous socio-environmental cost: evictions of sea-front kampung communities and destruction of the nearby islands in the Bay through sand mining. Kampung Kojan, 10 km away from the first artificial island, is under pressure from the surrounding commercial activities. In addition to the risk of its inhabitants being evicted, the Kampung would receive more intra-urban migration and also suffer acute infrastructural crises mainly due to a disrupted water cycle.

–   Privileged settlements and unbundled infrastructure planning procedures

With Jakarta's postcolonial economic growth, its middle class rose and became a privileged target group of urban spatial planning (Goldblum and Wong, 2000; Rimmer and Dick, 2009). In contrast to poor settlements, higher middle-class ones have benefited from state-led investment in public space, commercial facilities and gated residencies (Dorleans, 2000; Goldblum and Wong, 2000; Cairns, 2002; Kusno, 2002; 2010; Firman, 2004). The Kalideres subdistrict with Kampung Kojan and its surroundings are a microcosm of Jakarta's spatial fragmentation and social segregation (see Figure 3).

In general, upper and higher middle-class settlements like those adjacent to Kampung Kojan are equipped with small-scale collective water infrastructures utilizing advanced technology, beyond what some authors call 'the archipelagos' of state piped networks (Bakker, 2003; Gopakumar, 2014). In the absence of satisfactory state-led service provision this has been the strategy of many property developers to meet the need for clean water and sanitation services. One developer widened the canal that passes Kampung Kojan, to channel the water to a private water treatment facility. Thanks to Mercy Corps, its sanitary education program and the septic-tank construction projects, open defecation in the Kampung has ended, and pollutants in the canal have significantly diminished. Thus the water also became treatable, ironically enough, to serve the middle-class housing estates in the kampung's surroundings.

But the unbundling of water services has created new shortages and postponed structural solutions to the problems at the neighbourhood level. Due to unreliable small-scale piped water supply systems, not only housing estates but also nearby factories have, often illegally, exhausted the groundwater through digging artesian wells.[13] Many experts have urged the provincial government to forbid private enterprises to overuse groundwater because this increases saltwater intrusion and land subsidence in the coastal area. The government of DKI Jakarta has responded by increasing the groundwater tax significantly. This has had an adverse impact. The tax increase reduced the revenue of PDPAL Jaya, the provincial wastewater company that manages the sewerage system in the central parts of Jakarta as some private enterprises opted to disconnect from the sewerage network and many proprietors of high-rise buildings recycle their wastewater as an alternative to using ground water and paying taxes on that use.[14]

Thus the state groundwater tax mentioned above stimulates decentralized improvements only within high-capital-intensive property development projects, such as shopping malls, high-rise office towers and luxurious apartments. Low-rise housing estates surrounding Kampung Kojan, built in the 1970s are not equipped with wastewater treatment facilities for recycling wastewater. One director of PDPAL

---

13   A local leader of Kalideres and a founder of Kalideres Cooperative, in an interview on 8 November 2011.
14   During an interview on 17 January 2011.

FIGURE 3 Spatial fragmentation around Kampung Kojan (*sources*: compiled and redrawn by the main author based on maps issued in the Jakarta Master Plan 2030 as well as data and maps issued by the Jakarta Housing Agency, 2004 and 2008)

Jaya explained that the regulations for wastewater management had not been strictly imposed on housing developers. They stipulate that developers must connect their housing estates to the sewerage network if the main sewer passes through the area, otherwise they should provide local collective systems. He added:

> But this [technical requirement] has not been enforced by law ... We haven't had a [mandatory] guideline for developers ... [for example] one collective system for every 30 units ... There is no definitive master plan ... [it has not been decided if] certain collective systems [are] suitable for this or that area.[15]

This regulatory ambiguity was confirmed by a high official of the Planning Agency of West Jakarta Municipality, which is responsible for regulating spatial development in the Kalideres Subdistrict. He declared:

> We issue planning permits for developers. For areas above 5,000 square metres, we give planning advice [to follow] ... the size of the land parcels, land ratio for roads ... open space ... drainages ... but not for wastewater treatment systems.[16]

Some policymakers and inhabitants of the 'better' compounds consider kampungs—which are often their 'neighbours'—as settlements full of polluters and sanitation-illiterate populations. But environmental practices in the housing estates are no better than those in the kampungs. Many households in the estates utilize individual septic tanks.[17] If faecal wastewater leaks or overflows from individual tanks, there are good drainage systems to discharge unwanted water away from the estates, nevertheless it still pollutes nearby rivers, the soil and aquifers. This illustrates how better-quality infrastructure in some areas enhances social stratifications in residential patterns. Housing is not only a conspicuous consumption good that reflects income inequality within cities (Saunders, 1984), but it often also metabolically reinforces the unequal access to basic infrastructure (see also Kaika and Swyngedouw, 2000; Jewitt, 2011).

– Reciprocal regularization of water handling in the kampungs

Time and again kampung communities fall victim to land-grabbing for real estate developments and mega construction projects. The Jakarta Legal Aid Institute (LBH Jakarta) reported that in 2015 alone there were 113 cases of forced eviction in Jakarta, directly affecting more than 8,000 households and 6,000 units of community business. Evictions of kampung communities have debilitated associative social relations. Oligopolistic, often global market players in the real estate sector have directly and indirectly spurred both the expansion and densification of informal settlements. Surviving enclaves of kampung communities are also threatened by service homogenization and unaffordable prices induced by the market- and state-driven institutionalization procedures adopted in the surrounding settlements, such as the piped water infrastructure in the housing estates neighbouring Kampung Kojan.

Nevertheless, there are opportunities to integrate different types of services, their technology and their modes of governance into a sustainable ensemble of socio-infrastructural networks. As observed in Kampung Kojan, in addition to benefiting from state-and-market-organized collective provisions, households in different social contexts satisfy their basic needs individually, develop 'new' habits or establish associative processes through informal institutionalization of redistribution and non-monetary exchange in solidarity and self-help networks (see Mingione, 1991: 85,

15   During an interview on 20 January 2011.
16   During an interview on 09 January 2012.
17   An official of Building Authority Agency (Dinas P2B), North Jakarta Municipality, during an interview on 19 October 2012.

132, 262–65). In cooperation with the local communities, (international) civil society organizations have taken on a significant facilitating role in the provision of water and sanitation services in the kampungs. These organizations also have a role as mediators between the state, the corporate sector and kampung communities.

Fieldwork in Kampung Kojan revealed how civil society organizations can help in weaving new associative relations. During the Mercy Corps PUSH project, tenants were willing to collectively build new latrines while Mercy Corps helped construct shared septic tanks. Around 35 semi-private septic tanks were constructed for the benefit of the people living in rental settlements, who are generally the poorest members of the community. Access to a toilet that is located near their rooms and has a tap-water connection enables women to enjoy more privacy in their sanitary activities, and saves more time for other (domestic) work that may increase their real income. Modes of usage were developed stepwise and interactively.

NGOs like Mercy Corps are not developers, instead they seek to make creative use of the porous social space within communities and adjust the ambitions of the districts and subdistrict authorities to the regulatory vacuum left by the national state and the corporate players. Local inhabitants might benefit from initiatives led by NGOs, as shown above; but it remains an open question under which conditions urban populations can act as active communities, capable of controlling their social reproduction spheres in ways that improve the well-being of the community members, while keeping them from becoming passive and individualist consumers instead of active citizens (see McFarlane, 2008).

Concluding remarks: through institutional hybridization towards community-based governance of the waterscape

This article explains the complex configuration of socio-ecological conditions from which different types of water provision and sanitation services—structural components of the overall urban waterscape—emerged to meet the needs of competing human activities, communities and territories in Jakarta. It makes use of three interconnected layers of analysis: the historical-geographical metabolic development of the water provision and sanitation system; the role of informality in meeting water and sanitation needs in interaction with the state and corporate sector; and the multiple and interconnected forms of institutionalization in the water sanitation sector.

It unravels water sanitation problems as the unsatisfied needs of various communities in search of healthy living conditions for which the protection of (traditional) water sources is essential. Meeting these needs would require environmental governance systems in which the local communities play a decisive role. Thus, the future water and sanitation service system should not only rely on the institutionalization of state and corporate sector infrastructures and practices, but also on the regularization of robust informal service practices.

The *first layer of the analytical framework* provides a basis for understanding the contemporary socio-ecological system of water and sanitation provision as the historical-geographical outcome of development trajectories that do not always square up. A coherent ensemble of city-wide infrastructures that could serve the needs of all urban population groups is missing; instead the water sanitation system consists of a patchwork of different modes of provision that are often territorially conflictive and socio-politically exclusive. Yet this diversity of modes of sanitation offers a rich laboratory in which opportunities for applying more decentralized and diverse technologies and integrating them into a city-wide ensemble of water and sanitation services can be studied. The water cycle, although socially, technically and institutionally fragmented, does form a unity and is badly needed as a means of restoring the balance between the qualities that humans require for different water uses.

The *second analytical layer* stresses the symbiosis between the formal and informal water economy, especially at the neighbourhood level. It highlights the characteristics of the informal sector: combinations of traditional and modern practices of water provision and sanitation by households, groups of inhabitants, small enterprises; modes of cooperation based on reciprocity, but also on loose forms of association with corporate players and state agencies; a high level of adaptability to changing socio-ecological conditions. Symbiosis with the 'formal' market and state sectors is everywhere and confirms the necessity of considering informality as the community-based twin rather than the antagonist of market and state regularity in the institutionalization process. This process involves a mixture of building codes and modes of cooperation at the level of the kampung or district, procedures for access to water and sanitation services including network use-rights among major players (developers, industries, groups of tenants, and others), unsatisfactory yet influential state regulation, etc.

The *third layer* then examines how various methods of institutionalizing water and sanitation service provision fit, comply or even collide with different modes of spatial arrangement. These modes have hampered or reinforced each other, mutated, or negotiated symbiotic forms of service provision. These symbiotic forms refer to combinations of different technologies as well as their modes of operation and regulation and they have a great potential for building an integrated yet heterogeneous water and sanitation service system across Jakarta's kampungs.

The failure of the formal systems and the growing informal service provision have pressured the state and private sector to integrate and institutionalize informal practices within the current development model (see Hardoy *et al.*, 2005; Gerlach and Franceys, 2010). By regulating informal services, including standardizing service quality and increasing the scale of operations, the state and private sector assume that proper basic sanitation service provision for all can be achieved. However, the analysis in this article suggests that it is not a matter of technologically integrating the systems outside the piped infrastructure networks—'informal', 'low-tech', 'non-state', 'community', or 'decentralized', whatever you want to call them—into the piped networks that are governed by institutions instigated by the corporate sector and operated by the central state. Such a homogenizing approach to governance would lead to a further loss of control of the water cycle by the urban communities, especially those in the kampungs. Instead, different technologies and their modes of use should be recognized and connected by a multiplex but more coherent governance system. As Mingione argued, '[the] informalization process has served to increase the importance of some local characteristics as against universal patterns' (Mingione, 1991: 177).

The application of the *three-layered analytical framework* shows that institutional hybridization in a capital- and profit-driven society can put reciprocity as the basis of informality under pressure. But other forms of institutionalization are possible, in which the reciprocity networks are improved (Mingione, 2002). Highly informal community services often serve as both productive economic and socially reproductive activities, sustaining the well-being of the community members. Improved reciprocity networks can be associated with a community-governed waterscape and water-wastewater cycle with relatively autonomous environmental sanitation systems capable of ensuring public health and sustaining bio-hydrological balance at the local level.

Prathiwi W. Putri, Department of Food and Resource Economics, University of Copenhagen, Rolighedsvej 25, 1958 Frederiksberg, Denmark, pwp@ifro.ku.dk

Frank Moulaert, Planning and Development Unit, Faculty of Engineering, KU Leuven, Kasteelpark Arenberg 1, B-3001 Leuven, Belgium, frank.moulaert@asro.kuleuven.be

References

Abeyasekere, S. (1989) *Jakarta: a history,* Revised edition, Oxford University Press, Singapore.

Angelo, H. and D. Wachsmuth (2015) Urbanizing urban political ecology: a critique of methodological cityism. *International Journal of Urban and Regional Research* 39.1, 16–27.

Bakker, K. (2003) Archipelagos and networks: urbanization and water privatization in the South. *The Geographical Journal* 169.4, 328–41.

Bakker, K. (2007) Trickle down? Private sector participation and the pro-poor water supply debate in Jakarta, Indonesia. *Geoforum* 38.5, 855–68.

Braadbaart, O. (2005) Privatizing water and wastewater in developing countries: assessing the 1990s' experiments. *Water Policy* 7.4, 329–44.

Brenner, N. (2001) The limits to scale? Methodological reflections on scalar structuration. *Progress in Human Geography* 25.4, 591–614.

Cairns, S. (2002) Troubling real-estate: reflecting on urban form in Southeast Asia. In T. Bunnell, L. Drummond and K.C. Ho (eds.), *Critical reflections on cities in Southeast Asia,* Times Media Private Limited and Brill Academic Publishers, Singapore and Leiden.

Castells, M. and A. Portes (1989) World underneath: the origins, dynamics, and effects of the informal economy. In A. Portes (ed.), *The informal economy: studies in advanced and less developed countries,* John Hopkins University Press, Baltimore, MD.

Dagdeviren, H. (2008) Waiting for miracles: the commercialization of urban water services in Zambia. *Development and Change* 39.1, 101–21.

Dorleans, B.R.G. (2000) From kampung to residential development. Some trends in the development of the Greater Jakarta Area. In K. Grijns and P.J.M. Nas (eds.), *Jakarta- Batavia: socio-cultural essays,* KITLV Press, Leiden.

Elson, R.E. (1986) Sugar factory workers and the emergence of 'free labour' in nineteenth-century Java. *Modern Asian Studies* 20.1, 139–74.

Firman, T. (2004) New town development in Jakarta Metropolitan Region: a perspective of spatial segregation. *Habitat International* 28.3, 349–68.

Gandy, M. (2008) Landscapes of disaster: water, modernity, and urban fragmentation in Mumbai. *Environment and Planning A* 40.1, 108–30.

Gerlach, E. and R. Franceys (2010) Regulating water services for all in developing economies. *World Development* 38.9, 1229–40.

Goldblum, C. and T-C. Wong (2000) Growth, crisis and spatial change: a study of haphazard urbanisation in Jakarta, Indonesia. *Land Use Policy* 17.1, 29–37.

Gopakumar, G. (2014) Experiments and counter-experiments in the urban laboratory of water-supply partnerships in India. *International Journal of Urban and Regional Research* 38.2, 393–412.

Graham, S. (2000) Constructing premium network spaces: reflections on infrastructure networks and contemporary urban development. *International Journal of Urban and Regional Research* 24.1, 183–200.

Graham, S. (2002) On technology, infrastructure and the contemporary urban condition: a response to Coutard. *International Journal of Urban and Regional Research* 26.1, 175–82.

Hardoy, A., J. Hardoy, G. Pandiella and G. Urquiza (2005) Governance for water and sanitation services in low-income settlements: experiences with partnership-based management in Moreno, Buenos Aires. *Environment and Urbanization* 17.1, 183–99.

IndII. (2010) *Jatiluhur-Jakarta pipeline and water treatment plant. Pre-feasibility study* [WWW document]. URL: http://www.indii.co.id/images/dx_publication_ file/8379/jatiluhur-jakarta-pipeline-and-water-treatment-plan-pre-feasibility-study.pdf (accessed 2 November 2017).

Jewitt, S. (2011) Geographies of shit: spatial and temporal variations in attitudes towards human waste. *Progress in Human Geography* 35.5, 608–26.

Jonas, A.E.G. (2006) Pro scale: further reflections on the 'scale debate' in human geography. *Transactions of the Institute of British Geographers* 31.3, 399–406.

Kaika, M. and E. Swyngedouw (2000) Fetishizing the modern city: the phantasmagoria of urban technological networks. *International Journal of Urban and Regional Research* 24.1, 120–38.

Kesteloot, C. and H. Meert (1999) Informal spaces: the geography of informal economic activities in Brussels. *International Journal of Urban and Regional Research* 23.2, 232–51.

Kooy, M. (2014) Developing informality: the production of Jakarta's urban waterscape. *Water Alternatives* 7.1, 35–53.

Kooy, M. and K. Bakker (2008) Splintered networks: the colonial and contemporary waters of Jakarta. *Geoforum* 39.6, 1843–58.

Kusno, A. (2002) Architecture after nationalism: political imaginings of Southeast Asian architects. In T. Bunnell, L.B.W. Drummond and K.C. Ho (eds.), *Critical reflections on cities in Southeast Asia,* Times Media Private Limited and Brill Academic Publishers, Singapore and Leiden.

Kusno, A. (2010) *The appearances of memory. Mnemonic practices of architecture and urban form in Indonesia.* Duke University Press, Durham, NC.

Lambooy, J.G. and F. Moulaert (1996) The economic organization of cities: an institutional perspective. *International Journal of Urban and Regional Research* 20.2, 217–37.

Loftus, A. (2007) Working the socio-natural relations of the urban waterscape in South Africa. *International Journal of Urban and Regional Research* 31.1, 41–59.

Loftus, A. (2009) Rethinking political ecologies of water. *Third World Quarterly* 30.5, 953–68.

Lund, C. (2014) Of what is this a case? Analytical movements in qualitative social science research. *Human Organization* 73.3, 224–34.

Massey, D. (2005) *For space.* Sage Publications Ltd, London.

McFarlane, C. (2008) Sanitation in Mumbai's informal settlements: state, 'slum' and infrastructure. *Environment and Planning A* 40.1, 88–107.

McFarlane, C. (2012) Rethinking informality: politics, crisis, and the city. *Planning Theory and Practice* 13.1, 89–108.

Miller, J.M. (2006) Support to DKI Jakarta for wastewater management. Unpublished draft final report provided in person by a government official to the main author. The World Bank–WSP EAP, Jakarta.

Mingione, E. (1991) *Fragmented societies: a sociology of economic life beyond the market paradigm.* Basil Blackwell, Oxford.

Mingione, E. (2002) The use of the concept of reciprocity for the interpretation of contemporary advanced industrial societies: ambiguities and assets. *ENDOXA: Series Filosoficas* 15, 51–58.

Miraftab, F. (2004) Neoliberalism and casualization of public sector services: the case of waste collection services in Cape Town, South Africa. *International Journal of Urban and Regional Research* 28.4, 874–92.

Miraftab, F. (2005) Informalizing and privatizing social reproduction: the case of waste collection services in Cape Town, South Africa. In N. Kudra and L. Beneria (eds.), *Rethinking informalization: precarious jobs, poverty and social protection,* Cornell University Open Access Repository, Ithaca, NY.

Moulaert, F., B. Jessop and A. Mehmood (2016) Agency, structure, institutions, discourse (ASID) in urban and regional development. *International Journal of Urban Sciences* 20.2, 167–87.

Moulaert, F. and J. Nussbaumer (2008) *La logique sociale du développement territorial* [The social logic of territorial development]. PUQ, Québec.

Putri, P. (2017) Moulding citizenship: urban water and the (dis)appearing kampungs. In S. Bell, A. Allen, P. Hofmann and T-H. Teh (eds.), *Urban water trajectories,* Springer International Publishing, Switzerland.

Rangan, H. and C.A. Kull (2009) What makes ecology 'political'? Rethinking 'scale' in political ecology. *Progress in Human Geography* 33.1, 28-45.

Ranganathan, M. (2014) Paying for pipes, claiming citizenship: political agency and water reforms at the urban periphery. *International Journal of Urban and Regional Research* 38.2, 590-608.

Rimmer, P.J. and H.W. Dick (2009) *The city in Southeast Asia: patterns, processes and policy*. NUS Press, Singapore.

Roy, A. (2005) Urban informality: toward an epistemology of planning. *Journal of the American Planning Association* 71.2, 147-58.

Roy, A. (2010) Informality and the politics of planning. In J. Hillier and P. Healey (eds.), *The Ashgate research companion to planning theory: conceptual challenges for spatial planning*, Ashgate, Farnham.

Saunders, P. (1984) Beyond housing classes: the sociological significance of private property rights in means of consumptions. *International Journal of Urban and Regional Research* 8.2, 202-27.

SUEZ Environment and Mercy Corps (2010) Access to sanitation: generating environmental improvements and economic benefits for the urban poor in Jakarta.

Unpublished Technical Report provided in person to the main author (version 6 September 2010).

Swyngedouw, E. (1997) Neither global nor local: 'glocalization' and the politics of scale. In K.R. Cox (ed.), *Spaces of globalization: reasserting the power of the local*, Guilford/Longman, New York/London.

Swyngedouw, E. (2004) *Social power and the urbanization of water: flows of power*. Oxford University Press, Oxford.

Swyngedouw, E., M. Kaika and E. Castro (2002) Urban water: a political-ecology perspective. *Built Environment* 28.2, 124-37.

Walker, G. (2014) A theoretical walk through the political economy of urban water resource management. *Geography Compass* 8.5, 336-50.

Yachiko Engineering (2012) *The project for capacity development of wastewater sector through reviewing the wastewater management master plan in DKI Jakarta in the Republic of Indonesia. Final Report, Summary*. JICA, Ministry of Public Work, DKI Jakarta, PD PAL Jaya [WWW document]. URL: http://open_jicareport.jica.go.jp/pdf/12078622_01.pdf (accessed 29 March 2012).

INTERNATIONAL JOURNAL OF URBAN AND REGIONAL RESEARCH
DOI:10.1111/1468-2427.12583

— WRITING ACROSS CONTEXTS: Urban Informality and the State in Tallinn, Bafatá and Berlin

HANNA HILBRANDT, SUSANA NEVES ALVES AND TAURI TUVIKENE

Abstract

Urban research has long related informality to a lack of state capacity or a failure of institutions. This assumption not only fails to account for the heterogeneous institutional relations in which informality is embedded, but has also created a dividing line between states. Whereas some states are understood to manage urban development through functioning institutions, others, in this view, fail to regulate. To deconstruct such understandings, this article explores informal practices through a multi-sited individualizing comparison between three case studies of water governance, parking regulation and dwelling regimes in Bafatá (Guinea-Bissau), Tallinn (Estonia) and Berlin (Germany), respectively. Our approach to understanding informality starts from the negotiation and contestation of order between differently positioned actors in the continuous making of states. From this point of view, informality is inherent in the architecture of states—emerging through legal systems, embedded in negotiations between and within institutions, and based on conflicts between state regulations and prevailing norms. Tracing how order takes shape though negotiation, improvisation, co-production and translation not only highlights how informality constitutes a modus operandi in the everyday workings of the state in all three cases, but also provides a way to talk across these cases, i.e. to bring them together in one frame of analysis and overcome their presumed incommensurability.

Introduction

How can we talk about informality across contexts? That is, how can we compare informality across the globe while acknowledging the different histories and trajectories of states? While the geographical spread of research that builds on the notion of informality suggests that it is related to the experiences of cities across the world, these questions confront at least two major challenges.

The first is an epistemological difficulty concerning the definition of informality that has haunted urban studies for quite some time (see Bunnell and Harris, 2012: 339). The multiplicity of processes being discussed under this label makes it hard to pinpoint common dynamics or objects of analysis—even in one context. Finding a common definition across dissimilar sites raises further difficulties. Whereas research in states that are understood to manage cities through coherently functioning institutions tends to regard informality as a marginal phenomenon, investigations into states that are presumed to have weak institutions frequently use the notion of informality to point to a plethora of processes that are key to different areas of urbanization, including housing and economies. As these approaches have enlisted the cities of the South in an alleged trajectory of development or modernization (Comaroff and Comaroff, 2012), they have drawn a dividing line between the economic hubs of the Northern and the Southern megalopolis that hampers meaningful conversation through informality as an analytical frame. As a result, authors variably relate informality to a lack of state capacity

We thank Jennifer Robinson and Suzanne Hall plus three very helpful IJURR reviewers for their comments on an earlier version of this article, and William Gray for the time and effort he invested in proofreading and editing this article. Susana Neves Alves' research was funded by the Portuguese funding institution FCT (Fundação para a Ciência e Tecnologia). Research done by Tauri Tuvikene was supported by the Estonian Research Council grants IUT3-2, PUT690 and PUTJD580.

or to a failure of institutions, a 'mode of urbanization' (Roy, 2005: 148), itself produced through the state, or a marginal phenomenon at the peripheries of the 'modern' state. In short, informality is understood to point to different processes that hardly allow for a comparison across presumed global divides.

This article constitutes an attempt to defy this supposed incommensurability. More precisely, we seek to advance a comparative analysis of informality to sort out and test if and how informality can serve as a global analytic that allows us to talk across very distinct cases, i.e. to bring these cases together in one frame of analysis. In order to employ informality as an analytical and comparative concept of governance relations, we need to further scrutinize the conceptions of states that underlie informality. Our approach to understanding the state underlines the impact of everyday practices in the production of states (Mitchell, 1991; Painter, 2006). This understanding not only illustrates that institutions hardly work as an overarching, coherent entity, but also reveals the incoherencies, breaks and gaps within the workings of all states. In this light, informality appears to be produced by different actors in the construction of order: it points to the continuous contestation and negotiation in the enforcement of order rather than to a fixed process or practice. Most importantly, this understanding allows for a more nuanced reading of informality that promises to hold true across different sites.

The second challenge that a global comparison of informality confronts concerns the methodological difficulties of comparative urbanism. Drawing comparisons between cities in very dissimilar regions is commonly seen as an insurmountable task, in particular when these comparisons are drawn across the conceptual boundaries of the global North and South. This article builds on research developed around a literature on 'comparative urbanism' (see Robinson, 2004; Nijman, 2007; Ward, 2010; McFarlane and Robinson, 2012) that has argued for the expansion of urban theorizing to cities deemed 'off the map' (Robinson, 2002), meaning those formerly categorized as 'third-world' or 'second-world' cities (see Ferenčuhová, 2012; Grubbauer, 2012; Wiest, 2012). These accounts attempt to scrutinize understandings of certain cities as being in need of 'development' or 'catching up' with the 'Western world' and aim to work towards a more equal and global urban theory in which any city constitutes a site of theorization (Robinson, 2011a). But while these approaches have increasingly challenged the long-standing perception of 'incommensurability' (Robinson, 2011b) between cities in different parts of the world (although, to be sure, many still see it as a 'problem' to combine cities in different regional context; see, for example, Kantor and Savitch, 2005), it is less clear how such comparisons can be drawn practically.

This project confronts these challenges by relating three distinct cases in cities in different regions, whereby each co-author contributes intimate knowledge of one case study. Each study has a specific focus, although all three cases converge in terms of their interest in informality or, more precisely, the relations of informality to state practices. Our comparison is analytical, which means that we make the cases commensurable by focusing on similar processes that further a conceptual understanding of informality in and across these sites. We term this strategy a *multi-sited individualizing comparison*. Briefly, the approach combines two aims. On the one hand, in providing an in-depth analysis of each individual case, it accounts for contextual particularities. On the other hand, in allowing a juxtaposition of the insights gained from one case with those gained from other cases, it opens up the comparison to generalizations. Based on this understanding, the empirical sections of this article examine similar instances of informality in the use and governance of different urban infrastructures, namely infrastructures of water provisioning in Bafatá,[1] of parking in Tallinn[2] and of dwelling

---

1   This case draws on research conducted by Susana Neves Alves between 2011 and 2016. For further detail on methodology and data, see Neves Alves (2016).
2   This case draws on research conducted by Tauri Tuvikene between 2012 and 2014. For further detail on methodology and data, see Tuvikene (2015).

in Berlin.³ These cases cross presumed North–South divides and appear to have divergent contextual particularities. But rather than being selected according to these or other categories, our joint analytical interest brought us into a conversation about the ways in which a meaningful frame of analysis would enable a joint understanding of informal processes in different contexts. Each co-author contributed a case study to this conversation, based on individual research (for a more detailed explanation of this approach, see Tuvikene *et al.*, 2017).

This article traces how order takes shape though negotiation, improvisation, co-production and translation within the governance mechanisms we observed across our cases. Based on this comparison, our central argument is twofold. On the one hand, we contend that informality constitutes a modus operandi in the continuous formation of the state. On the other hand, we suggest that such an understanding of informality—as embedded in everyday state practices—provides a way to talk across and overcome the presumed incommensurability of informality in Northern or Southern cities. Although informality plays out through similar mechanisms across what are presumed to be incommensurable sites, differences in the role of state institutions, the implementation of laws, or the leverage of civil actors in the production and contestation of order alter the relevance of these mechanisms and the ways in which they manifest themselves in each case. Crucially, our comparison also highlights the negotiated nature of order across all sites. Our comparison finds informality to be inherent in the architecture of states: it emerges through the limits and ambiguities of legal systems, is embedded in the inconsistencies between and within institutions, and is based on conflicts between state regulations and prevailing norms that govern social interaction.

The article has three parts. In the first part, we scrutinize some of the key work on informality, focusing on the possibilities of these analyses regarding the 'comparative gesture' (Robinson, 2011b) we seek to develop. In doing so, we introduce some of the ways in which these accounts imagine the state and complement this discussion with insights that state ethnographies may bring into the informality debate. Secondly, we introduce our cases. Finally, we probe our analytical framework through a discussion of the three cases and draw some conclusions on the exigencies and possibilities for informality to work as a comparative concept.

Informality as a comparative analytic

It is now commonplace to criticize conceptions of informality that reproduce formal–informal binaries, that is, to define the 'informal' as clearly distinct from 'formal' order (see, for example, Bunnell and Harris, 2012). Thus conceived, researchers long assumed informality to constitute a separate sphere. They associated the concept with specific groups (for example, the poor), spaces (such as slums), or modes of governing (for example, self-governing) that were predominantly found in cities of the 'developing' world (Chen, 2007).

In the past decade, these binaries have been challenged by more complicated theorizations that have recognized that these divisions are more fluid and complex. Today, the multiple ambiguities constituting the formal–informal divide are well rehearsed: various authors, including Laurent Fourchard (2011), Ilda Lindell (2008), Ryan Devlin (2011) and Colin McFarlane (2012), have examined the ways in which informal processes are strongly linked to the workings of state institutions and have illustrated how social spheres are embedded in a mesh of different relations that can be formal and informal at the same time. Moreover, this work has disentangled the notion from a development trajectory in which informality results from a lack of modernity and will disappear as 'developing' cities 'modernize'. Instead, as McFarlane notes, 'we

---

3   This case draws on research conducted by Hanna Hilbrandt between July 2013 and July 2014. For further detail on methodology and data, see Hilbrandt (2016).

cannot assume a priori that cities in the global south are "more" informal than cities in the global north' (McFarlane, 2012: 104).

–   Informality and the state

If this latter body of work is united in its criticism of binaries between informality and formality, divergent views prevail concerning the ways in which different scholars relate informality to the state. As existing theorizations of informality tend to rely on different and frequently under-defined understandings of the state, an analytical and comparative use of the concept remains a challenge. In addition, despite much critical engagement, less has been written about the rather fundamental question of how to approximate a conceptual understanding of informality that would allow addressing empirical concerns across diverse contexts. Instead, the contemporary literature operates predominantly with an understanding of informality that builds on empirical explorations of how informality is used and experienced locally and in a particular field, and hardly constitutes what Robert Merton would term a 'theory of the middle range', that is, 'a set of assumptions from which empirical generalizations have themselves been derived' (Merton, 2012 [1949]: 533). Thus, to use informality as an analytic to talk across different sites, this section examines the conceptual underpinnings of the state in understandings of informality through theories of the state.

First, in the literature informality is discussed as 'produced by the state itself' (Roy, 2005: 149). For example, Yiftachel's (2009a; 2009b) investigations into urban Israel examine how state institutions use informality in an instrumental way. His work describes how the Israeli state strategically manipulates informality, formalizing and informalizing certain forms of order to advance the interests of particular groups. Yiftachel (2009a: 92) identifies these processes as the 'whitening' and 'blackening' of urban practices. He debunks, as he notes, 'the tendency of the system to "launder" gray spaces created "from above" by powerful or favourable interests', while the 'graying' of other spaces allows the state to further delegitimize or marginalize poor groups, leading to 'destruction, expulsion or elimination' (*ibid.*). The state appears here as a coherent, hegemonic entity acting strategically to pursue specific aims.

In a similar vein, Roy (2011a: 233) considers the 'valorization of elite informalities and the criminalization of subaltern informalities' in urban India to highlight the ways in which states manage urban informality. Roy's account is primarily based on research on the Indian state, which she describes through the multiple contradictions of state practices. However, as Roy argues, these ambiguities hardly indicate weakness; rather, they conceal an 'activist' state for which governance failures constitute a strategy in itself (2011b: 262). In this account, informality emerges in decentralized and privatized modalities of governing, entailing moments of social and political agency and constituting, as Roy (2005: 148) writes, 'a system of norms that governs the process of urban transformations itself'. In line with Yiftachel's account, Roy points to the ways in which the state acts in essentially strategic ways to manage informality (*ibid.*: 149). Their analytical focus on these state strategies graphically illustrates some of the workings of informality as produced by the Indian or Israeli state. However, this analytical approach is less helpful for the purpose of our comparative exercise. As it does not unpack comparative mechanisms, practices, resources or actor constellations through which this production is brought about, this approach poses challenges for generalizations across different settings.

Secondly, researchers have examined informality through the ambiguities of the state's own architecture, the room for discretion, or the malleability of legal frames—in short, through the routine but incoherent workings of state institutions and their agents. Devlin's (2011) account of street economies and the ambiguous and flexible practices of regulation thereof in New York is an interesting case in point. As he argues, 'on the street formal law does not act like a blueprint structuring social action and spatial form;

it exists mostly as a point of departure for spatial negotiations and manoeuvres by all actors involved' (*ibid.*: 54). Devlin's account of street governance explicitly turns away from the idea of a coherent set of regulations, but shows how informality works through variegated power structures and through the gaps, flexibilities and ambiguities of porous laws that are applied in diverse ways.

In contrast to Weberian understandings of the state, which tend to suppose the rationality of institutions, Devlin's analysis suggests that multiple and divergent projects constitute the state. Mariana Valverde (2011) follows the same line of thought to suggest that even if institutions may form one entity, they tend to govern with discordant aims or follow their own rationalities. Both authors thus point to the pervasive and commonly accepted room for manoeuvre in the governing practices of state authorities. Rather than investigating the action of a 'state' that acts coherently through concerted efforts, they understand the state—and in Devlin's account the production of informality— through the multiple practices of individuals.

Thirdly, theorizations that have developed predominantly from research conducted in African cities consider informality through the multiplicity of governance arrangements that produce order beyond formal policies and projects. Lindell's (2008) and Fourchard's (2011) investigations of markets in Maputo and Lagos, respectively, demonstrate how various state institutions and actors, operating at different levels, shape the workings of these markets and thereby challenge observations that portray these places as self-regulatory systems created to overcome states' inability to deliver urban services. Thus, like Roy and Yiftachel, they discard views of informality as a separate or independent domain. However, their account differs in the ways in which they conceive of the actor constellations that produce urban governance. Lindell and Fourchard argue that the order of the markets they investigate does not lie beyond the reach of the state's actors, policies or regulations. Instead, governing is perceived through the complex entanglement of practices within and beyond state institutions. Thereby, these accounts highlight the inescapable messiness and incoherencies of state institutions and governing instruments as well as the relevance of these complexities for an understanding of urban governance. From their perspective, practices of informality are not necessarily ingrained in wider strategies of governing, as they tend to be described in Roy's and Yiftachel's accounts. Informality emerges as a consequence of the complexity and the multiplicity of interests and practices that are intrinsic to the everyday workings of states. This understanding provides the basis from which we advance the central task of this article: to develop an analytic that allows us to bring our cases together in one frame of analysis to speak about informality in the production of order in and beyond the state.

Similar concerns with institutional structures and the regulation of space have been subject to close scrutiny in a body of empirical investigations on states and their workings in everyday practice (Mitchell, 1991; Gupta, 1995; Mbembe, 2001; Shore and Wright, 2011). This mostly anthropological body of work has explicitly turned against an abstract theorization of states in which the state is seen as a coherent, unitary entity that is divided from and exists 'outside' or 'above' society as a directing or antagonistic force (Ferguson and Gupta, 2008). Painter, for instance, defines the state as a bundle of 'spatialized social practices', which, he argues, 'are to a greater or lesser extent institutionalized (in a "state apparatus") and which involve claims to authority which are general in social scope and which secure at least partial compliance through either consent, or coercion, or both' (Painter, 1995: 34). Consequently the state, as Mountz (2003: 640) writes, 'does not exist outside of the people who comprise it, their everyday work, and their social embeddedness in local relationships' and thus requires an analysis of the state 'from within' through ethnographic explorations into the mundane mechanisms of its operation (Corbridge *et al.*, 2005; Nugent, 2007).

If the state, to follow these accounts, is not necessarily characterized by bureaucratic rationality that encompasses the legitimacy and regulations or statutory frames of a distant legislator, informality can neither sit apart from it, nor can it be employed by the state. In other words, an account of the state that considers the diversity of actors and practices involved in the formation of states challenges the boundaries between formal and informal domains. From this point of view, informality emerges at the heart of state practices. It provides a lens through which to examine the negotiation and contestation of order between differently positioned actors in the continuous making of states.

This approach provides a crucial starting point for the construction of a comparative frame. As a view 'from within', neither starting from ingrained and situated assumptions of rational and coherently functioning institutions nor from the presumption of the state's failures, gaps or breakdowns, the approach avoids situating the three different states in which our cases are located on an evolutionary path. Instead, our perspective allows us to compare small-scale mechanisms in the making of order that manifest themselves across all case sites. As this view accounts for the involvement of actors of all sorts, it poses problems that cut across different realms and matter in each research site. Based on this understanding of informality, the sections that follow set out to talk across informality in governance processes in Bafatá, Tallinn and Berlin in an attempt to overcome the supposed incommensurability of these sites.

Informality in Bafatá, Tallinn and Berlin

A comparison of informality in the workings of the state in Guinea-Bissau, Estonia and Germany would merit an extensive discussion of these systems. However, as this comparison is focused on the ways in which order is negotiated and contested in the everyday workings of the state, we limit ourselves to introducing the actor constellations and key points of negotiation in each case before talking across the cases in the subsequent section.

– Water supply in Bafatá

The Bafatá case explores the city's piped water supply, focusing on the everyday water practices of state and non-state actors who shape this urban service.[4] The Associação de Saneamento Básico Protecção da Água e do Ambiente (ASPAAB), a local non-profit association, took over responsibility for the management of the city's piped water network in 2006. At the time, the network comprised only one operational standpipe and around ten known home connections, and the service being provided was extremely irregular. By 2015, the city's piped water network functioned on a daily basis, serving 23 standpipes and around 104 home connections (ASPAAB, 2009; TESE, 2012). The evolution of the city's piped water supply over these years must be understood in the context of the implementation of two major projects targeting the city's water infrastructure. These projects, implemented between 2010 and 2014, were funded by international donors and implemented by a range of national and international organizations, including local and national state departments. However, ASPAAB and the regional offices of the Department of Water Resources, alongside other state and non-state actors also played key roles. First, they were key actors in managing and mobilizing a range of resources—material, organizational and knowledge—as well as in securing compliance and support at all levels. Secondly, they were essential in negotiating, translating and appropriating projects and policies according to local priorities and institutions (Neves Alves, 2016).

The notion of informality provides a useful analytic for an analysis of the ways in which the evolution of this urban service related to a range of national and international policies and regulatory frameworks. When the transfer of management responsibilities

4   Bafatá, with a population of approximately 30,000, holds the title of second city of Guinea-Bissau and is an important urban centre. For more information on access to safe water in Guinea-Bissau, see MEPIR (2011).

to ASPAAB took place in 2006, it remained based on an (informal) verbal agreement between this organization and the Regional Director of the Department of Water Resources until 2012, when a five-year concession contract was signed by ASPAAB and the Ministry of Natural Resources. However, the process of formalizing this institution did not transform the myriad ways in which state actors and institutions were already shaping water provision in the city or the ways in which ASPAAB and other actors related to different organizations and institutions. This situation highlights how the formalization process has become a resource that is mobilized in the negotiation of legitimacy and order.

–   Parking provisioning in Tallinn
       The Tallinn case study examines the regulation of car parking provided by private companies on large vacant lots in Tallinn, which are characterized by minimal design and often have no permanent surface covering. Tallinn, the capital city of Estonia, with its 430,000 inhabitants, is a city of average size that has experienced rapid suburbanization (see, for example, Leetmaa et al., 2009) accompanied by a sizeable growth in car ownership, in a context of lax planning regulations (see Ruoppila, 2007). The existence of more than 100 such parking lots in Tallinn can partly be attributed to these processes. The total number of parking spaces they offer approximately matches kerbside parking in the city (about 6,000 parking spaces, according to information from city officials). These private parking lots thus constitute significant business and provide a noteworthy form of parking in the city. Yet, despite their importance, these parking spaces remain outside of municipal ordinances and governing capacities. Thus, despite the municipality's will to regulate this business, they are neither governed by urban or transport policies, nor is their establishment restricted or directed. Simultaneously, the companies that operate them are registered, pay taxes and comply with the general legal requirements of private businesses.
       Like all key actors in our three studies, these private businesses operate within a combination of rules and norms that define parking spaces in ambiguous ways. In the face of these ambiguities, the power relations between and differing interests of all actors involved work to shape the governance of parking provisioning. State institutions at different government scales disagree over the definition of these spaces: for state officials,[5] they are a regular business, whereas the city planning department in Tallinn sees the parking lots as disorderly additions to the urban landscape.[6] These definitional ambiguities provide a tactical tool that is adopted by business actors. Moreover, the rapidly expanding driving public seeking parking spaces for their cars in the city centre would not widely support regulations that lead to the disappearance of these parking lots. Here, too, informality emerges as a relational product of different actors and activities entangled in state procedures.

–   Dwelling in Berlin
       The Berlin case focuses on the experiences of Berliners who live in allotment gardens. These compounds were established during a period of industrialization at the turn of the twentieth century, with the aim of 'toughening up' young city dwellers through gardening in fresh air (Urban, 2013). Since then, approximately 958 compounds have provided half a million members with gardening land on 3,018 hectares of inner-city space (BDG, n.d.). Here, Berliners garden according to strict rules, on private-use plots of about 300 to 500 square metres that are commonly leased from the city for an undetermined period. However, although the Federal Allotment Law[7] prohibits

5   Official response by the Ministry of Economic Affairs to a request for information dated 22 March 2013.
6   This interview was conducted at the Tallinn Planning Department on 18 September 2012.
7   The *Bundeskleingartengesetz* (Federal Allotment Law) prohibits allotment huts being constructed for permanent habitation.

permanent inhabitation of these plots, gardeners take up residence in the small allotment huts that have been erected on these plots, particularly during summer.[8]

Allotment land is predominantly owned by the city, but rented out to an association of allotment gardeners that takes over the management of all compounds in one district and then commonly sublets single colonies, which, in turn, sublet individual plots. At the district level, this system is supervised by a small number of allotment garden administrators, who represent the landowner—the city—and oversee the work of the gardening associations. At the level of the municipality, Berlin finances one additional position in the city administration to look after the approximately 74,000 plots (SenStadt, 2012). As the management of this gardening land is not a small task, this capacity hardly suffices. Through the organizational set-up and a lack of capacity to regulate land use, there are multiple hurdles to governing the allotments, which lead to different mechanisms through which all those concerned negotiate order on these sites (see also Hilbrandt, 2015; 2016).

In this context, informality offers a useful lens through which to examine the negotiation of order through institutional organizations, legal frameworks and social relations. However, as local media and public opinion frequently relate informality to poverty or migration, the phenomenon continues to be seen as imported, or as a product of cultural change in the context of an orderly functioning state. Analysis of the negotiation of dwelling practices helps us reconsider certainties about the functioning of order and to highlight mechanisms through which informality emerges within and outside of state institutions.

Negotiation and contestation: regulatory systems, institutions and social norms

How, then, can we compare informality in governance processes, or the negotiation and contestation of order between differently positioned actors in the continuous workings of states in Tallinn, Bafatá and Berlin? In our comparison, we focus our analysis on three interrelated dimensions, in which the negotiation and contestation of order play out. These dimensions allow us to define certain areas of negotiation in the governance of the infrastructures we are comparing and to point out more clearly how informality operates in similar ways across our cases. Although some dimensions were slightly more prominent in one case than in another, these three dimensions emerged as important entry points to understanding the making of order in the reiterative process of comparing material. First, we explore the role of regulatory systems, with the aim of comparing how the systems both stabilize and unsettle order, as the different actors involved in and beyond the state use them as a resource to define order in their own interest. Secondly, we analyse negotiations and conflicts between, within and beyond institutions to illustrate how informality emerges through the power play between the different actors who are involved. Last, we examine negotiations between social norms and regulatory systems to consider how these conventions influence the making of order when state regulations conflict with common practices.

Together, these aspects highlight how the everyday workings of states produce informality through continuous power play between different actors who seek to shape order. Moreover, tracing informality through these dimensions illustrates some of the similarities and differences through which informality emerges across the contextual differences of the three seemingly incommensurable cases.

---

8   While a limited number of gardeners hold permits to reside in their allotment sheds, an unknown number of Berliners dwell in such sheds informally, particularly in compounds that have a functioning infrastructure throughout the year. Others move into the gardens in early spring and return to their flats in late autumn (Hilbrandt, 2015).

–   Negotiating regulatory systems

While the relevance of law and state regulations differs from case to case, in all cases the regulatory frameworks are part of the continuous negotiations that constitute informality. Our three studies exemplify how actors in and beyond the state use regulations as a resource to claim legitimacy in conflicts between institutions or to enforce the status quo through legal ambiguities. Crucially, order is never secured in these negotiations, even in settings where laws are designed to predefine the order in place. Rather, our cases underline how informality emerges in continuing power play around the definition of order, as different actors mobilize the law or translate its meaning to different sites according to their own interests and needs. In this sense the notion of informality—as a modus operandi in governance—provides a lens through which to look at the ways and means by which order is negotiated in and beyond state institutions and frameworks across our cases.

First, the law is mobilized by different institutional actors to legitimize their practices. The implementation and use of the law thus depends on the power and intent of the different actors who define how order is put in place. For instance, the Tallinn case illustrates how internal differences and power play between the municipality and the central state hamper the regulation of parking spaces and create room for manoeuvre for the parking providers. With an aim to move away from what was perceived as the excessive and arbitrary power of the Soviet state in a country that regained independence, the current law and constitution crucially shape the independence of the municipality and other state authorities in their decision making (Tuvikene, 2016). In this context, the municipality's attempt to limit businesses' operations and use of private property has evoked the image of the totalitarian Soviet state in parliamentary discussions, media opinion pieces, and affected significant decisions by constitutional institutions. However, the law not only curtails local state actors; statutory systems also allow municipal discretion in certain spheres. Thus, a parking business operating in a parking garage requires permission from the local state, but owing to the unpaved surface of the lots, businesses fall outside the remit of these regulations and can bypass the existing legal tools (mainly the planning instruments) of local government. From the perspective of the local state, these boundaries to their sphere of influence limit the making of order and empower the businesses, which are thus able to provide parking without the intervention of city authorities.

Conversely, in Bafatá legality neither emerges as a key factor shaping social order, nor as a key tool to be used by those who are involved in water supply. Rather, the water governance model that is in place has evolved independently from national or international policies or regulations. Moreover, most interactions between ASPAAB, different state actors and institutions as well as other relevant agents routinely take place through local step-by-step negotiations that are rarely defined by legal or policy frameworks. This has remained the case even after the formalization of ASPAAB's role in 2012. At first sight, the minor importance of state regulation in the present case appears to challenge the central aim of this article—to find a notion of informality that allows us to talk across contexts. Nevertheless, the signing of the concession contract[9] in 2012 highlights some of the ways in which this contract, and legality, were strategically used by different actors. Similar to officials in Tallinn, state officials based in Bissau, the capital city of Guinea-Bissau and previously rather distant from the realm of water supply in Bafatá, have sought to expand their symbolic influence through the expansion of their legal realm to water supply in Bafatá. The formalization of ASPAAB allowed them to claim a role for the state in water provisioning for the city. ASPAAB, having

---

9   As mentioned, in 2012, ASPAAB and the Ministry of Natural Resources of Guinea-Bissau signed a contract that formalized the role of ASPAAB as the operator of the piped water network in Bafatá. This happened six years after ASPAAB de facto taking over of the management of the system.

recognized the importance that international organizations and NGOs attach to formal law and the supposed security that legality entails, has also strategically employed legal concession as a tool for mobilizing international funds. Thus, while in Bafatá the law does not emerge as a key tool for framing relations between different parties, as these remain negotiated outside of statutory frames, legality has been strategically embraced by different actors in their attempts to mobilize resources. In both the Tallinn and the Bafatá cases, regulatory systems are used in conflicts between institutions, but also by actors who employ them beyond the law to legitimize their practices and negotiate ways in which order is enacted and ensured.

Secondly, order is negotiated through the translation of (frequently ambiguous) regulatory texts or contracts to specific sites. The legal ambiguities of informal dwelling in Berlin illustrate this clearly. Even though current laws define regulatory responsibilities, the implementation of order requires negotiating multiple and, at times, contradictory legal ideas. For instance, the ways in which 'dwelling' is defined and framed by the law give city officials and allotment holders room for manoeuvre regarding the regulation of common residential practices in these sites. While more recent amendments to the Federal Allotment Law permit allotment holders to occasionally spend a night in their allotment sheds, following national law, the character of the hut may not be designed for permanent stay. As neither the notion of 'occasionally' spending the night nor of 'permanent' stay is clearly defined, there is considerable room for manoeuvre, and interpretation of these notions is thus at the discretion of allotment holders and regulators. While some bureaucrats allow allotment holders to spend vacations on these sites, others tolerate weekend stays only. Allotment dwellers use these ambiguities to respond both to the necessities of permanent dwelling as well as to the requirements of the law through a plethora of creative approaches to the design of their huts that play with the materiality of the site.

Similar ambiguities of definition and material manoeuvres characterize the Tallinn case, in which actors circumvent regulation through the design of the surface of the parking spaces. Estonian planning and construction laws only necessitate the regulation of developments that substantially alter the land plot, such as a new house, a canal or a parking garage. However, the parking lots we focus on are deliberately 'built' as impermanently as possible—without tarmac, fixed buildings, fences or other constructions—to make the business cheaper, more flexible and viable. In fact, their impermanence is what makes them possible at all. As the legal definition of these sites as parking spaces is circumvented by these means, the local state has only limited capacity to influence the design of signs at the entrance to the lots. From the perspective of the municipality, suitable legal instruments are currently missing. In both cases, laws that have weight in the negotiation of order do exist. However, legal voids and semantic ambiguities complicate the municipality's regulatory practices. Allotment dwellers and parking providers, aware of these ambiguities, act in keeping with the law as they translate its meanings according to their needs. Leeway in terms of the law is, in other words, constructed through the law itself.

The case studies we consider here differ in terms of the weight and meanings of the applicable laws, that is, in terms of the leverage and resources the institutions have which legitimize or enforce these laws. Consequently, in the case-specific processes of negotiation, regulatory systems play different roles. On the one hand, in a context in which state institutions lack the resources to legitimize or enforce the law, as is the case in Bafatá, the law has important effects but is not necessarily key in the negotiation of order. On the other hand, cases of negotiation in Tallinn and Berlin exemplified ways in which institutions manoeuvre the law or the ways in which regulations are put in place. To analyse these cases within an overarching conceptual framework, informality can neither be understood as emerging beyond the law, nor as used strategically by the state (for this argument, see, for instance, Yiftachel, 2009a). Rather, it is useful to consider the normal working mechanisms through which regulatory systems are put in place: beyond an understanding of the law as a means to fix or stabilize order, in all cases regulatory systems provide a resource in the interest of groups in and beyond the state, as they also work to contest or shape the order that the local state would seek to advance.

–   Negotiating institutions

Secondly, order is negotiated through conflicts between institutions at multiple scales, involving actors within and beyond the state. Positioning our case studies side by side reveals how negotiations around responsibilities and spheres of influence shape the production of informality in at least two ways.

On the one hand, actors in different state institutions negotiate fields of responsibility through which they can define how order is implemented. For instance, in Tallinn order is produced through inter-administrative conflict around the regulation of parking spaces. Based on the formal division of responsibilities, the local state handles issues of transport, planning and aesthetics, while central state authorities regulate the finances of the companies that provide private parking. As the businesses formally register and pay taxes, the central state does not require further regulation. However, the municipality problematizes both the aesthetics of the sites as well as the municipality's inability to influence how parking is provided in the city. Although Tallinn's municipality is one of the most influential in the country, local-level government nevertheless lacks resources and skilled employees to enforce its claims against state authorities at other scales. Similarly, in Bafatá, the increasing recognition of ASPAAB's success in managing the city's piped water supply highlights ongoing competition and conflict between actors in different institutions. State representatives within the regional offices of the Department of Water Resources have been strongly involved in the work of ASPAAB, which is seen to be furthering the department's goals of improving access to water. While government officials in other departments have occasionally supported ASPAAB, they have also looked at this organization as an opportunity to raise revenue through the collection of disputable taxes. The legal basis of such taxes is not always clear to ASPAAB and even other state institutions, who challenge their validity. The divergent interests of the various state institutions have unveiled conflicts between different local state institutions. Although the ensuing negotiations have taken place predominantly beyond formal bureaucracies, state regulations and duties are routinely mobilized in these negotiations between representatives of different organizations. In contrast to the institutional conflicts discussed in the case of Tallinn, state regulations do not clearly define the responsibilities of these actors. Nevertheless, ongoing negotiations over the legitimacy of their practices, which often refer to laws and regulations, determine the shape of water provisioning in the city. Informality is also produced here as a result of discrepant interests between different state institutions.

On the other hand, informality emerges through governance arrangements between civil and state institutions. In the context of Bafatá, state actors at the national level have used the formalization of ASPAAB and their subsequent legal expansion to the realm of water supply to symbolically extend their presence in the city. In other words, the formalization of ASPAAB has allowed state actors to capture the work of this organization, thereby furthering their own goals by framing it as an organization that is working under their oversight. ASPAAB, in turn, similarly tries to benefit from this recognition to increase its influence, while simultaneously striving to remain independent and pursue its own strategies. In these processes, national institutions stabilize their power, but also increase room for manoeuvre for actors beyond the state. Order is thus defined in the process of determining responsibilities and influence.

In Berlin, the inability to control 'summer dwelling' is similarly interlinked with questions of institutional responsibility. Comparable to water provisioning in the Bafatá case, allotment dwelling is governed predominantly by a non-state organization—an association of allotment gardeners that manages the allotments through its own bureaucracy of lay professionals. The organization functions as lessor and contractual partner to the city, which is the owner of most allotment land. Moreover, similar to the governance of water provisioning through ASPAAB, the gardening organization's long tradition of involvement and far-reaching expertise serve to legitimize it. However, this arrangement results in a regulatory dilemma: since the officials of the associations are not only the contractual partners of the individual allotment holders, but also gardeners themselves, technically, these officials regulate their peers. As a result, the associations are prone to turning a blind eye to residents who live in the dwellings on their plots beyond the legally allowed period, so that legal infringements frequently remain under the radar. However, as the city is dependent on these associations, because no other institution can handle the task it performs, Berlin's bureaucratic leadership cannot afford to alter these governance structures.

The Bafatá and Berlin cases both illustrate how state institutions use civil organizations to implement order, but also point to how this process of 'formalization' strengthens the same organizations that gain power to enforce their own needs. Certainly, the contexts differ in crucial ways. In Bafatá, a city in which order is rarely implemented through written rules, the state uses formalization to expand its power over different actors. Conversely, in Berlin, the state not only recognizes the involvement of the allotment association based on the necessity of outsourcing the work of managing the gardens, but also because of a conception of governance that promotes civil engagement. Yet, independently of the multiple rationales behind these different arrangements, the involvement and recognition of civil actors by state institutions fosters conflict around the ways in which order is defined.

Overall, this analysis shows how order is negotiated through conflicting interests between institutions. On the one hand, as shown in the case of Tallinn and Bafatá, conflicts between the local and national state frequently emerge through legal ambiguities, thus allowing third parties—such as Tallinn's parking businesses—to define order. On the other hand, examples from Bafatá and Berlin point to ways in which processes of negotiation around the realm and responsibilities of the state work to define order. In these cases, inter-institutional conflict around influence and responsibility, rather than a top-down implementation of rule by a strategically acting state, govern the emergence of informality.

–   Negotiating social norms
Finally, informality emerges in similar ways across our three cases, as actors in and beyond the state accommodate social norms and contradictory regulations. The resultant mechanisms of negotiating provide further possibilities for comparing informality in the three divergent contexts. An exploration of these negotiations challenges an understanding of order as fixed, settled or ever fully formalized, but points instead to continuous conflicts around the ways in which order is enacted in everyday practices.

On the one hand, a focus on the conflict between social norms and state rule underlines how governing practices are undergirded not only by the legal or state norms, but also by norms that civil society brings to processes of negotiation. Take, for instance, the case of Berlin: Berliners first moved into allotment dwellings following the destruction of the city in both world wars. For a limited period, the city permitted allotment dwelling to shelter those who were in dire need of housing. By the 1970s, Berlin had largely been rebuilt, and dwelling in allotment sheds for an extended period became illegal. But, by and large, the sociotechnical infrastructures of allotment dwelling, consisting of administrations, neighbourhood ties, water connections and extensive allotment sheds, were still approved and remained intact. Besides the reasons discussed above, authorities faced difficulties in enforcing the ban on dwelling practices because most gardeners widely approved of inhabiting sheds.

Similarly, in the case of Tallinn, social norms influence the ways in which private parking business is perceived and regulated. Demands for parking spaces grew in tandem with the rapid increase of motorization since the demise of the Soviet Union in 1991. Hence, drivers both criticize and accept these parking lots. Motorists require more parking spaces, but simultaneously express negative sentiments towards disorderly parking, contesting the access that the parking companies have to vehicle registry data and voicing criticism over the general lack of maintenance and care of the parking plots. Discontented motorists are expecting more formality and at times even disobey the requirement to pay for parking, causing numerous problems for the operating companies. Yet drivers' desire to park their cars in the city centre tends to trump their will to limit themselves to more organized parking spaces. In a research interview, even a city representative refrained from criticizing privately operated parking lots, because he was generally happy that these parking spaces were provided at all.[10] In this case, the broader expectation to have access to parking guides the normative evaluation of these spaces and contributes to maintaining the status quo. As these cases exemplify, norms not only guide the micro-politics of everyday engagement by civil actors, but also drive actors in state institutions.

Similar to Berlin, but on a different scale, regulations in Bafatá have been changed despite common norms in a process in which water policies have sought to shift deeply ingrained water sharing practices. The adoption of cost-recovery and user-payer principles in water management, which have been established through national policies, contradicts existing social norms related to the sharing of water resources. Water meters, installed on each public standpipe, have become an essential tool for cost-recovery and user-payer principles and have transformed daily interactions between users and their infrastructures. But operators and users alike contest the meters, since they interfere with long-standing sharing practices. Despite plans to discipline the operators, who have to submit exact revenue, as well as the consumers, who are forced to pay for all water they consume, people's daily routines have long involved the sharing of water resources. Wells, the most common source of water in the city, are typically built and maintained by individual households. But although these wells are privately owned, even in times of water scarcity they remain accessible to the public. At the time of writing, most standpipe operators regularly worked with huge defaults, since the volume of water supplied through standpipes far exceeded the revenues that were collected from the consumers. The importance given to the non-monetary value of water, in conjunction with ongoing practices of sharing resources, has fostered resistance to the adoption of user-payer principles and cost-recovery measures in water management. Thereby, national policies fostered the informalization of existing accepted practices to institutionalize new modes of getting things done.

While the practices we focused on in Berlin contradict the rules of the local state, but remain tolerable exceptions, the most common way of getting things done in Bafatá involves local norms that often contradict statutory rules. Similarly, the municipality of Tallinn, restrained in its regulatory incapacity, accepts conditions that in some aspects—such as the capacity to have a place to park—are enforced through prevailing norms. Thus, despite differences in the specificities of each case, deeply ingrained norms have presented a barrier to regulation across the three different research sites. In all cases, the rules of state institutions specify the intended effects of the legislator, but as different rationalities prevail in the ways in which order is put in place, these intentions fail to define the order that is in place. The crucial question remains to what extent different institutions sanction transgressions. However, such sanctioning also tends to depend on local norms and power structures. In this process, regulations and norms continue to shift as parties constantly negotiate with and through the state. As

10   Interview with the head of the Transport Department on 25 September 2012.

we have argued throughout this article, in this sense too, informality is inherent to the continuous processes of enacting and forming the state.

Conclusion

This article has launched a conversation between three case studies in cities that differ significantly in terms of location, history and institutional structure. We aimed to conduct an analysis that would allow us to understand the processes at work across these sites and thereby engage in one of the challenges that comparative urbanism has posed to urban studies: to set cities in different locations on an equal footing in urban theorizing. In this section, we draw some conclusions regarding the possibilities and limitations of such a comparison, the similarities and differences of governance processes in these divergent sites, and the lessons to be learnt for theorizations of informality and the state.

Conducting such a comparison requires approximating an understanding of informality that applies to our three case study sites. In reviewing different approaches that relate informality to the state, we argued that these approaches hamper a comparison across our cases, as their use of informality was frequently context-dependent, that is, the notion of informality referred to different phenomena in different sites. By relating these approaches to anthropological understandings of the state that account for the ambiguities and inconsistencies at the core of any state, we pointed to the fragility of order and the ways in which order is continuously redefined inside and outside of state institutions. This literature allowed us to conceive of informality as embedded in the nature of states, rather than to define informality as the result of exceptional failures, the state's weaknesses or arbitrary strategies. Based on this definition, we argued for an understanding of informality as a lens through which to view the normal workings of state practices, that is, the contestation and negotiation of rules in the continuous enactment and production of states. Smaller-scale mechanisms of state enactment by different actors point, in particular, to three dimensions through which the various parties negotiate order: through legal and other regulatory systems; through inter- and intra-institutional relations; and through the ways in which rules are employed in the face of prevailing norms.

First, we highlighted that negotiations evolve in processes of translating and manoeuvring regulatory systems. As laws or regulations never work as blueprints, order is defined only by how these laws and regulations are applied. Certainly, in Tallinn and Berlin, the law has more weight than in the regulatory processes we discussed in Bafatá, as in the former two cases, the relevant institutions are better equipped to implement these regulations. But our discussion of informality in Tallinn and Berlin also showed that, even in these cases, order is not fixed. Rather, actors use institutional conflict to manoeuvre the law or translate regulations to specific sites. Informality evolves as order is defined, not through the law, but through the negotiability of the law. Secondly, our cases unveil how order is produced through power play between different institutions that compete for responsibility to define the rules of the game. Informality emerges through the contradictions inherent in inter- and intra-institutional relations between actors in and beyond the state, rather than through the actions of civil actors against the state, or vice versa. Our cases differ significantly in terms of the roles, aims and resources of the institutions involved. But juxtaposing these three cases also shows that, in the face of the different interests of the multiple authorities involved, order continues to shift, regardless of the degree of institutionalization of the actors or the supposed modernity of the different states. Thirdly, we explored how informality is negotiated through inconsistencies between state regulations and prevailing social norms. In all three cases prevailing norms shape how regulations are put in place, as in all three cases, local legitimacy was in conflict with local or national law.

Throughout the three case studies—located in states with very different histories—constant struggles around the definition of order by different authorities in and outside of institutions produce order through the continuous negotiations that constitute informality. Such a conclusion defies claims to modernization and developmentalism, allowing us to show instead that these negotiations are neither indicative of different stages in the processes of state consolidation nor signs of underdevelopment, or of historical and contextual particularities. Moreover, this analysis of informality makes it necessary to reconsider the nature of states, or, in the words of Magnusson (2011: 2), to call for 'a different ontology of the political', in which one ought to accept 'that a multiplicity of political authorities in different registers is the rule rather than the exception' (*ibid.*). However, an analysis that confronts idealized imaginaries of the colonial, modern, authoritarian or hegemonic state also challenges the analytical separation between theories of informality and theories of the state. A joining of these two bodies of work highlights how negotiation, improvisation, co-production and translation characterize the everyday enactment of the state. As a common modus operandi in the continuous formation and deformation of the state, informality allows us to talk across and overcome presumed incommensurability in the nature of and our approaches to understanding the state.

Hanna Hilbrandt, HafenCity Universität Hamburg, Überseeallee 16, 20249 Hamburg, Germany, hanna.hilbrandt@complicity.de

Susana Neves Alves, Department of Geography, University College London, Gower Street, London WC1E 6BT, UK, susana.alves.11@ucl.ac.uk

Tauri Tuvikene, Centre for Landscape and Culture, Tallinn University, Uus-Sadama 5, 10120 Tallinn, Estonia, tauri.tuvikene@tlu.ee

References

ASPAAB (Associação de Saneamento Básico Protecção da Água e do Ambiente) (2009) *Relatório da situação geral do abastecimento de água—cidade de Bafatá* [Report on the performance of the water supply system of the city of Bafatá]. ASPAAB, Bafatá.

BDG (Bundesverband Deutscher Gartenfreunde e.V.) (n.d.) Zahlen und Fakten [Figures and facts] [WWW document]. URL http://www.kleingarten-bund.de/de/portrait/zahlen-und-fakten/ (accessed 6 June 2017).

Bunnell, T and A. Harris (2012) Re-viewing informality: perspectives from urban Asia. *International Development Planning Review* 34.4, 339–48.

Chakrabarty, D. (2009) *Provincializing Europe: postcolonial thought and historical difference*. Princeton University Press, Princeton, NJ, and Oxford.

Chen, M.A. (2007) Rethinking the informal economy: linkages with the formal economy and the formal regulatory environment. DESA Working Paper No. 46 [WWW document]. URL: http://www.un.org/esa/desa/papers/2007/wp46_2007.pdf (accessed 9 October 2017).

Comaroff, J. and J.L. Comaroff (2012) *Theory from the South: or, how Euro-America is evolving toward Africa*. Paradigm, Boulder, CO.

Corbridge, S., G. Williams, M. Srivastava and R. Véron (2005) *Seeing the state: governance and governmentality in India*. Cambridge University Press, Cambridge and New York, NY.

Devlin, R.T. (2011) 'An area that governs itself': informality, uncertainty and the management of street vending in New York City. *Planning Theory* 10.1, 53–65.

Ferenčuhová, S. (2012) Urban theory beyond the 'East/West divide'? Cities and urban research in postsocialist Europe. In T. Edensor and M. Jayne (ed.), *Urban theory beyond the West: a world of cities*, Routledge, London and New York, NY.

Ferguson, J. and A. Gupta (2008) Spatializing states: toward an ethnography of neoliberal governmentality. In J.X. Inda (ed.), *Anthropologies of modernity*, Blackwell, Oxford.

Fourchard, L. (2011) Lagos, Koolhaas and partisan politics in Nigeria. *International Journal of Urban and Regional Research* 35.1, 40–56.

Grubbauer, M. (2012) Toward a more comprehensive notion of urban change: linking post-socialist urbanism and urban theory. In M. Grubbauer and J. Kusiak (eds.), *Chasing Warsaw: socio-material dynamics of urban change since 1990*, Campus Verlag, Frankfurt and New York, NY.

Gupta, A. (1995) Blurred boundaries: the discourse of corruption, the culture of politics, and the imagined state. *American Ethnologist* 22.2, 375–402.

Harris, A. (2012) The metonymic urbanism of twenty-first-century Mumbai. *Urban Studies* 49.13, 2955–73.

Hilbrandt, H. (2015) Housing constellations: three faultlines of informality research. In G. Theune and S. Quadflieg (eds.), *Nadogradnje: urban self-regulation in post-Yugoslav cities*, M-Books, Weimar.

Hilbrandt, H. (2016) Negotiating formalities: everyday rule in Berlin's allotment gardens. PhD dissertation, Department of Geography, The Open University, Milton Keynes.

Kantor, P. and H.V. Savitch (2005) How to study comparative urban development politics: a research note. *International Journal of Urban and Regional Research* 29.1, 135–51.

Leetmaa, K., T. Tammaru and K. Anniste (2009) From priority-led to market-led suburbanisation in a post-communist metropolis. *Tijdschrift voor Economische en Sociale Geografie* 100.4, 436–53.

Lindell, I. (2008) The multiple sites of urban governance: insights from an African city. *Urban Studies* 45.9, 1879–901.

Loftus, A. and F. Lumsden (2008) Reworking hegemony in the urban waterscape. *Transactions of the Institute of British Geographers* 33.1, 109–26.

Magnusson, W. (2011) *Politics of urbanism: seeing like a city*. Routledge, Abingdon and New York, NY.

Mbembe, A. (2001) *On the postcolony*. University of California Press, Berkeley, CA.

McFarlane, C. (2010) The comparative city: knowledge, learning, urbanism. *International Journal of Urban and Regional Research* 34.4, 725–42.

McFarlane, C. (2011) *Learning the city: knowledge and translocal assemblage*. John Wiley & Sons, Chichester.

McFarlane, C. (2012) Rethinking informality: politics, crisis, and the city. *Planning Theory and Practice* 13.1, 89–108.

McFarlane, C. and J. Robinson (2012) Introduction. Experiments in comparative urbanism. *Urban Geography* 33.6, 765–73.

McFarlane, C. and M. Waibel (2012) *Urban informalities*. Ashgate, Farnham and Burlington, VT.

MEPIR (Ministério da Economia, do Plano e Integração Regional) (2011) *Segundo documento de estratégia nacional de redução da pobreza da Guiné-Bissau (DENARP II – 2011–2015)* [Second national poverty reduction strategy paper for Guinea-Bissau]. MEPIR, Bissau.

Merton, R. (2012 [1949]) On sociological theories of the middle range. In C. Calhoun, J. Gerteis, J. Moody, S. Pfaff and I. Virk (eds.), *Classical sociological theory*, John Wiley & Sons, Malden, MA.

Mitchell, T. (1991) The limits of the state: beyond statist approaches and their critics. *The American Political Science Review* 84.1, 77–96.

Mountz, A. (2003) Human smuggling, the transnational imaginary, and everyday geographies of the nation-state. *Antipode* 35.3, 622–44.

Neves Alves, S. (2016) Creole water supply: states, neoliberalism and everyday practices in a secondary African city. PhD dissertation, Department of Geography, University College London, London.

Nijman, J. (2007) Introduction: comparative urbanism. *Urban Geography* 28.1, 1–6.

Nugent, D. (2007) Governing states. In J. Nugent and J. Vincent (ed.), *A companion to the anthropology of politics*, Wiley-Blackwell, Oxford.

Painter, J. (1995) *Politics, geography and political geography: a critical perspective*. E. Arnold, New York, NY.

Painter, J. (2006) Prosaic geographies of stateness. *Political Geography* 25.7, 752–74.

Robinson, J. (2002) Global and world cities: a view from off the map. *International Journal of Urban and Regional Research* 26.3, 531–54.

Robinson, J. (2004) In the tracks of comparative urbanism: difference, urban modernity and the primitive. *Urban Geography* 25.8, 709–23.

Robinson, J. (2005) *Ordinary cities: between modernity and development*. Routledge, London and New York, NY.

Robinson, J. (2011a) 2010 *Urban Geography* plenary lecture—The travels of urban neoliberalism: taking stock of the internationalization of urban theory. *Urban Geography* 32.8, 1087–109.

Robinson, J. (2011b) Cities in a world of cities: the comparative gesture. *International Journal of Urban and Regional Research* 35.1, 1–23.

Rose, N. and P. Miller (1992) Political power beyond the state: problematics of government. *British Journal of Sociology* 34.2, 173–205.

Roy, A. (2005) Urban informality: toward an epistemology of planning. *Journal of the American Planning Association* 71.2, 147–58.

Roy, A. (2009) Why India cannot plan its cities: informality, insurgence and the idiom of urbanization. *Planning Theory* 8.1, 76–87.

Roy, A. (2011a) Slumdog cities: rethinking subaltern urbanism. *International Journal of Urban and Regional Research* 35.2, 223–38.

Roy, A. (2011b) The blockade of the world-class city: dialectical images of world-class urbanism. In A. Roy and A. Ong (eds.), *Worlding cities: Asian experiments and the art of being global*, John Wiley & Sons, Chichester.

Ruoppila, S. (2007) Establishing a market-orientated urban planning system after state socialism: the case of Tallinn. *European Planning Studies* 15.3, 405–27.

SenStadt (Senatsverwaltung für Stadtentwicklung und Umwelt) (ed.) (2012) *Das bunte Grün—Kleingärten in Berlin* [Colourful green—allotment gardens in Berlin] [WWW document]. URL www.stadtentwicklung.berlin. de/umwelt/stadtgruen/kleingaerten/downloads/ Kleingartenbroschuere.pdf (accessed 23 March 2017).

Shore, C. and S. Wright (2011) Introduction. Conceptualising policy: technologies of governance and the politics of visibility. In C. Shore, S. Wright and D. Però (ed.), *Policy worlds: anthropology and the analysis of contemporary power*, Berghahn Books, Oxford and New York, NY.

TESE (2012) *Projecto Bafatá misti iagu: relatório narrativo final* [Bafatá water supply project: completion report]. TESE, Lisbon.

Tuvikene, T. (2015) Freedom to park: post-socialist automobility in Tallinn, Estonia. PhD dissertation, Department of Geography, University College London, London.

Tuvikene, T. (2016) Strategies for comparative urbanism: post-socialism as a de-territorialized concept. *International Journal of Urban and Regional Research* 40.1, 132–46.

Tuvikene, T., S. Neves Alves and H. Hilbrandt (2017) Strategies for relating diverse cities: a multi-sited individualising comparison of informality in Bafatá, Berlin and Tallinn. *Current Sociology* 65.2, 276–88.

Urban, F. (2013) The hut on the garden plot: informal architecture in twentieth-century Berlin. *Journal of the Society of Architectural Historians* 72.2, 221–49.

Valverde, M. (2011) Seeing like a city: the dialectic of modern and premodern ways of seeing in urban governance. *Law and Society Review* 45.2, 277–312.

Ward, K. (2010) Towards a relational comparative approach to the study of cities. *Progress in Human Geography* 34.4, 471–87.

Wiest, K. (2012) Comparative debates in post-socialist urban studies. *Urban Geography* 33.6, 829–49.

Yiftachel, O. (2009a) Theoretical notes on 'gray cities': the coming of urban apartheid? *Planning Theory* 8.1, 88–100.

Yiftachel, O. (2009b) Critical theory and 'gray space': mobilization of the colonized. *City* 13.2/3, 246–63.

– SYMPOSIUM

– SPATIAL SPILLOVERS REVISITED: Innovation, Human Capital and Local Dynamics

TUZIN BAYCAN, PETER NIJKAMP AND ROGER STOUGH

Abstract

This symposium focuses on understanding key territorial-level innovation trends and processes by country, region and technology. It questions various widely accepted assumptions, offers fresh perspectives, both conceptually and methodologically, and challenges a paradigm shift in the field of innovation and spatial dynamics. It consists of three articles analysing at different scales (urban, regional and national) the territorial dynamics of innovation and their determinants. The innovation process, with local symbiosis and spatial spillovers at its core, is analysed within the conceptual framework of national and regional innovation systems and regional economic development. Based on a discussion of spatial spillovers and the way they shape the evolutionary and symbiotic relationships between local agents and actors, including university, industry and local development agencies, the symposium highlights the relevance of this framework for a better understanding of the transformation of local economic development processes. It investigates the differences in the geography of innovation regarding different institutional settings, different systems of innovation, and different national innovation strategies. While addressing mainly the EU, the US, and emerging countries such as China and India, the contributions also highlight the critical role of current innovation policies from a general perspective. In so doing, the symposium recognizes a contrarian perspective that argues that contemporary information and communication technologies (ICTs) provide a way to leapfrog the dominant role of proximity in innovation processes, creating a complimentary rather than a substitution effect for more remote and peripheral places. That said, this symposium focuses primarily on an urban network view of the innovation process and proximal effects in this context.

Introduction

In an open and globalizing world, cities and regions tend to act increasingly as spatial 'powerhouses' whose energy and economic forces radiate out to all regions worldwide. The world becomes an interconnected system of localities which—through competitive strategies in global networks—are outwardly oriented. This 'centrifugality' trend of localities, cities and regions prompts important and strategic questions about human capital, entrepreneurship, innovation strategies and complex spatial dynamics from the perspective of spatial spillovers. Spatial linkages are becoming a key feature in modern spatial planning and geography. They may also play a critical role in current economic-crisis phenomena, in which a downturn in one region may have a severe impact on others. Cities and regions are permanently 'in motion'.

Spatial dynamics are nowadays an intrinsic feature of a knowledge-based and innovation-oriented economy. A main driver of pronounced differences in the modern, evolving space economy is caused by productivity development in different regions or cities. Productivity is a key force in competitive, efficiency-driven strategies in geographical space. Consequently, the world is not flat, but exhibits a spiky landscape in terms of economic performance. Productivity differentials are not only caused by differences in the use of human capital, physical capital and natural resources, but also by a range of spatial externalities, in particular agglomeration economies and social capital. Spatial agglomeration advantages no doubt provide added value to the economic performance of regions and cities. Such benefits relate to the production, organization, absorption and dissemination of innovative and creative resources and may create far-reaching footprints in the space economy. Yet it is important to recognize the potential contemporary information and communication technology offers in an age of knowledge-based innovation: namely, that it not only connects distant places and thus complements expertise and knowledge at a specific place, but also connects remote or peripheral places in a way that can complement their otherwise disadvantageous relative location (Grillitsch and Nilsson, 2015).

In the past decades, regions and cities have turned from 'islands of isolation' into open network constellations, not only at interregional scales, but increasingly also at global scales. The rising openness of regions and cities and, to some extent, more remote places in a globalizing world has prompted a wide array of spatial interactions and spatial spillovers. As a consequence, a contemporaneous spatial system is not an economic oasis characterized by tranquillity, but a dynamic systemic configuration that often develops swiftly as a result of competitive innovation strategies, mobile human capital flows (including migration) and local entrepreneurial initiatives. In this vein, important policy questions are emerging on the vulnerability of interdependent systems of regions or cities to external shocks. Likewise, important issues may arise regarding the critical role of innovativeness and human capital in a dynamic regional system striving for resilience and symbiosis.

This symposium offers a critical perspective. It raises a set of research questions to interrogate various widely accepted assumptions, offering fresh perspectives, both conceptually and methodologically, and provides new departures for the field of innovation and spatial dynamics. The research questions raised and the core issues addressed in this symposium are:

- What are the most important abilities of the local workforce for economic growth and how should we label these abilities?
- How are different types of knowledge, such as creativity, entrepreneurship and human capital—including the ways they are traditionally measured—symbiotically interrelated?
- Do different types of knowledge and entrepreneurial skills have complementarities in creating an environment for local or regional economic growth?
- What are the different territorial patterns of innovation and the contextual conditions (internal and external to the locality or region) that accompany such innovation patterns?
- Why do similar economies show different patterns of inter- and intra-regional socio-economic inequalities and development trajectories?
- Will emerging countries follow the innovation path of the EU or the US, or are they following their own path and building their own indigenous systems of innovation?
- How and where does innovation take place in emerging economies and to what extent do the territorial systems of innovation in emerging countries differ from those in the EU or the US?

In an attempt to answer these strategic research questions, the articles in this collection offer a novel and comparative exploration of relevant concepts and assumptions, and provide empirical evidence in different geographical contexts and spatial scales ranging from countries to metropolitan regions, cities and counties, including more remote areas. The articles focus on different dimensions of innovation and spatial dynamics, examine themes at the intersection of important new concepts, and thus offer complementary original insights on local synergy and spatial spillovers.

The main premise of this symposium is that in open spatial systems innovation is key to the competitive performance of regions and cities. In the spirit of modern (endogenous) growth theory, the critical role of innovation and human capital in creating advances in economic, institutional and technological performance will be highlighted. Similarly, economic growth is not space neutral, but is shaped and influenced by a wide range of spatial external and synergetic agglomeration forces. Spatial symbiosis regards a regional or urban economy as a set of mutually reinforcing drivers of spatial-economic growth. This concept has played an important role in traditional regional growth theories (such as in Marshallian industrial districts, growth pole and growth centre concepts, development corridor strategies, or Porterian industrial cluster notions). In recent years, the role of innovation and human capital in spatial symbiosis has gained more prolific attention, as is evident from concepts such as open (spatial) innovation systems and local resilience, in which the governance of such systems is receiving more attention too.

The articles in this symposium focus on different dimensions of innovation and spatial dynamics; the arguments developed reflect a new perspective in which they share a common, comprehensive and integrated understanding of innovation as a key element in spatial symbiosis. The central and common concepts of the symposium are as follows:

- Innovation processes, networks and globalization are fundamentally linked to territory, and this territorial orientation furthers our understanding of the connection between innovation and space (Capello, 2017; Crescenzi and Rodríguez-Pose, 2017, both in this issue)
- Innovation often takes place in symbiotic networks and such networks are not necessarily local; in general, global connections and value chains become increasingly relevant to any new conceptualization of innovation and space (Capello)
- the factors that stimulate new knowledge, invention, innovation and innovation diffusion differ (Capello; Crescenzi and Rodríguez-Pose)
- Research capacity and innovation are not spread evenly across countries, regions and cities; the geography of innovative activity is territorially very uneven (Capello; Crescenzi and Rodríguez-Pose; Faggian *et al.*, 2017, this issue)
- Local innovation dynamics are caused by external as well as internal factors; likewise, local innovation processes may, through spillover channels and filters, have an impact elsewhere (Capello; Crescenzi and Rodríguez-Pose)
- In some cases, local and regional development is not necessarily linked to local and regional innovation (Capello; Crescenzi and Rodríguez-Pose; Faggian *et al.*)
- The presence of advanced sectors and of functions such as R&D and higher education may induce innovation paths, which, though important, cannot be considered necessary and/or sufficient conditions for innovation (Capello; Faggian *et al.*)
- National and regional institutional frameworks may affect innovation systems, while regional characteristics and endowments may favour different innovation patterns, although combinations—and over time, changes in these combinations—may also occur (Capello; Crescenzi and Rodríguez-Pose).

These new concepts are discussed in remainder of this introductory article. The following section addresses human capital and local agents of economic growth and examines the critical role of human capital in innovation and economic development.

The third section investigates innovation in terms of national and regional innovation systems, with different stages of the innovation processes and different levels of innovation performance of regions. The fourth section focuses on the spatial clustering of innovation and local dynamics, and highlights the drivers of the geography of innovation. On the basis of these new arguments, the closing remarks offer broader conclusions on the symposium about innovation and spatial dynamics, and highlight challenges and future prospects.

Human capital and local agents of economic growth

Human capital plays an important role in innovation and economic development. Human capital provides, on the one hand, a workforce offering the necessary knowledge, skills and expertise for economic development, and on the other hand, different ideas and perspectives, leading to creative, innovative and entrepreneurial approaches and diverse new concepts for economic development (Baycan et al., 2011). Human capital refers, on the one side, to 'the knowledge, skills and competencies embodied in individuals that increase their productivity' (Faggian, 2005: 362), and on the other to entrepreneurship as 'the recognition of a pure profit opportunity that had previously gone unnoticed' (Kirzner, 1997). This recognition also refers to niche markets that provide a competitive advantage to firms of all sizes, but especially to small and medium-sized enterprises (SMEs). The article by Faggian, Partridge and Malecki in this symposium focuses on the role of human capital in innovation and economic development and investigates human capital in terms of the abilities of the workforce.

It is clear that the abilities of the workforce are crucial for economic growth. But which 'abilities' are most important and how should these abilities be identified or labelled? Faggian et al. (this issue) investigate the relationship between three knowledge-based attributes, namely creativity, entrepreneurship and human capital. They first propose new conceptual ways to portray the interrelationship of these knowledge-based attributes and then empirically test how these different types of knowledge—and the ways they are traditionally measured—are interrelated, and whether they have complementarities in creating an environment for regional economic growth. Contrary to earlier contributions (see Faggian, 2005), they test the joint effect of entrepreneurship, human capital and creativity measures and find that human capital as measured by educational attainment and the intensity of small and medium-sized firms are statistically associated with subsequent growth, while other factors, such as the share of creative-class workers or advanced technology industries, are insignificant.

The question as to which abilities are the most important for economic growth, as raised by Faggian et al. (this issue) with a specific focus on the workforce clearly also has broader implications. In their study on the geography of innovation, Crescenzi and Rodríguez-Pose (this issue) draw attention to migrants and transnational communities in facilitating innovation by spreading ideas and developing globalized production systems. On the basis of their surveys, Crescenzi and Rodríguez-Pose argue that large cities and trade entry points in China and India have become gateways for diaspora migrants and transnational communities. They also evaluate the recent evolution of the endowment of skilled human capital in both China and India, which points to a greatly enhanced potential to generate new knowledge and to assimilate externally generated innovation. Their comparative evaluation of the number of graduates between the US, EU, China and India reveals a considerable catching-up process in the two emerging countries.

Although Capello (this issue) and Crescenzi and Rodríguez-Pose (this issue) do not focus specifically on human capital, in their articles they view the concept of abilities differently from Faggian et al. (this issue). Instead of taking ability as the feature of individuals (the workforce), Crescenzi and Rodríguez-Pose investigate the abilities of firms and economic organizations in China and India to develop new products and services, whereas Capello describes the regions as agents of economic growth according to their abilities as collective actors in a symbiotic relationship.

An overall evaluation of the articles in this symposium highlights that the abilities of individuals (the workforce), firms and economic organizations, and regions as collective actors play an important synergetic role in local, regional or national economic growth. The skills of the workforce and entrepreneurs matter, and a well-educated workforce and entrepreneurs enhance productivity, which is the key mechanism for economic growth.

Innovation systems, processes and performances

In a knowledge-based society, creativity, innovation and technological progress are key factors of economic development. Creativity refers to the innovative capacity of individuals (human capital), groups and organizations (particularly firms), and cities and regions (creative milieu). Innovation and technological progress are a source of entrepreneurial opportunity (new firm formation or market expansion), while entrepreneurship is the real engine of economic growth (Baycan et al., 2011) in that it is the entrepreneur who manages the innovation process. In a knowledge-based economy, economic performance depends on competition as a driver of improved productivity, while innovation in the form of new technologies, techniques and ways of working also drive improved productivity. However, in an increasingly dynamic and global economy, the institutional infrastructure has remained ineffective at moving innovations to the marketplace and society. In recent years, the question of how to facilitate and foster knowledge commercialization has become hotly debated in academic and policy circles (Litan et al., 2007, PricewaterhouseCoopers, 2007; Bercovitz and Feldman, 2008; Mitchell, 2010; Baycan, 2013; Baycan and Stough, 2013), while the commercialization and valorization of knowledge has come to be considered an important stimulus of economic growth, particularly for improving the development capabilities and economic performance of regions (Baycan, 2013; Baycan and Stough, 2013).

Innovation systems are the result of an interactive process of knowledge generation, diffusion and application. The importance of knowledge interaction has been emphasized in the literature on innovative milieu (Camagni, 1991), knowledge spillovers (Bottazi and Peri, 2003), innovation networks (Powell and Grodal, 2005) and innovation systems (Edquist, 2005). The innovation-systems approach regards innovation as an evolutionary, non-linear and interactive endeavour that requires intensive communication and cooperation between firms and other organizations such as universities and other public research facilities, technology centres, educational establishments, financing institutions, standard-setting bodies, industry associations and government agencies (Edquist, 1997; 2005). Within the systems-of-innovation approach, the creation, selection and transformation of knowledge takes place within a complex matrix of interactions between different actors and within a diverse economic, institutional, social, political, cultural and geographical context.

The innovation systems literature argues that institutions relevant to a specific sector (Sectoral Innovation Systems, or SIS), country (National Innovation Systems, or NIS) or region (Regional Innovation Systems, or RIS) have an influence on innovation (Tödtling et al., 2009). Innovation processes are generally evaluated within the frameworks of NIS and RIS. The NIS approach is defined as the flows and mechanisms of technology and information between people, enterprises and institutions that are the key elements of the innovation process at the national level (OECD, 1997). Various researchers have quickly applied the NIS concept in studying RIS (Braczyk et al., 1996; Cooke et al., 1997; Morgan and Nauwelaers, 1999; Cooke, 2001; Koschatzky et al., 2001; Doloreux, 2002). While NIS specifically focuses on how a system of innovation shapes competitive advantage, the RIS approach emphasizes economic and social interactions between agents, spanning the public and private sectors to engender and diffuse innovation within regions. RIS more specifically examines innovating firms in the context of external institutions, government policies, competitors, suppliers, customers, value systems and social and cultural practices that affect their innovation activities within a geographical area that is larger than a city, but smaller than a nation (Kumaresan and Miyazaki, 1999; OECD, 1999; van Hemert and Nijkamp, 2010; van Hemert *et al.*, 2013). These areas or regions are originally embedded in national systems, but increasingly RIS is considered to be included in a complex web of relations, not only of national but also of international agencies and innovation systems (Trippl, 2010). While the RIS approach traditionally highlights the disparities in innovation across regions (Autio, 1998; de la Mothe and Paquet, 1998; Howells, 1999; Acs, 2000; Cooke *et al.*, 2000; Doloreux, 2002; Fornahl and Brenner, 2003; Cooke *et al.*, 2004; Asheim and Gertler, 2005; Doloreux and Parto, 2005; Tödtling and Trippl, 2005; Asheim and Coenen, 2006), the NIS approach shows that countries may also differ enormously with respect to their economic structures, R&D bases, institutional setups and innovation performances (Edquist, 2001).

Owing to its regional unit of analysis, the RIS literature has focused more specifically on knowledge spillover and interaction processes. At least three forms of knowledge spillover can be distinguished (Boschma and Frenken, 2006): spinoff firms, labour mobility and R&D collaboration. These topics have, over the past years, been addressed systematically in empirical research (Uzzi, 1996; Almeida and Kogut, 1999; Breschi and Lissoni, 2003; Giuliani, 2007; Klepper, 2007; Ponds *et al.*, 2007; Morrison, 2008). Key assumptions of RIS (Trippl and Tödtling, 2007) are: innovation activities exhibit a very distinctive geography (see, among others, Howells, 1999; Breschi, 2000; Paci and Usai, 2000); knowledge spillovers are often spatially bounded (i.e. localized) (Jaffe, 1989; Jaffe *et al.*, 1993; Audretsch and Feldman, 1996; Anselin *et al.*, 1997; Bottazzi and Peri, 2003); tacit knowledge remains important for successfully carrying out innovation (Howells, 2002; Gertler, 2003); the exchange of tacit knowledge presupposes trust and personal contacts, which are essentially facilitated by spatial proximity (Storper, 1997; Morgan, 2004); and subnational territories tend to differ strongly in terms of their institutional settings and political decision-making abilities (Cooke *et al.*, 2000). Again, it is important to recognize the evolving argument that ICTs provide a potential vehicle for remote and peripheral regions to overcome their non-proximal location by providing a communication link with the more dominant urban network innovation framework (Grillitsch and Nilsson, 2015). However, the potential for linking up at this time has more of a complementary than a substitute role.

The NIS and RIS approaches focus mainly on the exploration stage of innovation. However, various researchers now argue that the focus should be on the innovation processes in an NIS/RIS context rather than on systems activities. While positioning innovation in local, regional and international contexts, the articles in this symposium focus, in particular, on the innovation processes that highlight the main assumptions of the systems-of-innovation approaches and outline the different paths and patterns of innovation. The articles in this symposium by Capello and by Crescenzi and Rodríguez-Pose critically examine the literature of innovation, drawing attention to some of the assumptions of innovation theory that remain insufficient to explain current innovation patterns, and highlighting the different innovation processes as well as the different territorial paths and patterns of innovation at regional and national levels. Capello focuses on contextual conditions of innovation patterns at the regional level, and Crescenzi and Rodríguez-Pose investigate different innovation paths at the national level while addressing territorial systems of innovation in emerging countries.

What are the different territorial patterns of innovation and the contextual conditions that accompany each innovation pattern? Capello investigates the way in which regions innovate and critically evaluates the current conceptual approach in regional innovation theory. She argues, first of all, that the presence of advanced sectors and advanced functions such as R&D and higher education displays specific features of only *some of the possible innovation paths* and that these—although important—cannot be considered as necessary or sufficient preconditions for innovation; and secondly, that the emphasis on symbiotic interaction per se among the different actors of knowledge development as the crucial factor in knowledge creation and diffusion is not entirely satisfactory. She establishes the need for a new conceptual framework for the determinants of innovation capability at the regional level that goes beyond some simplified assumptions that still accompany even recent analyses, and then offers a novel conceptual framework interpreting the different patterns of territorial innovation, defined as a combination of contextual conditions (internal and external to the region), and specific modes of performing the different phases of the innovation process. She describes three patterns of innovation, namely *an endogenous innovation pattern in a scientific network, a creative application pattern* and *an imitative innovation pattern*. This new interpretative paradigm that Capello recognizes as 'the innovation patterns paradigm' brings to light the complex interplay between phases of the innovation process and the spatial context or territorial conditions. On the basis of this novel conceptual framework she also expresses some doubts on the usefulness of EU policy and proposes, instead, thematically and regionally focused innovation policies.

The variation in local dynamics manifests itself at a global scale too. How and where does innovation take place in leading emerging countries and to what extent do territorial systems of innovation in emerging countries differ from those in the EU or the US? Crescenzi and Rodríguez-Pose (this issue) explore the geography of innovation in two emerging countries, China and India, by concentrating on understanding key territorial-level innovation trends by country, region and technology field, while using the US and the EU as benchmarks. In contrast to the general tendency to assume that 'emerging countries are in an earlier stage of the innovative process than the EU or the US and that they will tend to follow a similar path towards innovation and development in the future' (Crescenzi and Rodríguez-Pose, this issue, 2), they highlight that the pace of change currently experienced by emerging countries is virtually unparalleled in history and that both India (around Delhi and in the South) and China's coastal regions display highly concentrated territorial patterns of innovation that significantly surpass those found in the US and the EU. Based on their comparative exploration they also highlight that the differences in the geographies of innovation between China and India as well as between these countries and the developed world are rooted in different institutional settings, different systems of innovation, and different national innovation strategies.

Both the articles by Capello and by Crescenzi and Rodríguez-Pose argue that the factors that stimulate new knowledge, invention, innovation and innovation diffusion differ and that the geography of innovative activity is territorially very uneven. While Capello highlights the disparities in innovation across regions, Crescenzi and Rodríguez-Pose show that countries differ enormously with respect to their economic structures, R&D bases, institutional setups and innovation performances. The articles suggest that innovation can be the result of different forces and mechanism patterns and that the diversity of development and innovation paths explains the failure of a 'one-size-fits-all' policy for innovation.

Spatial clustering of innovation and local dynamics

How does innovative activity concentrate or spread out? How do local dynamics affect the spatial concentration or distribution of innovative activities? What is the connection between local R&D, local knowledge creation and local innovation? Under what circumstances does local innovation lead to positive local outcomes? The literature on spatial aspects and local dynamics of innovation focuses on these key research questions. Research capacity and innovation are not spread evenly across countries, regions and cities. Different streams of literature (the linear model of innovation, geographical analyses of knowledge spillovers, and theories about institutions and regional systems of innovation) explain the level of concentration of innovative activities by knowledge spillovers and the spatial dynamics of innovation (see e.g. Jaffe *et al.*, 1993; Audretsch and Feldman, 1996; Malmberg *et al.*, 1996; Acs *et al.*, 2002; Carlino *et al.*, 2007; Bathelt and Cohendet, 2014). Research on knowledge spillovers emphasizes the fact that innovation does not diffuse costlessly in space and highlights the presence of relatively strong distance decay effects both in Europe (Moreno *et al.*, 2005; Rodríguez-Pose and Crescenzi, 2008) and in the US (Anselin *et al.*, 1997; Varga, 2000; Sonn and Storper, 2008). This stream of literature explains the geographically concentrated innovation capacity of agglomeration economies as often linked to urbanization, spatial proximity, economic symbiosis and path dependency. At the same time it is again of use to recognize the evolving argument that ICTs provide a way for peripheral regions to be a complementary part of a networked innovation system (Bathelt and Turi, 2011; Grillitsch and Nilsson, 2015).

Various studies show that in industries where new economic knowledge plays an important role, innovation tends to cluster geographically. Therefore, one may expect that innovative activity is likely to occur within close geographic proximity to the source of that knowledge (Audretsch and Feldman, 1996; Warren *et al.*, 2008). Spatial proximity is seen as the main, but not only, factor explaining the channels through which knowledge spreads (Torre and Wallet, 2014). The central insight is that proximity facilitates innovation; ICT considers the concomitant complementary role of peripheral areas. Specific regional factors such as the presence of universities and public agencies, networks and institutions, in conjunction with national-level factors and institutions, determine the economic performance of individual firms and local actors. Moreover, the dynamics that are at work prior to commercialization of knowledge (Baycan, 2013) develop at local geographic levels, including local clusters, megacenters and regions (Uranga *et al.*, 2007). Venture capitalists and universities are important actors within networks of local or regional clusters of knowledge-based activities or systems of regional innovation (Cooke *et al.*, 2004; Huggins, 2008). Most venture capitalists seek to invest in ventures and activities that are relatively proximate to their own location, in the same locality or region (Huggins, 2008). Start-up companies are predominantly local and the 'industry helix' is embedded in local network relationships (Uranga *et al.*, 2007). Collaborations between universities and non-academic agents and organizations are localized geographically and according to Frenken and Oort (2004), the capacity to collaborate and cooperate is often more important than the ability to produce knowledge. This capacity to collaborate is determined by the 'absorptive capacity' of different actors within a region and the cognitive base of actors and organizations, while their potential for learning may differ substantially (Qian *et al.*, 2013).

Geographic proximity is a spatial symbiosis factor for the development of strong ties within local and regional networks to promote the transfer of complex knowledge. The argument related to geographic proximity suggests that strong ties promote the transfer of complex knowledge, while weak ties promote the transfer of simple knowledge (Bathelt *et al.*, 2004; Huggins, 2008). Weak ties or poor network conditions may also lead to information asymmetries between potential investors and investees (Shane, 2004). A lack of existing and effective networks may have a negative effect on the commercialization of knowledge, not only in terms of financing, but also in terms of exchanging expertise and experience (Huggins, 2008). Development of strong ties requires face-to-face interaction and the geographic proximity of network actors facilitates this interaction. Therefore, the existence of established spatially proximate networks plays an important role in regional knowledge commercialization. In more advanced clusters, territories and network drivers are more biased towards creating conditions for commercializing knowledge, and to a lesser extent, to government intervention to foster development (Uranga *et al.*, 2007).

However, the globalization of production and the globalization of R&D (Bruche, 2009; Lundvall, 2009; Yeung, 2009; Fu and Soete, 2010; Kuchiki and Tsuji, 2010) has in the past few decades created a complex web of relations connecting regional innovation systems not only to national but also to international organizations and innovation systems (Trippl, 2010). This web has led to the innovative success of regions as well as countries depending not only on how to internationalize and exploit local innovations, but also on how much knowledge and technology is transferred by multinational corporations and to what extent local firms are able and capable of branching into global scientific and technology networks. This complex web of relations also differentiates emerging and developing countries from developed countries, based on country- and locality-specific factors such as institutions, networks and norms (Lundvall *et al.*, 2006; Crescenzi and Rodríguez-Pose, this issue). While internationalization has increasingly become a critical success factor in regional innovation systems, scarce or inadequate innovation agents, limited capacity for collaboration among different actors, a limited presence of multinational firms and limited institutional capacity and fragmented governance represent barriers to the development of innovative capacity. Of course, contemporary ICTs provide, to some extent, a caveat to this conclusion, but, as noted earlier, the ability of ICTs to provide substitution effects are at best at a nascent stage.

The articles in this symposium investigate how innovative activity concentrates or distributes and how local dynamics affect the spatial concentration or distribution of innovative activity. Given the limited knowledge existing about the geography of innovation in emerging countries, as well as the low level of systematic comparative analysis, the symposium also highlights the organizational and institutional settings that shape innovation and innovation systems in different countries, as well as the differing territorial dynamics of innovation in the EU and the US, and in emerging countries. While the articles focus closely on the purported connection between local R&D, local knowledge creation and local innovation, they develop new arguments in contrast to general assumptions in the innovation literature on the spatial clustering of innovation and local dynamics. The symposium highlights four main arguments: first, local innovation dynamics result from external as well as internal factors; likewise, local innovation processes may lead to outcomes elsewhere (Capello, this issue; Crescenzi and Rodríguez-Pose, this issue); secondly, in some cases local and regional development is not linked to local and regional innovation (Capello, this issue; Crescenzi and Rodríguez-Pose, this issue; Faggian *et al.*, this issue); thirdly, the presence of advanced sectors and functions such as R&D and higher education are special features of only some of the possible innovation paths and, although they are important, cannot be considered as necessary or sufficient preconditions for innovation (Capello, this issue; Faggian, *et al.*, this issue); and fourthly, national institutional conditions affect innovation systems (Capello, this issue; Crescenzi and Rodríguez-Pose, this issue).

The symposium articles by Crescenzi and Rodríguez-Pose and Faggian *et al.* offer empirical evidence that supports a conclusion that geographically, innovation capacity is concentrated at country and county levels. Crescenzi and Rodríguez-Pose highlight that innovation in China, India and the US is geographically concentrated, while the East and West Coast are two important innovation cores in the US, the more innovative regions being located on the western and eastern seaboards and in the Great Lakes region (Michigan, Wisconsin), while less innovative areas are relatively less populated and include parts of the Midwest other than the Great Lakes region, as well as the Western Plains and the Deep South counties. In China, the leading regions for innovation also tend to lie in coastal areas, especially in the larger cities and in the South. In addition, the authors highlight that in both China and India, the top human capital regions also appear in the most innovative regions lists. Their comparative evaluation reveals a high level of concentration in a limited number of provinces and shows that this geographical agglomeration of innovation is greater in China than in the US. Empirical evidence offered by Faggian *et al.* (this issue) supports this geographic concentration of innovation capacity at the county level in the US. Their analysis demonstrates that accessibility to large metropolitan areas (especially above a threshold of 250,000 and 500,000 inhabitants) plays a positive role in economic growth at both the level of metropolitan and non-metropolitan areas. Their analysis also demonstrates that knowledge workers want to be located near larger agglomerations that are already growing swiftly and that urban areas, particularly metropolitan areas, have more to gain from increasing human capital, perhaps owing to larger knowledge production and spillovers. Once again it is important to temper this conclusion with the potential ICTs create for more remote and peripheral regions to effectively link into national and subnational regional innovation systems.

Crescenzi and Rodríguez-Pose and Faggian *et al.* empirically demonstrate the important role of spatial proximity in regional innovation. Their findings also highlight that, although the availability of highly educated human capital significantly explains the innovative capacity of regions, the existence of advanced technology industries does not necessarily determine higher innovative regional performance (Faggian *et al.*, this issue), while the spread of human capital, R&D investments and patenting can be highly selective and exhibit different patterns that may lead to territorial polarization of innovation (Crescenzi and Rodríguez-Pose, this issue). Given these empirical results, the symposium highlights that linear innovation and endogenous growth theories are insufficient to explain the complex relations at the local level between local R&D, local knowledge creation and local innovation, and are insufficient at the global level for understanding the more complex relations between local and global agents of innovation, the internal and external factors and conditions that determine the capacity of innovation, and the increasing internationalization of knowledge and technology transfer and its projection at the local level.

Conclusion

This symposium offers a focused view on the geography of cities and regions as symbiotic hubs of innovation, knowledge creation and economic dynamics. Both conceptually and empirically, there is much scope for a thorough analysis of the centrifugal position of cities and regions in an open spatial-economic system. Spatial spillovers—including spatial externalities and connectivities—reflect the rising importance of complex spatial networks, in which cities and regions display internal network elements while being part of broader globally oriented networks. These network features do not show a uniform or homogeneous picture, but exhibit a multi-faceted mosaic.

This symposium aims at a better understanding of key territorial-level innovation trends and processes by country, region and technology field; analyses the territorial dynamics of innovation and their determinants; and investigates differences in the geography of innovation regarding differing institutional settings, systems of innovation and national innovation strategies. While reflecting on the rising importance of complex spatial networks, the symposium highlights a set of new arguments: first, invention and innovation are not necessarily intertwined, which gives rise to very different and multi-faceted situations. Secondly, regions are not homogeneous in terms of their orientation regarding innovations; rather, they contain within them a diversity of economic activities and capacities, while research capacity and innovation are not spread evenly across countries, regions and cities. Thirdly, the factors that stimulate new knowledge, invention, innovation and innovation diffusion differ; while in some cases local and regional development are not linked to local and regional innovation and the presence of advanced sectors, R&D and higher education cannot be considered as necessary or sufficient preconditions for innovation. Fourthly, innovation takes place in networks and these networks are not necessarily local but sometimes even global, so that local innovation processes may lead to outcomes elsewhere. And fifthly, national institutional conditions affect innovation systems at different levels of scale; the institutional framework and the regional characteristics and endowments might favour different innovation patterns, including more endogenous, more creative applications or more imitative ones in regions, although combinations may occur too, and changes in these combinations may happen over time.

Against the background of these arguments, this symposium underlines the need for a better understanding of the complexity of innovation processes and spatial dynamics as well as for a more integrated framework. It offers a new framework that considers a 'multiple-solution model of innovation', whereby innovation builds on internal knowledge, or local creativity induces—despite lack of local knowledge—an innovative application of knowledge developed elsewhere and acquired through scientific linkages, or innovation is made possible by imitation of innovations developed outside the region. While we recognize that innovation can be the result of differing patterns and a diversity of development and innovation paths, the symposium highlights that uniform spatial policies are by no means successful or effective vehicles for urban or regional development. A critical review of the potential policy handles alluded to in this symposium brings to light the need for tailor-made, strategic policy initiatives that transcend the traditional administrative borders of cities and regions and are based on the self-organizing and evolutionary capacities of these areas rather than on top-down steered policy instruments. Indeed, the rising relevance of spatial spillovers (economic, social, innovation, knowledge, mobility) challenges the principles of traditional urban and regional development policy. Mobilization of spatially interlinked local and regional growth resources may be viewed as an adequate response to current economic recession phenomena.

The contributions in this symposium, on the basis of a critical review of the literature as well as on empirical investigations, also highlight the challenges for both policy and research perspectives. From a research perspective, there is an obvious need to examine more closely the purported connection between local R&D, local knowledge creation and local innovation. Given the complexity of spatial connections from the local to the global level, there is also a need for a spatial symbiotic approach, not in the sense of regions or territories but in the sense of space-bridging networks and connections. From a policy perspective, there is a need for an alternative analysis of regional innovation systems to the 'one-size-fits-all' approach. This alternative analysis requires an integrated and place-based approach to innovation policy design and delivery to be developed, which underlines the importance of innovation policies tailored to the local context while acknowledging that there are different pathways for regional innovation and development. What emerges clearly from this approach is that each territorial innovation pattern calls for specific ad hoc innovation policy goals. Another challenge from a policy perspective is to develop strategies to attract and retain highly educated workers and to build a diverse small and medium-sized business foundation. Current economic development strategies are sometimes too focused on attracting large outside firms and advanced technology firms, while insufficient attention is given to building a foundation of competitive small and medium-sized firms. This challenge is not limited to innovation policy, but also refers to immigration policy that may encourage diversity of economic activities and capacities and may facilitate labour-force mobility. These fresh perspectives call for a paradigm shift in the field of innovation and spatial dynamics with a focus on open spatial symbiosis.

Finally, while this symposium focuses on a territorial approach to innovation in a highly global, national and regional networked framework, it recognizes that ICTs are increasingly creating a vehicle for less proximal regions and places to enjoy a role in innovation in this evolving symbiotic context (McCann, 2007; Bathelt and Turi, 2011; Shearmur, 2011; Huber, 2012; Rodríguez-Pose and Fitjar, 2013; Grillitsch and Nilsson, 2015; Ruten, 2017). The relatively minor role that the symposium affords the potential to link in remote places lays a strong rationale for a follow-on symposium that focuses on this potential. Such compilation of research on this topic will promote a much-needed and improved understanding of the role of ICTs in the integration of remote and peripheral places into the evolving networked system of innovation that has been emphasized in this symposium.

Tuzin Baycan, Department of Urban and Regional Planning, Istanbul Technical University, Taskisla 34437 Taksim, Istanbul, Turkey, tbaycan@itu.edu.tr

Peter Nijkamp, Faculty of Geography, Adam Mickiewicz University, Ul. Bogumila Krygowskiego 10, 61-680 Poznan, Poland, pnijkamp@hotmail.com

Roger R. Stough, Schar School of Policy and Government, George Mason University, 3351 Fairfax Drive, MS 3B1, Arlington, Virginia 22201, USA, rstough@gmu.edu

References

Acs, Z. (ed.) (2000) *Regional innovation, knowledge and global change*. Pinter, London.

Acs, Z.J., L. Anselin and A. Varga (2002) Patents and innovation counts as measures of regional production of new knowledge. *Research Policy* 31.7, 1069-85.

Almeida, P. and B. Kogut (1999) Localization of knowledge and the mobility of engineers in regional networks. *Management Science* 45.7, 905-17.

Anselin, L., A. Varga and Z. Acs (1997) Local geographic spillovers between university research and high technology innovations. *Journal of Urban Economics* 42.3, 422-48.

Asheim, B. and L. Coenen (2006) Contextualising regional innovation systems in a globalising learning economy: on knowledge bases and institutional frameworks. *Journal of Technology Transfer* 31.1, 163-73.

Asheim, B. and M. Gertler (2005) The geography of innovation: regional innovation systems. In J. Fagerberg, D.C. Mowery and R.R. Nelson (eds.), *The Oxford handbook of innovation*, Oxford University Press, Oxford.

Audretsch, D. and M. Feldman (1996) Innovative clusters and the industry life cycle. *Review of Industrial Organisation* 11.2, 253-73.

Autio, E. (1998) Evaluation of RTD in regional systems of innovation. *European Planning Studies* 6.2, 131-40.

Bathelt, H. and P. Cohendet (2014) The creation of knowledge. *Journal of Economic Geography* 14.5, 869-82.

Bathelt, H. and P. Turi (2011) Local, global and virtual buzz: the importance of face-to-face contact in economic interaction and possibilities to go beyond. *Geoforum* 42.5, 520-29.

Bathelt, H., A. Malmberg and P. Maskell (2004) Clusters and knowledge: local buzz, global pipelines and the process of knowledge creation. *Progress in Human Geography* 28.1, 31-56.

Baycan, T. (ed.) (2013) *Knowledge commercialization and valorization in regional economic development*. Edward Elgar, Cheltenham.

Baycan, T. and R.R. Stough (2013) Bridging knowledge to commercialization: the good, the bad, and the challenging. *Annals of Regional Science* 50.2, 367-405.

Baycan, T., P. Nijkamp and R.J. Stimson (2011) Editorial: Innovative business resources in economic development: analysis and policy. *International Journal of Foresight and Innovation Policy* 7.1-3, 1-6.

Bercovitz, J. and M. Feldmann (2008) Academic entrepreneurs: organizational change at the individual level. *Organization Science* 19.1, 69-89.

Boschma, R.A. and K. Frenken (2006) Why is economic geography not an evolutionary science? Towards an evolutionary economic geography. *Journal of Economic Geography* 6.3, 273-302.

Bottazzi, L. and G. Peri (2003) Innovation and spillovers in regions: evidence from European patent data. *European Economic Review* 47.4, 678-710.

Braczyk, H.J., P. Cooke and M. Heidenreich (1996) *Regional innovation systems*. University College London, London.

Breschi, S. (2000) The geography of innovation: a cross-industry analysis. *Regional Studies* 34.3, 213-29.

Breschi, S. and F. Lissoni (2003) Mobility and social networks: localised knowledge spillovers revisited. CESPRI Working Paper 142 [WWW document]. URL http://www.cespri.unibocconi.it/ (accessed 1 June 2013).

Bruche, G. (2009) *A new geography of innovation: China and India rising*. Columbia FDI Perspectives, Vale Columbia Center, Columbia University, New York, NY.

Camagni, R. (1991) Local 'milieu', uncertainty and innovation networks: towards a new dynamic theory of economic space. In R. Camagni (ed.), *Innovation networks: spatial perspectives*, Belhaven Press, London.

Capello, R. (2017) *Towards a new conceptualization of innovation in space: territorial patterns of innovation*. *International Journal of Urban and Regional Research* 41.6, 976-96.

Carlino, G., S. Chatterjee and R. Hunt (2007) Urban density and the rate of invention. *Journal of Urban Economics* 61.3, 389-419.

Cooke, P. (2001) Regional innovation systems, clusters and knowledge economy. *Industrial and Corporate Change* 10.4, 945-74.

Cooke, P., P. Boekholt and F. Tödtling (2000) *The governance of innovation in Europe: regional perspectives on global competitiveness*. Pinter, London.

Cooke, P., M. Heidenreich and H.J. Braczyk (eds.) (2004) *Regional innovation systems: the role of governances in a globalized world*. Routledge, London.

Cooke, P., M.G. Uranga and G. Etxebarria (1997) Regional innovation systems: institutional and organizational dimensions. *Research Policy* 26.4, 475-91.

Crescenzi, R. and A. Rodríguez-Pose (2017) The geography of innovation in China and India. *International Journal of Urban and Regional Research* 41.6, 1010-27.

de la Mothe, J., and G. Paquet (eds.) (1998) *Local and regional systems of innovation*. Kluwer, Boston, MA.

Doloreux, D. (2002) What we should know about regional systems of innovation. *Technology and Society* 24.3, 243-63.

Doloreux, D. and S. Parto (2005) Regional innovation systems: current discourse and unresolved issues. *Technology in Society* 27.2, 133-53.

Edquist, C. (1997) *Systems of innovation: technologies, institutions and organizations*. Pinter, London.

Edquist, C. (2001) The systems of innovation approach and innovation policy: an account of the state of the art. DRUID conference working paper, 12-15 June, Aalborg.

Edquist, C. (2005) Systems of innovation—perspectives and challenges. In J. Fagerberg, D. Mowery and R. Nelson (eds.), *The Oxford Handbook of innovation*, Oxford University Press, Oxford.

Faggian, A. (2005) Human capital. In R. Caves (ed.), *Encyclopaedia of the city*, Routledge, New York, NY.

Faggian, A., M. Partridge and E. Malecki (2017) *Creating an environment for economic growth: creativity, entrepreneurship or human capital?* International Journal of Urban and Regional Research 41.6, 997-1009.

Fornahl, D. and T. Brenner (eds.) (2003) *Cooperation, networks and institutions in regional innovation systems*. Edward Elgar, Cheltenham.

Frenken, K. and F.G. van Oort (2004) The geography of research collaboration: theoretical considerations and stylized facts in biotechnology in Europe and the United States. In P. Cooke and A. Piccaluga (eds.), *Regional economics as knowledge laboratories*, Edward Elgar, Cheltenham.

Fu, X. and L. Soete (eds.) (2010) *The rise of technological power in the South*. Palgrave Macmillan, Basingstoke.

Gertler, M. (2003) Tacit knowledge and the economic geography of context or the undefinable tacitness of being (there). *Journal of Economic Geography* 3.1, 75–99.

Giuliani, E. (2007) The selective nature of knowledge networks in clusters: evidence from the wine industry. *Journal of Economic Geography* 7.2, 139–68.

Grillitsch, M. and M. Nilsson (2015) Innovation in peripheral regions: do collaborations compensate for lack of local knowledge spillovers? *The Annals of Regional Science* 54.1, 299–321.

Howells, J. (1999) Regional systems of innovation. In D. Archibugi, J. Howells and J. Michie (eds.), *Innovation policy in a global economy*, Cambridge University Press, Cambridge.

Howells, J.R. (2002) Tacit knowledge, innovation and economic geography. *Urban Studies* 39.5/6, 871–84.

Howells, J. and J. Bessant (2012) Introduction. Innovation and economic geography: a review and analysis. *Journal of Economic Geography* 12.5, 929–42.

Huber, F. (2012) On the role of interrelationships of spatial, social and cognitive proximity: personal knowledge relationships of R&D networks in the Cambridge information cluster. *Regional Studies* 46.9, 1169–82.

Huggins, R. (2008) Universities and knowledge-based venturing: finance, management and networks in London. *Entrepreneurship and Regional Development* 20.2, 185–206.

Jaffe, A. (1989) The real effects of academic research. *American Economic Review* 79.5, 957–70.

Jaffe, A., M. Trajtenberg and R. Henderson (1993) Geographic localization of knowledge spillovers as evidenced by patent citations. *Quarterly Journal of Economics 79 (August)*, 577–98.

Kirzner, I.M. (1997) Entrepreneurial discovery and the competitive market process: an Austrian approach. *Journal of Economic Literature* 35.1, 60–87.

Klepper, S. (2007) Disagreements, spinoffs, and the evolution of Detroit as the capital of the US automobile industry. *Management Science* 53.4, 616–31.

Koschatzky, K., M. Kulicke and A. Zenker (2001) *Innovation networks: concepts and challenges in the European perspective*. Fraunhofer Institute for Systems and Innovation Research, Heidelberg.

Kuchiki, A. and M. Tsuji (eds.) (2010) *From agglomeration to innovation: upgrading industrial clusters in emerging economies*. Palgrave Macmillan, Basingstoke.

Kumaresan, N. and K. Miyazaki (1999) An integrated network approach to systems of innovation—the case of robotics in Japan. *Research Policy* 28.6, 563–85.

Litan, R.E., L. Mitchell and E.J. Reedy (2007) Commercializing university innovations: alternative approaches. *Innovation Policy and the Economy* 8, 31–57.

Lundvall, B.Å. (ed.) (2009) *Handbook of innovation systems and developing countries: building domestic capabilities in a global setting*. Edward Elgar, Cheltenham.

Lundvall, B.Å., P. Intarakumnerd and J. Vang (2006) *Asia's innovation systems in transition*. Edward Elgar, Cheltenham.

Malmberg, A., O. Sölvell and I. Zander (1996) Spatial clustering, local accumulation of knowledge and firm competitiveness. *Geografiska Annaler Series B: Human Geography* 78.2, 85–97.

McCann, P. (2007) Sketching out a model of innovation, face-to-face interaction and economic geography. *Spatial Economic Analysis* 2.2, 117–34.

Mitchell, L. (2010) From lab to bench to market: house subcommittee holds hearing on improving commercialization. Testimony by Lesa Mitchell, 10 June [WWW document]. URL http://www.kauffmann.org (accessed 1 June 2013, URL no longer available).

Moreno, R., R. Paci and S. Usai (2005) Spatial spillovers and innovation activity in European regions. *Environment and Planning A* 37.10, 1793–812.

Morgan, K. (2004) The exaggerated death of geography: learning, proximity and territorial innovation systems. *Journal of Economic Geography* 4.1, 3–21.

Morgan, K. and C. Nauwelaers (1999) *Regional innovation strategies*. The Stationery Office, London.

Morrison, A. (2008) Gatekeepers of knowledge within industrial districts: who they are, how they interact. *Regional Studies* 42.6, 817–35.

OECD (Organisation for Economic Co-operation and Development) (1997) *The Oslo manual: the measurement of scientific and technological activities*. OECD, Paris.

OECD (Organisation for Economic Co-operation and Development) (1999) *Managing national innovation systems*. OECD, Paris.

Paci, R. and S. Usai (2000) Technological enclaves and industrial districts: an analysis of the regional distribution of innovative activity in Europe. *Regional Studies* 34.2, 97–114.

Ponds, R., F.G. van Oort and K. Frenken (2007) The geographical and institutional proximity of research collaborations. *Papers in Regional Science* 86.3, 423–43.

Powell, W. and S. Grodal (2005) Networks of innovators. In J. Fagerberg, D. Mowery and R. Nelson (eds.), *The Oxford handbook of innovation*, Oxford University Press, Oxford.

PricewaterhouseCoopers (2007) *Staying in control while unlocking the knowledge*. Published in cooperation with TechnoPartner.

Qian, H., Z. Acs and R. Stough (2013) Regional systems of entrepreneurship: the nexus of human capital, knowledge and new firm formation. *Journal of Economic Geography* 13.4, 559–87.

Rodríguez-Pose, A. and R. Crescenzi (2008) R&D, spillovers, innovation systems and the genesis of regional growth in Europe. *Regional Studies* 42.1, 51–67.

Rodríguez-Pose, A. and R.D. Fitjar (2013) Buzz, archipelago economies and the future of intermediate and peripheral areas in a spiky world. *European Planning Studies* 21.3, 355–72.

Ruten, R. (2017) Beyond proximities: the socio-spatial dynamics of knowledge creation. *Progress in Human Geography* 41.2, 159–77.

Shane, S.A. (2004) *Academic entrepreneurship: university spinoffs and wealth creation*. Edward Elgar, Cheltenham.

Shearmur, R. (2011) Innovation, regions and proximities: from nero-regionalism to spatial analysis. *Regional Studies* 45.9, 1225–43.

Sonn, J.W. and M. Storper (2008) The increasing importance of geographical proximity in technological innovation: an analysis of U.S. patent citations, 1975–1997. *Environment and Planning A* 40.5, 1020–39.

Storper, M. (1997) *The regional world*. Guilford Press, New York, NY.

Tödtling, F. and M. Trippl (2005) One size fits all? Towards a differentiated regional policy approach. *Research Policy* 34.8, 1203–19.

Tödtling, F., P. Lehner and A. Kaufmann (2009) Do different types of innovation rely on specific kinds of knowledge interactions? *Technovation* 29.1, 59–71.

Torre, A. and F. Wallet (2014) *Regional development and proximity relations*. Edward Elgar, Cheltenham.

Trippl, M. (2010) Developing cross-border regional innovation systems: key factors and challenges. *Tijdschrift voor Economische en Sociale Geografie* 101.2, 150–60.

Trippl, M. and F. Tödtling (2007) Developing biotechnology clusters in non-high technology regions—the case of Austria. *Industry and Innovation* 14.1, 47–67.

Uranga, M.G., G.E. Kerexeta and J. Campàs-Velasco (2007) The dynamics of commercialization of scientific knowledge in biotechnology and nanotechnology. *European Planning Studies* 15.9, 1199-214.

Uzzi, B. (1996) The sources and consequences of embeddedness for the economic performance of organizations: the network effect. *American Sociological Review* 61.4, 674-98.

van Hemert, P. and P. Nijkamp (2010) Knowledge investments, business R&D and innovativeness of countries: a qualitative meta-analytic comparison. *Technological Forecasting and Social Change* 77.3, 369-84.

van Hemert, P., P. Nijkamp and E. Masurel (2013) From innovation to commercialization through networks and agglomerations: analysis of sources of innovation, innovation capabilities and performance of Dutch SMEs. *Annals of Regional Science* 50.2, 425-52.

Varga, A. (2000) Local academic knowledge spillovers and the concentration of economic activity. *Journal of Regional Science* 40.2, 289-309.

Warren, A., R. Hanke and D. Trotzer (2008) Models for university technology transfer: resolving conflicts between mission and methods and the dependency on geographic location. *Cambridge Journal of Regions, Economy and Society* 1.2, 219-32.

Yeung, H.W.C. (2009) Regional development and the competitive dynamics of global production networks: an East Asian perspective. *Regional Studies* 43.3, 325-51.

DOI:10.1111/1468-2427.12556

— TOWARDS A NEW CONCEPTUALIZATION OF INNOVATION IN SPACE: Territorial Patterns of Innovation

ROBERTA CAPELLO

Abstract

This article investigates the way in which regions innovate. Its conceptual framework departs from the simple notion that scientific activities equate with knowledge, which assumes that the presence of local knowledge produced by research centres, universities and firms is a necessary and sufficient condition for increasing the innovative capacities in local firms, fed by local spillovers. In particular, the paradigmatic jump in interpreting regional innovation processes lies in a conceptual framework interpreting not a single phase of the innovation process, but the different modes of performing different phases of the innovation process. This article conceptually identifies different territorial patterns of innovation and highlights the context conditions (internal and external to the region) that accompany each innovation pattern. Based on this debate, I express some doubts on the usefulness of EU policy aims for achieving a figure of 3% of the EU's GDP (public and private) to be invested in R&D/innovation and instead strongly support normative suggestions towards thematically and regionally focused innovation policies.

The need for a new conceptual approach in regional innovation

The importance of innovation and—in the most recent conception—of knowledge in explaining the competitiveness of economic systems has led to a resurgence of interest and inspiration for policymakers over the past ten years. The Lisbon Agenda, formulated by the Lisbon and Luxembourg ministerial meetings at the start of the previous decade (in 2000 and 2005), committed the EU to becoming the most competitive and dynamic knowledge-based economy in the world. The main target was to increase EU R&D investment intensity from 1.8% of GDP in the late 1990s to about 3% by 2010.

Despite these policy goals, in 2009 R&D intensity was still stable at the level of 1.84% of GDP, and although some EU member countries such as Sweden and Finland recorded a relatively high R&D intensity (Sweden had already exceeded 3% several years previously), the figure for the majority of EU countries and regions lay significantly below 2% (Čenys, 2009).

The notion of increasing competitiveness through knowledge and innovation has not been abandoned, however. Instead, it has been relaunched as part of the Europe 2020 strategy document, in terms of which the goals for smart growth again call for 3% of the EU's GDP (public and private) to be invested in R&D/innovation, with the aim of making Europe a knowledge-based society through the production and use of advanced technologies (CEC, 2010).

Scientific debate on the role of knowledge and innovation as strategic elements of the competitiveness of regions and countries has always strongly supported this policy framework. The interpretative approach adopted in the 1980s emphasized the importance of pervasive and horizontal functions such as R&D and higher education for the process of knowledge creation and innovation diffusion. 'Scientific regions' hosting large and well-known scientific institutions, were studied deeply, and relationships between these institutions and the industrial fabric were analysed, with some disappointments regarding an expected but not often visible direct linkage (MacDonald, 1987; Monk *et al.*, 1988; Massey *et al.*, 1992; Storey and Tether, 1998). Indicators of

R&D inputs (such as public and private research investment and personnel) and increasingly indicators of R&D output (such as patenting activities) were studied in order to understand the commitment of firms and territories to knowledge, regarded as a necessary long-term precondition for continuing innovation (Dasgupta and Stiglitz, 1980; Antonelli, 1989; Griliches, 1990). This approach equated knowledge with scientific research, on the assumption that the presence of local knowledge produced by research centres and universities was a necessary and sufficient condition for increasing the innovation capacities of local firms that were fed by local spillovers.

The difficulties encountered in achieving the Lisbon Agenda stimulated reflections on the need for a new innovation policy style and scope by a group of scholars, who stressed the need to replace a thematically and regionally neutral and generic innovation policy—a 'one-size-fits-all approach'—with a policy built on the smart specialization of R&D activities in different regions and on exploiting advantages stemming from specialized R&D concentrations (CEC, 2008; Foray, 2009).

These arguments seem rather persuasive. A smart specialization is a way out of the thematically/regionally neutral and generic orientation of R&D funding investments. Core regions can be seen as natural places for general-purpose technologies (GPT), which can achieve a critical mass of scientists and knowledge for achieving increasing returns on R&D, giving 'peripheral' regions the role of co-inventors of applications in their technological domain (Foray, 2009). Based on this logic, R&D funding investments become targeted in a thematic and regional sense: general-purpose technological R&D investments find their most efficient destination in core regions, while R&D funding in specific innovation applications is allocated to peripheral regions, each fulfilling a specific role based on its comparative advantage in a knowledge-production hierarchy (Pontikakis *et al.*, 2009).

These recent reflections show that there is space for developing a further conceptual framework of analysis about the reasons for the failure of the Lisbon Agenda and on possible new innovation policy styles. What is required in particular is a new conceptual framework on the determinants of innovation capability at regional level that goes beyond some of the simplified assumptions that still accompany even the most recent analyses. In particular, the notions of a simple equation between knowledge and scientific research, of a simple core–periphery dichotomy in R&D activities, and of R&D expenditure as the only way to boost innovation processes, require some additional thinking within a new conceptual framework that is able to overcome these limitations and to drive normative interventions towards thematically/regionally focused innovation policies.

Our discussion starts from the assumption that the presence of advanced sectors and advanced functions such as R&D and higher education are special features of only some of the possible innovation paths and, although they are important, cannot be considered as necessary or sufficient preconditions for innovation. Furthermore, emphasizing interaction among the different actors of knowledge development in itself as the crucial factor in knowledge creation and diffusion is not completely satisfactory.

Instead, all valid scientific contributions produced in the field of knowledge creation (Dasgupta and Stiglitz, 1980; Antonelli, 1989; Griliches, 1990) and of knowledge spillovers (Acs *et al.*, 1994; Audretsch and Feldman, 1996; Anselin *et al.*, 2000; Paci and Usai, 2009) can form the basis for a new conceptual framework aimed at interpreting the different patterns of territorial innovation, defined as a combination of *context conditions* and *specific modes of performing the different phases* of the innovation process. This article presents preliminary reflections on this.

The structure of the article is as follows. The next section presents a survey of the theoretical achievements in regional innovation and knowledge approaches and highlights the challenges that still remain. In the third section, I present a new conceptual approach that addresses these remaining challenges. Section four sets out the possible conceptual innovation patterns, while the concluding section considers the policy implications of such an approach.

Theoretical achievements in regional innovation approaches

Innovation diffusion at the regional level first attracted the interest of regional economists and geographers towards the end of the 1960s, when the neoclassical paradigm of innovation, as 'manna from heaven', being equally distributed among firms and in space, was questioned. These approaches viewed innovation as an exogenous event that propagates through specific territorial channels to generate a positive impact on local areas from outside. Analyses should therefore examine the territorial routes by which innovation reaches a particular area—routes formalized in models of the spatial diffusion of innovation, whose main feature consists in the epidemic nature of diffusion. The pure likelihood of contact between people who have already adopted an innovation and its potential adopters explains innovation diffusion in this model, which implicitly assumes that every potential adopter has the same opportunity to adopt the innovation, and that spatial variations in adoption can be attributed solely to information flows that spread territorially at different times (Hägerstrand, 1967) (see Table 1). According to this approach, information means innovation, and innovation means higher economic performance in a natural and undisputed short-circuit. The role of space in this theory is that of spatial friction to information flows. The latter arise naturally in large cities and then propagate through cities at the lower level of the urban hierarchy owing to infrastructures and economic flows.

The notion that the spatial diffusion of innovation is influenced less by geographic distance among adopters than by economic distance was introduced into the model of spatial innovation by economists: the amount of productive activity in an area, and the latter's levels of income, consumption and investment, can straightforwardly explain the greater receptiveness of an adoption area (Griliches, 1957; Mansfield, 1961; Metcalfe, 1981). Moreover, empirical analyses developed more recently in different technological trajectories, namely robotics and ICT development, bear witness to the importance of the stage of economic development for interpreting technological penetration rates, speed of adoption and the historic moment of first adoption (Camagni, 1985; Capello, 1988).

When the need for an endogenous approach to regional innovation was felt, the conditions for innovation creation came to the fore as a second stage of reflection. In this literature, innovation was interpreted as being produced by high-tech goods or services, on the assumption that there is an immediate link between invention and innovation within individual firms (or their territories) operating in advanced sectors. R&D facilities, in fact, are strictly linked to production facilities, while firms tend to cluster in high-tech districts in order to take advantage of all sorts of proximity externalities. According to this approach, the mere presence of high-tech sectors was a condition for a region to innovate. The spatial conditions behind local innovation were empirically identified. Externalities arising from the presence of advanced education facilities were invoked to explain innovation capacity, while international accessibility, advanced urban atmosphere, and traditional industrial competencies under reorientation (Malecki, 1980; Saxenian, 1996) were also suggested.

When many knowledge-based advances were actually achieved by 'traditional' sectors—such as textiles and car production—in their path towards rejuvenation, it became evident that the 'sector-based' approach was not sufficient, and knowledge creation became the main aspect of scientific interest. Conceptual efforts were made to explain the different regional capacities in generating knowledge.

A first wave of studies mainly interpreted the capacity of a region to create knowledge owing to the presence of pervasive and horizontal functions such as R&D and higher education (MacDonald, 1987; Monk et al., 1988; Massey et al., 1992; Storey

TABLE 1 Alternative approaches to knowledge and innovation studies

	Innovation Diffusion	Innovation Creation	Knowledge Creation		Knowledge Diffusion	
			Functional Approach	Cognitive Approach	Spatial Approach	Evolutionary Approach
Aim of the theory	Identification of the spatial channels supporting innovation diffusion	Identification of the reasons for local innovation creation	Identification of the reasons for local knowledge creation		Identification of the reasons for local knowledge diffusion	
Knowledge-innovation linkage	Information-adoption short-circuit	Invention-innovation short-circuit	Spin-offs, spatial spillovers	Collective learning, local synergies; entrepreneurship	Spin-offs, spatial spillovers	Common cognitive codes
From innovation to performance	Adoption-performance linkage	Radical innovation, Schumpeterian profits	Technological breakthrough, royalties on patents	Continuing innovation, productivity increases	Knowledge-performance linkage	
Location of regions	Regions along the urban hierarchy	Advanced regions	Scientific regions	Milieux; learning regions	Networking regions	
Role of space	Barrier to information diffusion	Proximity economies, specialization advantages	Agglomeration economies	Uncertainty reduction, relational capital	Proximity economies	
Period	From the end of the 1960s to the 1970s	From the middle of the 1980s	From the end of the 1980s to the end of 1990s	From the end of the 1980s to the end of the 1990s	From the middle of the 1990s onwards	From the middle of the 2000s onwards
Key references	Hägerstrand, 1952; Griliches, 1957; Mansfield, 1961; Metcalfe, 1981; Camagni, 1985; Capello, 1988	Malecki, 1980; Saxenian, 1996	MacDonald, 1987; Monk et al., 1988; Massey et al., 1992; Storey and Tether, 1998	Camagni, 1991; Perrin, 1995; Capello, 1999; Keeble & Wilkinson, 1999; Lundvall & Johnson, 1994; Cappellin, 2003a	Acs et al., 1994; Audretsch & Feldman, 1996; Anselin et al., 2000	Rallet & Torre, 1995; Boschma, 2005; Capello, 2009

SOURCES: author's own research

and Tether, 1998). The link between knowledge creation and innovation was interpreted as resulting from a sort of division of labour between R&D/higher education facilities on the one hand, and innovating firms on the other. Their interaction produced academic spinoffs or knowledge spillovers flowing from the former to the latter, which were subject to strong distance decay effects (Acs *et al.*, 1994; Audretsch and Feldman, 1996; Anselin *et al.*, 2000).

At the beginning of the 1990s, knowledge creation was studied from a different perspective, whereby the degree of knowledge creation by a region was mainly based on its cognitive capability (Foray, 2000). The emphasis in this approach was on interaction, synergy and cooperation among local actors as the main source of collective learning processes, and therefore of knowledge creation. Areas, or local milieus, as they are called, were pointed to as the loci for the construction of knowledge (Camagni, 1991; Perrin, 1995; Capello, 1999; Keeble and Wilkinson, 1999; 2000; Cappellin, 2003a) through network relations (long-distance, selective relationships), interaction, creativity and recombination capability, nourished by spatial proximity and atmosphere effects.

The 'learning' region was also identified as the place where such cognitive processes play a crucial role to combine existing but dispersed know-how, interpretations of market needs, and information flows with intellectual artefacts such as theories and models, allowing the exchange of experiences and cooperation (Lundvall and Johnson, 1994).

The cognitive approach explicitly highlights the link between knowledge and innovation adoption as being the result of a link between knowledge and entrepreneurship. The ensuing idea posited is that investments in knowledge by incumbent firms and research organizations such as universities will generate entrepreneurial opportunities, because not all of the new knowledge will be pursued and commercialized by the incumbent firms. The 'knowledge filter' (Acs *et al.*, 2004) refers to the extent to which new knowledge remains un-commercialized by the organization creating that knowledge. It is these residual ideas that generate the opportunity for entrepreneurship. The capabilities of economic agents within the region to access and absorb such knowledge and ultimately utilize it to generate entrepreneurial activity are not assumed to be invariant with respect to geographical space, contrary to what had always been thought. In particular, diversified areas, in which differences among people result in different appraisals of any new idea, were expected to gain more from new knowledge.

Therefore, in the 1990s and early 2000s, the two approaches to knowledge creation were set aside, leaving space for a debate on how knowledge spreads at the local level. Spatial proximity was initially seen as the main factor for explaining the channels through which knowledge spreads. Based on the original contributions on innovation diffusion made in the 1960s by the geographer Hägerstrand, the new theory of spatial spillovers explained that the pure likelihood of contact between a knowledge creator (an R&D laboratory) and a potential recipient (a firm, a university, another R&D centre) was the main vehicle of knowledge transmission, based on a pure epidemic logic (Acs *et al.*, 1994; Audretsch and Feldman, 1996; Anselin *et al.*, 2000). The theory of technological spillovers developed in the 1990s linked the spatial concentration of innovative activities with the increasing returns that concentrated location generates on those innovative activities themselves. According to this theory, cross-fertilizations, dynamic interactions between customers and suppliers, and synergies between research centres and local production units occur within circumscribed geographical areas such as highly specialized metropolitan areas. They do so as a result of the rapid exchange of information and transmission of tacit knowledge made possible by face-to-face encounters. In a concentrated location, the beneficial effects of a firm's research and development activities are not confined within the boundaries of firms: they 'spill over' into the surrounding environment, to the advantage of innovative activity by other firms.

A large number of empirical analyses, mainly econometric, successfully measured the technological spillovers and knowledge advantages enjoyed by spatially concentrated firms. Space is purely geographical in this approach: it is the physical distance among actors, a pure physical container of spillover effects that come about—according to the epidemiological logic adopted—simply as a result of contact among actors, the probability of which increases in a limited geographical area.

The simplicity of this approach soon became evident, and a vigorous debate arose about the need to enrich spatial proximity with cognitive aspects to differentiate the absorptive capacity of different actors within a region. Knowledge creation and innovation, it was argued, are in fact cumulative and localized outcomes of search (Antonelli, 1989); as a result, the cognitive bases of actors and organizations and their potential for learning differ substantially. Different concepts of proximity, from social, to institutional, cultural and cognitive, were added as interpretative elements in knowledge spillovers, enriching the conceptual tools for interpreting knowledge diffusion (Rallet and Torre, 1995; Boschma, 2005; Capello, 2009; Boix-Domenech and Soler-Marco, 2017).

These approaches are all interesting per se, and over time they have provided a rich scientific apparatus for analyses of how knowledge and innovation take place in space. Testifying to their richness are the multiple scientific paradigms on which they draw—economic geography, evolutionary theory of innovation, neo-Schumpeterian theories on local development, evolutionary geography—to enrich the understanding of local innovation processes.

However, they have a feature in common that represents the limits of current scientific know-how on local knowledge and innovation: all these theories consider *one particular phase* of the innovation process, often interpreted as the crucial one—either knowledge creation, innovation creation, innovation diffusion or knowledge diffusion. Some theories even interpret knowledge and innovation as coinciding processes, taking it for granted that if knowledge is created locally, this inevitably leads to innovation—or if innovation takes place, this is attributable to local knowledge availability. A similar short-circuit is assumed between knowledge/innovation and performance, with the expectation of productivity increases in all cases in which a creative effort, a learning process and an interactive and cooperative atmosphere characterize the local economy.

Instead, factors that enhance the implementation of new knowledge may be quite different from the factors that stimulate invention and innovation. Invention, innovation and diffusion are not necessarily intertwined, not even at the local level. The firms and individuals leading an invention are not necessarily also leaders in innovation or in the widespread diffusion of new technologies. The real world is full of examples of this kind: the fax machine, first developed in Germany, was turned into a successful worldwide product by Japanese companies. Similarly, the anti-lock braking system (ABS) was invented by US car makers but became prominent primarily owing to adoption by German automotive suppliers (Licht, 2009; Boix-Domenech and Soler-Marco, 2017).

Moreover, it is by no means always true that technological catch-up shows a positive correlation with economic convergence; the strong economic growth performance of Eastern European countries up to 2008 was certainly not related to knowledge-economy growth, as these countries (and their regions) witnessed no technological catch-up in those years. Regional economic growth is weakly related to different scientific indicators, both of input (R&D) and of output (patenting activity). This has been demonstrated by a simple correlation run on a sample of 286 NUTS2 regions (basic regions for the application of regional policies) in Europe between regional growth in the years 2006 to 2008 and R&D on GDP in 2007, which showed a negative (and significant) value (–0.33); the value of the Pearson correlation index remained negative and significant (–0.23) when the correlation was measured between regional growth in the years 2006 to 2008 and patents per capita for the years 2005 to 2006.

All this suggests that innovation can be the result of different patterns, and of different modes of performing each phase of the innovation process. The variety of innovation modes explains the failure of a 'one-size-fits-all' policy for innovation, such as the thematically/regionally neutral and generic R&D incentives expected to develop a knowledge economy everywhere. On the contrary, innovation modes typical of each specific area have to be identified so that ad hoc and targeted innovation policies can be devised.

Territorial patterns of innovation: a proposed definition and a framework

There certainly seems to be space for further conceptual reflections that help policymakers devise effective policies to launch European competitiveness based on a knowledge economy. In particular, the paradigmatic jump in interpreting regional innovation processes today stems from the capacity to take the single approaches developed for the interpretation of knowledge and innovation and use them to build a conceptual framework interpreting not a single phase of the innovation process, but the different modes of performing the different phases of the innovation process, and highlighting the context conditions (internal and external to the region) that accompany each innovation pattern. In other words, regional innovation follows differentiated innovation patterns obtained by separating the various steps of a knowledge–invention–innovation process and by recombining them in space, following a relational logic of exchange of knowledge (Camagni, 2015; Capello and Lenzi, 2017). In this way, it will be possible to consider alternative situations in which innovation builds on internal knowledge, or in which local creativity allows, even when local knowledge is lacking, an innovative application thanks to knowledge developed elsewhere and acquired via scientific linkages, or in which innovation is made possible by an imitative process of innovation outside the region.

This new interpretative paradigm—the innovation patterns paradigm emphasizing complex interplay between phases of the innovation process and spatial context or territorial conditions—adds two new elements to the previous theoretical paradigms.

First of all, it disentangles knowledge from innovation, addressing the two as different (and subsequent) phases of an innovation process; thus, each phase requires specific local elements for its development and a different natural location depending on the presence of the factors that support their development. This approach rejects the assumption of an invention–innovation short-circuit taking place inside individual firms (or their territories) operating in advanced sectors, as well as an immediate interaction between R&D/higher education facilities, on the one hand, and innovating firms on the other, brought about by spatial proximity. The necessarily temporal sequentiality between knowledge source and innovation, and between innovation and economic performance—which we refer to here as the 'linear model of innovation'—has been heavily criticized because it is rooted in the notion that innovation can be analysed as a 'rational' and 'orderly' process (Edgerton, 2004). However, I strongly believe that, first, in many cases, scientific advance is a major source of innovation, while fully recognizing that this is neither a necessary nor a sufficient condition for innovation to take place. Secondly, an alternative model, in which 'everything depends on everything else', with no specific structure of the innovative system fully and clearly specified, does not help us generate a conceptual analytical model that is able interpret the systemic, dynamic and interactive nature of innovation. And thirdly, self-reinforcing feedbacks from innovation to knowledge and from economic growth to innovation and knowledge play an important role in innovation processes. The impact of science on innovation does not merely reside in the creation of new opportunities to be exploited by firms, but rather in increasing research productivity and therefore returns on R&D through solving and exploiting technical problems, eliminating research directions that have been proven wrong from a scientific perspective, and providing new research technologies (Nelson, 1959; Mowery and Rosenberg, 1998; Balconi et al., 2010). I therefore strongly support the concept of a 'fragmented (spatially diversified) linear model of innovation', in which the pattern of innovation is a linearization, or partial block linearization, of an innovation process in which feedbacks, interconnections and non-linearities, in the form of increasing returns, play a prominent role.

Secondly, the concept of 'patterns of innovation' calls for identification of the context conditions, both internal and external to the region, that support the various innovation phases. These context conditions become integral to the definition of a *territorial pattern of innovation*. In this sense, the approach does not look for territorial capabilities that allow territories (in general) to exploit innovation and knowledge, such as the presence of human capital. The conceptual framework looks for the territorial specificities (context conditions) that are behind different modes of performing the different phases of the innovation process and which become integral parts of a territorial pattern of innovation.

An integrated conceptual framework such as this identifies the local conditions that guarantee: the shift from local knowledge to innovation; the acquisition of external knowledge to innovate locally; and the acquisition of external innovation for imitation with different degrees of creativity. It builds on the different modes of performing innovation as well as on the context conditions that guarantee the different phases of the innovation process. The conceptual effort required, therefore, is to identify the combination of context conditions that accompany each phase of the innovation process and give rise to alternative patterns of innovation.

A territorial pattern of innovation is therefore defined as a combination of context conditions and of specific modes of performing the different phases of the innovation process. The basic elements of a territorial pattern of innovation are:

1 *Agents/collective actors.* In a territorial pattern of innovation, agents in regions are identified as collective actors, where innovation and knowledge processes take place across regions. Local firms and non-corporate entities are the referent agents where intra-regional flows of innovation and knowledge are considered.

2 *Phases of the innovation process: knowledge/innovation/performance.* An innovation pattern conceptualizes the innovation process as starting from a knowledge source, which is then transmitted to other agents (locally or among regions) and turned into an innovative application. When innovation has taken place, this leads to increasing productivity and economic performance.

3 *Territorial conditions for local interaction.* As the evolutionary theory of innovation has stated since the 1980s, firms do not innovate in isolation; therefore, innovation must be seen as a collective process involving other firms as well as a number of other non-corporate entities, such as universities, research centres, government agencies, and so on (Nelson and Winter, 1977; Dosi, 1982; Nelson and Winter, 1982). The behaviour and specific nature of these agents and, more importantly, the relationships among them, have a crucial influence on how an innovation process works and performs. The mechanisms that facilitate interaction among firms and non-corporate agencies at the local level reside, according to our approach, in the territorial conditions of the local area. The capacity of actors to interact, to cooperate and to share a path towards innovation is, in our approach, embedded in a region's socioeconomic context, which generates and supports collective learning processes at the local level, or allows interactive effects to take place between two socio-economic contexts that share common social values, a similar scientific background and a cognitive base. These arguments have been developed in terms of neo-Schumpeterian regional innovation theories that highlight space as a source of dynamic externalities, and as a generator of collective learning that reduces the uncertainty and risks associated with innovation processes.

4   *Territorial conditions for knowledge and innovation diffusion between regions.* A territorial pattern of innovation highlights in particular the conditions that ensure that a region will interact with other regions, thus attracting knowledge and innovation that is not present locally. In line with evolutionary economic geography theory, which applies interdisciplinary insights from social, cultural and political sciences to explain interaction in innovation processes, these conditions cannot be looked for only in spatial proximity; they require a wider interpretative base for knowledge spillovers. While a spatial perspective can explain knowledge flows within a region, with clear distance decay effects, its application at the interregional level loses any conceptual meaning and merely takes on a gravity-type approach. Instead, wider use of 'proximity effects', such as cultural and cognitive proximity advantages, may be extremely useful for our understanding of interaction among regions. The networking approach to innovation through long-distance cooperation among different places finds explanations for it in the cognitive and social nature of the different areas involved.

Different kinds of territorial patterns of innovation
–   Differentiated patterns of innovation
A territorial pattern of innovation is made up of a combination of territorial specificities (context conditions) that lie behind different modes of performing the different phases of the innovation process. Among all possible combinations, the most interesting are:

- An *endogenous innovation pattern* in a scientific network, where local conditions are all present to support the creation of knowledge, its local diffusion and transformation into innovation and its widespread local adoption so that higher growth rates can be achieved. Given the complex nature of knowledge today, this pattern is expected to be tightly linked with the creation of knowledge with other regions, and therefore belonging to an international scientific network.

- A *creative application pattern*, characterized by the presence of creative actors who are interested and curious enough to look for knowledge that is lacking within a region in the external world, and creative enough to apply external knowledge to local innovation needs.

- An *imitative innovation pattern*, where actors base their innovation capacity on imitative processes that can be applied with differing degrees of creativity to adapt an already existing innovation.

Each territorial pattern of innovation is characterized by different innovative models and by different outcomes from interregional cooperation; each also requires different territorial preconditions. Therefore, each territorial pattern of innovation has a natural place where it may take place (see Table 2). Finally, each pattern has specific innovation policy aims (Table 2), as explicitly mentioned in the subsections that follow.

–   Endogenous innovation patterns in a scientific network
A straightforward territorial pattern of innovation is an endogenous one, in a situation in which a region is endowed with local conditions for knowledge creation and for turning knowledge into innovation so as to guarantee a productivity increase and regional growth. This model relies on specific *internal context conditions* that explain knowledge creation and diffusion, as well as innovation, by looking at the internal structural conditions of a region.

Knowledge creation is in general dependent on an urban environment where material and non-material elements supporting scientific knowledge find a natural location. Table 3 summarizes the main elements identified as the sources of knowledge

TABLE 2   Characteristics of the different innovation patterns

Characteristics	Endogenous Innovation Pattern in a Scientific Network	Creative Application Pattern	Imitative Innovation Pattern
Knowledge/technology	Basic, general-purpose technologies (GPT)	Applied technologies	Creative imitation
Innovative model	Supply-driven	Supply-driven	Supply-driven
Role of the region in the innovation process	Active role	Active role	Passive role
Outcome of interregional cooperation	Knowledge creation	Creative innovation adoption	Innovation diffusion
Territorial preconditions behind interregional flows of knowledge and innovation	Territorial receptivity	Territorial creativity	Territorial attractiveness
Natural regional context associated with the innovation pattern	Metropolitan regions	Second-ranked urban regions	Catching-up regions
Innovation policy aims	Maximum return on R&D investment	Maximum return on co-inventing applications	Maximum return on imitation

SOURCE: author's own research

TABLE 3   Urban elements and knowledge creation

Source of Urban Increasing Returns	Indivisibility (agglomeration)	Synergy (proximity)
Type of element supporting knowledge: material	Fixed social capital; high-level functions	City as a node of national and international transport networks
Type of elements supporting knowledge: non-material	Large markets of inputs; large market of qualified human capital; diversified productive systems; creative capital accumulation	High availability of information; transcoding system of knowledge and information; R&D and higher-education integration

SOURCE: author's own research

creation. These are material and non-material, stemming from indivisibility and synergies, that is, from agglomeration and proximity—the two elements characterizing urban environments:

- urban size per se (McCann, 2004), especially concerning the creation of large human capital pools and wide labour markets (Lucas, 1988; Glaeser, 1998; Burgalassi *et al.*, 2016);

- diversity concerning the variety of activities and the possibility for specializations in thin subsectors and specific types of production, owing to the size of the overall urban market (Jacobs, 1969; 1984; Quigley, 1998);

- contacts and interactions allowing face-to-face encounters, which reduce transaction costs (Scott and Angel, 1987; Storper and Scott, 1995);

- synergies owing to proximity, complementarity and trust (Camagni, 1991; 1999); in more formalized models, these same effects stem from the complexity of the urban system and synergetics (Haken, 1993);

- a reduced risk of unemployment for households owing to thick and diverse urban labour markets (Veltz, 1993);

- trans-territorial linkages emerging from the international gateway role of large cities, which are crucial, particularly in a globalizing world (Sassen, 1994).

The literature has not confined itself to the identification of territorial factors in knowledge creation. Studies have explored the *territorial elements* that explain the capacity of a region to use its knowledge for innovative activities. In particular, creativity and recombination capability to translate basic or applied scientific knowledge into innovative applications require a relational space where functional and hierarchical economic and social interactions are embedded in a geographical space. Geographical proximity (agglomeration economies, district economies) and cognitive proximity (shared behavioural codes, common culture, mutual trust and sense of belonging) guarantee the socio-economic and geographical substrate on which collective learning processes can be incorporated, mainly owing to two main processes (Camagni and Capello, 2002): high mobility of professionals and skilled labour—between firms, but internal to the local labour market defined by the district or the city, where this mobility is maximal, and intense cooperative relations among local actors, and in particular customer–supplier relationships in production, design, research and, finally, knowledge creation.

The translation of knowledge into innovation is facilitated by interaction and cooperation, by the reduction of uncertainty (especially concerning the behaviour of competitors and partners), of information asymmetries (thus reducing mutual suspicion among partners) and of the probability of opportunistic behaviour under the threat of social sanctioning (Camagni, 1991; 2004)— all these elements have been confirmed by various regional economics schools (Bellet *et al.*, 1993; Rallet and Torre, 1995; Cappellin, 2003b).

The foregoing discussion on the role of territorial variables and the centrality of local conditions should not be taken as suggesting a return to an anti-historical localism or territorial autarchy. On the contrary, local milieus should be perfectly accessible, open and receptive to external flows of information, knowledge, technologies, organizational and cognitive models, and always ready to combine local knowledge and external knowledge anew. What is really meant by referring to the importance of local territories is the fact that, while some important production factors such as financial capital, general information, consolidated technologies and codified knowledge are today readily available virtually everywhere, the ability to organize these 'pervasive' factors into continuously innovative production processes and products is by no means pervasive and generalized, but instead exists selectively in some places, where tacit knowledge is continuously created, exchanged and utilized, and business ideas find their way to real markets (Camagni and Capello, 2009).

In this respect, the knowledge filter theory of entrepreneurship put forward by Acs *et al.* (1994) envisages an explicit link between knowledge and entrepreneurship within spatial contexts, in which entrepreneurs are interpreted as the innovative adopters of new knowledge. This theory posits that investments in knowledge by incumbent firms and research organizations such as universities will generate entrepreneurial (innovation) opportunities because not all of the new knowledge will be pursued and commercialized by the incumbent firms. The knowledge filter (Acs *et al.*, 2004) refers to the extent to which new knowledge remains un-commercialized by the organization creating that knowledge. Residual ideas are those that generate opportunities for entrepreneurship. The interesting aspect of this theory is that the capabilities of economic agents within the region to access and absorb such knowledge and ultimately utilize it to generate entrepreneurial activity is no longer assumed to be invariant with respect to geographical space, contrary to earlier thought. In particular, diversified areas in which differences among people foster alternative appraisals of a given information set (resulting in different appraisal of new ideas) are expected to gain more from new knowledge.

Notwithstanding internal capacities to generate knowledge, given the complex and systemic nature of knowledge and innovation, in most cases regions reinforce and complement their internal knowledge with external knowledge. This process may happen through diffusive, mostly unintentional, knowledge patterns based on spatial proximity ('spatial linkages'), which are subject to strong distance decay effects, as well as through intentional relations based on a-spatial networks or non-spatially mediated channels ('a-spatial linkages') that may take place both over short and long distances, depending on the organization of forms of transfer and exchange of information and knowledge other than pure spatial proximity.

An innovation pattern of this kind can be labelled an 'endogenous innovation pattern in a scientific network' (see Figure 1). In the face of a territorial pattern of innovation of this kind, the natural innovation policy aim is to achieve a maximum return on R&D investments—an aim that emphasizes the importance of a specialization in R&D at the European level that guarantees a critical mass of researchers, equipment and R&D resources. This critical mass is interpreted as crucial to attaining the desired goal—effective research work and achieving an acceptable research performance (see Table 2).

Based on the indivisibility rule associated with research activities in general, and with general-purpose technologies in particular, the idea of a smart specialization in R&D activity has permeated the innovation economic debate, with a call for a European Research Area to enable agglomeration processes to occur and to give rise to centres of excellence. This can only be done within an integrated research space, where knowledge is exchanged within a solid and efficient network among centres of excellence that become regions specialized in basic inventions. A region exhibiting 'an endogenous innovation pattern in a scientific network' can become one of these centres; the specialization of each centre in general-purpose technology research activities can become a policy mission.

The innovative model in this territorial innovation pattern is a typical supply-driven model: from scientific activities, from an invention, the subsequent co-invention of applications leads to a number of innovations mainly by inventors and co-inventors of applications.

The condition for a region to acquire knowledge from outside its boundaries can be regarded as *territorial receptivity* (see Table 4), broadly defined as the capability of the region to interpret and use external knowledge for complementary research and science advances, or more generally the absorptive capacity of a region *à la* Cohen and Levinthal (1990). More specifically, receptivity is made up of different aspects according to the nature of knowledge and its diffusion. If a modern view of knowledge is adopted, learning and interaction processes are put at the forefront, and knowledge is considered to be complex semi-public or cooperative. Its diffusion is subject to strong spatial barriers and follows largely unpredictable creative processes. Knowledge creation and learning often depend on combining diverse, complementary capabilities of heterogeneous agents.

Given these characteristics, receptivity is first of all dependent on the *relational capability* required to ensure that a region is in general made up of individuals, firms and institutions oriented towards cooperation and synergy nourished by trust and a sense of belonging, to guarantee collective and interactive learning processes.

Moreover, spatial proximity facilitates the overcoming of spatial friction; the exchange of knowledge, mainly tacit knowledge, seems to be subject to strong distance decay effects. *Spatial proximity* to a region may therefore be another component of receptivity. However, this kind of proximity is not enough. The complexity of science and knowledge evolution, together with the bounded rationality that generates cognitive constraints on actors, induces economic agents to search in close proximity to their existing knowledge base, thus providing opportunities and setting constraints on further improvement (Boschma, 2005). Knowledge evolution therefore takes place in a cumulative way, localized around a technological paradigm, in cooperation among

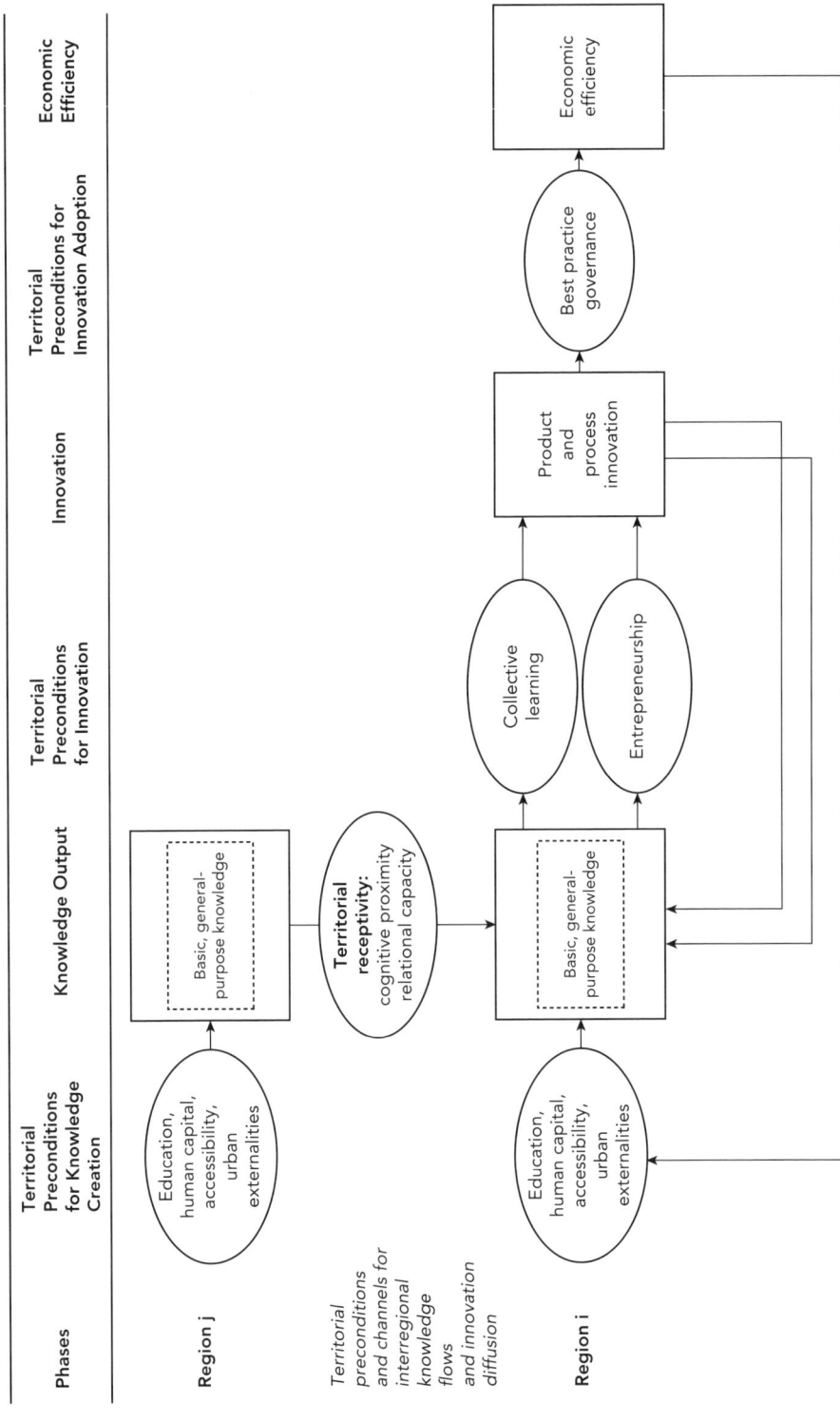

FIGURE 1 An endogenous innovative pattern in a scientific network (*source:* author's own work, originally published in Capello, 2012)

TABLE 4   Preconditions for the interregional exchange of knowledge and innovation

	Territorial Receptivity	Territorial Creativity	Territorial Attractiveness
Preconditions to receive	Relational capacity	Openness to innovation	Limited labour costs
Preconditions to exchange	Social proximity; cognitive proximity	Technological proximity	Income differentials
Channels for exchange	Scientific networks; co-patenting; migration of inventors	Participation in industrial associations	Foreign direct investments (FDI)

SOURCE: author's own research

actors with a strong complementarity within a set of shared competencies. For this reason, a third component of territorial receptivity is *cognitive proximity* among regions, which is necessary for one region to acquire knowledge from another, and to understand and use it in a creative way (see Table 4).

All these features are more easily found in metropolitan areas. The latter are the main sites of innovative activity, the 'incubators' of new knowledge: cities are the principal centres of research, given their large pools of expertise and the availability of advanced services (finance and insurance) that are ready to carry the risk of any innovative activity. The fuel for continuing knowledge and innovation processes in cities consists in the density of external, particularly international, linkages maintained and developed by individuals, groups, associations, firms and institutions—what is increasingly called 'relational capital' (Camagni, 1999)—coupled with a large diversity of competencies, based on which complementary knowledge can find common cognitive ground (Burger and Meijers, 2016; Glaeser *et al.*, 2016).

–   Creative application patterns

Reality has shown that some regions are latecomers and mainly users of basic general-purpose technologies. Experience has also shown that being a latecomer in a core technology has serious long-lasting implications that are difficult to reverse. First and foremost, technological leaders are enabled to expand into new science and technology fields and create the conditions for reiterating such processes in further emerging science and technology areas.

However, in reality, there are many examples of invention and innovation not being intertwined. Factors that enhance the implementation of new knowledge can differ quite widely from factors that stimulate invention and innovation. Invention, innovation and diffusion are not necessarily intertwined, not even at the local level.

The linkage between basic knowledge and innovation is therefore in many cases not evident, and there are many regions in which innovation takes place on the basis of basic knowledge acquired from outside, and of specific know-how in local application sectors. In such a case, innovation activity stems from a merger of general-purpose technology knowledge derived from networking with leading regions and local specialized knowledge in the region (Figure 2). In this pattern, a particular case consists of investments in the 'co-invention of applications'—that is, development of applications in one or several important domains of the regional economy—without embarking on expensive basic R&D activities with an insufficient critical mass of human and financial resources (Foray, 2009; Foray *et al.*, 2009).

In this innovation pattern, regions must develop original and unique knowledge domains based on their productive vocations; therefore, regions must discover the research and innovation areas in which they can hope to excel. This discovery has been made by firms that have to achieve combinations of technologies with various elements of the value chain, and need to construct very different and unpredicted specific niches of competitive advantage. In this sense this innovation pattern is supply-driven, as it

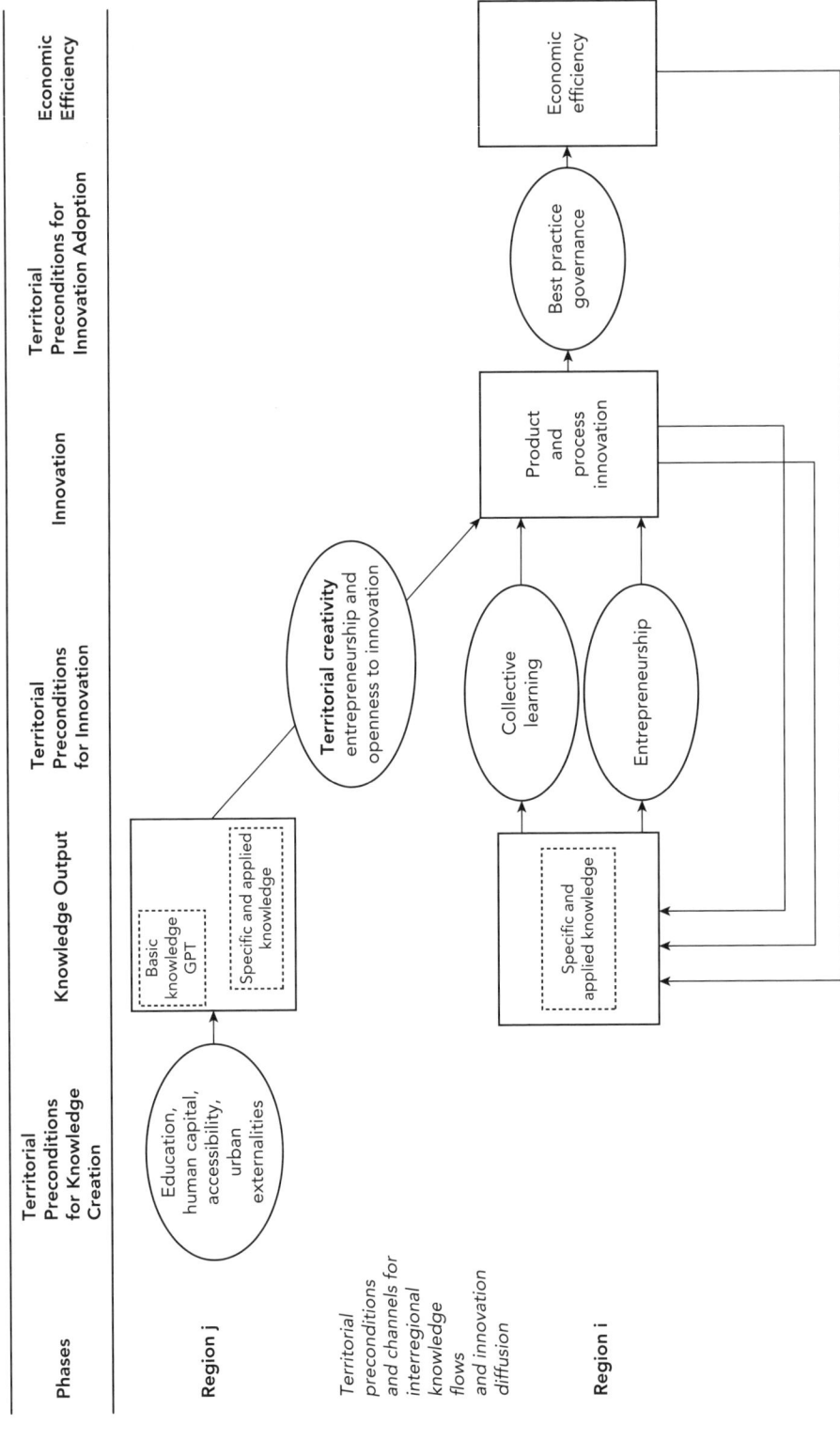

FIGURE 2 A creative application pattern (*source: author's own work, originally published in Capello, 2012*)

depends on the creativity and recombination capability of potential innovating firms, which—owing to their internal specific knowledge—identify a gap in a possible application of general-purpose technologies and devote their creative efforts to closing that gap.

This does not necessarily mean that regions must specialize in one or a few knowledge domains. In a creative innovation pattern, the evolutionary trajectories of innovation can either be specialized, or they can progress by means of the evolution of 'platforms' combining many technologies. But they can also be the result of differentiated technological fields within which local firms operate. The features shared by all these possible forms in which this innovation pattern can take place is that the move from invention to innovation resides in creativity, recombination capability, the ability to simultaneously identify new needs and the right basic technology of local actors, and the ability to recombine local knowledge and external knowledge anew. In this sense, the innovation process results from the active role collective actors play in a region, especially potential innovators/adopters. This leads to innovation despite a lack of ability to create knowledge.

The maximum return on R&D investments is not the natural policy aim of this pattern; the innovation policy aim in this case is maximum return on co-inventing applications (that is, typical Schumpeterian profits), which depends closely on the ability of regions to change rapidly in response to external stimuli (such as the emergence of a new technology) —in other words, it depends on the ability to promote a 'shift' from old to new uses.

The networking activity between scientific core regions in which basic knowledge is created and co-innovating application regions finds an economic rationale in the dynamic feedback loops that link invention and application. Invention gives rise to the co-invention of applications, which in turn increase the return on subsequent inventions. When this virtuous cycle takes place, a long-term dynamic develops, consisting of large-scale investments in R&D that provide high levels of social and private marginal rates of return. Myriad economically important innovations result from the co-invention of applications; in addition, the amount of application co-invention increases the size of the general technology market and improves the economic return on invention activities relating to it (Foray, 2009).

The territorial conditions necessary for this innovation pattern to occur are linked to the concept of *territorial creativity*. This creative process is driven by entrepreneurs who are able to access and absorb the knowledge produced in the world and ultimately utilize it to invent co-applications—which happens more readily in a context that is open to innovation and nourishes itself with external knowledge that is useful for its local purposes and needs. Regions with similar technological vocations are most likely to interact in this kind of innovative pattern. Participation in industrial associations and/or the exploitation of external experts are the channels through which knowledge flows into the region (see Table 4).

Regions in which this innovation pattern finds a natural location are second-ranked urban regions characterized by high accessibility to leading metropolitan regions, with a local labour market fed by human capital generally formed in the first-ranking urban areas. But this pattern is also found in highly specialized areas, such as local districts where specialized knowledge cumulates over time and where the need for technological jumps is often resolved by merging specific local competencies with new basic knowledge from outside through what has been labelled 'trans-territorial networking' (Camagni, 1991). In the milieu innovation theory, these networking capabilities have always been regarded as a way to feed local specialized knowledge with technological novelties at the frontier, to adopt a new technological paradigm— something that is impossible to achieve by only cumulating specialized technological knowledge inside the area. The latter carries the inevitable risk of locking the area into a technological pattern that leaves no possible way out.

–   Imitative innovation patterns

Another innovation pattern that can be envisaged is an imitative innovation pattern, in regions that innovate because they receive innovation from outside. This can be considered an adoption innovation pattern, with technological developments at the local level resulting from a region's passive attitude—in terms of invention, knowledge creation and innovation generation—being fed by external innovation that has been developed elsewhere (see Figure 3).

This imitative pattern is not necessarily the least productive and least efficient innovation pattern; regions can be creative and rapid in the imitation phase if they deepen and improve productivity in existing uses, adapt existing uses to specific local needs, adjust products to local market interests, and forge innovation processes on local productive needs. Regions can also be more passive and imitate innovation from outside as conceived elsewhere.

Especially in the latter case, the right innovation policy for this pattern has nothing to do with efficiency in R&D activities, or with supporting co-inventing applications. In this case, policy actions must be devoted to achieving the maximum return on imitation. This aim is accomplished through creative adaptation of already existing innovation, that is, through adoption processes driven by creative ideas on how already existing innovation can be adapted to respond to local needs.

A channel through which innovation is acquired from the outside is, in fact, through foreign direct investments (FDI) (see Table 4). Products, processes, and managerial and organizational innovation embedded in large multinationals can be the channel through which innovation is brought into regions that are catching up. *Territorial attractiveness* is the precondition for regions to acquire external innovation; a large final market (market seeking) and/or labour cost competitiveness (efficiency seeking) are the preconditions for becoming attractive areas for FDI (Dunning, 2001; 2009; Cantwell, 2009). Regions exchanging innovation through FDI are regions with strong income differentials.

Imitative innovation patterns are typical of the Eastern countries that, over the past two decades, have shown significant economic performance mainly based on FDI and on the innovative capacity brought in by multinationals. The efficiency of this innovation pattern may be high, giving rise to strong positive feedback loops from growth to innovation through higher financial resources to invest in the innovation process. The high rate of growth may produce higher living standards and a higher quality of life in these countries. The ways in which innovation is attracted from outside the region may evolve into a second stage that includes other channels, such as mobility of inventors, the determinants for which are economic growth potential, expected high wages and high quality-of-life potential.

Conclusions and policy implications

The main idea put forward in this article is that pathways towards innovation and modernization can be differentiated among regions according to local specificities, and that this differentiation explains why a single overall strategy is unlikely to provide the right stimuli and incentives in these differing contexts.

The article commenced with the notion that R&D equals knowledge and that knowledge equals innovation. The distinction between, on the one hand, the process of invention in general-purpose basic technology, pervading different sectors horizontally once invention has turned into an innovation and, on the other hand, the process of inventing an application of basic knowledge in a specific sector innovating in new products and new market niches is vital for understanding current patterns of innovation. This becomes even more important if we consider that the factors that stimulate new knowledge, invention, innovation and innovation diffusion differ. Invention and innovation are not necessarily intertwined. This gives rise, even at the local level, to very

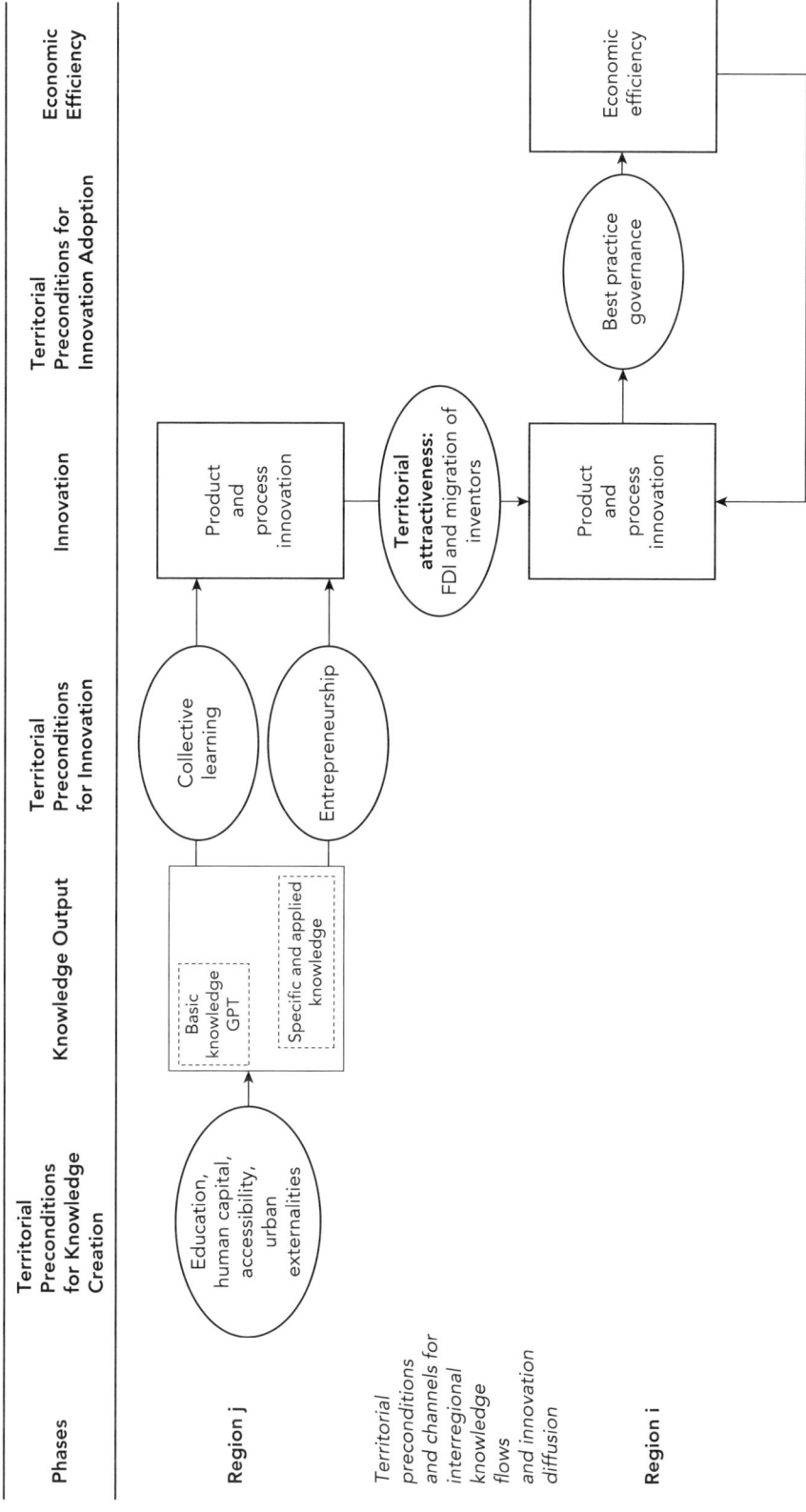

FIGURE 3   An imitative innovation pattern (*source:* author's own work, originally published in Capello, 2012)

different and multi-faceted situations. Some regions have the capacity to go through all phases of the 'linear model' from knowledge creation to innovation and growth, with all feedbacks that can be foreseen from growth to knowledge and innovation. Other regions reinforce this 'linear model' by exchanging knowledge with other regions to gain complementary assets through a scientific network. There is, however, a completely different situation too, in which regions innovate by combining their creative thinking with basic knowledge cumulated in other regions to develop co-inventing applications. Finally, another territorial innovation pattern consists of situations in which regions innovate by creative imitation of innovation developed elsewhere.

All these innovation patterns are the result of specific contextual conditions that support one innovation pattern more than another. A necessary condition for entering scientific networks is territorial receptivity, defined as a region's capacity to understand knowledge coming from outside—cognitive proximity, understood *à la* Boschma as the presence in a region of complementary knowledge within competencies shared with another region. Territorial creativity is a *sine qua non* for a region to exploit external knowledge in order to launch internal innovation processes driven by an entrepreneurial process of discovery. Territorial attractiveness is the local condition for imitating innovation from outside.

Importantly, what emerges clearly from this approach is that each territorial innovation pattern calls for specific ad hoc innovation policy goals: the maximum return on R&D investment can be the right goal for a region specialized in knowledge creation, but it cannot at the same time be the right policy goal for regions that innovate by exploiting external knowledge, or for regions that imitate innovation processes. For the former, the ad hoc policy goal is the maximum return on co-inventing applications, which happens when the region promotes changes in response to external stimuli (such as the emergence of a new technology). A maximum return on imitation, pushing towards creative imitation, is instead the right policy aim for regions that rely on external innovation processes. Each region must be able to discover its territorial innovation pattern, and only through awareness of the original and unique territorial innovation pattern can a region hope to excel at exploiting innovation efficiency, in line with the smart specialization strategy launched by the European Union (Foray *et al.*, 2009; Coffano and Foray, 2014; Capello and Kroll, 2016).

There is no pattern that is by definition superior to the others in terms of the efficiency and effectiveness of innovation in terms of growth; on the contrary, each territorial pattern may provide efficient use of research and innovation activities for generating growth. But this impression must be proven empirically.[1]

Roberta Capello, Department of Architecture, Built Environment and Construction Engineering, Politecnico di Milano, Piazza Leonardo da Vinci 32, 20131 Milan, Italy, roberta.capello@polimi.it

References

Acs, Z., D. Audretsch and M. Feldman (1994) R&D spillovers and recipient firm size. *Review of Economics and Statistics* 76.2, 336–40.

Acs, Z.J., D.B. Audretsch, P. Braunerhjelm and B. Carlsson (2004) The missing link: the knowledge filter and entrepreneurship in endogenous growth. Discussion Paper, Centre for Economic Policy Research (CEPR), London.

Anselin L., A. Varga and Z. Acs (2000) Geographic and sectoral characteristics of academic knowledge externalities. *Papers in Regional Science* 79.4, 435–43.

Antonelli, C. (1989) A failure inducement model of research and development expenditure: Italian evidence from the early 1980s. *Journal of Economic Behaviour and Organization* 12.2, 159–80.

Audretsch, D. and M. Feldman (1996) R&D spillovers and the geography of innovation and production. *American Economic Review* 86.3, 630–40.

Balconi, M., S. Brusoni and L. Orsenigo (2010) In defense of a linear model. *Research Policy* 39.1, 1–13.

Bellet, M., G. Colletis and Y. Lung (1993) Introduction au numero special sur economie et proximité [Introduction to the special issue on economy and proximity]. *Revue d'Économie Régionale et Urbaine* 3 (Special issue), 357–61.

1   An empirical analysis has identified the territorial patters of innovation (Capello and Lenzi, 2013a) and tested their efficiency (Capello and Lenzi, 2013b), concluding that there is no superior pattern.

Boschma, R. (2005) Proximity and innovation: a critical survey. *Regional Studies* 39.1, 61–74.

Boix-Domenech, R. and V. Soler-Marco (2017) Creative service industries and regional productivity. *Papers in Regional Science* 96.2, 261–79.

Burgalassi, D., S. Iommi and D. Marinari (2016) Dimensione e offerta funzionale nella crescita urbana: alcune evidenze nel periodo 2001–2011 [Aspects and functional size in urban growth: some evidence for the period 2001–2011]. *Scienze Regionali/Italian Journal of Regional Science* 15.2, 37–60.

Burger, M.J. and E.J. Meijers (2016) Agglomerations and the rise of urban network externalities. *Papers in Regional Science* 95.1, 5–15.

Camagni, R. (1985) Spatial diffusion of pervasive process innovation. *Papers of the Regional Science Association* 58, 83–95.

Camagni, R. (1991) Technological change, uncertainty and innovation networks: towards dynamic theory of economic space. In R. Camagni (ed.), *Innovation networks: spatial perspectives*, Belhaven-Pinter, London.

Camagni, R. (1999) The city as a milieu: applying the Gremi approach to urban development. *Revue d'Économie Régionale et Urbaine* 3 (Special issue), 591–606.

Camagni R. (2004) Uncertainty, social capital and community governance: the city as a milieu. In R. Capello and P. Nijkamp (eds.), *Urban dynamics and growth: advances in urban economics*, Elsevier, Amsterdam.

Camagni, R. (2015) Towards creativity-oriented innovation policies based on a hermeneutic approach to the knowledge–space nexus. In A. Cusinato and A. Philippopoulos-Mihalopoulos (eds.), *Knowledge-creating milieus in Europe: firms, cities, territories*, Springer, Berlin.

Camagni, R. and R. Capello (2002) Milieux innovateurs and collective learning: from concepts to measurement. In Z.J. Acs, H.L.F. de Groot and P. Nijkamp (eds.), *The emergence of the knowledge economy*, Springer, Berlin.

Camagni, R. and R. Capello (2009) Knowledge-based economy and knowledge creation: the role of space. In U. Fratesi and L. Senn (eds.), *Growth and competitiveness in innovative regions: balancing internal and external connections*, Springer, Berlin.

Cantwell, J. (2009) Location and multinational enterprise. *Journal of International Business Studies* 40.1, 35–41.

Capello, R. (1988) La diffusione spaziale dell'innovazione: il caso del servizio telefonico [The spatial diffusion of innovation: the case of telephone services]. *Economia e Politica Industriale* 58, 141–75.

Capello, R. (1999) Spatial transfer of knowledge in high-technology milieux: learning vs. collective learning processes. *Regional Studies* 33.4, 353–65.

Capello, R. (2009) Spatial spillovers and regional growth: a cognitive approach. *European Planning Studies* 17.5, 639–58.

Capello, R. (2012) Territorial patterns of innovation. In R. Capello, F. Ferlaino and P. Rizzi (eds.), *La città nell'economia della conoscenza* [The city in the knowledge economy], FrancoAngeli, Milan.

Capello, R. and H. Kroll (2016) From theory to practice in smart specialization strategy: emerging limits and possible future trajectories. *European Planning Studies* 24.8, 1393–406.

Capello, R. and C. Lenzi (2013a) Territorial patterns of innovation: a taxonomy of innovative regions in Europe. *The Annals of Regional Science* 51.1, 119–54.

Capello, R. and C. Lenzi (2013b) Territorial patterns of innovation and economic growth in European regions. *Growth and Change* 44.2, 195–227.

Capello, R. and C. Lenzi (2017) Regional innovation patterns from an evolutionary perspective. An investigation of European regions. *Regional Studies*. https://doi.org/10.1080/00343404.2017.1296943

Cappellin, R. (2003a) Territorial knowledge management: towards a metrics of the cognitive dimension of

agglomeration economies. *International Journal of Technology Management* 26.2-4, 303–25.

Cappellin, R. (2003b) Networks and technological change in regional clusters. In J. Bröcker, D. Dohse and R. Soltwedel (eds.), *Innovation clusters in interregional competition*, Springer, Berlin.

CEC (Commission of the European Communities) (2008) Green paper on territorial cohesion: turning territorial diversity into strength. COM, Brussels.

CEC (Commission of the European Communities) (2010) Europe 2020: a strategy for smart, sustainable and inclusive growth. COM, Brussels.

Čenys, A. (2009) R&D specialisation and the Lisbon strategy. In D. Pontikakis, D. Kyriakou and R. van Bavel (eds.), *The question of R&D specialisation: perspectives and policy implications*, JRC/European Commission, Brussels.

Coffano, M. and D. Foray (2014) The centrality of entrepreneurial discovery in building and implementing a smart specialization strategy. *Scienze Regionali/Italian Journal of Regional Science* 13.1, 33–50.

Cohen, W. and D. Levinthal (1990) Absorptive capacity: a new perspective on learning and innovation. *Administrative Science Quarterly* 35.1, 128–52.

Dasgupta, P. and J. Stiglitz (1980) Uncertainty, industrial structure and the speed of R&D. *Bell Journal of Economics* 11.1, 1–28.

Dosi, G. (1982) Technological paradigms and technological trajectories: a suggested interpretation of the determinants and directions of technical change. *Research Policy* 11.3, 147–62.

Dunning, J. (2001) The eclectic (OLI) paradigm of international production: past, present and future. *International Journal of the Economics of Business* 8.2, 173–90.

Dunning, J. (2009) Location and the multinational enterprise: John Dunning's thoughts on receiving the *Journal of International Business Studies* 2008 decade award. *Journal of International Business Studies* 40.1, 20–34.

Edgerton, D. (2004) The linear model did not exist: reflections on the history and historiography of science and research in industry in the twentieth century. In K. Grandin, N. Worms and S. Widmalm (eds.), *The science-industry nexus*, Science History Publications, Sagamore Beach, MA.

Foray, D. (2000) *L'Économie de la connaissance* [The knowledge economy]. La Découverte, Paris.

Foray, D. (2009) Understanding smart specialisation. In D. Pontikakis, D. Kyriakou and R. van Bavel (eds.), *The question of R&D specialisation: perspectives and policy implications*, JRC/European Commission, Brussels.

Foray, D., P. David and B. Hall (2009) Smart specialisation—the concept. *Knowledge Economists Policy Brief* 9 (June).

Glaeser, E. (1998) Are cities dying? *Journal of Economic Perspectives* 12.2, 139–60.

Glaeser, E., G.A.M. Ponzetto and Y. Zou (2016) Urban networks: connecting markets, people and ideas. *Papers in Regional Science* 95.1, 17–59.

Griliches, Z. (1957) Hybrid corn: an exploration in the economics of technological change. *Econometrica* 25.4, 501–25.

Griliches, Z. (1990) Patent statistics as economic indicators: a survey. *Journal of Economic Literature* 18.4, 1661–707.

Hägerstrand, T. (1952) The propagation of innovation waves. *Lund Studies in Geography, Series B: Human Geography* 4, 3–19.

Hägerstrand, T. (1967) Aspects of the spatial structure of social communication and the diffusion of innovation. *Papers of the Regional Science Association* 16, 27–42.

Haken, H. (1993) Synergetics as a theory of creativity and its planning. In A. Andersson, D. Batten, K. Kobayashi and K. Yoshikawa (eds.), *The cosmo-creative society: logistical networks in a dynamic economy*, Springer, Berlin.

Jacobs, J. (1969) *The economy of cities*. Random House, New York, NY.

Jacobs, J. (1984) *Cities and the wealth of nations*. Random House, New York, NY.

Keeble, D. and F. Wilkinson (1999) Collective learning and knowledge development in the evolution of regional clusters of high-technology SMEs in Europe. *Regional Studies* 33.4, 295-303.

Keeble, D. and F. Wilkinson (2000) *High-technology clusters, networking and collective learning in Europe*. Ashgate, Aldershot.

Licht, G. (2009) How to better diffuse technologies in Europe. Paper by Research Commissioner Janez Potočnich's expert group 'Knowledge for Growth', European Communities, Luxembourg.

Lucas, R. (1988) On the mechanics of economic development. *Journal of Monetary Economics* 22.1, 3-42.

Lundvall, B.A. and B. Johnson (1994) The learning economy. *Journal of Industry Studies* 1.1, 23-42.

MacDonald, S. (1987), British science parks: reflections on the politics of high technology. *R&D Management* 17.1, 25-37.

Malecki, E. (1980) Corporate organisation of R&D and the location of technological activities. *Regional Studies* 14.3, 219-34.

Mansfield, E. (1961) Technological change and the rate of imitation. *Econometrica* 29.4, 741-66.

Massey, D., P. Quintas and D. Wield (1992) *High-tech fantasies: science parks in society, science and space*. Routledge, London.

McCann, P. (2004) Urban scale economies: statics and dynamics. In R. Capello and P. Nijkamp (eds.), *Urban dynamics and growth: advances in urban economics*, Elsevier, Amsterdam.

Metcalfe, J.S. (1981) Impulse and diffusion in the study of technological change. *Futures* 13.5, 347-59.

Monk, C.S.P., R.B. Porter, P. Quintas, D. Storey and P. Wynarczyk (1988) *Science parks and the growth of high technology firms*. Croom Helm, London.

Mowery, C.D. and N. Rosenberg (1998) *Path of innovation: technological change in 20th-century America*. Cambridge University Press, New York, NY.

Nelson, R. (1959) The simple economics of basic scientific research. *Journal of Political Economy* 67.3, 297-306.

Nelson, R. and S. Winter (1977) In search of a useful theory of innovation. *Research Policy* 6.1, 36-76.

Nelson, R. and S. Winter (1982) *An evolutionary theory of economic changes*. Harvard University Press, Cambridge, MA.

Paci, R. and S. Usai (2009) Knowledge flows across European regions. *Annals of Regional Science* 43.3, 669-90.

Perrin, J-C. (1995) Apprentissage collectif, territoire et milieu innovateur: un nouveau paradigme pour le developpement [Collective learning, territory and innovative environment: a new paradigm for development]. In J. Ferrão (ed.), *Políticas de inovação e desenvolvimento regional et local* [Innovation policies and regional and local development], Ediçáo do Instituto de Ciencias Sociais de Universidade de Lisboa.

Pontikakis, D., G. Chorafakis and D. Kyriakou (2009) R&D specialisation in Europe: from stylized observations to evidence-based policy. In D. Pontikakis, D. Kyriakou and R. van Bavel (eds.) *The question of R&D specialisation: perspectives and policy implications*, JRC/European Commission, Brussels.

Rallet, A. and A. Torre (eds.) (1995) *Économie industrielle et économie spatiale* [Industrial economics and space economics]. Economica, Paris.

Quigley, J.M. (1998) Urban diversity and economic growth. *Journal of Economic Perspectives* 12.2, 127-38.

Sassen, S. (1994) *Cities in a world economy*. Pine Forge Press, Thousand Oaks, CA.

Saxenian, A. (1996) *Regional advantage: culture and competition in Silicon Valley and Route 128*. Harvard University Press, Cambridge, MA.

Scott, A.J. and D.P. Angel (1987) The US semiconductor industry: a locational analysis. *Environment and Planning A* 19.7, 875-912.

Storey, D.J. and B.S. Tether (1998) Public policy measures to support new technology-based firms in the European Union. *Research Policy* 26.9, 1037-57.

Storper, M. and A.J. Scott (1995) The wealth of regions: market forces and policy imperatives in local and global context. *Futures* 27.5, 505-26.

Veltz, P. (1993) D'une geographie des coûts a une géographie de l'organisation: quelques thèses sur l'evolution des rapports entreprises/territoires [From a geography of costs to a geography of the organization: some theses on the evolution of relations between companies]. *Revue Economique* 44.4, 445-81.

INTERNATIONAL JOURNAL OF URBAN AND REGIONAL RESEARCH
DOI:10.1111/1468-2427.12555

— CREATING AN ENVIRONMENT FOR ECONOMIC GROWTH: Creativity, Entrepreneurship or Human Capital?

ALESSANDRA FAGGIAN, MARK PARTRIDGE AND EDWARD J. MALECKI

Abstract

Scholars and policymakers interested in the growth and prosperity of regions have long recognized that talent and knowledge are fundamental. Yet the question is what types of talent are needed in a growing twenty-first-century economy: human capital, creativity and innovation, or entrepreneurship? The latter we define broadly to include any type of risk taking, and not only radical innovation. The literature does not clearly point to one factor as being the most essential. This study assesses this question separately for rural and urban United States (US) counties. We find that human capital—measured by educational attainment—is considerably more conducive to employment growth than the share of creative occupations. Likewise, the share of small and medium businesses is also very conducive to local growth, although this does not apply to the self-employment share. Rural and urban areas experience similar patterns, although the magnitude thereof tends to be larger for urban counties, whereas high-technology employment share has had a positive effect in rural areas. Policy conclusions suggest that enhancing small business development and increasing educational attainment are the two strategies that are most likely to succeed.

Introduction

What are the key drivers of economic growth? This question has been at the heart of economics and economic geography since their very beginnings. Centuries of studies on the subject have produced a plethora of complementary (and sometimes competing) theories, but a high degree of uncertainty remains. What is undisputed is that the skills of the workforce matter. Especially as we progressed towards a 'knowledge-based' economy in the latter part of the twentieth century, it became clear that the abilities of the workforce are a crucial feature of economic growth. Yet it is debatable what 'abilities' are most important and how we should label these abilities. Clearly, the answers are important not only to academics interested in regional growth, but also to policymakers trying to boost struggling local economies in an age of austerity.

In 1911, Schumpeter contended that entrepreneurial skills are paramount and that an increase in the number of entrepreneurs leads to economic growth. Yet, Becker (1962; 1964) argued that what matters is the collective know-how and skills of workers, referred to as 'human capital'. A well-educated workforce will result in enhanced productivity, which is the key to economic growth. More recently, Florida (2002) popularized the term 'creativity' as the key driver for economic success. The knowledge strategies we describe relate to the skills embodied in workers and the population. An alternative 'knowledge' strategy is to attract innovation-intensive or advanced-technology firms to induce growth (see e.g. Yu and Jackson, 2011, for a discussion of these strategies by the US federal government). Such sectoral strategies are often related to cluster strategies (see Porter, 1998; Porter and Stern, 2001; Feser *et al.*, 2008). In terms of policy, the difference then relates to attracting 'smart people' versus attracting 'smart firms/industries'. Although we consider both, we focus primarily on the former.

The aim of this article is twofold. First, on the theoretical front, it aims to clarify the relationship between different concepts of 'knowledge', i.e. creativity, entrepreneurship and human capital. Secondly, it empirically tests how these different types of knowledge—and the ways they are traditionally measured—are interrelated and whether they have complementarities in creating an environment for regional economic growth. US counties are used for our empirical appraisal. Contrary to most previous contributions, we jointly test the effect of entrepreneurship, human capital and creativity measures—while controlling for a series of other possible explanatory variables—and also account for possible endogeneity problems. This is a crucial point, as endogeneity is very likely, because workers and firms will naturally self-sort to places where they can expect to grow faster subsequently, creating a spuriously positive relationship between knowledge measures and growth. The vast majority of previous contributions have disregarded this issue.

In the section that follows, we present a theoretical background and summarize the results of a subset of key studies on the role of entrepreneurship, human capital and creativity. The third section describes our unique database, which combines information from a variety of sources at both county and metropolitan level in the US. Section four describes our empirical modeling strategy, while the concluding section presents and discusses the implications of our findings for policy and future research.

Theoretical background: creativity, entrepreneurship or human capital?

One of the most popular labels of modern society is that of the 'knowledge economy', a society in which what people know and how they use that knowledge is paramount. Knowledge has few apparent boundaries and is not subject to the same constraints as other resources. A key feature of endogenous growth theory (Lucas, 1988) is that knowledge does not show decreasing returns at all or depreciate like other production factors. Knowledge can also easily 'flow' over space, either because people interact and exchange it through knowledge spillovers or—perhaps more importantly— because highly skilled and educated individuals are generally highly mobile (Yankow, 2003; Faggian et al., 2006; 2007; Faggian and McCann 2009a; 2009b). Yet regions need to have the absorptive capacity to benefit from these knowledge spillovers or from a so-called 'social filter' (Rodríguez-Pose, 1999; Crescenzi, 2005; Rodríguez-Pose and Crescenzi, 2008).

That knowledge is a main engine of our society is uncontroversial, but it is unclear whether all knowledge matters in the same way—or whether there are particular types of knowledge that are more crucial for economic growth.

In economics, several terms have been linked to the concept of 'knowledge'. Probably the most comprehensive term in describing the abilities and skills of a person is 'human capital'. Although dating as far back as Adam Smith, the concept was formalized by Nobel Prize winner Gary Becker in 1964. Human capital per se is a very general concept that 'refers to the knowledge, skills and competencies embodied in individuals that increase their productivity' (Faggian, 2005: 362). Such a general concept is almost impossible to quantify and hence, in the decades after Becker's contribution, it has been empirically 'operationalized' using formal education—mostly measured in years of schooling—as a proxy.

This empirical simplification of the concept of human capital has led to much criticism and, ultimately, to the creation of alternative 'labels' to identify knowledge that matters. A whole stream of literature underlines the importance of 'entrepreneurship', as opposed to human capital, as the key factor for societal economic success. Although a univocal definition of entrepreneurship does not exist, the concept is usually linked to that of innovation. In a recent survey, Wennekers and Thurik (1999: 46) associate the term 'entrepreneurial' with 'the manifest ability and willingness of individuals, on their own, in teams, within and outside existing organizations, to perceive and create new economic opportunities (new products, new production methods, new organizational schemes and new product–market combinations)'.

Kirzner (1997: 73) offers a more concise but effective definition of entrepreneurship as the recognition of 'pure profit opportunities' previously unnoticed.

There is also an underlying assumption that an entrepreneur is an individual who is willing to take risks—as Schumpeter (1911) originally put it, a sort of 'revolutionary' who can reform the pattern of production by exploiting an invention and is willing to face uncertainty and overcome obstacles in order to succeed. Hence, while much of the academic focus on entrepreneurs has been on radical innovations, successful small and medium-sized enterprises (SMEs) are typically defined by an owner who sees a niche profit opportunity and is willing to take some risk in order to succeed.

Whereas the concept of entrepreneurship is appealing, it presents the same problem as the concept of 'human capital' when it comes to be operationalized for empirical testing. Measuring 'entrepreneurship' is challenging, because it is defined on many dimensions, such as innovation, risk taking, and identifying markets and proxies to measure these dimensions need to be used. However, while in the case of human capital, education is almost universally accepted as a good proxy, in the case of entrepreneurial abilities, it has been hard to reach consensus on an appropriate definition (Cunningham and Lischeron, 1991; Malecki, 1994). Three of the most popular proxies are self-employment rate, share of SMEs and new firm formation.

Self-employment rates are relatively easy to measure, so they have become standard in much of the empirical work (Evans and Jovanovic, 1989; Acs et al., 1994; Blanchflower and Oswald, 1998; OECD, 1998; Blanchflower, 2000; Parker and Robson, 2004; Glaeser, 2007; Goetz and Rupasingha, 2007; Shrestha et al., 2009; Stephens and Partridge, 2011). Self-employed individuals are proprietors (and partnerships) that own or operate businesses that range from employing no one else to medium-sized enterprises that employ thousands.[1] The assumption behind this proxy is that self-employed individuals are most likely to exhibit entrepreneurial characteristics such as greater risk taking and the ability to innovate and to commercially exploit inventions. Although these are reasonable assumptions, this proxy does not account for individuals who are highly entrepreneurial but work within an organization, labeled *intrapreneurs* by some (Gibb, 1990; Wennekers and Thurik, 1999). As Glaeser (2007) acknowledges, this measure is biased towards the smallest entrepreneurs and makes little distinction between 'Michael Bloomberg and a hot dog vendor'. Another concern with the self-employment measure is that it may include those who are the not particularly entrepreneurial, such as those who start a business out of necessity because there are few other job opportunities. Yet Stephens and Partridge (2011) contend that even 'necessity entrepreneurs' could serve a useful role if their businesses take off, or at the very least, if these further diversify the local economy.

An alternative to the self-employment rate is the share of SMEs (see e.g. Chinitz, 1961). The assumptions behind this measure are not dissimilar from the ones behind the use of self-employment. SMEs can be very innovative and hence very 'entrepreneurial'. However, the use of the share of SMEs as a proxy for entrepreneurship does not solve the problem that arises when using self-employment as a measure. Measured either by the self-employment rate or by the share of SMEs, entrepreneurship might seem to decline in industries where entrepreneurs have been successfully expanding their companies into 'large' firms.

New firm formation has been used by some researchers (Armington and Acs, 2002; Kirchoff et al., 2002) as yet another measure of entrepreneurship. Shapero (1984) calls the decision to start a new company the 'entrepreneurial event'. However, although creating a new business clearly demonstrates a willingness to take risks and the ambition to commercialize new ideas, this measure still has its shortcomings in that it does not account for entrepreneurial activities that are not 'new'. (Neither does it tell us how

---

1   Of course, there could be privately held companies that employ tens of thousands, but these are usually organized as corporations. Specifically, for the US Bureau of Economic Analysis (BEA) data we employ here, the BEA defines self-employment or non-farm proprietors as 'the number of sole proprietorships and the number of individual business partners not assumed to be limited partners'.

successful these new activities are, as new firms often fail.) Moreover, data availability is more of a problem, as many countries do not compile data on newly created and closed businesses, much less on re-registered businesses, and there are serious comparability issues (Vale, 2005). Hence we will not employ this measure in this study.

What is clear, however, is that an entrepreneur has certain characteristics that are desirable for an economy. To varying degrees, he or she is the 'innovative' type, who has an idea—a 'vision'—and is willing to face uncertainty to succeed. Although education is not a prerequisite for becoming an entrepreneur, a certain degree of overlap between being 'educated' and being 'entrepreneurial' has been found (Evans and Leighton, 1989; Bates, 1993; Audretsch and Fritsch, 1994; Malecki, 1994; Bregger, 1996; Robson, 1998; Goetz and Freshwater, 2001).

A more recent extension of the relationship between knowledge and economic growth is the introduction of the concept of 'creative class' (Florida, 2002). Florida and his followers argue that it is not only the education a person possesses that really matters, but whether they are 'creative'. Hence, 'creativity' is a 'driving force in regional economic growth and prosperity' (Florida, 2002: xxvii). Florida and his fellow researchers contend that the best way of measuring creativity is by considering an individual's profession. Based on this, Mellander and Florida (2007) and Florida *et al.* (2008) argue that a particular set of occupations compose the 'creative class', and that this measure of human capital outperforms the conventional use of educational attainment because it accounts for utilized skills rather than mere *potential* talent. Marlet and van Woerkens (2004: 2) state that 'the creative class sets a better standard for measuring human capital'.

Few would dispute that creativity matters and that not all who are 'educated' are also 'creative'. However, the concept of creativity suffers from the same empirical problems as the concept of human capital and entrepreneurship: it is an elusive concept, and very difficult to operationalize. Many authors dispute that the set of professions included in the creative class concept outperforms the use of simple educational attainment as human capital proxy. Hansen (2007) showed that the correlation between creative class and educational attainment is 0.94, and that a very high correlation was also found in Finland, Denmark and Norway (0.96, 0.84 and 0.85, respectively).[2] Glaeser (2005) observed that, if the creative class has an effect over and above the traditional measure of human capital, then it should be positive in a model in which both variables are included. However, by estimating a simple regression based on US metropolitan areas, he found that while the percentage of adults with a college education had a positive and statistically significant impact on growth, the share of workers in the 'super-creative core' was statistically insignificant when the schooling variable was included. Moreover, the two variables were also highly correlated (0.75). Other contributions, such as those by Wojan *et al.* (2007), Rausch and Negrey (2006) and Donegan *et al.* (2008) also showed that the creative class measure of human capital performed very similarly to the traditional education measure.

If we take the concept of human capital in its broadest sense, being creative or possessing entrepreneurial abilities are only parts of possessing higher human capital. Since human capital is very difficult to measure and education is a very imperfect measure, creativity and entrepreneurship measures can only be regarded as a way of better measuring human capital in a more comprehensive way. Although these measures might have considerable overlap, they do capture different aspects of 'knowledge'.

It should be noted that fostering new firms locally, rather than attracting them from elsewhere, is part of 'high-road' regional economic development policies (Malecki, 2004). The entrepreneurial climate is likely to be more influential than other local amenities in new firm formation (Goetz and Freshwater, 2001). Marlet and van Woerkens (2007) find that in Dutch cities and towns, higher levels of human capital are correlated with employment

2   See Andersen *et al.* (2010)

growth, largely as a result of growth in commercial, mainly financial, services and to newly started companies. They conclude that both a highly productive labor force and the right atmosphere for starting up new businesses emerge in places that have high levels of skilled and creative people. Concentrations of such people emerge as individuals 'choose to locate on the basis of some sort of structured match between their talents and the forms of economic specialization and labor demand to be found in the places where they eventually settle' (Storper and Scott, 2009: 162).

In this article, by using a unique comprehensive data set, we simultaneously build proxies to measure education, entrepreneurship and creativity in an effort to shed more light on what type of knowledge really matters for economic growth. At the same time we correct for possible endogeneity problems that might lead to bias in our results.

Methodology and data

To test the joint effect of creativity, entrepreneurship and education on economic growth we use US counties as a case study. The wealth of publicly available data in the US allows for the creation of a rich database that serves the purposes of our empirical model. One of the key challenges that is typically underappreciated in related research is that self-sorting entrepreneurs or knowledge workers tend to locate in places that are growing, which can create a spuriously positive association between our knowledge measures and growth.[3]

The most popular economic model describing movement of firms and people across locations is the spatial equilibrium approach, which is summarized by Glaeser and Gottlieb (2008). The key aspect of the model is that firms and households will relocate to places that offer them the highest expected future profits or future utility. Thus, firms, entrepreneurs and workers may be prone to migrate to or locate in places they think will perform well in future in terms of job availability, wages or profits. Alternatively, there could be a negative bias in the human capital/creativity coefficients if, for example, the least productive high-human-capital (or -creativity) people relocate to fast-growing places because they are unable to get a job in their initial location (all else being equal)—for example, unemployed arts majors. The problem such sorting would cause is that individual actors may use information that is unavailable to the researcher, such as election of a competent politician, investment in key public services or infrastructure, business attitudes or general buzz surrounding a place, and financial struggles or successes of key firms. Of course, many of these factors can be discovered in newspaper searches, but quantitative studies will find it nearly impossible to find common variables to measure such events for their entire sample. Statistically, these omitted variables can create endogeneity bias in our entrepreneur and human capital variables if they are sorting or moving in response to these events.[4]

3　For example, Low et al. (2005) found that business formation in rural areas could be attributed to fewer economic opportunities. Similarly, using instrumental variables, Stephens and Partridge (2011) found larger effects from small business formation in the depressed Appalachian region after accounting for the fact that people were more prone to start businesses when they expected less future job creation. Likewise, McGranahan et al. (2010) and Stephens and Partridge (2011) found evidence that entrepreneurship and amenities (which also support growth) have a reinforcing effect in promoting growth.

4　The recent literature on household and business location has been keenly focused on endogeneity through omitted variables in which households and firms self-sort based on future expectations or where there is an omitted fixed factor that may be correlated with the explanatory variables of interest. Policymakers may also implement certain policies based on their expectations about future growth. One solution to these endogeneity concerns is to implement natural experiment matching, in which a counterfactual is obtained to compare to the control group. For example, Hanson and Rohlin (2011) create counterfactuals to address the concern that government policies were developed based on policymakers' expectations of future conditions. As noted, another solution is using instrumental variables. For example, Duranton and Turner (2011) instrument for interstate highway infrastructure because policymakers may provide additional infrastructure (or less infrastructure) based on their expectations of whether a region may become a future leading or lagging region. One final example that has some similarities to our case may be found in Glaeser et al. (2012). The authors of this article argue that historical coal mining communities have lower economic growth both directly as a result of productivity growth in coal mining and indirectly because of coal mining creating an atmosphere that does not nurture entrepreneurship and small-firm formation. Thus, in their model of local growth, they instrument for small-firm intensity with distance to historic coal mines.

To mitigate this endogeneity problem, we need to control for the key factors that underlie growth so that we minimize omitted variable bias. Though we are careful to account for supply and demand factors that influence economic activity, there could be residual endogeneity in that forward-looking firms and individuals will choose to locate in places that they expect will have faster growth beyond what our measures of economic activity already suggest. Likewise, omitted persistent effects such as culture may also bias the regression results. Instrumental variables are one solution to correct for these types endogeneity, as we describe below.

We adopted a tripartite modeling strategy. First, we estimate a simple ordinary least squares or OLS model (see equation [1]) with employment growth as dependent variable and a series of explanatory variables, including two proxies for entrepreneurship (ENT1 and ENT2), 'traditional' human capital (in the form of education, EDU) and creativity (CREA).

$$EMPGR_i = \alpha + \beta_1 EDU_i + \beta_2 CREA_i + \beta_3 ENT1_i + \beta_4 ENT2_i$$

$$+ \beta_5 AME_i + \beta_6 HT_i + \beta_7 POP_i + \sum_{j=8}^{11} \beta_j ACC_i^j + \text{State Fixed Effects} + \varepsilon_i \qquad (1)$$

where $i = 1,...,3065$ identifies the US counties in the lower 48 states and the District of Columbia. Employment growth is calculated between the years 2000 and 2007. Our employment growth measure represents the number of jobs, but does not differentiate between full-time and part-time employment.[5] The explanatory variables all refer to the initial year (2000) to avoid direct simultaneity with the dependent variable. We consider metropolitan counties separately from non-metropolitan counties to account for heterogeneity in urban and rural environments. A description of how the variables are constructed and their sources is reported in Table 1.

We also control for the share of employment in 2000 accounted for by high-technology industries. Thus, our results compare the influence of knowledge embodied across the entire workforce to the influence of having knowledge-intensive industries. This comparison is important, because attraction of high-technology firms often forms the heart of innovation and cluster strategies used by economic development practitioners.

To account for faster growth in high-natural-amenity locations, we control for a one-to-seven natural amenity scale. The amenity scale uses climate (warm winters, less humid summers, clear days), access to water, and topography (such as mountains) in its construction. The log 1990 population is included to account for agglomeration effects. Moreover, we include different accessibility measures to reflect the distance penalty across the urban hierarchy, which Partridge et al. (2008a; 2008b) found to be a key factor driving spatial differences in growth. First we consider distance to reach a metropolitan area, adding incremental distances to reach a Metropolitan Statistical Area (MSA) of at least 250,000, 500,000 and 1.5 million people, respectively. Polèse and Shearmur (2004) found that industry composition follows similar patterns of urban proximity, with the highest-order and most human-capital-intensive firms located near the largest urban centers. Beyond these regional economic linkages, Shearmur (2010) notes that innovation spillovers and regional innovation systems have similar proximity relationships in the urban hierarchy (see also Doloreux and Shearmur, 2011). Overall, not controlling for distance, amenities and population would confound the independent effects of 'entrepreneurship' and knowledge intensity with the likely fact that businesses

---

5   Job growth is a key measure of economic prosperity that is also correlated with population growth. Job growth also reflects the highest economic priority in the American economy since the year 2000, when job growth slowed markedly. Yet, our job growth measure does not account for part-time workers or the share of 'high'- or 'low'-wage jobs. Another indicator of economic wellbeing is average income or wage. We do not pursue these measures, because average income may only reflect what is happening at the upper end when there are rapid increases in income inequality, as in the US. Likewise, high income may not translate to high utility, because it may only be compensating for disamenities (see Glaeser and Gottlieb, 2008).

TABLE 1 Description of variables

Variable	Description	Source
EMPGR	Employment growth between the years 2000 and 2007	US Bureau of Economic Analysis
EDU	Percentage of people with a bachelor or graduate degree (2000)	US Census Bureau
CREA	Percentage of people in 'creative occupations' in 2000 (based on two-digit occupational codes as per Florida, 2002)[6]	Own calculations based on US Census Bureau data
ENT1	Self-employment (non-agricultural) (in the year 2000)	US Bureau of Economic Analysis
ENT2	Share of SMEs (in the year 2000)	US Census Bureau—county business patterns
HT	Employment share in high-tech sectors (in the year 2000)	EMSI consulting company data; see Dorfman et al. (2011) for a detailed discussion of EMSI data. Our definitions of high-technology (or advanced-technology) industries is based on the US Department of Labor (see Hecker, 2005).
AME	Natural Amenity Index 1999 (values from 1 to 7, with 7 the highest amenities)	US Department of Agriculture
POP	Log population 1990	US Bureau of Economic Analysis
ACC8	Distance in km to nearest MSA	Partridge et al. (2008a; 2008b)
ACC9	Incremental distance to MSA > 250,000 population	Partridge et al. (2008a; 2008b)
ACC10	Incremental distance to MSA > 500,000 population	Partridge et al. (2008a; 2008b)
ACC11	Incremental distance to MSA > 1,500,000 population	Partridge et al. (2008a; 2008b)

SOURCE: Authors' own analysis

and knowledge workers want to locate near larger agglomerations that are already growing faster than others.

Secondly, we address endogeneity problems by estimating a two-stage least squares (2SLS) regression analysis with appropriate instruments for the endogenous independent variables. As noted above, many of the variables in our model, except for the amenity index and the accessibility variables, might potentially suffer from endogeneity. We follow a common approach in the literature (Card and DiNardo, 2000), using deep lags for the independent variables we suspect have potential contemporaneous endogeneity. In particular, we use the population of 1950, the share of 'creative' people (managers and professionals) in 1950, the percentage of the population over 25 with three or more years of college in 1970, the share of non-agricultural self-employment in 1970, the percentage of SMEs in 1974, and the percentage of high-tech firms in 1990.

We also include 'industry mix employment growth' (INDMIX_GR) (Bartik, 1991; Blanchard and Katz, 1992) as an instrument for the effects of persistent local economic growth as a key measure of underlying growth.[7] We use the growth rate between 1990 and 2000 ($n = 10$) to avoid simultaneity with the dependent variable. Industry mix growth represents the hypothetical employment growth rate if the county's industries grew at the national average over the sample period and it should be exogenous to the county because it is based on national patterns.

Thirdly, to correct for spatial autocorrelation we use Conley's (1999) 2SLS generalized method of moments (GMM) estimator for spatially correlated errors. Conley's code uses a weighting function that declines linearly until the distance reaches a certain threshold, where it becomes zero. We use three degrees of latitude and

---

6   We thank Kevin Stolarick for providing us with the appropriate occupational census codes.

7   The industry mix employment growth rate for a state (s) in the period (t, t+n) is defined as:

$$INDMIX\_GR_s = \sum_i S^t_{is} * EMP\_GR^{t,t+n}_{i,USA},$$

where S^t_{is} is the county's employment share in industry (i, one-digit SIC) in the initial year (t) and $EMP\_GR^{t,t+n}_{i,USA}$ is the growth rate in industry (i) for the whole of the US in the period (t, t+n). Changes in *national industry* demand are the exogenous shifters for each county.

longitude as our thresholds, which correspond to a square of about 200 by 160 miles (at 40 degrees latitude). The results are not sensitive to changing these thresholds.

Fourthly, state fixed effects account for common features about each state that may be driving its growth, including differently sized counties, historic settlement, access to coasts, tax policy, business regulations and public infrastructure. For state fixed effects, all variable coefficients reflect the effects of within-state movements of the explanatory variables.

Results and discussion

The results of our estimations are reported in Table 2. Columns 1 and 2 report the results of the OLS estimation for non-metropolitan (non-MSA) and metropolitan (MSA) areas, respectively. The OLS results would be the preferred results to the extent that our concerns about endogeneity are not warranted. However, as reported in note

TABLE 2   OLS and 2SLS spatial GMM results

Dependent Variable: Employment Change 2000-2007 (%)	OLS		2SLS SPATIAL GMM	
	1 Non-MSA	2 MSA	3 Non-MSA	4 MSA
EDU	0.66***	1.31***	1.25***	3.16***
	(7.07)	(4.97)	(3.72)	(3.51)
CREA	0.10	-0.66***	-1.84***	-3.76***
	(0.74)	(-2.79)	(v2.75)	(-3.18)
ENT1	37.04***	74.02***	-31.33**	-9.45
	(10.92)	(4.71)	(-2.27)	(-0.25)
ENT2	114.39***	249.73***	409.93***	616.60***
	(3.63)	(2.46)	(5.53)	(3.44)
AME	2.05***	-1.40	1.90***	0.53
	(5.33)	(-1.42)	(4.62)	(0.55)
HT	13.89*	-11.31	15.93*	24.47
	(1.89)	(-0.77)	(1.71)	(1.40)
POP	2.87***	-0.06	-1.08	-5.39***
	(7.42)	(-0.73)	(-1.02)	(-3.19)
ACC8	-0.024***	–	-0.046***	–
	(-4.30)		(-5.14)	
ACC9	-0.014***	-0.038***	-0.020***	-0.047***
	(-3.47)	(-3.44)	(-4.28)	(-4.09)
ACC10	-0.011**	-0.024***	-0.007	-0.027***
	(-2.35)	(-2.80)	(-1.28)	(-2.86)
ACC11	-0.002	-0.002	-0.006*	-0.005
	(-0.60)	(-0.28)	(-1.65)	(-0.61)
State fixed effects			Yes	
Constant	-158.89***	-237.11**	-376.28***	-531.31***
	(-5.13)	(-2.40)	(-5.53)	(-3.29)
Test for overidentifying restrictions	–	–	13.35	11.45
R-squared	0.31	0.45	–	–
Number of observations	2,247	818	2,247	818

*10% significance level; **5% significance level; ***1% significance level
NOTES: (a) To rule out possible multicollinearity problems, we calculated the variance inflated factor (VIF) for each regressor (values below 10 show no multicollinearity problem). In model 1, the maximum VIF value—associated with the amenity variable AME—is 4.17, and the average VIF for all regressors is 2.14. In model 2, the maximum VIF—associated with the Alabama state fixed effects—is 5.58, and the average VIF is 2.26. (b) Although we do not present these results here, we also estimated the 'non-spatial' version of the 2SLS model (using the 'ivreg2' Stata command). The endogeneity test for the regressors (implemented with the 'endog' command) showed that we indeed had an endogeneity issue. The null hypothesis that the education, entrepreneurship and creativity regressors were exogenous was rejected with a value of the χ^2 test equal to 65.29 and a P-value = 0.000.
SOURCE: Authors' own analysis

B at the bottom of Table 2, endogeneity seems to be a problem in our model. Columns 3 and 4 report the results of the 2SLS spatial GMM. We omit the results of the non-spatial 2SLS, as they are very similar to the spatial model, the only difference being in the standard errors, which are corrected for potential spatial dependence.[8]

Starting with the control variables, most of the OLS results are in line with expectations. Better accessibility of large MSAs (especially above the thresholds of 250,000 and 500,000 inhabitants) has a positive effect on growth in both MSA and non-MSA areas. Amenities are significant only for non-MSA areas, although this is consistent with previous studies, which have found that amenities are a strong determinant of growth in non-metropolitan areas (see e.g. Deller *et al.*, 2001; McGranahan *et al.*, 2010). One caveat is that the USDA amenity index measures only natural amenities.[9] MSAs are likely to offer urban man-made amenities linked to agglomeration economies that are not captured by this index.

The high-tech share is less important than some may expect, playing a marginal role (10% level significance) only in non-MSA areas. Even though not strong, the positive relationship between high-tech share and subsequent growth in non-metropolitan areas seems to suggest that product-cycle models might apply. As these high-tech technologies 'mature', they disperse to low-cost rural areas for manufacturing. Nonetheless, Malecki (1981) noted that the likely success of high-technology strategies varies across different settings.

The most interesting results are those for the proxies for 'human factors', i.e. education, entrepreneurship and creativity. The OLS results show that education and both measures of entrepreneurship have a positive and significant effect on growth, while creativity—measured in the traditional way—is either insignificant or negative. Although a variance inflated factor (VIF) test does not indicate multicollinearity among the regressors, removing the education variable does not change the results for creativity. Yet, a more restrictive definition of creative class works better; for example, if we restrict the creative class measure only to professionals and managers, both the education and restricted creative class variables are positive and statistically significant (see McGranahan and Wojan, 2007). Nonetheless, the larger metropolitan human capital coefficient suggests a stronger affect for metropolitan counties than for non-metropolitan counties, suggesting that urban areas have more to gain from increasing human capital (perhaps as a result of larger knowledge spillovers; see Abel *et al.*, 2012).

Note (b) at the bottom of Table 2 reports the results of the endogeneity test, in which the null hypothesis is that human capital, entrepreneurial and creativity variables are exogenous. The results suggest that the null hypothesis can be rejected, hence making the OLS results biased. Columns 3 and 4 report the 2SLS results that adjust for endogeneity effects such as self-sorting or future anticipation effects. Correcting for endogeneity and spatial autocorrelation does not significantly alter the results on accessibility, amenities or high-tech. However, the role of 'size' in terms of population does change. While in the OLS model, there appears to be some evidence of agglomeration economies in non-metropolitan areas, the 2SLS spatial GMM results suggest that congestion effects dominate in MSAs.

Regarding the control variables, the results on the other variables of interest do not vary much when correcting for endogeneity and spatial autocorrelation, the only exception being self-employment rate (although the magnitude of the education

---

8   Note that all of conventional first-stage tests for the strength of our instruments show that we do not have a weak instruments problem with F-values exceeding the 10 threshold (Stock and Watson, 2007). The 2SLS spatial GMM results also include a test for overidentifying restrictions. The tests do not reject the null hypothesis of orthogonality between the instruments and the error term (at 5% level) showing that our instruments are valid. For more details on this test, see Carvalho *et al.* (2005).

9   We need to bear in mind that state fixed effects are included in the model. For amenities, this means that the influence of, say, all Minnesota counties being cold and all Arizona counties being warm are captured in the state fixed effects. The amenity variable only reflects the influence of changes in the amenity scale within, say, Minnesota or Florida.

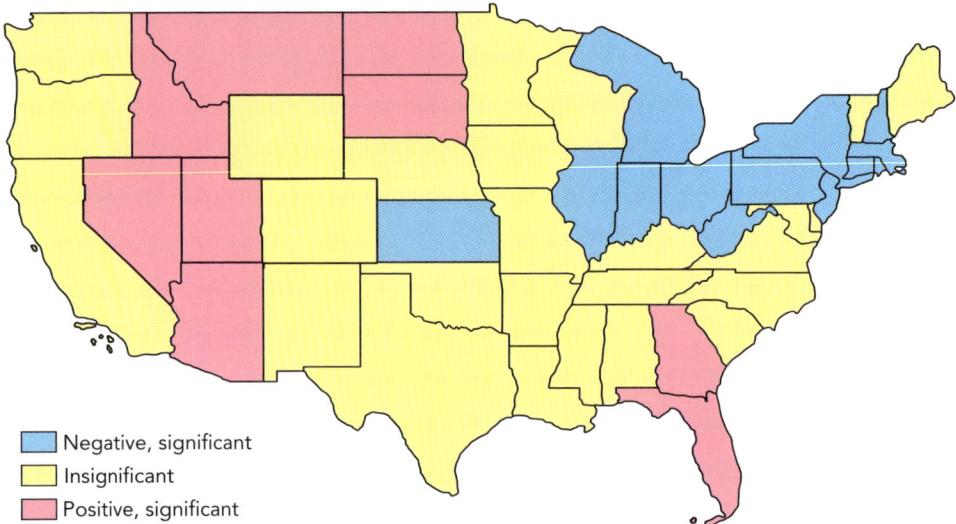

Negative, significant
Insignificant
Positive, significant

FIGURE 1   State fixed effects (*source*: based on authors' own analysis)

coefficient increases), which loses its significance in metropolitan areas and even becomes negative in non-metropolitan areas. We further note that removing either the self-employment or the SME variable does not change the result for the other coefficient, suggesting that this finding is not an artifact of multicollinearity.

The negative coefficient on self-employment after addressing endogeneity suggests that self-sorting may explain the general OLS result in previous studies that self-employment (ENT1) is positively linked to growth.[10] However, it may also reflect that having a greater share of small and medium-sized businesses (ENT2) that tend to buy locally or are locally owned is of paramount importance (Fleming and Goetz, 2011). The role of SMEs is also consistent with Audretsch and Thurik's (2001) contention that, as comparative advantage shifts towards knowledge-based economic activity, SMEs become more and more important for growth. However, while further research would be needed to fully assess this point, it does suggest that state and local development efforts aimed at luring outside big firms to a region through generous subsidies and incentives is misguided when compared to cultivating home-grown small businesses (see e.g. Goetz *et al.*, 2011).

Although we do not report the state fixed effects results in the table due to lack of space, Figure 1 provides a graphical representation for the 2SLS GMM spatial model that includes all counties (MSA and non-MSA).

Everything else being equal, these results suggest that the states in the Northeast and the Rustbelt are underperforming. This is not surprising, as they are characterized by their unattractive climate, weak industry composition, poor local government, fragmented governance and perceived high tax rates. The over-performers are high-amenity mountain and Sunbelt states with pro-business climates and, especially in the case of North Dakota, commodity-driven growth. Some results may be a little surprising, such as the non-significant parameter of California, which performed poorly in the period under investigation. On the opposite end of the spectrum there seem to be relatively fast-growing states, such as Washington, Colorado and North Carolina, that do not have positive and significant fixed effects (suggesting that the other control variables explain their growth).

---

10   We caution that removing creativity seems to increase the importance of self-employment.

Conclusions

Human capital (proxied by education), entrepreneurship and creativity have often been treated as separate phenomena. Most contributions have focused on one of these only or, at most, on the relationship that links two. In this article we argue that creativity, entrepreneurship and education are all part of a more broadly defined concept of human capital, which is the most essential production factor in knowledge societies.

We also argue that empirical measures for creativity, entrepreneurship and human capital are highly imperfect, and that combining them might get us closer to capturing the complexity of human abilities that account for economic growth. To assess their relative roles, we built a model explaining economic growth of US counties over the period from 2000 to 2007, in which we simultaneously consider the role of human capital, entrepreneurship and creativity, while controlling for other important factors such as accessibility, amenities and share of high-tech industries.

We have found that when we include all three factors, education seems to prevail, followed by the entrepreneurship measure associated with a concentration of local SMEs. Creativity—traditionally measured—does not appear as a dominant factor, although different results are found for more 'restrictive' definitions. Likewise, other studies have found positive creativity effects in more specific local contexts—for example, Stephens et al. (2013) for the Appalachian region. Our results are robust after correcting for potential endogeneity problems and spatial autocorrelation. In fact, our results on human capital are strengthened in the final 2SLS spatial GMM model. Nevertheless, the results support arguments that the best economic development strategies center on attracting and/or retaining highly educated workers and building a diverse small and medium-sized business foundation (Malecki, 1994; Yigitcanlar et al., 2007; Glaeser and Gottlieb, 2008; Glaeser et al., 2010; Partridge and Olfert, 2011). Conversely, we find little evidence that, despite its popular appeal, attracting high-technology industries contributes to subsequent growth in urban areas. Nonetheless, while having more educated workers is conducive to growth, we did not address the nagging question of how to attract (or create) these workers through migration or through own schools. More research is needed to examine this vexing policy challenge (see Brown and Scott, 2012, as a starting point).

The results on creativity do not necessarily imply that the concept itself has no value, but rather that the direction of causality is important and that endogeneity should always be accounted for. Creative people might be very efficient at self-sorting themselves in places they expect to grow faster. Moreover, as creativity is a relatively young concept, better measures might still be needed. Fine-tuning the proxies for creativity or dissecting the creative class into more detailed and homogeneous subcomponents (see Comunian et al., 2010) might influence the results. This is something that should be explored in future research.

In conclusion, we have noted that these findings apply mainly to the US and may not apply to other countries. Different economic structures, a varying propensity for migration, and differing governmental policies mean that the underlying growth processes may also differ. These possibilities are left to future research.

Alessandra Faggian, Social Sciences, Gran Sasso Science Institute, Viale Francesco Crispi 7, 67100 L'Aquila, Italy, alessandra.faggian@gssi.it

Mark Partridge, Department of Agricultural, Environmental, and Development Economics, The Ohio State University, 2120 Fyffe Road, Columbus, OH 43210, USA, markd.partridge@gmail.com

Edward J. Malecki, Department of Geography, The Ohio State University, 1036 Derby Hall, 154 North Oval Mall, Columbus, OH 43210, USA, malecki.4@osu.edu

References

Abel, J.R., I. Dey and T.M. Gabe (2012) Productivity and the density of human capital. *Journal of Regional Science* 52.4, 562-86.

Acs, Z.J., D.B. Audretsch and D.S. Evans (1994) Why does the self-employment rate vary across countries and over time? CEPR Discussion Paper No. 871, Centre for Economic Policy Research, London.

Andersen, K.V., H.K. Hansen, A. Isaksen and M. Raunio (2010) Nordic city regions in the creative class debate: putting the creative class thesis to a test. *Industry and Innovation* 17.2, 215-40.

Armington, C. and Z. Acs (2002) The determinants of regional variation in new firm formation. *Regional Studies* 36.1, 33-45.

Audretsch, D.B. and M. Fritsch (1994) The geography of firm births in Germany. *Regional Studies* 28.4, 359-65.

Audretsch, D. and R. Thurik (2001) What's new about the new economy? Sources of growth in the managed and entrepreneurial economies. *Industrial and Corporate Change* 10.1, 267-315.

Bartik, T.J. (1991) Who benefits from state and local economic development policies? Upjohn Institute, Kalamazoo, MI.

Bates, T. (1993) Theories of entrepreneurship. In R.D. Bingham and R. Mier (eds.), *Theories of local economic development*, Sage Press, Newbury Park, CA.

Becker, G.S. (1962) Investment in human capital: a theoretical analysis. *Journal of Political Economy* 70.5, 9-49.

Becker, G.S. (1964) *Human capital*. The University of Chicago Press, Chicago, IL.

Blanchard, O. and L.F. Katz (1992) Regional evolutions. *Brookings Papers on Economic Activity* 23.1, 1-75.

Blanchflower, D.G. (2000) Self-employment in OECD countries. *Labour Economics* 7.5, 471-505.

Blanchflower, D.G. and A.J. Oswald (1998) What makes an entrepreneur? *Journal of Labor Economics* 16.1, 26-60.

Bregger, J.E. (1996) Measuring self-employment in the United States. *Monthly Labor Review* 119.1/2, 3-9.

Brown, W.M. and D.M. Scott (2012) Human capital location choice: accounting for amenities and thick labor markets. *Journal of Regional Science* 52.5, 787-808.

Card, D. and J.E. DiNardo (2000) Do immigrant inflows lead to native outflows? *The American Economic Review* 90.2, 360-67.

Carvalho, A., D. da Mata and K. Chomitz (2005) Estimation of multiequation cross-section models in the presence of spatial autocorrelation. Discussion Paper no. 1111, Instituto de Pesquisa Econômica Aplicada (IPEA), Brasilia.

Chinitz, B. (1961) Contrasts in agglomeration: New York and Pittsburgh. *The American Economic Review* 51.2, 279-89.

Comunian, C., A. Faggian and Q.C. Li (2010) Unrewarded careers in the creative class: the strange case of Bohemian graduates. *Papers in Regional Science* 89.2, 389-410.

Conley, T. (1999) GMM estimation with cross sectional dependence. *Journal of Econometrics* 92.1, 1-45.

Crescenzi, R. (2005) Innovation and regional growth in the enlarged Europe: the role of local innovative capabilities, peripherality, and education. *Growth and Change* 36.4, 471-507.

Cunningham, J. and J. Lischeron (1991) Defining entrepreneurship. *Journal of Small Business Management* 29.1, 45-61.

Deller, S.C., T-H. Tsai, D.W. Marcouiller and D.B.K. English (2001) The role of amenities and quality of life in rural economic growth. *American Journal of Agricultural Economics* 83.2, 352-65.

Doloreux, S. and R. Shearmur (2012) Collaboration, information and the geography of innovation in knowledge intensive business services. *Journal of Economic Geography* 12.1, 79-105.

Donegan, M., J. Drucker, H. Goldstein, N. Lowe and E. Malizia (2008) Which indicators explain metropolitan economic performance best? Traditional or creative class. *Journal of the American Planning Association* 74.2, 180-95.

Dorfman, J., M.D. Partridge and H. Galloway (2011) Are high-tech employment and natural amenities linked? Answers from a smoothed Bayesian spatial model. *Spatial Economic Analysis* 6 (December), 397-422.

Duranton, G. and M.A. Turner (2011) The fundamental law of road congestion: evidence from US cities. *The American Economic Review* 101.6, 2616-52.

Evans, D.S. and B. Jovanovic (1989) An estimated model of entrepreneurial choice under liquidity constraints. *Journal of Political Economy* 97.4, 808-27.

Evans, D.S., and L.S. Leighton (1989) Some empirical aspects of entrepreneurship. *The American Economic Review* 79.3, 519-35.

Faggian, A. (2005) Human capital. In R.W. Caves (ed.), *Encyclopaedia of the city*, Routledge, New York, NY.

Faggian, A. and P. McCann (2009a) Human capital, graduate migration and innovation in British regions. *Cambridge Journal of Economics* 33.2, 317-33.

Faggian, A. and P. McCann (2009b) Universities, agglomerations and graduate human capital mobility. *Journal of Economic and Social Geography* 100.2, 210-23.

Faggian, A., P. McCann and S. Sheppard (2006) An analysis of ethnic differences in UK graduate migration behaviour. *Annals of Regional Science* 40.2, 461-71.

Faggian, A., P. McCann and S. Sheppard (2007) Some evidence that women are more mobile than men: gender differences in UK graduate migration behaviour. *Journal of Regional Science* 47.3, 517-39.

Feser, E., H. Renski and H. Goldstein (2008) Clusters and economic development outcomes: an analysis of the link between clustering and industry growth. *Economic Development Quarterly* 22.4, 324-44.

Fleming, D. and S.J. Goetz (2011) Does local firm ownership matter? *Economic Development Quarterly* 25.3, 277-81.

Florida, R. (2002) *The rise of the creative class (and how it's transforming work, leisure, community and everyday life)*. Basic Books, New York, NY.

Florida, R., C. Mellander and K. Stolarick (2008) Inside the black box of regional development—human capital, the creative class and tolerance. *Journal of Economic Geography* 8.5, 615-49.

Gibb, A.A. (1990) Entrepreneurship and intrapreneurship—exploring the differences. In R. Donckels and A. Miettinen (eds.), *New findings and perspectives in entrepreneurship*, Avebury, Aldershot.

Glaeser, E.L. (2005) Review of Richard Florida's *The Rise of the Creative Class*. *Regional Science and Urban Economics* 35.5, 593-96.

Glaeser, E.L. (2007) Entrepreneurship and the city. NBER Working Paper No. 13551, Cambridge, MA.

Glaeser, E.L. and J.D. Gottlieb (2008) The economics of place-making policies. *Brookings Papers on Economic Activity* 39.1 (spring), 155-254.

Glaeser, E.L., W.R. Kerr and G.A.M. Ponzetto (2010) Clusters of entrepreneurship. *Journal of Urban Economics* 67.1, 150-68.

Glaeser, E.L., S. Pekkala and W.R. Kerr (2012) Entrepreneurship and urban growth: an empirical assessment with historical mines. NBER Working Paper No. 18333, Cambridge, MA.

Goetz, S.J. and D. Freshwater (2001) State-level determinants of entrepreneurship and a preliminary measure of entrepreneurial climate. *Economic Development Quarterly* 15.1, 58-70.

Goetz, S.J. and A. Rupasingha (2007) Determinants of growth in non-farm proprietor densities in the US, 1990-2000. *Small Business Economics* 32.4, 425-38.

Goetz, S.J., M.D. Partridge, D.S. Rickman, and S. Mujumdar (2011) Sharing the gains of local economic growth: race-to-the-top versus race-to-the-bottom economic development. *Environment and Planning C: Politics and Space* 29.3, 428-56.

Hansen, H. (2007) Technology, talent and tolerance—the geography of the creative class in Sweden. *Rapporter och Notitser* 169, Department of Social and Regional Geography, Lund University, Lund.

Hanson, A. and S.M. Rohlin (2011) Do location-based tax incentives attract new business establishments? *Journal of Regional Science* 51.3, 427–49.

Hecker, D.E. (2005) High-technology employment: a NAICS-based update. *Monthly Labor Review* 128.7, 57–72.

Kirchhoff, B., C. Armington, I. Hasan and S. Newbert (2002) The influence of R&D expenditures on new firm formation and economic growth. Research report for the US Small Business Administration, Washington, DC.

Kirzner, I.M. (1997) Entrepreneurial discovery and the competitive market process: an Austrian approach. *Journal of Economic Literature* 35.1, 60–87.

Low, S., J. Henderson and S. Weiler (2005) Gauging a region's entrepreneurial potential. *Economic Review Federal Reserve Bank of Kansas City* QIII, 61–89.

Lucas, R. (1988) On the mechanics of economic development. *Journal of Monetary Economics* 22.1, 3–42.

Malecki, E.J. (1981) Science, technology, and regional economic development: review and prospects. *Research Policy* 10.4, 312–34.

Malecki, E.J. (1994) Entrepreneurship in regional and local development. *International Regional Science Review* 16.1/2, 119–53.

Malecki, E.J. (2004) Jockeying for position: what it means and why it matters to regional development policy when places compete. *Regional Studies* 38.9, 1101–20.

Marlet, G. and C. van Woerkens (2004) Skills and creativity in a cross-section of Dutch cities. Discussion Paper Series 04-29. Tjalling C. Koopmans Research Institute, Utrecht.

Marlet, G. and C. van Woerkens (2007) The Dutch creative class and how it fosters urban employment growth. *Urban Studies* 44.13, 2605–26.

McGranahan, D. and T. Wojan (2007) Recasting the creative class to examine growth processes in rural and urban counties. *Regional Studies* 41.2, 197–216.

McGranahan, D.A., T.R. Wojan and D.M. Lambert (2010) The rural growth trifecta: outdoor amenities, creative class and entrepreneurial context. *Journal of Economic Geography* 11.3, 529–57.

Mellander, C. and R. Florida (2007) The creative class or human capital? Explaining regional development in Sweden. KTH/CESIS, Electronic Working Paper Series in Economics and Institutions of Innovation Paper No. 79, Stockholm.

OECD (Organisation for Economic Co-operation and Development) (1998) *Fostering entrepreneurship*. OECD, Paris.

Parker, S.C. and M.T. Robson (2004) Explaining international variations in self-employment: evidence from a panel of OECD countries. *Southern Economic Journal* 71.2, 287–301.

Partridge, M.D. and M.R. Olfert (2011) The winners' choice: sustainable economic strategies for successful 21st-century regions. *Applied Economic Policy Perspectives* 33.2, 143–78.

Partridge, M.D., D.S. Rickman, K. Ali and M.R. Olfert (2008a) Employment growth in the American urban hierarchy: long live distance. *The B.E. Journal of Macroeconomics* 8.1, Article 10.

Partridge, M.D., D.S. Rickman, K. Ali and M.R. Olfert (2008b) Lost in space: population growth in the American hinterlands and small cities. *Journal of Economic Geography* 8.6, 727–57.

Polèse, M. and R. Shearmur (2004) Is distance really dead? Comparing industrial location over time in Canada. *International Regional Science Review* 27.4, 431–57.

Porter, M.E. (1998) *On competition*. Harvard Business School Press, Cambridge, MA.

Porter, M.E. and S. Stern (2001) Innovation: location matters. *MIT Sloan Management Review* 42.4, 28–39.

Rausch, S. and C. Negrey (2006) Does the creative engine run? A consideration of the effect of creative class on economic strength and growth. *Journal of Urban Affairs* 28.5, 473–89.

Robson, M.T. (1998) Self-employment in the UK regions. *Applied Economics* 30.3, 313–22.

Rodríguez-Pose, A. (1999) Innovation prone and innovation averse societies: economic performance in Europe. *Growth and Change* 30.1, 75–105.

Rodríguez-Pose, A. and R. Crescenzi (2008) Research and development, spillovers, innovation systems, and the genesis of regional growth in Europe. *Regional Studies* 42.1, 51–67.

Schumpeter, J.A. (1911) *The theory of economic development*. Harvard University Press, Cambridge, MA.

Shapero, A. (1984) The entrepreneurial event. In C.A. Kent (ed.), *The environment for entrepreneurship*, Lexington Books, Lexington, MA.

Shearmur, R. (2010) Innovation, regions and proximity: from neo-regionalism to spatial analysis. *Regional Studies* 45.9, 1225–43.

Shrestha, S.S., S.J. Goetz and A. Rupasingha (2007) Proprietorship formations and US job growth. *Review of Regional Studies* 37.2, 146–68.

Stephens, H. and M.D. Partridge (2011) Do entrepreneurs enhance economic growth in lagging regions? *Growth and Change* 42.4, 431–65.

Stephens, H., M.D. Partridge and A. Faggian (2013) Innovation, entrepreneurship and economic growth in lagging regions. *Journal of Regional Science* 53.5, 778–812.

Stock, J.H. and M.W. Watson (2007) *Introduction to econometrics*. Second edition, Pearson, Boston, MA.

Storper, M. and A.J. Scott (2009) Rethinking human capital, creativity and urban growth. *Journal of Economic Geography* 9.2, 147–67.

Vale, S. (2005) International data on business start-ups: factors affecting comparability. CEPR Discussion Paper No. 871, Centre for Economic Policy Research, London.

Wennekers, S. and A.R. Thurik (1999) Linking entrepreneurship and economic growth. *Small Business Economics* 13.1, 27–55.

Wojan, T.R., D.M. Lambert and D.A. McGranahan (2007) Emoting with their feet: Bohemian attraction to creative milieu. *Journal of Economic Geography* 7.6, 711–36.

Yankow, J. (2003) Migration, job change and wage growth: a new perspective on the pecuniary return to geographic mobility. *Journal of Regional Science* 43.3, 483–516.

Yigitcanlar, T., S. Baum and S. Horton (2007) Attracting and retaining knowledge workers in knowledge cities. *Journal of Knowledge Management* 11.5, 6–17.

Yu, J. and R. Jackson (2011) Regional innovation clusters: a critical review. *Growth and Change* 42.2, 111–24.

DOI:10.1111/1468-2427.12554

— THE GEOGRAPHY OF INNOVATION IN CHINA AND INDIA

RICCARDO CRESCENZI AND ANDRÉS RODRÍGUEZ-POSE

Abstract

The BRICS countries in general, and China and India in particular, are now widely regarded as the areas of the world likely to challenge the economic leadership of the United States (US) and the European Union (EU). A large part of this challenge will come from rapid technological catch-up by China and India. Yet, despite a recent rise in interest, there is limited knowledge about how and where innovation takes place in these two leading emerging countries and to what extent the Chinese and Indian territorial systems of innovation differ from those in the EU or the US. In this article we explore the geography of innovation in China and India, concentrating on understanding key territorial-level innovation trends by country, region and technology field, using the US and the EU as benchmarks. We find significant contrasts between the geography of innovation in China and India and that of the US and the EU. First, the degree of concentration of innovative activities in both countries is extremely high. Levels of agglomeration of innovation in the coastal provinces of China, as well as in Delhi and the South of India, significantly exceed the levels of agglomeration found in the USA and the EU. Secondly, China has witnessed a more rapid increase in the degree of concentration of innovation than India. We posit that the differences in the geography of innovation between, on the one hand, China and India and, on the other hand, between these countries and the developed world are rooted in different institutional settings, different systems of innovation and different national innovation strategies.

Introduction

Considerable attention has been focused on the similarities and differences in the territorial dynamics of innovation between the European Union (EU) and the United States (US) (see, for example, Freeman, 2002; Dosi *et al.*, 2006; Crescenzi *et al.*, 2007; Navarro *et al.*, 2009). Their status as leading innovation and technology hubs of the world warranted this attention. However, their position as the most innovative poles is being challenged by emerging countries, specifically by the BRICS countries (Brazil, Russia, India, China and South Africa; or BRIICS countries, which include Indonesia) bursting onto the scene. The growing academic and policy interest in these countries—and especially in India and China—reflects their increasing economic importance as well as their demographic potential. BRICS countries have rapidly transformed themselves, gaining significant economic and political clout in the process (Crescenzi *et al.*, 2012; Rodríguez-Pose and Wilkie, 2016; Crescenzi and Jaax, 2017). Spectacular urbanization in India and in China in particular has been the most visible symbol of this transition (He and Mao, 2016). India's cities alone could generate 70% of net new jobs up to 2030 and by then represent more than 70% of its GDP, to reflect urban population growth from 290 million in 2001 to 340 million in 2008, and to a projected 590 million in 2030 (MGI, 2010). Similarly, China's urban population is expected to increase from 636 million in 2010 to 905 million by 2030 (UN Population Division, 2011). Rapid changes and sustained high levels of growth are likely to place the BRICS countries—and, fundamentally, China and India—among the key economic players of the future. China is already the second largest economy in the world and is catching up quickly with the US. An influential Goldman Sachs report, 'Dreaming with

The authors are grateful to Peter Nijkamp, Tüzin Baycan and Roger Stough, as well as to two anonymous IJURR referees for helpful suggestions on earlier drafts of this article. Financial support under the European Union's Horizon 2020 Program (H2020/2014-2020), Grant Agreement No. 639633-MASSIVE-ERC-2014-STG, is gratefully acknowledged.

BRICS', suggests that by 2040, China will be the largest economy and India the third largest, surpassing the economies of Japan, Germany, France and Great Britain (Wilson and Purushothaman, 2003; see also Jacques, 2012).

In terms of innovation, the past two decades have seen the globalization of production and R&D (Bruche, 2009; Lundvall, 2009; Yeung, 2009; Fu and Soete, 2010; Kuchiki and Tsuji, 2010). China and India have been at the forefront of these shifts (Leadbeater and Wilsdon, 2007; Popkin and Iyengar, 2007; Parayil and D'Costa, 2009) and their economic dynamism is increasingly based on endogenous innovative capacity rather than on mass production and cheap labour (Friedman, 2005). Yet, despite the growing economic importance of the BRICS countries and the phenomenal changes in innovation capacity in China and India, very little is known about the geography of innovation in these emerging countries. Little systematic comparative analysis exists and past analyses have been fundamentally limited to describing the major 'inputs' for the generation of innovation, such as the quantity and quality of innovative efforts or the different levels of human capital accumulation, the structure of the educational system, and the capacity to attract, generate and retain top-level scientists (Winters and Yusuf, 2007). Alternatively, research has focused on the organizational and institutional settings that shape innovation and the innovation systems (see, for example, Lundvall *et al.*, 2006; Lundvall, 2009), but analysis of indigenous factors and their geography has been more limited, with literature generally being based on case studies (see, for example, Lewis, 2007; Chaminade, 2010) and, sometimes, on anecdotal evidence. By and large, there has been a tendency to assume, in a Rostovian way (Rostow, 1959), that emerging countries are in an earlier stage of the innovative process than the EU or the US and that they will tend to follow a similar path towards innovation and development in the future (World Bank, 2009). However, this assumption flies in the face of facts that indicate that, first, the pace of change currently experienced by emerging countries has virtually no parallels in history (Henderson, 2010) and that, secondly, even between the EU and US the territorial dynamics of innovation have differed widely (Crescenzi *et al.*, 2007). Hence, the limited knowledge we have about the evolutionary trajectories of countries such as China or India, coupled with the diversity of development and innovation paths of countries now at the forefront of science and technology, raise numerous questions about the territorial dimension of the process of technological development in China and India (Crescenzi *et al.*, 2012). How have global changes in the production of ideas affected Chinese and Indian regions and cities? What role are regions and cities playing in the shifting geography of innovative activity? Will China and India follow the innovation path of the EU, or are they more likely to move in the direction of the US? Or will they follow their own path and build their own unique systems of innovation?

This article represents a first exploration of the geography of innovation in China and India, using the US and the EU as benchmarks and paying special attention to developments at subnational level. This is why, in the next section, we look at the spatial distribution of innovative activity, proxied by patents, taking into account differences by country, region and technological sectors (ICT, biotech and nanotech). In the third part we revisit these stylized facts for China and India in light of the main theories of innovation and development to interpret existing evolutionary processes and identify emerging trends. In the final section, we present our main conclusions.

Innovation in China and India vs. Europe and the US: the broad picture in territorial perspective

–   A country-level comparative perspective

The first stage of our analysis involves an overview of the comparative 'innovation performance' of China and India, using the US and the EU as benchmarks. We first focus on patents as the most commonly used, albeit highly imperfect, innovation 'output'.[1] An important caveat to using patent data in China and India is that it partly reflects patenting activity by multinational firms (MNEs). MNE patents may be filed in any office around the world, regardless of where invention thereof actually took place, making it hard to assign patents to a specific territory (Li and Pai, 2010). There are close links between foreign firms, MNE clusters and patenting clusters in India and China. For example, Duan and Kong (2008), in a study of Chinese patents from 1988 to 2007, observe that most 'Chinese' applications to the United States Patent and Trademark Office (USPTO) are owned by foreign applicants. Da Motta e Alburquerque (2003) suggests a similar pattern for India. Patenting is also related to firm size. Patenting data over-represents innovations in large firms (often located in major agglomerations), while underestimating innovation in smaller firms, which also tend to be located outside the main centres of innovation. Finally, patenting is bound to significantly under-represent certain types of innovation, such as process innovation, and incremental innovation conducted by generally local firms. However, despite all the imperfections of patenting data for China and India—which reproduce the imperfections of patenting data elsewhere in the world—lack of alternative and comparable territorial data on innovation implies the need to resort to patents as the only suitable available indicator of innovation, while relying on data based on patent applicants' location capture the innovative performance of local firms to the maximum extent possible.

Figure 1 illustrates the evolution of patenting trends in China and India, relative to the US and the EU, in the period before the global crisis—between 1995 and 2007. A striking feature of patent intensity is China and India's heavy investment in innovation 'inputs'—increasing literacy rates and higher education enrolment, raising production of engineering graduates and increasing expenditure on R&D—have been translated into rapidly rising patenting rates (clearly visible in the corresponding trend lines in Figure 1). However, while China and India matched each other during the 1990s, the

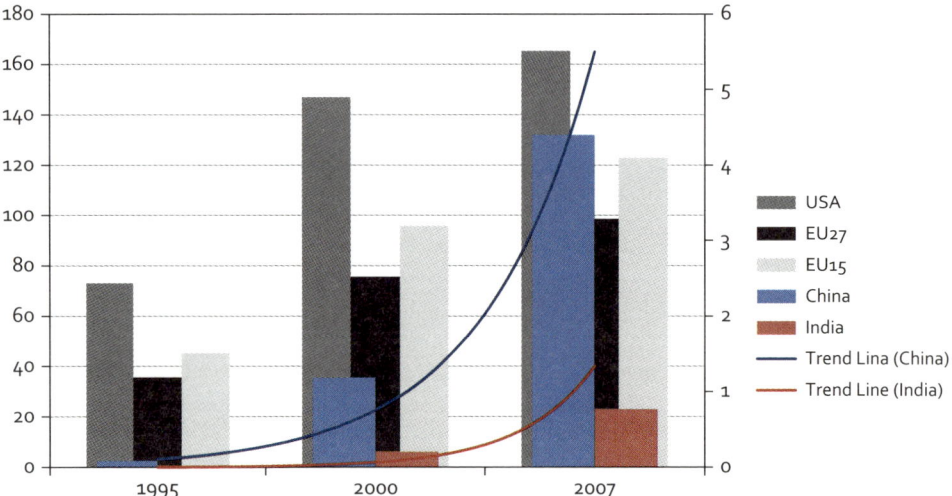

NOTES: US, EU27 and EU15 on primary axis (left-hand scale), China and India on secondary axis (right-hand scale); Patent Cooperation Treaty (PCT) patents per million inhabitants used in the calculation.

FIGURE 1   Patent intensity in China, India, the US and the EU (1995-2007) (*source*: authors' own research, based on OECD patent databases)

---

1   Our data stem from OECD Patent Cooperation Treaty (PCT) patent applications, thus avoiding problems that might arise from using domestic Chinese or Indian data (Li and Pai, 2010; Wadhwa, 2010).

2000s witnessed a divergence between the two countries. Indian patenting started to stall from 2003 onwards, precisely as China's patents took off. Between 2000 and 2007 patent intensity in China rose fourfold up to 4.4 patents per million inhabitants. By contrast, patenting in India had by 2007 not yet exceeded the threshold of 0.8 patents per million inhabitants (see Figure 1).

Despite this non-negligible catch-up, in particular by China since 2000, the gap between the US and the EU, on the one hand, and China and India, on the other, is still considerable. In 2007, in absolute terms the EU filed almost eight times more patent applications than China and almost 39 times more than India. Taking into account that this ratio was 156:1 with respect to China and more than 2,000:1 with respect to India in 1994, there has certainly been rapid convergence. But rapid convergence does not hide the sheer dimension of the innovation output gap between the leading developed countries and the leading emerging countries (see Figure 1).

However, a quick look at the evolution of innovation 'inputs' indicates that the convergence rate of innovation outputs is not only likely to continue, but—as more recent data indicate—to accelerate in years to come. The gap in R&D expenditure as a percentage of GDP, often regarded as one of the key innovation inputs, has been narrowing very rapidly since the turn of the century. This is particularly the case between China and the EU. Whereas in 1995 R&D expenditure relative to GDP in the EU almost tripled that of China, the significant effort made by the Chinese government and firms to catch up in R&D expenditure meant that the gap in 2007 was a mere 20% in favour of the EU (see Figure 2—in this figure, data for all countries are shown on the same axis and scale). The R&D gap had all but disappeared by 2013 (Rodríguez-Pose and Wilkie, 2016). The gaps in R&D expenditure between the US, the EU and India, by contrast, have remained more stable (see Figure 2). The comparison of the trend lines between China and India confirms the higher R&D dynamism of the former.

The evolution of the endowment of skilled human capital in both China and India also points towards greatly enhanced potential to create new knowledge and to assimilate externally generated innovation. The effort both countries put in to increase their human capital is starting to pay off. While the US still has significantly more graduates than India or China, the EU trails behind the US considerably, although it

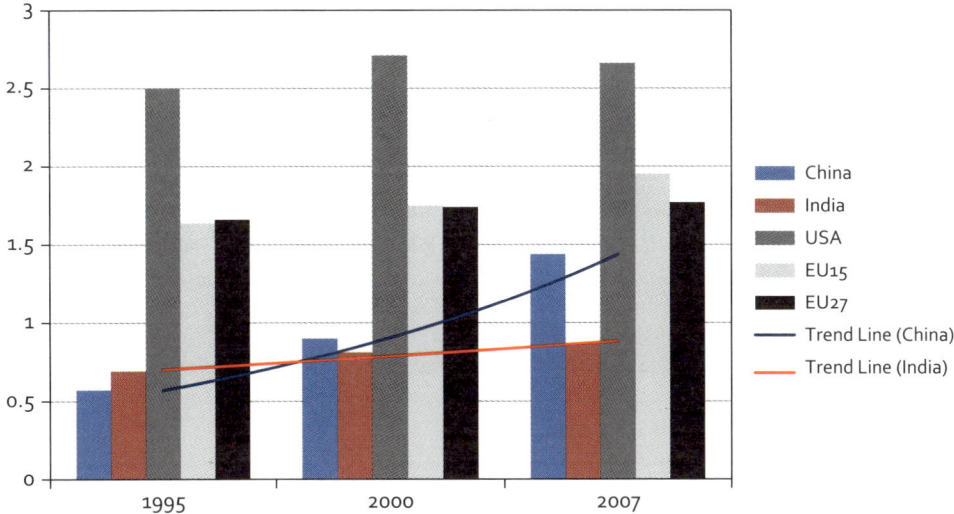

FIGURE 2 Evolution of R&D expenditure as a percentage of GDP for China, India, the US and the EU (1994–2007) (*source*: authors' own research, based on OECD patent databases)

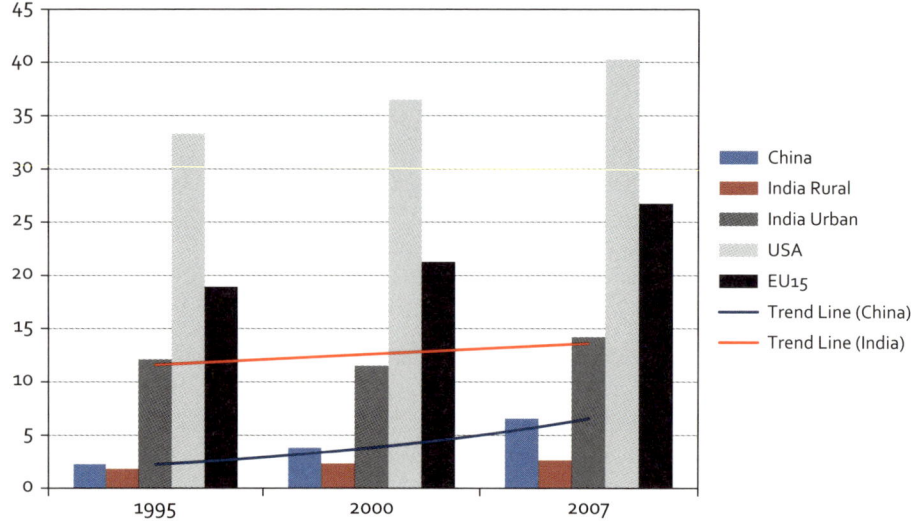

FIGURE 3   Share of population that has a tertiary education (1994–2007) (*source:* authors' own research, based on OECD patent databases)

has a relevant margin in terms of endowment of human capital relative to China and India (see Figure 3). However, there is evidence, especially since 2000, of considerable catch-up on the part of the two emerging countries. Particularly in certain technological fields the gap is vanishing rapidly. The number of engineering graduates in China (352,000 graduates) and in India (184,000 graduates) already clearly exceeded that of the US (76,000 graduates) as early as the year 2000 (Mitra, 2007). The quality of graduates has also improved. Not only have Chinese and Indian universities moved closer to the knowledge and technological frontier; China has, since 2000, also been sending its best graduates to foreign institutions in droves. In this respect China has been more aggressive than India, although Indian returnees have been crucial for the development of specific high-tech and scientific sectors in the country, such as the ICT sector (Saxenian, 2006). This internal effort has also translated into a rise in the number of scientists. China only trails behind the US in terms of overall number of researchers (Schaaper, 2009), whereas India's R&D worker intensity, which rose significantly in the 1990s and early 2000s, has stalled somewhat since then.

–   The territorial dimension of innovation in China and India

The country-level comparative perspective hides significant contrasts in how innovative capacity is distributed both within China and India, and how the geography of innovation in these two countries differs from that of the US and Europe.

Research capacity and innovation are not spread evenly across China and India. Indeed, the geography of innovative activity in China and India—as is the case in other emerging countries (Rodríguez-Pose and Villarreal Peralta, 2015; Crescenzi and Jaax, 2017)—is territorially very uneven. Patent counts at the subnational level indicate that the five EU regions with the highest shares of patent applications together represent 35% of all EU patenting; for the US the corresponding figure is about 50%. By contrast, the five most innovative Indian regions cover 75% of Indian patents; in China, the five regions with the highest patent share produce almost 80% of all patent applications.[2]

2   In each case the most appropriate comparable spatial unit has been selected under the constraint of regionalized patent data availability from the OECD—using Chinese provinces, Indian states, and, finally, the American Bureau of Economic Analysis (BEA) Economic Areas, as a benchmark.

Both India and China have innovation systems that tend to be significantly more spatially concentrated than in the US and, of course, the EU, where the heritage of national innovation systems is still evident. China's innovative capacity is spread along its coastal regions, especially in the larger cities and in the South (Sun, 2003; Wang and Lin, 2008; Rodríguez-Pose and Wilkie, 2016). Chinese data indicate that Guangdong, the leading province, accounted for 46% of total average patent applications over the period from 1994 to 2007. It was followed by the municipalities of Beijing (14%) and Shanghai (13%). The overall system was highly agglomerated, with the top three regions accounting for 73% of all patents.

In India, patent counts were highest in high-tech clusters such as Bangalore, Chennai, Delhi, Hyderabad, Mumbai and Pune (Mitra, 2007). At the regional level, da Motta e Alburquerque (2003) found that from 1981 to 2002 nearly half of all patents to Indian inventors were in two states: Maharashtra and Delhi. Our data confirm that Maharashtra (with Mumbai as its capital) and Delhi accounted for 26% and 24% of total average patents, respectively. The third was the former state of Andhra Pradesh (former capital Hyderabad, now the capital of the new state of Telangana) with 13%. The top three Indian states accounted for 64% of all patent counts over the period of analysis. One step below were the states around Delhi (Haryana—with 7% of total patent counts, as well as Punjab[3] and Himachal Pradesh) and some of the larger states of the South, such as Karnataka with 8.7% (capital Bangalore) and Tamil Nadu with 7% (capital Chennai).

The analysis of the geographical distribution of patent counts in the US puts the dimension of the geographical concentration of innovation activity in China and India into perspective. The US is acknowledged as the world leader on a range of innovation metrics and often considered the epitome of geographically self-contained innovation systems (Crescenzi *et al.*, 2007). Innovation in the US is indeed geographically concentrated, displaying two important innovation cores along the northeast (New England and the eastern part of the Atlantic States) and the West Coast (from Seattle to San Diego). However, the rest of the country is far from an innovation desert, as strong innovation hubs can be found throughout the country (for example, Minneapolis, Milwaukee-Madison, Cincinnati, Austin).

The US thus has a smoother spatial distribution of patent applications than either China or India, as can be seen in Table 1, which lists the twenty most innovative regions in China, India and the US in terms of patent intensity. In the US, the three leading regions were San Jose-San Francisco-Oakland (northern California), San Diego-Carlsbad-San Marcos (southern California) and Appleton-Oshkosh-Neenah (Wisconsin). These three accounted for only 32% of all patenting, compared to 73% and 64% shares for, respectively, the leading Chinese and Indian regions. Generally, the more innovative regions in the US were located on the western and eastern seaboards, or in the Great Lakes region (Illinois, Minnesota, Wisconsin). Less innovative areas were relatively less populated and tended to be confined to the Midwest—in particular, some of the Western Plains counties—and to the deep South (Louisiana, Mississippi, Alabama and southern Georgia). But even in these areas there were major innovation hubs, such as Austin (Texas), Houston-Baytown-Huntsville (Texas) and Denver-Aurora-Boulder (Colorado) (Lee and Rodríguez-Pose, 2016).

In China, as we have seen, the leading regions for innovation are in coastal areas. Outside these regions, very few provinces have accounted for more than 1% to 3% of total patenting. Fundamentally, these are in other coastal provinces (for example, Fujian, Liaoning, Jiangsu, Zhejiang and, to a lesser extent, Shandong). Among those that filed more than 1% of patents, only Sichuan (southwest) and Hunan (centre) are not on the coast. The centre and the West of China were less innovative, with western provinces

3   Indira Gandhi's raid on the Golden Temple in Amritsar in 1984 resulted in large-scale migration of the skilled Sikh population, which severely dented Punjab's innovation capacity.

TABLE 1 Top 20 innovative regions in terms of patent intensity (1994 to 2007)

	China	India	USA		China	India	USA
1	Beijing	Delhi	San Jose-San Francisco-Oakland, CA	11	Chongqing	Himachal Pradesh	Reno-Sparks, NV
2	Shanghai	Haryana	San Diego-Carlsbad-San Marcos, CA	12	Heilongjiang	West Bengal	New York-Newark-Bridgeport, NY-NJ-CT-PA
3	Guangdong	Chandigarh	Appleton-Oshkosh-Neenah, WI	13	Sichuan	Kerala	Gainesville, FL
4	Tianjin	Maharashtra	Minneapolis-St. Paul-St. Cloud, MN-WI	14	Shaanxi	Punjab	Seattle-Tacoma-Olympia, WA
5	Zhejiang	Andhra Pradesh	Boston-Worcester-Manchester, MA-NH	15	Jilin	Uttar Pradesh	Boise City-Nampa, ID
6	Fujian	Karnataka	Cincinnati-Middletown-Wilmington, OH-KY-IN	16	Hainan	Jharkhand	Chicago-Naperville-Michigan City, IL-IN-WI
7	Jiangsu	Goa	Rochester-Batavia-Seneca Falls, NY	17	Hubei	Rajasthan	Houston-Baytown-Huntsville, TX
8	Liaoning	Gujarat	Austin-Round Rock, TX	18	Shanxi	Madhya Pradesh	Hartford-West, Hartford-Willimantic, CT
9	Shandong	Tamil Nadu	Philadelphia-Camden-Vineland, PA-NJ-DE-MD	19	Inner Mongolia	Jammu and Kashmir	Raleigh-Durham-Cary, NC
10	Hunan	Pondicherry	Albany-Schenectady-Amsterdam, NY	20	Xinjiang	Orissa	Santa Fe-Espanola, NM

SOURCE: Authors' own research, based on OECD patent databases

such as Tibet and Qinghai, and central provinces, such as Ningxia, barely generating patent applications.

In India, little innovation is conducted outside the already mentioned innovation hubs of Mumbai, Delhi, Bangalore, Chennai, Hyderabad or Pune—at least, when measured by patents. Some of the largest and most populated states of the North—Bihar, Madhya Pradesh, Orissa, Rajasthan and Uttar Pradesh—produce little innovation, reflecting the presence of less dynamic or even dying sectors and industries and complex or outright problematic political environments and industrial relations. But even there, the situation is better than in the 'seven sister states' of the extreme northeast, which are virtually innovation deserts. Some of these had no patent applications until 2007, including some relatively large states such as Assam (located in northeast India, on the border with Bhutan and Bangladesh).

–   An increasing tendency towards concentration of innovation

An important factor worth noting is that the geographical concentration of innovative activity in China and India shows no sign of abating. If anything, the agglomeration of innovation is increasing very rapidly, in particular in China. Patenting in India and China is far more spatially agglomerated than in the US and, especially, the EU. In addition, differential levels of investment in innovation inputs also appear to influence where innovative activity takes place. Top patenting regions in China account for a considerably larger share of innovative activity than those in India.

However, rather than 'maturing' and following the same path as the US or the EU towards a more even geographical distribution of innovative activity, the pace of concentration of innovation accelerated during the period of analysis.

A comparison of Figures 4 and 5 signals the evolution of the geographical dimension of innovation over the period from 1994 to 2007: Figure 4 refers to the situation in 1994, whereas Figure 5 covers 2007. As had been highlighted by Sun (2003), we find evidence of increasing spatial agglomeration of innovative activity in China since the 1990s, as measured by patents, which since 2000 outstrips that of India. Between

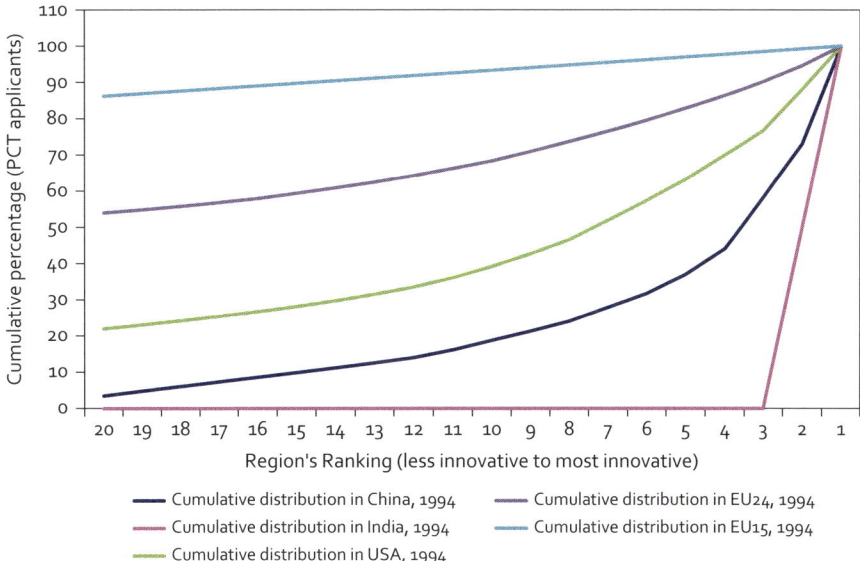

NOTES: China data 31 provinces; India data 24 states; USA data 179 BEA EA, EU24 data (Cyprus, Lithuania and Malta not included) 841 OECD TL3; EU15 data 653 OECD TL3

FIGURE 4 Cumulative distribution of average PCT applications: top 20 most innovative regions (1994) (*source*: author's own elaboration, based on OECD regional statistics and indicators)

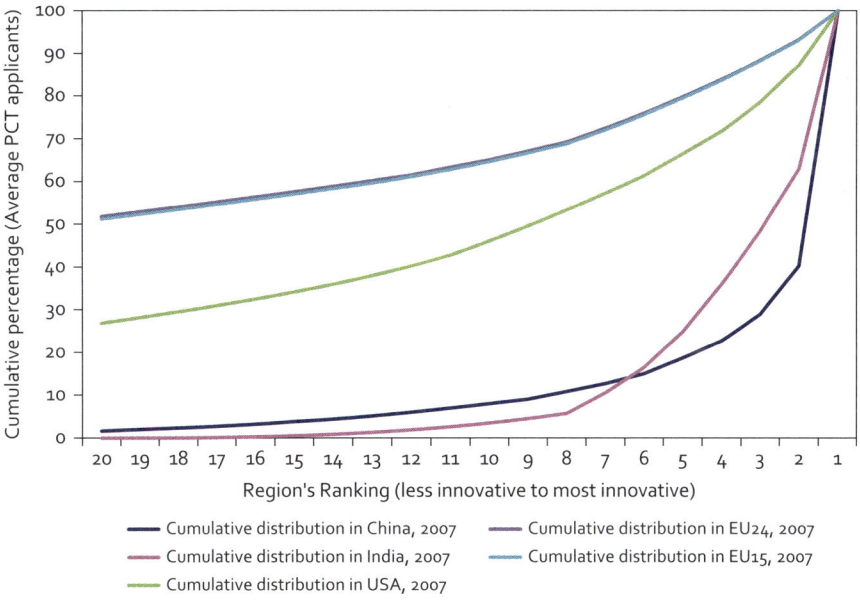

NOTE: China data 1994-2007, 31 provinces; India data 1994-2007, 24 states; USA data 1994-2007, 179 BEA EA; EU15 data 1994-2007

FIGURE 5 Cumulative distribution of average PCT applications: top 20 most innovative regions (2007) (*source*: author's own elaboration, based on OECD regional statistics and indicators)

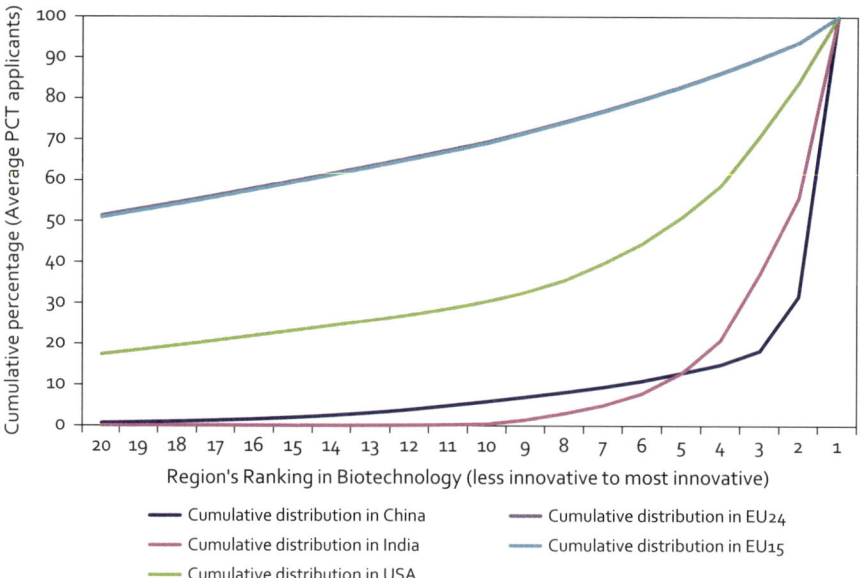

NOTES: China data 1994-2007, 31 provinces; India data 1994-2007, 24 states; USA data 1994-2007, 179 BEA EA; EU15 data 1994-2007

FIGURE 6 Cumulative distribution of average PCT applications in biotechnology: top 20 (1994-2007) (*source*: author's own elaboration, based on OECD regional statistics and indicators)

1994 and 2000 innovative activity in India was far more concentrated than in China. The majority of Indian states did not generate any patents at the beginning of the period of analysis (only seven patent applications were filed in India in 1994), meaning that all patenting activity was limited to two states (see Figure 5). At that time, innovation in China also exhibited a high level of concentration in a limited number of provinces. This geographical agglomeration of innovation was far greater in China than in the US and, in turn, higher in the US than in the EU. By the late 1990s the pattern began to change, and by 2007 patenting was already more clustered in Chinese provinces than in Indian states (Figure 5).

This concentration of innovation activity across Chinese provinces and Indian states is reproduced in every sector considered. When the overall patent count is broken down into technology fields, the resulting figures mimic the pattern already unveiled in previous figures. Figure 6 shows the spatial distribution of biotechnology patenting across the countries included in the analysis, for the whole period from 1994 to 2007. Although biotechnology patenting was somewhat more spatially agglomerated in China and India than overall patenting, the general trends are very similar (see Figure 6). In China, the top three biotech regions accounted for over 80% of overall patenting in the field. As was the case for overall counts, both countries have more concentrated biotech patenting activity than the US—where the top three regions accounted for just over 30% of all biotech patents—and the EU.

The same territorial patterns of innovation are reproduced for other technology fields, such as information and communications technology (ICT) and nanotechnology. In terms of ICT patents, sectoral activity is also more agglomerated in China than in India, with both countries having long tails of trailing regions. Again, both countries' ICT patenting was much more spatially clustered than in the US and the EU. Only in innovation in nanotechnology was India more territorially agglomerated than China.

The top three Indian regions accounted for over 80% of nanotech patenting, against a share of approximate 60% for the leading Chinese regions. As in the case of the other two industries, nanotech patenting in both these countries remains significantly more agglomerated than in the US or the EU.

–   The spatial clustering of innovation inputs

The spatial analysis of innovation inputs unveils some interesting dynamics in the geography of innovation in the different contexts. Table 2 reproduces the ranking analysis for R&D spending (in India and the US) and science and technology spending (in China). Expenditure is weighted by population to give comparable measures of intensity for these innovation inputs.

Patterns of agglomeration for R&D spending differ from those for patenting. For the US, San Jose-San Francisco-Oakland was at the top of both league tables, but only three locations (San Jose-San Francisco-Oakland, Seattle-Tacoma-Olympia, and Rochester-Batavia-Seneca Falls) remained in the top 10 ranking. Altogether 13 locations appear on both counts in the top 20. Notably, Detroit-Warren-Flint was the second highest region for R&D, but did not feature in the top 20 patenting areas.

Only three states appeared in India's top 10 rankings in R&D and science and technology intensity: Delhi, Haryana and Chandigarh, the top 3 locations for patenting, ranked 17th, 7th and 4th in R&D spending, respectively. Five of China's top 10 regions for science and technology also featured in the top 10 for patenting applications, and Beijing and Shanghai remained the top three regions (Guangdong is 3rd for patents but 17th for science and technology intensity).

TABLE 2   Top 5 regions in terms of R&D/science and technology intensity (% of regional GDP)

	China R&D (2007)		India R&D (1994-2006)		USA, BEA-EAs, Private R&D (1994-2007)	
1	Beijing	5.40	Uttaranchal	0.47	San Jose-San Francisco-Oakland, CA (EA)	(Not comparable—ranking only)
2	Shanghai	2.52	Himachal Pradesh	0.35	Detroit-Warren-Flint, MI (EA)	(Not comparable—ranking only)
3	Tianjin	2.27	Jammu and Kashmir	0.21	New York-Newark-Bridgeport, NY-NJ-CT-PA (EA)	(Not comparable—ranking only)
4	Shaanxi	2.23	Chandigarh	0.16	Davenport-Moline-Rock Island, IA-IL (EA)	(Not comparable—ranking only)
5	Jiangsu	1.67	Punjab	0.15	Seattle-Tacoma-Olympia, WA (EA)	(Not comparable—ranking only)

SOURCES: China—Intramural expenditure on R&D as percentage of regional GDP, China Statistical Yearbook on Science and Technology (various years); India—Combines central government extramural and state total expenditure in R&D as a percentage of regional GDP, R&D statistics (various years); USA—Regional private R&D expenditure as a percentage of regional total personal income, proxy for ranking purposes only, calculated based on Compustat firm-level data (various years)

Table 3 gives rankings for human capital inputs—measured by country population shares with a tertiary education or above. The spatial distribution of human capital again differs from that for patenting and R&D spending. China's territorial system was the most similar across inputs and outputs, with six of its top 10 human capital regions also in the most innovative regions list. As with R&D spending, Beijing and Shanghai remained in the top three, in identical positions to their patents rankings.

Four of India's top human capital regions appeared also in the ten most innovative regions lists, with Delhi and Chandigarh in the top three in both cases. There was substantial change in the rest of the top 20. In the case of the US, Washington-Baltimore-Northern Virginia was the economic area with the highest share of graduates, but did not even feature in the top 20 patenting regions. This is largely explained by

TABLE 3   Top 5 regions in terms of tertiary education achievements (1994–2007)

	China (1995-2007)		India (1995-2006)		USA, BEA-EAs (1990 and 2000)	
1	Beijing	0.20	Chandigarh	0.25	Washington-Baltimore-Northern Virginia, DC-MD-VA-WV (EA)	0.33
2	Shanghai	0.14	Delhi	0.21	Austin-Round Rock, TX (EA)	0.32
3	Tianjin	0.10	Himachal Pradesh	0.19	Denver-Aurora-Boulder, CO (EA)	0.31
4	Xinjiang	0.07	Goa	0.16	San Jose- San Francisco-Oakland, CA (EA)	0.30
5	Liaoning	0.07	Uttar Pradesh	0.15	Boston-Worcester-Manchester, MA-NH (EA)	0.29

SOURCES: China—People with college-level or higher degrees as a share of total provincial population (age 6 and above), China Statistical Yearbook (various years); India—People with college, diploma or higher degrees (in urban areas) as a share of total state population (age 7 and above)—National Sample Survey (various years); USA—People with bachelor's degree and higher as a share of total BEA EA population (age 25 and above), USA Census Bureau Counties Data Files (various years)

Washington DC's large community of graduates working in politics and public policy rather than in sciences or high-tech manufacturing. Austin-Round Rock is a well-known US tech cluster with a large university, explaining its presence high up in the patents, R&D and human capital tables. Denver-Aurora-Boulder was the third highest region in terms of graduate population share, but again did not feature in the top 20 patenting regions. There was some movement in the rest of the table, but the set of regions remained largely the same.

The drivers of the geography of innovation in China and India

The analysis of our data revealed a number of interesting trends and stylized facts. First was that the traditional global hierarchy of innovation capacity persists. The US remains the world leader in technology, outperforming the EU, China and India in R&D, R&D workforce, research quality and university-educated population shares. But the gap between the innovative capacity of the developed world and these emerging countries is closing fast. China and, to a lesser extent, India are setting the basis, in terms of innovation and human capital inputs, for the future generation of knowledge in a more competitive world. Secondly, the effort in R&D and human capital by these countries has been highly selective, favouring centres and sectors with greater potential and contributing to the emergence of highly unbalanced geographies of innovation. The territorial polarization of innovation in these countries is unprecedented and exceeds anything seen in the US and the EU, where in recent decades there has been some consolidation of the most dynamic innovation poles (see Crescenzi et al., 2007). The drive towards greater territorial polarization of innovation potential shows no sign of abating.

What are the reasons behind such a marked catch-up in innovation by China and India and the highly unbalanced geographical nature of the innovation efforts in these two countries? The reasons for these developments can be found in the different innovation policies adopted by China and India and can be interpreted through the analytical lenses of the different theories that have dominated how we think about innovation in recent decades: the linear model of innovation, geographical analyses of knowledge spillovers, and theories about institutions and (regional) systems of innovation.

Both India and China have adopted innovation strategies that can be directly extracted from linear innovation and endogenous growth theories. The linear model of innovation (Bush, 1945; Maclaurin, 1953) posits a relatively simple path towards innovation: innovation is the direct outcome of investing greater resources into science and technology and human capital. The greater the investment in R&D, the greater the capacity of a country to innovate. Although starting from a different perspective, endogenous growth theories also highlight the importance of human capital, technology and knowledge in advancing the technological frontier. Subsequent productivity gains drive long-term growth rates (Romer, 1990). In practice, national governments have tended to operationalize linear model innovation and endogenous growth ideas by seeking to raise overall levels of human capital and ideas production. Therefore, policy frameworks are effectively 'national innovation system' models that promote key innovative actors such as businesses, central government, universities and public research institutes (Liu and White, 2001), which closely resemble the 'national science systems' explored by David Mowery and others (Mowery, 1992; Mowery and Oxley, 1995). Analyses focus on countries' performance on key inputs—R&D spending, human capital stock, university investment—and their links to key outputs such as patenting rates and 'gazelle' firms, i.e. high-growth companies with annual growth rates of 20% or more, which approximate ideas generation and diffusion.

The trajectories of China and India in this respect have by no means been completely similar. China not only has a more globalized economy—its science and technology and innovation systems have also developed greater linkages to the rest of the world. China's economic opening started timidly in 1978, with the creation of special enterprise zones and, by the time India was starting to think about the liberalization of its economy in 1991, the networks between its economy and the rest of the world were more or less firmly established (Jian *et al.*, 1996; Liu and Buck, 2007; Dahlman, 2010). Consequently, China benefited from greater intakes of foreign direct investment (FDI) and inflows of foreign technology than the South Asian giant (Dahlman, 2010). By contrast, until the 1991 currency crisis forced an acceleration of economic liberalization, India's development strategy had been largely autarkic, based on import substitution (*ibid.*). Since then, the country has shifted from 'highly regulated, autarkic' development to more market-led models, with further acceleration in the early 2000s (Gajwani *et al.*, 2006, Fleischer *et al.*, 2010). More than China, India has since been able to make a virtue of cultural and historical specificities in developing innovative capacity—most obviously the English language and democratic political institutions (Bound, 2007; Bruche, 2009).

However, in terms of innovation, the similarities possibly outweigh the differences. China and India have not been shy of adopting national-level perspectives of innovation. Both countries have historically emphasized technology-led national growth (Leadbeater and Wilsdon, 2007). Both India and China have used innovation and technology-led development to pursue national prestige and international positioning, for example, via space flight and atomic weapons programmes (*ibid.*). The shift from heavily statist models of public policy towards market-led reforms (Jian *et al.*, 1996; Fan, 2008; Fleischer *et al.*, 2010) since the mid-1980s (China) to the early 1990s (India) has not implied an abandonment of national frameworks for innovation. China and India continue to invest heavily in 'innovation inputs', such as R&D and higher education (HE), while developing their domestic innovation capacities (Lundin and Schwaag Serger, 2007), which both feed into and feed from rapid macroeconomic growth.

The policy paths are similar but not necessarily the same. In 2006 China announced a medium- to long-term Science and Technology Development Programme. The main aim of this programme was to increase R&D spending from a level of 1.3% of GDP in 2006 to 2.5% by 2020. This implies a sustained effort and growth rates in R&D in the range of 10 to 15% per year. India, by contrast, has been less vocal on the R&D front and concentrated more on the development of human capital and the clustering of scientific and technological activity in science parks (Mitra, 2007). It has also sought to encourage the improvement of science and technology generation and innovative capacity by means of specific instruments, such as the increase of research grants for researchers and tax incentives and concessional loans for firms (Mani, 2004). The Indian government has also encouraged the emergence of venture capital to address some of the funding problems affecting innovative firms. Furthermore, India has promoted the adoption of foreign technology in specific sectors, such as ICT (Dahlman,

2010), while China has been more keen on enhancing the capacity of domestic science and technology sectors.

The main drawback of linear models of innovation activity is that they pay minimal attention to space—and thus do not explain why innovative activity is so spatially concentrated in China and India.

The phenomenal level of concentration of innovative activities in China and India can therefore be explained by resorting to research on knowledge spillovers and the spatial dynamics of innovation. Different streams of literature bring space into the picture by showing how agglomeration supports innovative activity via localized knowledge spillovers (see, for example, Jaffe *et al.*, 1993; Audretsch and Feldman, 1996; Malmberg *et al.*, 1996; Acs *et al.*, 2002; Carlino *et al.*, 2007). As neither agglomeration nor innovation can be measured directly, density and patenting are typically used as proxies (as in the data presented in the previous section of this article). Research on knowledge spillovers has put the emphasis on the fact that innovation does not diffuse in a costless manner in space. Indeed, analyses of innovation diffusion have tended to highlight the presence of relatively strong distance decay effects. This has been found to be true in Europe (Moreno *et al.*, 2005; Rodríguez-Pose and Crescenzi, 2008), as well as in the US (Anselin *et al.*, 1997; Varga, 2000; Sonn and Storper, 2008). Hence the combination of economies of agglomeration, often linked to urbanization, with high costs for the diffusion of innovation points to the fact that countries wanting to make a significant leap in innovation capacity may be better off by geographically concentrating their innovation inputs.

A number of studies suggest that proximity–spillover–innovation links also operate in developing country contexts, with strong evidence that urbanization boosts productive efficiency (Scott and Garofoli, 2007; Duranton, 2008; Xu, 2009). China and India are no exceptions. Sustained national inputs into innovation coupled with agglomeration and economic externalities have been key to the rapid emergence of cities such as Delhi, Mumbai, Bangalore and Hyderabad as innovation hubs in India, and to the prevalence of Beijing, Shanghai, Guangzhou and Shenzhen as the centres of innovation activity in China. Most indicators point towards these dynamic innovation poles sucking large resources from neighbouring areas, while so far providing limited evidence of large-scale diffusion of the knowledge being generated there. Both in China and India, backwash innovation effects still clearly prevail over spread effects (Crescenzi *et al.*, 2012). However, the dimension and evolution of backwash innovation effects may be constrained by the very pace of urbanization that is driving them. Specifically, rapid or chaotic urbanization can outstrip governments' ability to provide adequate infrastructure and public services (Venables, 2005; Cohen, 2006; Chen *et al.*, 2016). Thus, agglomerations are also strongly correlated with poverty and informal development and may undermine future innovative capacity.

Path dependency is another factor explaining the uneven geography of innovation (Martin and Sunley, 2006; Simmie *et al.*, 2008; Crescenzi and Jaax, 2017). This is particularly evident in the case of India, which has tended to suffer less from historical upheavals—at least in terms of the location of innovation and industrial activity—than China. Maharashtra's success has been partially built on an old concentration of pharmaceutical industries and on the industrial hubs in Mumbai-Pune-Nasik. Mumbai has also benefited from the presence of prestigious research institutes, such as the Tata Institute of Fundamental Research (TIFR) and the Indian Institute of Technology (IIT). The states in the South also enjoyed historical comparative advantages, such as the presence of an old hub of auto components in Tamil Nadu and some of the top Indian engineering schools in Karnataka. Gujarat in the West has built its innovation capacity on the back of a dynamic entrepreneurial class.

Inadequate institutional capacity may also become another important barrier to innovation in both countries. Country- and locality-specific factors—history, institutions, networks and norms—have a marked influence on innovation outcomes and have played an important role in the development of literatures on institutions and systems of innovation (see Freeman, 1987; Lundvall, 2009). Regional innovation systems (RIS) localize and spatialize these frameworks to specific regions and clusters (Piore and Sabel, 1984; Saxenian, 1994; Cooke et al., 1997; Storper, 1997; Cooke, 2002; Asheim and Gertler, 2005). The central insight is that proximity facilitates innovation, or as Asheim and Gertler (2005: 309–10) suggest, 'the geographic configuration of economic agents ... is fundamentally important in shaping the innovative capabilities of firms and industries'. RIS analysis heavily focuses on firms and their capabilities. Specific regional factors such as the presence of universities and public agencies, networks and institutions determine, in conjunction with national-level factors and institutions, the economic performance of individual firms and local actors. The interactions within RIS between the private sector, the public sector and universities confirm a 'triple helix' of relationships (Cooke, 2002) at the heart of the success (or lack thereof) of individual innovation systems.

RIS may not work in exactly the same way in emerging countries (see, for example, Scott and Garofoli, 2007; Lundvall, 2009; Padilla-Pérez et al., 2009). First, large sections of local innovative systems in China and India rely, to a much greater extent than in developed countries, on informal activities and even the informal sector. The institutional framework and social capital on which these systems rely are therefore shaped in a different way from what has been described in the developed world (Rodríguez-Pose and Di Cataldo, 2015). Secondly, both countries' systems—especially China's—have evolved swiftly as a consequence of rapid development and as result of the insertion of innovative actors into global production chains (Mitra, 2007; Bruche, 2009; Yeung, 2009). Thirdly, their international ascent has happened in the absence of robust, stable and high-quality institutions that are generally deemed essential for generating greater innovation, productivity and economic growth, producing the 'puzzle' of trying to explain the fast expansion of innovation under weak institutional conditions (Saxenian and Sabel, 2008).

Unlike innovation systems in developed countries, formal institutions remain weak in China and India, especially at the regional level. Intellectual property regimes provide only partial coverage and public agencies may not always be welfare-maximizing (Altenburg, 2009; Joseph, 2009). Capital and finance are often limited, and university–industry collaborations frail, with universities simply acting as suppliers of human capital (of varying quality) rather than of direct innovation-generating knowledge (Padilla-Pérez et al., 2009).

All of these factors place constraints on the ability of firms and economic organizations in China and India to develop new products and services—and limit managers' incentives to collaborate with other firms (Altenburg, 2009). In this context, MNEs become crucial providers of both capital flows (via FDI) and new technologies (via alliances, collaborations and spillovers) (Cantwell, 2005). More than half of global R&D is done within MNEs: in 2007 Toyota (at US $8.4 billion) and GM (at US $8.1 billion) each spent more on R&D than the Indian government (Dahlman, 2010). Also, in both China and India, multinational firms' location patterns closely follow those of patents, and vice versa. Between 60% and 80% of all MNEs in India and China were concentrated in Beijing and Shanghai and on the Bangalore-Pune-Delhi axis, respectively (Bruche, 2009).

Scarce or inadequate innovation agents, limited capacity to collaborate among firms, and limited presence of MNEs in inland China and in northeastern India thus represent insurmountable barriers to the development of innovative capacity in these areas. If we add inadequate institutions, it is not surprising that agglomeration and regional systems of innovation reinforce one another to create a very uneven and territorially unbalanced geography of innovation in China and in India.

Under such conditions, export markets and trade entry points become an important source of knowledge exchange and innovation, and the Chinese and Indian governments (and national policy frameworks) are, by the implementation of all sorts of different policies, contributing to the reinforcement of existing innovation hubs (Padilla-Pérez *et al.*, 2009). 'Discretionary public policies' in national development strategies are critical (Cimoli *et al.*, 2009). Moreover, large cities and trade entry points in China and India have become the gateways for diaspora migrants and transnational communities in facilitating innovation, by spreading ideas, developing globalized production systems and influencing institutional reform in 'home' countries (Saxenian, 2006; Saxenian and Sabel, 2008), thus further widening the internal gap between innovative and non-innovative territories (Rodríguez-Pose, 2012).

These developments combine themes from research on how the changes in global innovation networks have affected emerging countries (see, for example, Mowery, 2001). According to Archibugi and Iammarino (2002), the innovative success of emerging countries has tended to rely not only on how well individual countries managed to internationalize and exploit local innovations, but also on how much knowledge and technology was transferred by MNEs and on the extent to which local firms have been able to and capable of branching into global scientific and technology networks. In all these areas both China and India—despite following very different paths—have been successful on all counts. Both have managed to absorb knowledge and know-how from MNEs and to create a number of 'lead firms' capable of not only engaging and competing with leading firms elsewhere in the world, but also of developing the all-important local networks through which knowledge and innovation are distributed within clusters and then diffused across different parts of the country (Yeung, 2009). All these processes are at the origin of the very uneven geography of innovation observed in both China and India and shown by the data discussed in the previous section of this article.

Conclusion

This article has presented a first view into the geography of innovation in China and India, comparing it with that of developed spaces in the world, namely the US and the EU.

The picture that emerges from the analysis is one of countries still lagging in terms of innovation capacity, but which are laying the foundation for sustained and rapid catch-up in the endogenous generation of innovation. The impressive rate of convergence—albeit from very low initial levels—is possibly a sign of what is likely to happen in years to come: two countries rapidly rising up through the ranks of the world science and technology and innovation hierarchy, and which are developing innovation systems that differ from what is the norm in the developed world. In this respect, Jacques' (2012) prophecy that Chinese—and Indian—modernity will be very different from Western modernity is being reproduced in terms of their respective innovation systems.

The innovation effort in both China and India is, however, far from uniform and sustained in by what by all standards are very uneven geographies of innovation. National innovation strategies and policies, galloping urbanization and uneven institutional capacities across regions in China and India are combining in order to create innovation 'mountains' in large urban areas next to 'deserts', where innovation capacity is virtually absent. The location of FDI and MNEs in these 'mountains' further contributes to the emergence of self-reinforcing virtuous cycles of innovation in selected metropolises and trade entry hubs such as Beijing, Shanghai, Guangzhou and Shenzhen in China, or Delhi, Mumbai, Hyderabad and Bangalore in India. The picking of winners further exacerbates the territorial imbalance. The innovation 'mountains' are complemented by the 'deserts', where not only virtually no innovation takes place—namely, the 'seven sister' states of northeastern India and numerous provinces in the West of China—but where existing conditions are unlikely to trigger any kind of innovative surge in the near future. In fact, lack of a critical mass of innovative actors and national policies that involve picking winners, coupled with advantages of agglomeration economics and trade access for generating and diffusing knowledge, are likely to perpetuate what is already a very uneven and perhaps unsustainable geography of innovation in the two main emerging countries of the world.

Riccardo Crescenzi, Department of Geography and Environment, London School of Economics, Houghton Street, London WC2A 2AE, UK, r.crescenzi@lse.ac.uk

Andrés Rodríguez-Pose, Department of Geography and Environment, London School of Economics, Houghton Street, London WC2A 2AE, UK, a.rodriguez-pose@lse.ac.uk

References

Acs, Z.J., L. Anselin and A. Varga (2002) Patents and innovation counts as measures of regional production of new knowledge. *Research Policy* 31.7, 1069-85.

Altenburg, T. (2009) Building inclusive innovation systems in developing countries: challenges for IS research. In B.-Å. Lundvall, J. Vang, K.J. Joseph and C. Chaminade (eds.), *Handbook of innovation systems in developing countries*, Edward Elgar, Cheltenham.

Anselin, L., A. Varga and Z. Acs (1997) Local geographic spillovers between university research and high technology innovations. *Journal of Urban Economics* 42.3, 422-48.

Archibugi, D. and S. Iammarino (2002) The globalization of technological innovation: definition and evidence. *Review of International Political Economy* 9.1, 98-122.

Asheim, B. and M. Gertler (2005) The geography of innovation: regional innovation systems. In J. Fagerberg, D. Mowery and R. Nelson (eds.), *The Oxford handbook of innovation*, Oxford University Press, Oxford.

Audretsch, D. and M. Feldman (1996) Innovation in cities: science-based diversity, specialisation and local competition. *European Economic Review* 43.2, 409-29.

Bound, K. (2007) *India: the uneven innovator*. Demos, London.

Bruche, G. (2009) A new geography of innovation—China and India rising. Columbia FDI Perspectives, Vale Columbia Center, Columbia University, New York, NY.

Bush, V. (1945) *Science: the endless frontier*. Ayer, North Stanford.

Cantwell, J. (2005) MNCs, local clustering and science-technology relationships. In G. Santangelo (ed.), *Technological change and economic catch-up: the role of science and multinationals*, Edward Elgar, Cheltenham.

Carlino, G., S., Chatterjee and R. Hunt (2007) Urban density and the rate of invention. *Journal of Urban Economics* 61.3, 389-419.

Chaminade, C. (2010) Are knowledge-bases enough? A comparative study of the geography of knowledge sources in China (Great Beijing) and India (Pune). Centre for Innovation, Research and Competence in the Learning Economy (CIRCLE), Working Paper 2010/13, University of Lund, Lund.

Chen, Y., N. Salike, F. Luan and M. He (2016) Heterogeneous effects of inter- and intra-city transportation infrastructure on economic growth: evidence from Chinese cities. *Cambridge Journal of Regions, Economy and Society* 9.3, 571-87.

Cimoli, M., G. Dosi, R. Nelson and J. Stiglitz (2009) Institutions and policies in developing economies. In B-Å. Lundvall, C. Chaminade, K.J. Joseph and J. Vang (eds.), *Handbook of innovation systems and developing countries: building domestic capabilities in a global context*, Edward Elgar, Cheltenham.

Cohen, B. (2006) Urbanization in developing countries: current trends, future projections, and key challenges for sustainability. *Technology in Society* 28.1/2, 63-80.

Cooke, P. (2002) Regional innovation systems: general findings and some new evidence from biotechnology clusters *Journal of Technology Transfer* 27.1, 133-45.

Cooke, P., M. Uranga and G. Etxebarria (1997) Regional innovation systems: institutional and organizational dimensions. *Research Policy* 26.4/5, 475-91.

Crescenzi, R. and A. Jaax (2017) Innovation in Russia: the territorial dimension. *Economic Geography* 93.1, 66-88.

Crescenzi, R., A. Rodríguez-Pose and M. Storper (2007) The territorial dynamics of innovation: a Europe-United States comparative analysis. *Journal of Economic Geography* 7.6, 673-709.

Crescenzi, R., A. Rodríguez-Pose and M. Storper (2012) The territorial dynamics of innovation in China and India. *Journal of Economic Geography* 12.5, 1055-85.

Dahlman, C. (2010) Innovation strategies of three of the BRICS: Brazil, India and China—what can we learn from three different approaches? In X. Fu and L. Soete (eds.), *The rise of technological power in the South*, Palgrave MacMillan, Basingstoke.

da Motta e Albuquerque, E. (2003) Immature systems of innovation: introductory notes about a comparison between South Africa, India, Mexico and Brazil based on science and technology statistics. Textos para Discussão Cedeplar-UFMG, td221, Cedeplar, Universidade Federal de Minas Gerais, Belo Horizonte.

Dosi, G., P. Llerena and M. Sylos Labini (2006) The relationships between science, technologies and their industrial exploitation: an illustration through the myths and realities of the so-called 'European paradox'. *Research Policy* 35.10, 1450-64.

Duan, Y. and Y. Kong (2008) The role of R&D offshoring in explaining the patent growth of China and India at USPTO. Paper presented at the 2008 IEEE International Conference on Management of Innovation and Technology, Bangkok, 21-24 September.

Duranton, G. (2008) Viewpoint: From cities to productivity and growth in developing countries. *Canadian Journal of Economics/Revue Canadienne d'Économie* 41.3, 689-736.

Fan, P. (2008) *Innovation capacity and economic development China and India*. UNU World Institute for Development Economics Research, Helsinki.

Fleischer, B., H. Li and M.Q. Zhao (2010) Human capital, economic growth, and regional inequality in China. *Journal of Development Economics* 92.2, 215-31.

Freeman, C. (1987) *Technology policy and economic policy: lessons from Japan*. Pinter, London.

Freeman, C. (2002) Continental, national and sub-national innovation systems—complementarity and economic growth. *Research Policy* 31.2, 191-211.

Friedman, T. (2005) *The world is flat: a brief history of the twenty-first century*. Farrar, Straus and Giroux, New York, NY.

Fu, X. and L. Soete (eds.) (2010) *The rise of technological power in the South*. Palgrave MacMillan, Basingstoke.

Gajwani, K., R. Kanbur and X. Zhang (2006) *Comparing the evolution of spatial inequality in China and India*:

a fifty-year perspective. International Food Policy Research Institute, Washington, DC.

He, C. and X. Mao (2016) Population dynamics and regional development in China. *Cambridge Journal of Regions, Economy and Society* 9.3, 535–49.

Henderson, J.V. (2010) Cities and development. *Journal of Regional Science* 50.1, 515–40.

Jacques, M. (2012) *When China rules the world: the end of the Western world and the birth of a new global order*. Second edition, Penguin Books, Harlow.

Jaffe, A.B., M. Trajtenberg and R. Henderson (1993) Geographic localization of knowledge spillovers as evidenced by patent citations. *Quarterly Journal of Economics* 108.3, 577–98.

Jian, T., J. Sachs and A. Warner (1996) Trends in regional inequality in China. *China Economic Review* 7.1, 1–21.

Joseph, K.J. (2009) Sectoral innovation systems in developing countries: the case of India's ICT industry. In B.-Å. Lundvall, C. Chaminade, K.J. Joseph and J. Vang (eds.), *Handbook of innovation systems and developing countries: building domestic capabilities in a global context*, Edward Elgar, Cheltenham.

Kuchiki, A. and M. Tsuji (eds.) (2010) *From agglomeration to innovation: upgrading industrial clusters in emerging economies*. Palgrave Macmillan, Basingstoke.

Leadbeater, C. and J. Wilsdon (2007) *The atlas of ideas: how Asian innovation can benefit us all*. Demos, London.

Lee, N. and A. Rodríguez-Pose (2016) Is there trickle-down from tech? Poverty, employment, and the high-technology multiplier in U.S. cities. *Annals of the American Association of Geographers* 106.5, 1114–34.

Lewis, J.I. (2007) Technology acquisition and innovation in the developing world: wind turbine development in China and India. *Studies in Comparative International Development* 42.3/4, 208–32.

Li, X. and Y. Pai (2010) The changing geography of innovation activities: what do patent indicators imply? In X. Fu and L. Soete (eds.), *The rise of technological power in the South*, Palgrave MacMillan, Basingstoke.

Liu, X. and T. Buck (2007) Innovation performance and channels for international technology spillovers: evidence from Chinese high-tech industries. *Research Policy* 36.3, 355–66.

Liu, X. and S. White (2001) Comparing innovation systems: a framework and application to China's transitional context. *Research Policy* 30.7, 1091–14.

Lundin, N. and S. Schwaag Serger (2007) *Globalization of R&D and China: empirical observations and policy implications*. Research Institute of Industrial Economics, Stockholm.

Lundvall, B-Å (ed.) (2009) *Handbook of innovation systems and developing countries: building domestic capabilities in a global setting*. Edward Elgar, Cheltenham.

Lundvall, B-Å., P. Intarakumnerd and J. Vang (2006) *Asia's innovation systems in transition*. Edward Elgar, Cheltenham.

Maclaurin, W.R. (1953) The sequence from invention to innovation and its relation to economic growth. *Quarterly Journal of Economics* 67.1, 97–111.

Malmberg, A., O. Sölvell and I. Zander (1996) Spatial clustering, local accumulation of knowledge and firm competitiveness. *Geografiska Annaler Series B: Human Geography* 78.2, 85–97.

Mani, S. (2004) Institutional support for investment in domestic technologies: an analysis of the role of government in India. *Technological Forecasting and Social Change* 71.8, 855–63.

Martin, R. and P. Sunley (2006) Path dependence and regional economic evolution. *Journal of Economic Geography* 6.4, 395–437.

MGI (McKinsey Global Institute) (2010) India's urban awakening: building inclusive cities, sustaining economic growth. McKinsey Global Institute.

Mitra, R. (2007) India's emergence as a global R&D center: an overview of the Indian R&D system and potential. Working Paper R2007:012, Swedish Institute for Growth Policy Studies, Ostersund.

Moreno, R., R. Paci and S. Usai (2005) Spatial spillovers and innovation activity in European regions. *Environment and Planning A* 37.10, 1793–812.

Mowery, D. (1992) The U.S. national innovation system: origins and prospects for change. *Research Policy* 21.2, 125–44.

Mowery, D.C. (2001) Technological innovation in a multipolar system: analysis and implications for U.S. policy. *Technological Forecasting and Social Change* 67.2/3, 143–57.

Mowery, D.C. and J.E. Oxley (1995) Inward technology transfer and competitiveness: the role of national innovation systems. *Cambridge Journal of Economics* 19.1, 67–93.

Navarro, M., J.J. Gibaja, B. Bilbao-Osorio and R. Aguado (2009) Patterns of innovation in EU-25 regions: a typology and policy recommendations. *Environment and Planning C: Government and Policy* 27.5, 815–40.

OECD (Organisation for Economic Co-operation and Development) (n.d.-a) Patent databases (various years) [WWW document]. URL http://www.oecd.org/science/inno/oecdpatentdatabases.htm (accessed 26 September 2017).

OECD (Organisation for Economic Co-operation and Development) (n.d.-b) Regional statistics and indicators (various years) [WWW document]. URL http://www.oecd.org/cfe/regional-policy/regionalstatisticsandindicators.htm (accessed 26 September 2017).

Padilla-Pérez, R., J. Vang and C. Chaminade (2009) Regional innovation systems in developing countries: integrating micro and meso-level capabilities. In B-Å. Lundvall, J. Vang, K.J. Joseph and C. Chaminade (eds.), *Handbook of innovation systems and developing countries*, Edward Elgar, Cheltenham.

Parayil, G. and A. D'Costa (2009) *The new Asian innovation dynamics: China and India in perspective*. Palgrave Macmillan, Basingstoke.

Piore, M.J. and C. Sabel (1984) *The second industrial divide: possibilities for prosperity*. Basic Books, New York, NY.

Popkin, J.M. and P. Iyengar (2007) *IT and the East: how China and India are altering the future of technology and innovation*. Harvard Business School Press, Boston, MA.

Rodríguez-Pose, A. (2012) Trade and regional inequality. *Economic Geography* 88.2, 109–36.

Rodríguez-Pose, A. and R. Crescenzi (2008) R&D, spillovers, innovation systems and the genesis of regional growth in Europe. *Regional Studies* 42.1, 51–67.

Rodríguez-Pose, A. and M. Di Cataldo (2015) Quality of government and innovative performance in the regions of Europe. *Journal of Economic Geography* 15.4, 673–706.

Rodríguez-Pose, A. and E.M. Villarreal Peralta (2015) Innovation and regional growth in Mexico: 2000–2010. *Growth and Change* 46.2, 172–95.

Rodríguez-Pose, A. and C. Wilkie (2016) Putting China in perspective: a comparative exploration of the ascent of the Chinese knowledge economy. *Cambridge Journal of Regions, Economy and Society* 9.3, 479–91.

Romer, P. (1990) Endogenous technological change. *Journal of Political Economy* 98.5, 71–102.

Rostow, W.W. (1959) The stages of economic growth. *Economic History Review* 12.1, 1–17.

Saxenian, A-L. (1994) *Regional advantage: culture and competition in Silicon Valley and Route 128*. Harvard University Press, Cambridge, MA.

Saxenian, A-L. (2006) *The new argonauts: regional advantage in a global economy*. Harvard University Press, Cambridge, MA.

Saxenian, A-L. and C. Sabel (2008) Venture capital in the 'periphery': the new argonauts, global search and local institution-building. Roepke Lecture in Economic Geography. *Economic Geography* 84.4, 379–94.

Schaaper, M. (2009) *Measuring China's innovation system: national specificities and international comparisons*. Organisation for Economic Co-operation and Development (OECD), Paris.

Scott, A. and G. Garofoli (eds.) (2007) *Development on the ground: clusters, networks and regions in emerging economies*. Routledge, Oxford.

Simmie, J., J. Carpenter, A. Chadwick and R. Martin (2008) *History matters: path dependence and innovation in British city-regions*. National Endowment for Science, Technology and the Arts (NESTA), London.

Sonn, J.W. and M. Storper (2008) The increasing importance of geographical proximity in technological innovation: an analysis of US patent citations, 1975-1997. *Environment and Planning A* 40.5, 1020-39.

Storper, M. (1997) *The regional world: territorial development in a global economy*. The Guilford Press, New York, NY.

Sun, Y. (2003) Geographic patterns of industrial innovation in China during the 1990s. *Tijdschrift voor Economische en Sociale Geografie* 94.3, 376-89.

UN Population Division (2011) United Nations world urbanization prospects: the 2010 revision population database. United Nations, New York, NY.

Varga, A. (2000) Local academic knowledge spillovers and the concentration of economic activity. *Journal of Regional Science* 40.2, 289-309.

Venables, A.J. (2005) Spatial disparities in developing countries: cities, regions, and international trade. *Journal of Economic Geography* 5.1, 3-21.

Wadhwa, V. (2010) Chinese and Indian entrepreneurs are eating America's lunch. *Foreign Policy*, 28 December.

Wang, C. and G. Lin (2008) The growth and spatial distribution of China's ICT industry: new geography of clustering and innovation. *Issues & Studies* 44.2, 145-92.

Wilson, D. and R. Purushothaman (2003) Dreaming with BRICS: the path to 2050. Global Economics Paper 99, Goldman Sachs.

Winters, L.A and S. Yusuf (2007) Dancing with giants: China, India, and the global economy. World Bank, Washington, DC.

World Bank (2009) World development report 2009: reshaping economic geography. World Bank, Washington, DC.

Xu, Z. (2009) Productivity and agglomeration economies in Chinese cities. *Comparative Economic Studies* 51.3, 284-301.

Yeung, H.W.C. (2009) Regional development and the competitive dynamics of global production networks: an East Asian perspective. *Regional Studies* 43.3, 325-51.

― BOOK REVIEWS

Richard Florida 2017: *The New Urban Crisis: How Our Cities are Increasing Inequality, Deepening Segregation, and Failing the Middle Class ― and What We Can Do About It.* **New York: Basic Books**

Most urban scholars are familiar with Richard Florida's argument that the economic growth of cities depends on the presence of a critical mass of talent, what he calls the creative class. Spurring innovations, this class invents products and services, creates new businesses and stimulates employment. Since publication of *The Rise of the Creative Class* in 2002, he has been developing these ideas and advising policymakers on their implications.

In this book, Florida turns his attention away from the prosperity ostensibly produced by the knowledge-based economy and onto its less desirable consequences. The dynamic interplay of innovation and agglomeration, he argues, gives rise to income and wage inequality, concentrated poverty, deepening residential segregation by income and rising housing prices, pushing both the middle class and the aspiring working class out of the cities where economic opportunities are concentrated. This uneven development is the 'new urban crisis'.

Primarily focused on US cities, Florida provides extensive quantitative and comparative documentation of these consequences, with chapters exploring uneven development across neighborhoods, cities, suburbs, metropolitan areas and beyond. And while he indicts the cities where the creative class has congregated, he does not abandon his core argument. The book ends with policy recommendations to enable the creative economy to be more inclusive, so as to diminish the inequalities to which it gives rise.

There is much to discuss regarding Florida's historical positioning of innovation and agglomeration, his reliance on ecological correlations, the use of 'class', the primacy of economic concerns, his understanding of scale and his rhetorical style. In this review, though, I want to address the theme—contradictions—that frames his argument, what he labels 'winner-take-all urbanism'. Florida does not fully develop or sustain his argument about the contradictory nature of cities and it could be ungenerously interpreted as a rhetorical 'hook' meant to contrast this book with his earlier work. Nevertheless, Florida intends it to anchor the book intellectually and presents it as a pivot in the evolution of his thinking (p. xvi). Consequently, it is 'fair game'.

The argument is simple: contemporary urbanism is 'paradoxical and contradictory' (p. 4). To quote Florida: 'the very same force [urban clustering] that drives the growth of our cities and economy broadly also generates the divides that separate us and the contradictions that hold us back' (p. xviii) (full disclosure: I explore the theme of contradictions in my forthcoming work, *Cities in the Urban Age: A Dissent*). '[K]nowledge-based places don't just reflect inequality, they help create it' (p. 88), Florida asserts, with inequality a 'fundamental feature' (p. 94) of urban economies: 'Ironically and troubling—cities and metro areas can be both diverse and segregated at the same time' (p. 116). Prosperity and poverty exist together, with the implication being that prosperity depends on deprivation or, to state it bluntly, the rich are rich and creative cities are prosperous because other people and other places are exploited and marginalized. He avoids this extension of his argument. Instead, he mostly presents prosperity and poverty as co-related, and less often as causally or functionally related through urban clustering. The implications of the latter he leaves unacknowledged.

Indicative of this stance is his winner-take-all urbanism. Such an urbanism is not defined by paradox but rather by the unequal distribution of income, housing opportunities, education and place. As he states: 'Winner-take-all urbanism means that a few big winners capture a *disproportionate share* of the spoils of innovation and economic growth, while many more places stagnate or fall further behind' (p. 186, emphasis added). This is not an argument about contradictions but about distribution. It is not about how growth depends on stagnation and obsolescence; rather, it is about how economic and political power divides the spoils of growth and decline. The issue for Florida is exclusion, not exploitation. Or maybe he means to suggest another interpretation: the survival of the fittest, progress or meritocracy. Florida leaves us in the dark on this point. Moreover, because inequalities are presented as a matter of exclusion and he fails to address how this occurs, the implication is that including the disadvantaged in the knowledge-based economy will eliminate inequalities.

When Florida offers his policy recommendations, contradictions are absent, as is the moral outrage expressed in the opening pages. His goal is 'institutions that unleash the creative energy of people and neighborhoods' (p. 178). He wants to make the creative economy more sustainable and inclusive—'a more productive urbanism for all' (p. 191). Not willing to give up or even modify his core argument, he further distances himself from the theme of contradictions and posits a government that, devoid of contradictions, can do good without doing harm. This is most blatant when Florida presents creative cities as both the problem and the solution: 'the poor and the working classes have better prospects for upward mobility in them than in other places' (p. 50).

As for his policy recommendations, he begins by proposing investments in infrastructure (e.g. mass transit) and the imposition of a land value tax to encourage further clustering—'the key driver of economic growth' (p. 191). To this he adds more affordable housing, making 'low-wage service jobs into middle-class work' (p. 202), increasing minimum wages, investing in disadvantaged people and places, empowering local governments within the federal system and having the US lead a global effort to build resilient cities. Except for this last recommendation, all of the others are what I call 'recommendations to no one'; that is, good things that should be done by reasonable people.

I believe that cities amplify the contradictions prevalent in capitalist democracies and began the book hoping that Florida would take up the challenge of exploring how this occurs, rather than just documenting its consequences. He flinched. Read the book because it is Richard Florida and he is important in the worlds of urban studies and urban policy. Use the book because it offers a wealth of empirical material. But if you want to deepen your understanding of the contradictory nature of cities and the roots of this supposedly 'new' urban crisis, you will need to look elsewhere.

Robert Beauregard, Columbia University

Stephen Graham 2016: *Vertical: The City from Satellites to Bunkers.* **London: Verso**

Stephen Graham's book *Vertical* begins with the contention that 'attention to the vertical structuring of cities and urban life remains patchy and limited' (p. 6). Although true within the confines of the key urban geography texts he surveys in the introduction, it is testament to Graham's powers of collection and narration that the rest of this volume proves this first statement somewhat false. By assembling a wide range of secondary sources, including academic studies, journalism and blog posts, Graham is able to present a detailed overview of past and present vertical topographies and processes. The argument is brought to life through engaging writing and excellent use of figures.

The first part of the book is devoted to verticals 'above' ground. Some chapters discuss topics familiar from Graham's earlier work on military urbanism, such as drones and bombers. Others resonate closely with his thesis on splintering urbanisms, such as chapters covering helicopters and skywalk/skytrain/skydeck. In both cases, the discussions in *Vertical* usefully extend ideas presented elsewhere, or alternatively provide a useful synthesis of earlier work for those readers unfamiliar with it. However, perhaps the most interesting chapters are those that break new ground, such as the fascinating history of the elevator/lift (chapter 6) and the connections between air, urban heat islands and climate change (chapter 10).

Part two of *Vertical* goes below ground. Chapters in this section trace cities through the extraction of earth (chapter 11), the evolution of basements/cellars (chapter 12) and sewers (chapter 13), and a fascinating examination of mining in the final chapter, which links many of the previous foci (e.g. elevators, skyscrapers, earth extraction) together. The interconnection and imbrications of different verticals with each other is characteristic of the book overall.

A passionate denouncement of global capitalism, and the growing levels of inequality it produces, structures the text as a whole. Indeed, it is precisely these things that are positioned as the common cause of the various vertical topographies and their problems examined throughout. However, whether this causal thesis is sufficient remains to be seen. The recent Grenfell Tower fire in London was clearly a result of austerity politics, a cruel spectacle of the structural political-economic violence constantly inflicted upon the poor in the UK. And yet the populations disproportionally affected by this violence—black British and non-UK nationals—signify the need for a more nuanced understanding, putting capitalism in conversation with Britain's long colonial history and present racial and racist dynamics.

The book's one-page afterword identifies the key criticism many readers will have of it. As Graham notes, *Vertical* does not examine how people contest vertical axes of power. This lack of attention to forms of resistance or even practices of endurance means the book is infused with a slightly dystopian mood. However, this final *mea culpa* is perhaps more problematic because it creates the impression that studies of resistance can be simply bolted onto the foregoing 400 pages of analysis. What such an argument misses is the ways in which everyday practices and geographies of vertical life co-constitute and reshape the geographies and power relations they are enmeshed within. They are neither additive nor derivate, but rather creative in their own right. This is why Michel de Certeau (first cited here on p. 209) moves so swiftly in his *The Practice of Everyday Life* from the panoptic view from above to the inventiveness and 'the rumble of so many differences' (p. 211) of embodied urban subjects. A more recent study in the same vein, AbdouMaliq Simone's *Jakarta: Drawing the City Near*, demonstrates how topographies of urban life, no matter how fully three-dimensional, struggle to comprehend much of what is actually happening in cities if they neglect the co-constitutive topological relations in which the majority of residents are also ensconced.

Christopher Harker, Durham University

Oliver Coutard and Jonathan Rutherford (eds.) 2016: *Beyond the Networked City: Infrastructure Reconfigurations and Urban Change in the North and South*. **London: Routledge**

This collection comprises eleven chapters exploring the post-network city hypothesis. Editors Olivier Coutard and Jonathan Rutherford—both from LATTS, a research unit at Paris-Est University—began developing this idea a decade or so ago. The book represents a collective, sometimes contradictory, effort to explore and discuss the scope of a set of interrelated transformations affecting infrastructure and cities. All the chapters seek to challenge the domination of the network as a material infrastructure, an ideology and the object of political economy. According to the editors, the currently observed changes helping to define the post-networked city comprise 'a shift from ... homogeneity' to 'diversity (and targeted selectivity) of infrastructural spaces; reconfigurations and rescalings in the "spaces of solidarity" ... (large scale solidarities are recombining with forms of local "autonomy"); socio-spatial solidarity increasingly based on the division of resources ...; a shift from collective to more individualised or diversified practices, norms and expectations' (which leads to 'customized infrastructure'); 'the rise of new forms of individual and collective appropriation of infrastructure'; and 'international and interurban circulation of models supporting these shifts' (p. 7).

This research endeavor largely unfolds from debates initiated by the book *Splintering Urbanism*. Many authors who took part in those discussions, including Stephen Graham and Simon Marvin, feature in this book. The book comes back in a way to the interpretation of the causal link between the neoliberalization of infrastructure and urban fragmentation. The literature on global South cities highlights the fact that the modern infrastructural ideal was barely implemented in such cities and points instead to the prevailing infrastructural diversity. Research on urban environmental change and urban political ecology has also emphasized that the production of infrastructure is a strongly politically contested process which may result in unexpected changes in the way infrastructures are conceived and implemented, and in their urban impact. Specifically, environmental concerns for the preservation of resources and a more circular economy have garnered support in many cities. This, in turn, is believed to favor the advent of a post-network city.

A strength of the book is the wide diversity of case studies it uses to discuss this hypothesis. Regarding infrastructure, we find case studies on water supply, sanitation, waste collection and treatment, electricity and heat supply, as well as roads and (more surprisingly) volumetric urbanism (i.e. domes or—to use a phrase of Simon Marvin's—'domic ecologies'). Geographically, the case studies located in the global South (Vietnam, India, Brazil and Columbia, plus a broader review of sub-Saharan African cases) balance out those located in Europe (Paris, Berlin, Manchester, Birmingham and Aberdeen) and the US.

The main development emergent from the chapters is a shift from the post-network city hypothesis to what is encapsulated by the book's title: 'beyond the networked city'. 'Shifting forms of infrastructure never consist of big, paradigm-busting transitions from one large technical network to another' (p. 6), observe the editors. Instead, the authors depict incremental changes, small-scale adjustments and repairs, experiments and sometimes failures. The hypothesis helps us to properly address the diversity and coexistence of infrastructural systems that the chapters identify, illustrating the waning of exclusive belief in the network as the sole way to legitimately access urban services. In this respect, the experience of infrastructural diversity in the global South is very illuminating, at a time when many local authorities are beginning to recognize the contribution of non-networked solutions to resource delivery imagined by urban dwellers themselves. But what Sylvy Jaglin describes as 'a pragmatic turn' (that she identifies in African cities) doesn't mean that the network disappears from the aspirations of urban dwellers and city officials.

This trend towards diversity of infrastructural systems is also evident in cities of the global North, albeit less strikingly so than in the global South. There is, for instance, the recent promotion of heating districts in the UK, or the rediscovery of the value of the non-potable water network in Paris. In the UK, as well as in Berlin, the promotion of shorter circuits connects two arguments: one that envisions energy decentralization as a democratic development empowering local actors; and one that sees these new circuits as more environmentally sound. This argument is to be found in the European case studies alone. These examples also demonstrate how misleading the notion of post-network can be, since all these infrastructural systems still rely on networks: some at a meso-scale (heating districts), others still at city scale (Paris, Berlin). Barles *et al.* even propose the notion of 'the hyper-networked city' to acknowledge this fact. Other chapters also point to the fact that these networks in fact exceed the scale of the city, rendering the study of 'infrastructural hinterlands' essential.

On a final note, the editors stress that 'the socio-political significations of ongoing urban infrastructural transitions [are] fundamentally ambivalent' (p. 21). In some cases, they seem to reinforce neoliberal trends and social polarization, while in others they are seen as serving progressive agendas. Taking the case of Mumbai, Graham *et al.* analyze hydropolitics as the expression of a 'revanchist urbanism' by urban elites targeting illegal, as well as legal but provisory, connections in slum areas. De-networking the poor is the counterpoint of strategies of infrastructural secession among the middle and upper classes, thanks to rainwater harvesting and grey-water recycling. Jaglin interprets the African 'infrastructural pragmatic turn' in less dramatic terms. For her, legalizing 'hybrid delivery configurations [is] a way for African state authorities to negotiate the urban transition: a partial regularisation of the informal sector facilitates the provision of essential services, in exchange for a civil order that also benefits the urban elites and dominant classes' (pp.193–4), because they are among the customers of the new hybrid infrastructures. Several chapters also highlight (in contrast to the trend towards privatization) the increased role for public authorities in dealing with and planning for more diverse infrastructural systems.

Soundly grounded in theory, this book builds on rigorous and diverse case studies. It innovatively highlights the mutually constituting relations between changing infrastructure and urban environments. Its prudent conclusions open up avenues for future research focusing on the global inflexions of urban paradigms while also willing to grant due consideration to situated and contextualized trends.

Eric Verdeil, Sciences Po, Centre for International Studies (CERI), CNRS, Paris

Martina Löw 2016: *The Sociology of Space: Materiality, Social Structures, and Action.* **New York: Palgrave Macmillan**

A professor at Technical University Berlin, Martina Löw is arguably the most eminent scholar of space, place and cities in contemporary German sociology, besides being a notable contributor to the fields of gender and education. It is therefore more than timely that her seminal work *The Sociology of Space* (originally published in German in 2000 and followed by a French translation in 2015) is now available in English. Going well beyond Löw's English-language articles (e.g. in this journal in 2013), the book makes her sophisticated and original theory of space available in its entirety to a far wider international audience.

The book is clearly organized into seven chapters, with the compact first and last chapters functioning as justification and overall summary. Of particular interest perhaps to international readers is one of Löw's entry points stating that, despite increasing popularity in German urban and regional sociology, the concept of space (*Raum* in the original) has been undertheorized due to its historic associations with

Nazi ideology. Chapter 2 provides a solid foundation for Löw's theory by chronicling the transition from an absolute to a relativist conception of space in philosophy and science, as well as offering critiques of various urban sociology classics. Chapter 3 clarifies the need for a new 'processual' and 'relational' notion of space, in the light of fundamental social and spatial changes such as the rise of modern mobility, virtual space and globalization, while placing special emphasis on childhood socialization and embodiment. In chapter 4, Löw further zeroes in on her own theory by discussing agreements and disagreements with the spatial models of Elias, Lefebvre, Luhmann, Foucault, Harvey and Massey (among others).

Chapter 5 represents the longest and most important part of the book, a detailed description of Löw's 'dual' conception of space as informed by, yet going beyond, Gidden's structuration theory and Bourdieu's habitus. First, on the level of 'action', Löw understands space to be a 'relational arrangement of social goods and people (living beings) at places' (p. 188). Space is constituted through two distinct processes called 'spacing' and 'operation of synthesis'. While 'spacing' refers to the (primarily material) placement of goods, people and information, 'operation of synthesis'—unfortunately a somewhat unclear translation of the German *Syntheseleistung*—refers to the (primarily symbolic) linking of spatial elements into one unified space through 'processes of imagination, perception, and memory' (p. 189). As a result of placing and synthesis, spaces display 'atmospheres' which can be understood as sensual and emotional qualities that in turn influence action.

Of equal importance is the second level of Löw's theory of space relating to 'structure'. Social structures are generated and reproduced by the above constitution of space. Essentially, social structures (which may also include 'spatial' structures) are unequal and cemented in wealth, status, knowledge, organization and association-based hierarchies. In Löw's view, gender and class are fundamental aspects of all social actions, processes and structures, elevating them to the level of 'structural principles'. Because the reproduction of structures is often rendered invisible through institutionalization, routinization, embodiment and unintended consequences, social change is difficult to achieve yet it is ultimately possible. In sum, it is the dynamic 'duality of space' (p. 190) as rooted in action and social structure that gives Löw's theory its unique complexity and connectivity. Following this core part of the book, chapter 6 then attempts to demonstrate the empirical value of the theory through several analytic critiques and examples in the areas of education, gender and urban milieus.

Throughout the book, there are frequent previews and summaries which help guide non-expert audiences in particular through the occasional arid passage. Overall, the fluent and clear English translation results in an easily readable work of theory, especially when compared to some other key texts in this area. I particularly appreciated Löw's many examples, as well as her insightful references to significant works of modern art, adding both texture and color.

In a new preface to the English edition, Löw offers additional context and briefly responds to some of the questions raised by the original publication. For instance, she now clearly positions her work vis-à-vis the commonly invoked 'spatial turn', which nonetheless has not led to a satisfying inclusion of spatial theory in today's urban and regional sociology. Löw also clarifies her theory's connections with the concepts of place, boundary and time. I agree with Low's note that 'it will be and should be noticeable that the book was written in a specific cultural context; in my view, this determines not so much the contents as the authors with whom we debate, and makes certain systems of reference (e.g. Europe) more prevalent than others' (p. xvi). Indeed, international readers might find the strong attention to German conceptual schemes and empirical studies to be of limited interest, yet they should not discount the book's contributions to theory based on its somewhat dated and limited literature.

Just two items remain unfulfilled on my wish list. First, I would have appreciated a more in-depth theoretical exchange with paradigms beyond critical theory as well as approaches to space and place in other areas, such as Thomas Gieryn's interactionist notion of place or anthropologist Setha Low's theory of 'spatializing culture'. In my view, a firmer embrace of spatial ideas in relation to culture, identity, emotion and interaction could strengthen the 'action' side of Löw's theory. This would likely also lead to a more nuanced description of place which, despite additional comments, remains underdeveloped. Second, an international theory of space should not be lacking a conception of race, separate from ethnicity and religion, as an essential social structure and perhaps even a 'structural principle'. Overall, however, these shortcomings do little to tarnish a highly original and insightful book that should be obligatory reading for anyone working on space and place, and highly recommended for all urban scholars at graduate student level and above.

Margarethe Kusenbach, University of South Florida

Antonio Loris 2015: *Water, State and the City*. **London and New York: Palgrave Macmillan**

The relationship between the control and management of water and water-based services and the development of state institutions and political power is an enduring topic in history and social science. Antonio Ioris's book is a welcome contribution to this body of literature, combining elements of political economy, political ecology and critical geography, including the work of classical Marxist geographers like Henri Lefebvre and David Harvey.

The author's focus is on Latin American cities, looking at the experiences of very large metropolises: Mexico City, Lima and Rio de Janeiro (the chapters on these three cities are based on adaptations of previously published journal articles). One of the book's main arguments is that the 'urban question', including longstanding water-related problems affecting Latin American cities, is simultaneously a state concern and a result of the state's own failures. In this regard, Ioris attempts to 're-discuss' and 're-interpret' existing arguments about interrelations between the problems associated with large-scale urbanization and the development of the 'state apparatus' in Latin America. To this end, he adopts 'the megacity' and 'the dilemmas of the water sector' as his 'critical', 'privileged' analytical categories (pp. 8, 145). He also asserts there to be three driving forces that can explain the evolution of megacities, especially in Latin America. Summarizing his argument, these drivers are: (1) the consolidation of megacities being a product of the state apparatus acting on behalf of powerful 'social interests'; (2) Latin American megacities have become primary arenas of inequality and injustice owing to the region's history of dependent and elitist national development; (3) contemporary megacities are simultaneously the 'main locus' of 'mobilisation, creativity, and political action' and of 'experimentation of both top-down and bottom-up responses to collective problems' (p. 19). Ioris goes on to argue that 'the two most important mechanisms for the perpetuation of the power of national elites was the twin control of the city and the state' (p. 20). In addition, all-encompassing and perennial corruption—corruption as a 'totality'—as evident in Latin American megacities, is a major factor in the 'transformation from simple to complex capitalist societies' (p. 33). In this context, the specific problems of Latin America's water sector, such as 'water scarcity, the degradation of water bodies', together with the lack of safe water and sanitation affecting large sectors of the population, is 'directly or indirectly related to the persistence of corrupt practices and their synchronic and diachronic manifestation' (p. 33). Among these problems, 'water scarcity' is particularly relevant and Ioris proposes 'the concept of multiple scarcities' as an 'analytical device' to study 'the prevailing pattern of the lived space' characterized by social segregation, inequality and injustice (pp. 61–2).

As might be expected with a relatively short book, covering this highly complex topic in depth and giving due attention to the bewildering diversity of long-term historical processes and patterns characterizing five centuries of Western-led state formation in the continent was, even after reducing the scope to the interrelation between urban development and water management in three megacities, always going to be difficult. As a result, important sections are somewhat under-referenced, which may be understandable given the limited space available for additional bibliography. For example, some specialists in the long-established field of comparative analysis of Latin American development may want to know more about the methodological approach underpinning the research on the three megacities. Also, the author takes aim against rival arguments without providing a reference to the actual actors and their work. For example, he makes statements such as 'most references ... have been quite superficial and failed to discuss' (p. 12) and 'the now commonplace interpretations of Latin American urban questions' (p. 14), or mentions 'the theorists of ecological modernization' (p. 59) but does not refer specifically to the targets of his criticism. In other passages, he makes some sweeping generalizations, the most egregious perhaps being 'The dirty and scarce waters of Latin American cities' (p. 34), which serves as a section subtitle. Undeniably, dirtiness and (to use the author's own words) 'multiple scarcities' are a characteristic of many Latin American cities, including the three addressed in this book. But surely the statement will raise a few eyebrows, as Latin America also has some excellent examples of well-managed urban water systems. A reference to some counterexamples, and a more measured statement, would have helped to strengthen what is otherwise a correct argument.

There are other aspects that some readers may find controversial or not sufficiently substantiated, particularly in relation to the main objective of the book, which is the elucidation of the interlinkages between state formation, water management and the development of the megacity as a socio-historical phenomenon. As I mentioned above, it would be extremely difficult to provide a convincing account, duly grounded using empirical evidence, of such highly complex and extensive issues in a relatively short book. Nevertheless, I believe that the work provides a welcome reinstatement of ongoing debates that will retain great relevance for the foreseeable future. The book is a provocative invitation to expand these debates, revising existing assumptions and conceptual frameworks while at the same time revisiting classical arguments.

José Esteban Castro, CONICET, National University of General Sarmiento (UNGS), Argentina and Newcastle University, UK

Rowland Atkinson and Sarah Blandy 2017: *Domestic Fortress: Fear and the New Home Front.* **Manchester: Manchester University Press**

We have grown inured, perhaps, to the steady drip of news from the US or Australia of homeowners opening fire on suspected intruders (who turn out to be trick-or-treaters or drivers seeking help for their broken-down cars), the sound of burglar alarms blaring incessantly across even the most bucolic British villages and signs outside homes warning of 'Armed Response', if not (yet) to reports of spectacular, fortified, underground domestic redoubts excavated below otherwise unremarkable London townhouses. At the same time, we nearly intuitively understand 'home' to be among the highest achievements for self and family, not just on account of its structure, but for its social and psychic life making us who we are (which is one reason why homeless people and homelessness are so unsettling to homed society, why the destruction of home in war and violent natural disaster is so wrenching, and why domestic violence is a violation of more than its primary victims alone).

In *Domestic Fortress* urban sociologist Rowland Atkinson and legal scholar Sarah Blandy set out to unravel and explain what is perhaps the central contradiction of home in the global North (the book focuses particularly on the UK, Australia and the US): why it is that, as a stable, secure and (most importantly) owned home has become achievable for a greater portion of the population than ever before (despite grossly distorted housing markets that price so many out, ever-increasing homelessness and other countervailing forces), more and more homes are heavily fortified, with their owners increasingly fearful (and frequently armed) even as crime rates are falling. Nowadays, the authors make clear, it is not just the super-rich who establish their homes as fortresses (as the elite always have) but nearly everyone, or so it seems. 'Fear', they state at the outset, 'has been democratized [popularized would be more accurate] and, where resource exists to do so, the sense of concealment, protection and defence is ever more apparent in the designs and adaptations now being deployed' (p. 1). Taking their lead from Zygmunt Bauman, they ask: 'why do we witness the presence of anxiety and fear among many of the globe's most affluent people and how does this translate into a kind of urban life that offers both continuities and definite breaks with the built landscapes of even the recent past' (pp. 1–2)?

Their answers are not startling, but neither are they meant to be, since it is the very normalcy of this fear among the affluent (and then on down the class ladder) that is its most striking feature. Among those answers are the fact that the home (and not just the house, since the image of homeliness is so important) has become increasingly important as a store of wealth—for many the only store of wealth likely to see them through sickness and retirement until death—and so must be defended for that reason. Another is that, even as homeownership is apparently popularized, inequality continues to grow and this is perceived by many as an existential threat to their own relative security (in all senses of the term). A third answer is envy: as the homes of the rich and famous are brought into our homes through property and celebrity shows, we ache for what they have. A fourth, related, answer is vulnerability: as our neighbors 'fortress-up' we feel not just envy, but more and more like sitting ducks. A final explanation (perhaps a consequence of the others) is that the fortified home arises out of, and reinforces a new kind of, urban sociality that is highly private: 'staying in, protecting the home base, has become part of an elaborate shift of social centrality. Fear of crime, home consumption of alcohol, televisions and home cinemas keep us more house-bound and entertained than previous generations' (p. 178). As a result, 'the emphatic focus of our lives toward this interior space reflects one of the crucial binds of contemporary social existence: an apparent release from traditional forms of community, obligation, and identity has been partially supplanted by more atomized modes of living' (*ibid.*).

These explanations (and a lot more) unspool over the course of nine chapters. In the introductory chapter 1, the authors argue that what binds the processes—and consequences—of home fortification together is a social order defined by 'tessellated neoliberalism', which they define as 'the wider order and values of exchange and economic life that expand outwards from the micro-scale of a multitude of owned homes and into the fabric of the macro-economy, guided by prevailing ideologies and decisions by ruling parties and financial institutions' (p. 9). I never quite got this argument, perhaps because what makes this neoliberalism tessellated is never explained (to tessellate is to cover a floor with mosaics, or to cover a surface by using the same shape over and over; by extension something is tessellated—e.g. the dry bed of an intermittent stream underlain by shale, to use a geologist's favorite example—if it is paved by slightly overlapping similarly shaped stones or tiles: to 'expand outwards' doesn't strike me as a process of tessellation). Nor is any explanation given as to why this tessellation (if that is what it is) is neoliberal.

But never mind, the next eight chapters do not really need 'tessellated neo-liberalism' to make their arguments, beginning with chapter 2, an excellent historical (as well as contemporary) discussion of the myths of home security—and of the home as a form of social security—concluding that 'The home is therefore increasingly valued as a refuge, and the less secure we feel, the more likely we are to buy into the ideology of homeownership that promises territorial control and appreciating wealth' (p. 44), a key insight that helps drive much of the analysis in the book. Chapter 3 continues to explore the meaning of home, examining how it is figured as our protective carapace within and against society (even though within its walls can be a very violent place for some), while chapters 4 and 5 show how, since the home is our shell, 'invasions' of it—by the state as well as burglars, electronically as well as physically—are deeply felt (or deeply feared) violations of self. Chapter 6 explores the varied technologies (from motion-sensitive alarms to underground bunkers to facial recognition technology) that have arisen to assuage these felt and feared violations, the perceived limits of which perhaps help to explain the simultaneous rise of legalized fatal violence inflicted by homeowners defending their homes from perceived threats, the topic of chapter 7. Chapters 8 and 9 draw these analyses together to describe how cities are being recreated as 'fortress archipelagos' marked by gated communities, bunker homes and heavily armed (even castellated) redoubts of the wealthy and nearly wealthy, in which whatever social life exists is highly secluded, hardly public at all, a life that in fact imprisons those who think they are escaping the violence of the world.

As indicated, this is not a particularly startling story: we've been reading about and living in it forever, even as we feel its constant intensification. But in Atkinson and Blandy's hands it is a story very well told, one that adds up to a compelling and important account of our current domestic—and social—predicament. The authors end with a couple of pages on how to break out of the fortress we are building (or that is being built for us, which is why popularization of fear and of fortress architecture is a better term than democratization), pages that mostly only restate the problem, which is as it should be: what needs to be done is to begin to recognize the scope and the determinants of a problem that has been totally normalized. And that, the confusions of 'tessellated neoliberalism' notwithstanding, is precisely what *Domestic Fortress* does in compelling analytical detail.

Don Mitchell, Uppsala University

Françoise Montambeault 2016: *The Politics of Local Participatory Democracy in Latin America: Institutions, Actors, and Interactions*. **Stanford: Stanford University Press**

Françoise Montambeault is part of a new generation researching democratic innovations—most notably in Latin America—a field which combines two important qualities. First is the sharpness and dedication evident in field activities and subsequent treatment and systematization of data, making for an innovative empirical research tool, strongly supported by information generated in research processes. Second is the theoretical orientation regarding democratic innovations in Latin America, characterized by autonomy and freshness, contrasting with the work of analysts during the 1990s and 2000s (and the high expectations they generated). As Montambeault says, it is necessary to progress 'beyond the honeymoon' (p. 6).

These two qualities drive the author to answer difficult questions that have plagued experts over the last two decades. Can institutional change enhance the quality of democracy in Latin America? And (entering more properly into the subject matter of the book) to what extent can institutional reform foster the development of an autonomous civil society, capable of contributing to better-quality democracy (p. 2)?

For many years, the literature on democratic transition in Latin America was the scene of a clash between two bodies of research. Some saw transition processes from a purely institutional perspective—where, for example, respect for the results of periodic elections promoted by freely organized political parties represented a sufficient condition for defining transition. Others understood that an autonomous role for local civil societies in government affairs was a necessary condition for changing the authoritarian face of the state, dominated by traditional political elites perpetuating their power in starkly unequal societies.

In addressing participatory institutions—more specifically two participatory budgeting experiences in Brazil (Belo Horizonte and Recife, the latter over two periods, under Partido do Movimento Democrático Brasileiro and Partido dos Trabalhadores mandates) and two experiences of urban and participatory planning in Mexico (León and Nezahualcóyotl)—the author is working at the confluence of these two lines of study on Latin American democracy.

Montambeault's proposal is to understand state–society relations in two dimensions: the mobilization patterns of civil society and the levels of civil society autonomy within participatory institutions. This allows her to tackle the challenging theme of participatory institutions' effectiveness. For Montambeault, thinking about the success of participatory democracy is of necessity to consider its contribution to the transformation of state–society relationships.

The author realizes that, in assessing changes in state–society relations at the local level, the way institutional frameworks work at the national level does not matter. In addition to the institutional design of the participation mechanism itself, what matters is how civil society itself relates to it and to what extent local political partisanship engenders levels of more autonomous or more controlled participation by civil society.

Therefore, the mere existence of institutional participation mechanisms is insufficient to induce changes in local state–society relationships. Such mechanisms are related to a sociopolitical environment of competition between parties and within parties, so disputes about acting within these mechanisms just reinforce positions of this or that political faction.

But how does political competition relate to the idea of autonomy? The author shows how, in environments where government coalitions are not under fierce attack from their opponents, there is greater likelihood of autonomous civil society action. In more contentious environments, the political disputes permeating the mechanisms of institutional participation often make segments of civil society reinforce whichever party position is closer to their interests. Is it a loss of autonomy or a broader political clash in which social and political segments are articulated to achieve their goals? I think this is an interesting topic demanding further exploration beyond that which Montambeault laudably highlights in this work.

The heterogeneity of civil society (i.e. the diversity of positioning and political stance in the societal field) is a second element that 'tempers' analysis and acts as a brake on the influence of party competition in the participatory process. The circuit of success of the participation mechanisms closes when civil society is joined by a third element: an understanding on the part of societal and governmental actors that the very institutionalization of channels between state and society serves to support state action and also strengthen the ties of political representation. This is, perhaps, the least robust of all the analytical elements mobilized by the author; it is difficult to evaluate the perceptions of such multiple actors and, more than that, to analytically consider possible changes of perception regarding the participatory process in cases as expansive as those analyzed by Montambeault.

The Politics of Local Participatory Democracy in Latin America represents indispensable reading for scholars of participatory democracy seeking more than putative 'universal' models for resolving democratic deficits around the world. Participatory institutions do not exist in a vacuum, they fit into various political contexts and can even be trump cards in local political disputes. Montambeault's shrewd analysis helps us to better understand such phenomena.

Wagner de Melo Romão, University of Campinas (Unicamp) Brasil

Robert Saliba (ed.) 2015: *Urban Design in the Arab World: Re-conceptualizing Boundaries.* **Farnham and Burlington, VT: Ashgate**

A recent and prominent development in Arab cities is urban morphological change, brought about by multi-scalar urban design projects characteristic of neoliberal markets. This does not fit neatly with traditional scholarly research on Arab urbanism, which revolved around three themes: the geographical (wherein cities are compared across the Arab region); the historical (focusing on practices and subjugation of Western models during the colonial and post-colonial periods); and the thematic (mostly centered on postwar reconstruction and urban conservation). The contemporary discourse on what makes a city in the Arab World remains in flux, against a backdrop of religious extremism and moderation; peace and war; wealth and poverty; destruction and reconstruction; and globalization versus localization. *Urban Design in the Arab World* examines this dynamic phenomenon, compiling scholarly manuscripts and practice reflections emanating from the 'City Debates 2012' conference held in Beirut, revealing the complexities of this ongoing discourse.

In addition to its two introductory chapters, the book comprises five parts, each investigating current topical theory and practice via three cross-cutting themes: urban design as a distinct exploratory lens of city morphology (explicit from origins in other design disciplines); the confounding understanding of what constitutes the Arab World and city (due to conflicting usage of terms generating varying and sometimes conflicting frameworks); and (re)conceptualizing boundaries where the term 'margin' is employed to redefine periphery–core relationships and the transformation of identity from rootedness to constructiveness. Boundaries are thus redefined to requisition urbanism for emergent trends rather than for fixed concepts.

Part I ('The Discursive') presents diverse urban design approaches as an indicator of the flow of ideas across cities at the margins. The chapter titled 'The Cultural Discourse' examines the Aga Khan Award for Architecture as a normative benchmark to assess urban design practice, shifting the focus of Arab city (re)definition from an ideological overarching construct of Islam to collective community actions. In the next chapter, 'The Participative Discourse', the impact of public debate, community support and capacity building is examined as an alternative response to inaction of national institutions to urban space reconstruction through academic–professional emergency collaboration in the aftermath of the 2006 war. The subsequent chapter, 'The Corporate Discourse', is by contrast a narrative of long-term city rebuilding in Beirut following 15 years of civil strife (1975–90). A regional–globalization perspective repositions Beirut as the Levant's cosmopolitan and multi-faith center, in competition with other regional cities, promoting a transferable or 'franchisable' brand of successful place-making. An alternative view comes with the final chapter of part I, 'The Greening Discourse', which argues for an ecological approach to city-making that contests the dominant perception of idealized parks and 'vegetated green', framed within a regional perspective highlighting uncontrolled urbanization undermining the urban core–periphery relationship.

The next three parts of the book are separate but complementary threads. Part II ('The Hybrid') blurs the boundaries between design disciplines, utilizing recent theories of urbanism to examine potential hybridization in Beirut and Jeddah. For example, concepts of indeterminacy and 'machinic' processes (inspired by landscape urbanism) are applied to the Beirut River district for an emergent cultural infrastructure: a process-based intervention that locates marginalized subculture within marginal city spaces, motivating future change from within the community. In the two chapters comprising part II, local ecology is emphasized over morphology; informal network surface supersedes formal urban form; infrastructure is expanded to include the informal, social and cultural; and confluence of landscape, architecture, city and infrastructure emerges as an integrative disciplinary lens adapted to local conditions.

Part III ('The Operational') bridges research and practice to highlight the emerging accountability role of the designer vis-à-vis the community and the environment. Two partnerships are discussed as viable models for implementation of urban design initiatives: a cooperative partnership between a municipality (Aleppo, Syria) and an international donor, with planners playing a didactic role in the development of the city's master plan; and a partnership between a higher-education institution in Beirut and a local donor to upgrade a community market in a disadvantaged neighborhood. In both initiatives, research, inclusiveness and stakeholder involvement are starting points for project interventions. The significance lies in the formulation of alternative partner approaches under autocratic governance systems, mitigating complex socio-cultural webs manifest in intricate spatial negotiations.

Part IV ('The Visionary') places urban design as a mediator within dialectics of past and present approaches, ranging from Western-city replication to packaged historical landscapes for tourist consumption. As a consequence, diverse Arab contexts impose 'middle landscapes', generating new site typologies. In the four chapters comprising part IV, sites of globalization mediate local views of designers and global aspirations of clients (Riyadh); sites of worship reconcile places of primary worship with real estate speculation (Mekkah and Karbala); sites of conflict assimilate contradictions of city fragmentation due to continuing conflict (Baghdad); and sites of contestation bring together a practitioner's and a researcher's view of democratic expression (Tahrir Square, Cairo).

In the concluding part V ('Prospects'), environmental sustainability and a humanistic approach to city-making are presented as future trends for Arab cities. The 'Estidama' building rating system applied in Abu Dhabi is presented as an example of good practice adapted to regional conditions. Part V's second chapter links public health to infrastructure, with a focus on transforming vehicular infrastructure into pedestrian-friendly urban open space. In both cases, the emphasis is on urban design as a vessel to reduce land consumption in Arab cities.

This volume provides a well-curated array of urban design trends in the Arab World, contextualized within broader theory and practice, highlighting the complexities and dynamics of city-making. The questions posed as to what constitutes an Arab city are more pertinent than ever, especially amidst the turmoil engulfing the region. The diversity of ideas inform city-making in general, but also serve as a guide for eminent (re) construction efforts in the future. *Urban Design in the Arab World* is a valuable collection of manuscripts offering new ideas on a topic that is little published beyond conventional approaches. The book is an essential resource for scholars and practitioners seeking to expand their knowledge of cities in the Arab World.

Yaser Abunnasr, American University of Beirut, Lebanon

VOLUME 41   NUMBER 6   NOVEMBER 2017

The *International Journal of Urban and Regional Research* is published in 6 issues per year (January, March, May, July, September and November) by John Wiley & Sons Ltd, 9600, Garsington Road, Oxford OX4 2DQ, UK.

Institutional subscription prices for 2018 are: Print + Online: US $1,483 (USA), US $1,667 (Rest of World), €1008 (Europe), £792 (UK) Single issue prices are: US $20 (USA), £12 (Rest of World), €15 (Europe), £12 (UK)

Prices are exclusive of tax. Asia-Pacific GST, Canadian GST and European VAT will be applied at the appropriate rates. For more information on current tax rates, please go to www.wileyonlinelibrary.com/tax-vat. Subscription prices include online access to the current and all online back files to January 1st 2012, where available. For other pricing options, including access information and terms and conditions, please visit www.wileyonlinelibrary.com/access.

Delivery Terms and Legal Title: Where the subscription price includes print issues and delivery is to the recipient's address, delivery terms are Delivered Duty Unpaid (DDU); the recipient is responsible for paying any import duty or taxes. Title to all issues transfers FOB our shipping point, freight prepaid. We will endeavour to fulfil claims for missing or damaged copies within six months of publication, within our reasonable discretion and subject to availability.

US Mailing: *INTERNATIONAL JOURNAL OF URBAN AND REGIONAL RESEARCH* (ISSN: 0309-1317), is published bi-monthly in January, March, May, July, September and November.
US mailing agent: Mercury Media Processing, LLC, 1850 Elizabeth Avenue, Suite #C, Rahway, NJ 07065 USA. Periodical postage paid at Rahway, NJ.

Postmaster: Send all address changes to *INTERNATIONAL JOURNAL OF URBAN AND REGIONAL RESEARCH*, John Wiley & Sons Inc., C/O The Sheridan Press, Po Box 465, Hanover, PA 17331, USA.